D1585586

access to history

The American Dream: Reality and Illusion 1945–1980

VIVIENNE SANDERS

HODDER
EDUCATION
AN HACHETTE UK COMPANY

The Publishers would like to thank David Ferriby for his contribution to the Study Guide.

Caution: several of the historical extracts and quotations in this book contain words that are vulgar and offensive.

The Publishers would like to thank the following for permission to reproduce copyright material:

Photo credits: p3 Library of Congress, LC-USZ62-63361; **p6** Library of Congress, LC-USZ62-117122; **p33** Underwood Archives/Getty Images; **p40** Bettmann/Corbis; **p55** National Motor Museum/HIP/TopFoto; **p58** Library of Congress, LC-USZ62-104961; **p84** Library of Congress, LC-USZ62-126559; **p89** Scott Olson/Getty Images; **p98** Library of Congress, LC-USZ62-117124; **p101** TopFoto.co.uk; **p118** The Granger Collection/TopFoto; **p138** Library of Congress, LC-USZ62-13036; **p140** Yoichi Okamoto/ LBJ Presidential Library; **p142** Cecil W. Stoughton/White House Press Office (WHPO); **p165** Library of Congress, LC-USZ62-119478; **p173** Yankee Poster Collection, Library of Congress, LC-USZ62-91158; **p190** Everett Collection Historical/Alamy; **p193** Library of Congress, LC-USZ62-13037; **p205** The Granger Collection/TopFoto; **p213** Library of Congress, LC-DIG-ds-01512; **p234** Library of Congress, LC-USZ62-13038; **p235** Library of Congress, LC-USZCN4-116; **p262** Library of Congress, LC-USZ62-13040.

Acknowledgements: are listed on page 292.

Every effort has been made to trace all copyright holders, but if any have been inadvertently overlooked the Publishers will be pleased to make the necessary arrangements at the first opportunity.

Although every effort has been made to ensure that website addresses are correct at time of going to press, Hodder Education cannot be held responsible for the content of any website mentioned in this book. It is sometimes possible to find a relocated web page by typing in the address of the home page for a website in the URL window of your browser.

Hachette UK's policy is to use papers that are natural, renewable and recyclable products and made from wood grown in sustainable forests. The logging and manufacturing processes are expected to conform to the environmental regulations of the country of origin.

Orders: please contact Bookpoint Ltd, 130 Milton Park, Abingdon, Oxon OX14 4SB. Telephone: +44 (0)1235 827720. Fax: +44 (0)1235 400454. Lines are open 9.00a.m.–5.00p.m., Monday to Saturday, with a 24-hour message answering service. Visit our website at www.hoddereducation.co.uk

Contents

Dedication

Keith Randell (1943–2002)

The *Access to History* series was conceived and developed by Keith, who created a series to 'cater for students as they are, not as we might wish them to be'. He leaves a living legacy of a series that for over 20 years has provided a trusted, stimulating and well-loved accompaniment to post-16 study. Our aim with these new editions is to continue to offer students the best possible support for their studies.

CHAPTER 1

Truman and post-war America 1945–52

While most Americans experienced unprecedented prosperity in 1945–52, there were also fears and tensions. The greatest fear was Communism, whether at home or abroad. Anti-Communism generated a revolution in US foreign policy: traditional American isolationism became a distant memory as Cold War America engaged in worldwide interventionism. The greatest tensions were over race and industrial relations. President Truman steered the nation through (or, some would say, into) these problems, which are covered in the following sections:

★ The United States in 1945 and the legacies of the Second World War

★ The USA as a superpower

★ Truman and post-war reconstruction

★ African-Americans in the North and the South

★ Truman and post-war America: conclusions

The key debate on *page 25* of this chapter asks the question: Which side was to blame for the Cold War?

Key dates

1945	April	President Roosevelt died; Vice President Truman became president	1948	Nov.	Truman elected president
			1948–9		Berlin Blockade
	May	Germany surrendered	1949		Truman asked Congress for a 'Fair Deal'
	Aug.	US atomic bombs forced Japanese surrender	1950	Feb.	Senator McCarthy declared that there were Communists in the State Department
1946		Greatest number of strikes in US history			
1947	March	Truman Doctrine speech publicised containment		June	Outbreak of Korean War
	June	Marshall Plan speech			Three Supreme Court decisions eroded *Plessy* v. *Ferguson*
	Oct.	*To Secure These Rights* published	1952		Truman seized steel mills

KEY TERMS

Democrat Member of one of the two main political parties. In comparison to Republicans, more supportive of government interventionism and more on the left of the political spectrum.

Great Depression Beginning with the 1929 Wall Street crash, the US economy was characterised by unprecedented unemployment in the 1930s.

New Deal Roosevelt's plan to get the USA out of the 1930s' Depression; an unprecedented programme of federal aid to those most in need.

Congress The US equivalent of Britain's Parliament. It consists of the House of Representatives and the Senate. Each US state selects two senators, and a number of congressmen proportionate to its population.

Federal government The national or federal government, based in Washington DC, consists of the President, Congress (which makes laws) and the Supreme Court (which interprets laws).

Republican Member of one of the two main political parties. More conservative than Democrats, and generally opposed to federal government interventionism.

Supreme Court Issues rulings on whether or not laws and actions are in line with the Constitution.

1 The United States in 1945 and the legacies of the Second World War

▶ *What were the political, economic and social characteristics of the USA in 1945?*

In 1945, the victorious United States emerged from the Second World War as the wealthiest and most powerful nation in the world. This owed much to the **Democrat** President, Franklin Delano Roosevelt (FDR). Knowledge of the events of Roosevelt's presidency (1933–45) gives essential background to the USA in 1945 and illustrates the powers, potential and problems of a president.

The powers of the presidency: domestic affairs

The powers of the presidency increased under Roosevelt because of the two exceptional crises that faced the nation in 1933–45: the **Great Depression** and the Second World War.

When Roosevelt became president in 1933, 25 per cent of the workforce was unemployed. Roosevelt promised Americans a **New Deal** to lift the nation out of the economic depression and to ameliorate suffering. Roosevelt's New Deal proposals included job creation schemes, subsidies for farmers, and regulations to prevent another collapse of the banks. He needed **Congress** to grant him the unprecedented powers and money necessary to implement his programmes. Congress responded positively, for example, with the Social Security Act (1935), which guaranteed retirement payments for the over-65s, established federal insurance for the unemployed, and provided extra aid for the disabled, dependent women and children, and public health. Equipped with the necessary powers from Congress, his programmes helped end the Depression and transformed many Americans' ideas about the presidency and the **federal government**. His presidency was revolutionary in his promotion of large-scale federal government intervention in the economy and in society.

Roosevelt was also revolutionary in that he brought the presidency into the homes of the American people. He addressed them in a series of informal radio broadcasts. Families across the nation gathered around the radio to listen to their optimistic president who promised economic and social improvements. Not surprisingly, he was re-elected with a landslide victory in 1936.

The increase in the powers and prestige of the presidency under Roosevelt generated much criticism and even accusations of dictatorship. Arguably, Roosevelt's greatest opposition came from conservative justices appointed by his **Republican** predecessors to the **Supreme Court**.

Franklin Delano Roosevelt

1882   Born into a wealthy family in New York State

1900–4   Studied law at Harvard University

1905   Married a distant cousin, Eleanor Roosevelt

1913   Assistant Secretary of the Navy

1928–33   Popular and effective Governor of New York State

1933–7   First presidential **term** dominated by economic depression

1937–41   Second presidential term dominated by the deteriorating international situation

1941–5   Third presidential term: led the country through the Second World War

1945   Died in April, a few weeks into his fourth term as president

Although Roosevelt had great personal wealth, he empathised with the less privileged. Many thought this owed much to the polio infection he contracted in 1921 which left him paralysed from the waist down. Throughout his political career, the American press respectfully hid his disability: he could only stand with the help of heavy metal braces and needed a cane or crutch to enable him to swing each leg forward and 'walk'. The general public never knew they had a disabled president.

President Roosevelt used federal government power and expenditure to stimulate the economy during the Great Depression. The combination of his policies and wartime demand helped bring about economic recovery. Roosevelt led the nation through the war but died on the verge of victory.

Historians invariably rate Roosevelt as one of the greatest American presidents. His presidency was a turning point in US history in that it revolutionised the role of the federal government and saw the USA become the world's leading power. He was the first and last US president to be elected to serve four terms.

The President (the executive branch)

- Can recommend legislation to Congress and can veto their bills
- Appoints to the cabinet and federal bureaucracy
- Head of state
- Commander-in-chief of the armed forces

The American people vote for

Congress (the legislative branch)

- Consists of two houses: the Senate and the House of Representatives
- Each state elects two senators
- Congressmen who sit in the House of Representatives represent congressional districts. The number of Representatives per state depends on that state's population
- Congress passes bills, which then become laws

The Supreme Court (the judicial branch)

- Judges are appointed by the President but his nominees need the Senate's approval
- Decides (rules upon) whether actions are 'constitutional' (i.e. that they do not go against the US Constitution)
- Issues rulings (does not make laws)

🔑 **KEY TERM**

Term A US president is elected for a four-year term. Since FDR, he or she can only be re-elected for a second term.

Figure 1.1 Federal government in the USA.

Limitations on presidential power

President Roosevelt's power was limited by:

- The Supreme Court, which could rule his actions unconstitutional or illegal (it declared much of the New Deal legislation initiated by Roosevelt to be unconstitutional, but further congressional legislation rendered such rulings irrelevant).
- Public opinion, which could damage the electoral prospects of the president and/or his party, and could cause Congress to reject his proposals (public opinion caused him to stop trying to 'pack' the court with sympathetic justices).
- Congress, which could refuse to pass the legislation he suggested and which alone had the power to grant him the funds to carry out the work of government (by 1938, Roosevelt's own Democratic Party and the Republican Party were less supportive of the New Deal).

The main political parties

Although Roosevelt had great personal wealth, the Democrats were for the most part the party of poorer Americans. The Democratic Party was a loose coalition that included:

- the '**Solid South**'
- urban (mostly Catholic) ethnic voters in the North, for example Irish-Americans
- workers and the unemployed across the nation.

The Democrats were in the majority in the **House of Representatives** and the **Senate** throughout the 1930s. Democrat domination of Congress was essential for the passage of Roosevelt's New Deal legislation, but by 1937 powerful anti-New Deal opposition had developed within the Democratic Party and Roosevelt found it difficult to get further reforming legislation passed. The opposition was led by conservative Southern Democrats. White Southerners of all classes were determined to maintain the social, economic and political inferiority of black Americans in their region. They invariably voted Democrat because the Republican President Abraham Lincoln had led the North to victory over the South in the American Civil War (1861–5) and effectively ended black slavery. Most Southern Democrats were far more conservative and resistant to change than other Democrats.

Southern Democrat opposition to the New Deal was supported by the Republican Party, which was dominated by big business and the rich. Republicans loathed Roosevelt's higher taxes, support for labour unions and promotion of federal interventionism in the cause of economic and social reform.

Even as the New Deal seemed to have run out of steam, a new crisis dominated American politics: the foreign threat from two expansionist nations, Japan and Germany.

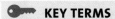 **KEY TERMS**

Solid South Before the Democratic Party became more liberal on race, the Southern states were dominated by the Democratic Party.

House of Representatives One of the two congressional chambers. Each state sends a number of congressmen proportional to its population to the House.

Senate One of the two chambers of Congress; two senators are elected from each state.

The powers of the presidency: foreign policy and war

For much of the 1930s, both Republicans and Democrats were **isolationist** and sought to keep the United States out of war. However, Roosevelt persuaded Congress to give material aid to Britain in its fight against Germany and to China in its struggle against Japan. When the Japanese attacked the US naval base at Pearl Harbor in Hawaii in December 1941, America declared war on Japan. Within days, Germany declared war on America.

Roosevelt led the nation through most of the Second World War. In wartime, the powers of the president inevitably increased because of his constitutional roles as **commander-in-chief** and **head of state**. Although it was Congress that had the constitutional power to declare war and to finance the nation's armed forces and production of **war materiel**, it was President Roosevelt who chose where to deploy those forces and resources. He made the foreign policy decisions that had a dramatic impact on post-war America, for example, over the division of Germany, the United Nations (UN) and Korea (see page 23).

The United States in 1945: the legacies of the world war

The war exhausted Roosevelt. By 1944, the dark patches under his eyes, along with his trembling hands and his weight loss, convinced his friends and aides that he would never survive a fourth term. Given his declining health, his choice of a **running mate** was particularly important for the fourth election. Roosevelt and his advisers decided that Missouri Senator Harry Truman would be the least likely to offend anyone. Roosevelt won the election (November 1944) and in January 1945, Truman became vice president. Just a few months later, on 12 April 1945, Roosevelt suffered a cerebral haemorrhage while at Warm Springs, Georgia. Americans were shocked and saddened at his death. He had been the only president that young Americans had ever known. To many Americans he was the president who had brought them successfully through two great crises, the Depression and the world war the United States was clearly winning. As the train carrying the dead president's coffin chugged slowly past, sombre crowds lined the railroad tracks all the way from Warm Springs to Washington.

Truman was now president. 'There have been few men in all history the equal of the man into whose shoes I am stepping,' he said. 'I pray God I can measure up to the task.'

Truman was president of a nation that was victorious in the war (Germany surrendered in May 1945, Japan in August 1945) and the wealthiest and most powerful in the world. Its wartime allies were exhausted, its wartime enemies totally devastated, and it was the sole possessor of the phenomenally powerful new atomic bomb. The USA was supreme both economically and militarily – an undoubted superpower.

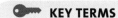 **KEY TERMS**

Isolationist Long-standing US foreign policy tradition (for example, Jefferson opposed entangling alliances); the avoidance of foreign entanglements.

Commander-in-chief Under the US Constitution, the president is commander-in-chief of the nation's armed forces.

Head of state Chief public representative of a country such as a monarch or president.

War materiel Military equipment such as guns, ammunition and so on.

Running mate The individual chosen to be a political party's presidential candidate has to choose a running mate, who will be vice president if the presidential candidate wins the election.

Harry Truman

1884	Born on a Missouri farm
1935	Elected senator for Missouri
1945	President Roosevelt died in April and Vice President Truman became president
1947	'Truman Doctrine' speech
1949	Established NATO. Republicans accused Truman and the Democrats of 'losing China'
1950	McCarthyite hysteria began
1950–3	Korean War ('Truman's war')
1953	Retired to Missouri
1972	Died

Many Americans felt that Truman, the very ordinary farm boy who became president, symbolised the **American Dream**. At Sunday school, aged six, he was smitten by pretty, wealthy Bess Wallace. For years she followed her mother's advice ('You don't want to marry that farmer boy, he is not going to make it anywhere') and refused his marriage proposals. Truman's first real success came in the First World War (1917), when he proved a popular and effective captain. When he returned home, Bess finally agreed to marry him.

At 'Boss' Thomas Pendergast's suggestion, Truman stood for local government office. He proved highly competent and exceptionally honest. In 1935,

Pendergast supported Truman's successful campaign to be senator for Missouri. Noting Truman's great modesty, Senator Hamilton Lewis of Illinois advised him, 'Harry, don't start out with an inferiority complex. For the first six months you'll wonder how the hell you got here, and after that you'll wonder how the rest of us got here.' Although initially known as 'the Senator from Pendergast', Truman gained great respect when his wartime Senate committee exposed corruption and inefficiency in the defence industries and probably saved taxpayers $15 billion. When Roosevelt told him his party and country needed him, Truman reluctantly agreed to be Roosevelt's running mate. He became president on Roosevelt's death in 1945.

President Truman failed to persuade Congress to pass the social reform legislation he suggested. He also failed to contain the McCarthyite hysteria (see page 36). He led the United States into the **Cold War** and successfully countered Communism through NATO, Marshall Aid and the Korean War, although the latter made him particularly unpopular.

The decisive and combative Truman was one of the most influential of American presidents because of his role in getting the United States into half a century of Cold War with the Soviet Union. It could perhaps be argued that he overestimated the **Communist** threat, but whether right or wrong, his anti-Communist ideas dominated US foreign policy for the next half-century. He began the exceptionally large defence expenditure that would cause the United States great economic problems by the 1970s.

KEY TERMS

American Dream Belief that the nature of US society enables an individual to fulfil his or her potential, especially through wealth.

Cold War The struggle between the capitalist USA and the Communist Soviet Union.

Communist Believer in economic equality brought about by revolutionary redistribution of wealth.

Post-war prosperity

Already very rich in natural resources such as coal, iron ore, oil, timber and minerals, the United States experienced an economic boom during the Second World War when the combination of factories working at full speed to produce war materiel and of millions of citizens serving in the military resulted in full and well-paid employment. Most Americans had never experienced so much disposable income. The aircraft, electrical, chemical, tobacco, food processing and pharmaceutical industries in particular flourished during the war: they helped make the American economy the most dynamic and successful in the world by 1945, and made a vital contribution to the exceptional post-war prosperity.

By the end of the 1940s, the United States had 7 per cent of the world's population but 42 per cent of its income. It produced half the world's manufactured goods – 57 per cent of the steel, 62 per cent of the oil and 80 per cent of the cars. In 1949, per capita income was nearly twice that of the other most prosperous nations such as Canada. Unemployment remained under 4 per cent throughout the decade. During the 1940s, the average American earned more in real dollars than his or her parents. With more disposable income and more products available, America was developing into a consumer society. When Americans purchased cars, vacuum cleaners, refrigerators and other goods, they raised their own standard of living and created employment for those involved in the production of these consumer goods. The American lifestyle was the envy of the world. It seemed that the American Dream was a reality.

The American Dream

The concept of the 'American Dream' was popularised by historian James Truslow Adams in his 1931 book, *Epic of America*. He said that the American Dream was 'not a dream of merely material plenty' but also 'a dream of being able to grow to fullest development as man and woman' unhampered by the rigid social orders characteristic of older nations. The unprecedented prosperity following the Second World War confirmed the belief of many Americans in the American Dream. They believed that hard work would bring them prosperity and that their children would do even better than they did, for this was the land of great opportunity and grand expectations.

Regional, ethnic and social divisions

Although the wealthiest and most powerful nation in the world, Harry Truman's America had its challenges. While wartime propaganda emphasised unity, there were great regional, ethnic and social differences among the people of the 48 states in 1945.

Regional divisions

The physical geography of the United States helped ensure great regional differences (see Figure 1.2), especially between the predominantly agricultural South with its acute racial tensions and the rest of America. The Northeast and Midwest had great cities such as Pittsburgh, Chicago and Detroit that were centres of manufacturing, and the war had brought defence industries that transformed West Coast cities such as Los Angeles. While big cities such as New York were more likely to respond favourably to change, conservatism was strong in the South and also in the great farmlands and small towns of the Midwest.

The war necessitated mobility which helped overcome regionalism. By 1945, out of the 140 million population of the United States:

- one in every nine had left their homes for training camps and three-quarters of them served overseas

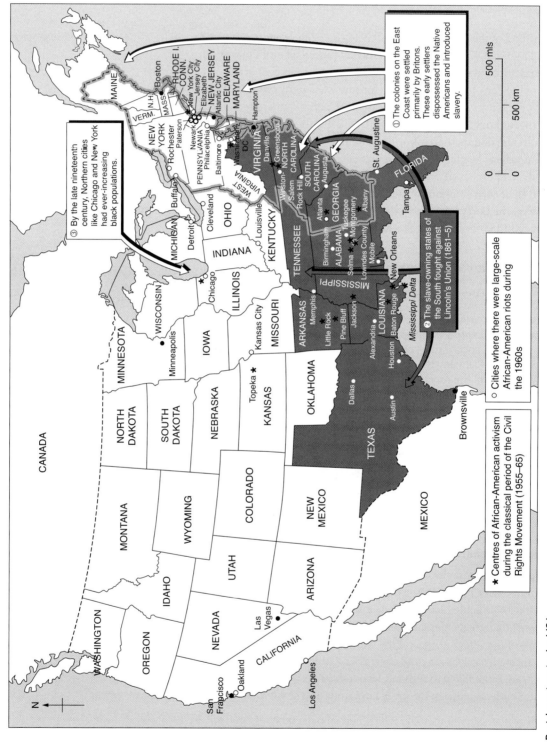

① The colonies on the East Coast were settled primarily by Britons. These early settlers dispossessed the Native Americans and introduced slavery.

③ By the late nineteenth century, Northern cities like Chicago and New York had ever-increasing black populations.

② The slave-owning states of the South fought against Lincoln's Union (1861–5)

○ Cities where there were large-scale African-American riots during the 1960s

★ Centres of African-American activism during the classical period of the Civil Rights Movement (1955–65)

500 mls

500 km

Figure 1.2 Racial tensions in the USA.

- one in every eight had changed their county of residence
- 8 million had made a permanent move to a different state, half of them to a different region.

The directional trend of this mass migration was from the predominantly agricultural South to the industrial North, and from the East to the West, especially to California. The West Coast population grew by one-third during the war, particularly in the cities that produced war materiel: San Diego, Los Angeles, Oakland, Portland and Seattle.

Regional differences were certainly decreasing (for example, **Sears** ceased producing catalogues for different regions), but they had not disappeared. The unique nature of the South in particular would be demonstrated during the struggle for civil rights (see page 39).

Ethnic divisions

The United States was a 'melting pot' of citizens from different ethnic groups, many of which were looked down upon by 'WASPs' (white, Anglo-Saxon and Protestant). Joseph Kennedy, the wealthy father of future President John F. Kennedy (1961–3), lamented that he was never fully accepted by Boston high society because of his Irish ancestry and Catholicism. Religious prejudice against Jews also remained strong. The Second World War accelerated the acceptance of the different ethnic groups, especially **white ethnics**. Wartime and post-war Hollywood films invariably showed a group of united, patriotic fighting men with names indicating Irish, Italian or Polish origin.

Although white ethnics were losing their inferior status, non-whites continued to suffer the greatest prejudice and discrimination. Most of the 14 million black Americans (10 per cent of the population), 1.2 million Hispanic Americans and 350,000 Native Americans were invariably treated as inferior. The social inferiority of black and Hispanic Americans was enshrined in law in the South, and in practice elsewhere (housing and schools were usually segregated outside the South). Black, Hispanic and Native American incomes were way below the national average.

Social divisions

There were massive disparities in wealth across the nation, ranging from billionaire dynasties such as the Rockefellers, rich families such as the Roosevelts, comfortable families such as those of Bess and Harry Truman, to the impoverished white people of the Appalachian mountains, the black **sharecroppers** of the South, and the Native Americans on their **reservations**. Such disparities were socially divisive and well illustrated in industrial relations. The membership and powers of the unions had increased under the sympathetic Roosevelt **administration**. Worker–employer tensions peaked in 1946, when 4.6 million workers went on strike and 116 million working days were lost.

 **KEY TERMS**

Sears A US department store chain.

White ethnics Groups of Americans such as Irish-Americans, Italian-Americans and Polish-Americans.

Sharecroppers Tenant farmers who give a share of the crops produced to the landowner as rent.

Reservations Lands to which white Americans confined Native Americans from the nineteenth century onwards.

Administration When Americans talk of 'the Truman administration', they mean the government as led by that particular president.

On the other hand, growing prosperity during and after the war decreased social tensions. Congress passed the GI Bill of Rights (1944) to assist returning military personnel with free vocational training and higher education and lower-interest loans for housing and the establishment of businesses. Due to this legislation:

● The percentage of college-educated Americans rose from 10 per cent in 1939 to 15 per cent in 1948, and a college education improved employment and economic opportunities.
● The number of new homeowners increased dramatically and their belief in the American Dream was confirmed.

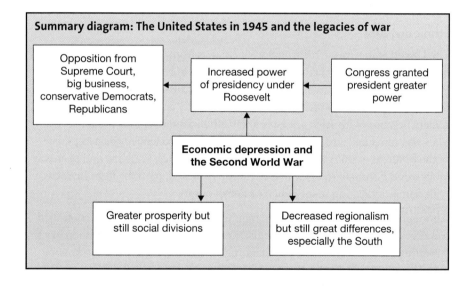

Summary diagram: The United States in 1945 and the legacies of war

Opposition from Supreme Court, big business, conservative Democrats, Republicans ← Increased power of presidency under Roosevelt ← Congress granted president greater power

Increased power of presidency under Roosevelt ↑ Economic depression and the Second World War

Economic depression and the Second World War → Greater prosperity but still social divisions

Economic depression and the Second World War → Decreased regionalism but still great differences, especially the South

 ## The USA as a superpower

▶ *What was the US reaction to the growth of Communism?*

 **KEY TERM**

USSR Several years after the Russian Revolution of 1917, Communist Russia became known as the Union of Soviet Socialist Republics (USSR) or the Soviet Union.

The USA and the **USSR** (also known as the Soviet Union) were allies in the Second World War but enemies soon after. The roots of Soviet–American antagonism dated to the Russian Revolution of 1917.

Soviet–American relations before Truman

After the Russian Revolution of 1917, Russia became the world's first Communist nation. The United States and the Soviet Union had very different ideologies and aims (see Table 1.1, page 11).

Table 1.1 Opposing ideologies and aims of the USA and the USSR

USA	USSR
Americans supported a capitalist system, with free trade and minimal government intervention in the economy	Communists favoured a state-controlled economy in which the government promoted economic equality through the redistribution of national wealth
Americans considered a multi-party state and free elections the hallmark of democracy	Communists argued that other parties were unnecessary as the Communist Party was the party of the people, and that economic rather than political equality characterised democracy
Americans thought Communist promotion of revolutions threatened US national security: it might leave the United States without trading partners and allies and Communist countries might attempt to export revolution to the United States	Many Communists advocated the promotion of Communist revolutions throughout the world

American antipathy to Communism was so great that it was 1933 before the United States gave the Soviet Union diplomatic recognition. However, when Nazi Germany attacked the Soviet Union and declared war on the United States during 1941, the two countries became wartime allies. There was considerable co-operation, but also a great deal of tension.

Wartime co-operation

United in their determination to defeat Germany, the Americans and the Soviets managed frequent and considerable co-operation during the war. Roosevelt, the Soviet leader **Josef Stalin** and British Prime Minister **Winston Churchill** held wartime conferences in Tehran (1943) and Yalta (February 1945), where they planned how to achieve victory. The discussions at Yalta were particularly important:

- They agreed that defeated Germany would be divided into four zones of occupation: one American, one Soviet, one British and one French. Although within the Soviet zone, Berlin would be similarly divided into four zones.
- For the most part, the Soviets and the Americans each kept the other out of the territories from which they drove the troops of Germany and its allies. Each promoted its own political and economic system in liberated countries. For example, as they fought their way to Berlin in 1944–5, Soviet forces promoted Communism in East European countries such as Poland. When Roosevelt and Churchill expressed great concern about this at Yalta, Stalin promised that Poland's Communist government would soon hold democratic elections (he lied).
- Roosevelt hoped that a new international organisation, the United Nations (UN), would keep the peace in the post-war world. Although wary, Stalin seemed in agreement at Yalta.

 KEY FIGURES

Josef Stalin (1878–1953)

Leader of the Soviet Union c.1925–53. Promoted industrialisation at home and brought the Soviet Union through the Second World War, having gained a new East European Empire.

Winston Churchill (1874–1965)

British Prime Minister 1940–5 and 1951–5. His relationship with President Roosevelt contributed greatly to the Allied victory in the Second World War.

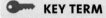
- As yet unaware of the enormous power of the untested atomic bomb, Roosevelt was desperate for Soviet aid in the war against Japan. Although **Chiang Kai-shek**'s China was a US ally, Roosevelt offered Stalin territorial and economic concessions in China at Yalta. Stalin in turn promised Soviet entry into the war in the Pacific three months after the defeat of Germany.

Wartime tensions

Two major causes of wartime tension were the atomic bomb and Poland. While the Americans (reluctantly) shared knowledge of the development of the atomic bomb with Britain, they kept it secret from their Soviet ally. However, Soviet spies kept Stalin informed. Disagreements over Poland in particular led Roosevelt to waver between optimism and pessimism over post-war Soviet–American relations until the day he died.

Soviet–American relations under Truman

Harry Truman had an inauspicious background for one who had to maintain the increasingly uneasy alliance with the USSR. He had focused on domestic politics throughout his political career and Roosevelt had not kept him informed on foreign and defence policies during his vice-presidency. The *Washington Post* said there was a 'great disparity between Mr Truman's experience and the responsibilities that have been thrust upon him'. Unsurprisingly, the inexperienced new president followed Roosevelt's policies and advisers.

Like Roosevelt, Truman was ambivalent about the Soviet Union. He had long held a reputation for plain-spoken honesty and subsequently claimed that he gave Soviet Foreign Minister Molotov a hard time when they talked about Poland in May 1945. However, he was pleased with the last **Big Three** wartime conference at Potsdam, Germany, in the summer of 1945 and said he thought he could work with Stalin. Subsequently, Truman ruefully recalled that, 'I liked the little son-of-a-bitch', but Stalin told a colleague that Truman was 'worthless'.

Potsdam

At Potsdam, there was relatively amicable agreement on the '5 Ds': the demilitarisation, deindustrialisation, decentralisation, denazification and democratisation of Germany. Stalin ignored Truman's and Churchill's protests about the imposition of Communism on Poland, but confirmed that he would join the war against Japan three months after the defeat of Germany. Unaware of Soviet spying talents, Truman triumphantly informed Stalin that the United States had successfully tested an amazing new weapon.

Japan and the bomb

As promised, Stalin declared war on Japan on 8 August 1945, three months to the day after the German surrender. However, it was the two atomic bombs that Truman ordered dropped upon Japan on 6 and 8 August 1945 that forced the Japanese surrender. Naturally, the United States worked to exclude the Soviets from the peace settlement with Japan. Stalin's successor, the Soviet leader Nikita Khrushchev (1955–64), recalled Stalin saying that the bomb had revolutionised the world balance of power. Stalin viewed Truman's America as a frightening economic, military and technological giant that was far more powerful than the Soviet Union, a nation devastated during the Second World War.

Post-war Soviet–American hostility

Post-war Soviet–American hostility was surely inevitable because of:

- their opposing ideologies
- long-term tensions
- disagreements during the Second World War, especially over Poland
- American secrecy over, and possession of, the atomic bomb
- the imbalance of power
- the personalities of Stalin and Truman.

The personalities of Stalin and Truman

The prospects for a good working relationship between Stalin and Truman were poor. Stalin was exceptionally suspicious and Truman lacked Roosevelt's emollient charm and patience. As Truman freely admitted, Roosevelt was a hard act to follow. As a result, the new president was keen to prove himself and determined to appear competent, tough and decisive. Regardless of personalities, it is unlikely that conflict between the two most powerful nations in the world could ever have been avoided, particularly given their opposing ideologies and the disparity in their power.

Post-war peace-making

In 1945, post-war peace treaties proved problematic due to Soviet–American tensions:

- *September 1945*: the first meeting of the Council of Foreign Ministers (of the USA, the USSR, Britain, China and France), held in London to draft peace treaties with defeated enemy states, broke down after nearly one month of unproductive discussions dominated by disagreements between the Soviets and the three Western nations.
- *December 1945*: the American, Soviet and British foreign ministers met in Moscow but the prospect of a peace treaty with Germany was increasingly poor because of disagreements over Iran, which both the Soviet Union and the United States sought to dominate. Truman was exasperated: 'I'm tired of babying the Soviets.'
- *February 1946*: the Truman administration was shocked by a speech in which Stalin declared the incompatibility of Communism with capitalism, and the inevitability of another war. Supreme Court Justice William Douglas described that speech as a 'Declaration of World War III'. Within days, American diplomat **George Kennan** sent his highly influential

 KEY FIGURE

George Kennan (1904–2005)
US diplomat who specialised in the USSR. His 'Long Telegram' and containment doctrine were very important in the origins of the Cold War: they helped persuade President Truman to oppose Communism.

'Long Telegram'
US diplomat George Kennan's 1946 telegram to Washington analysing Soviet expansionism and urging US resistance.

Containment US Cold War doctrine advocating military and diplomatic action to limit the expansion of Communism.

Iron Curtain Cold War accusation, notably by Churchill (1946), that the USSR had made the Soviet bloc countries (East Germany, Czechoslovakia, Poland, Romania, Bulgaria, Hungary) inaccessible and repressed.

Sovietised Made to resemble the social and political structure of the USSR.

Covert warfare
Undermining an enemy through subversion, for example with coups and spies.

War by proxy During the Cold War, the USA and the USSR often supported opposing sides in a war that was not initially a Cold War conflict but then became one as in the Korean War (see page 21) and the Vietnam War (see page 112).

'Long Telegram' from Moscow. Kennan argued that the Soviet Union was irredeemably expansionist and that the United States should resist it. This would become known as the doctrine of **'containment'**. Truman's Secretary of State James Byrnes called Kennan's analysis 'splendid' and began a series of speeches that demonstrated the hardening of the Truman administration's opposition to the Soviet Union.

- *March 1946*: the prospects for peace-making worsened because of the continuing disagreements over Iran and former British Prime Minister Churchill's speech at Fulton, Missouri. Churchill declared that the Soviets had brought down an **'Iron Curtain'** that separated **Sovietised** Eastern Europe from democratic and pro-American Western Europe and that they wanted 'the indefinite expansion of their power and doctrine.' Truman was taken aback when much of the American press reaction to the speech was hostile, and dishonestly denied that he had known and approved the speech in advance. US foreign policy under Truman was never made in a vacuum: during 1946 his policies towards the Soviets were criticised by liberal Democrats such as Henry Wallace as too harsh and by Republicans as too soft.

- *June 1946*: the Council of Foreign Ministers met in Paris and finalised draft treaties with Romania, Bulgaria, Hungary, Finland and Italy. There would be no peace treaty with Germany because Soviet–American relations had deteriorated further after March 1946, due to disagreements over Greece, Turkey and Germany, which signalled that what became known as the Cold War was underway.

The Cold War and 'containment' in Europe

The Cold War between the United States and the Soviet Union lasted from about 1946 to 1989. Although there was no direct Soviet–American military conflict, both countries used **covert warfare** and **war by proxy** as each sought to gain and maintain its own allies and to destabilise those of the other. The Cold War remained 'cold' because after 1949 both countries possessed nuclear weapons, so that resort to war would most likely have been suicidal. Nevertheless, both maintained readiness for war: they stockpiled nuclear weapons and prepared land, air and sea forces for a clash.

The Cold War has generated many debates, especially over when and why it started.

The origins and start of the Cold War

Despite ideological tensions that dated from the Russian revolutionary era, there was no real preparation for any possible Soviet–American conflict until after the Second World War. This suggests that it was events during the Second World War that triggered the Cold War. The most important of these were:

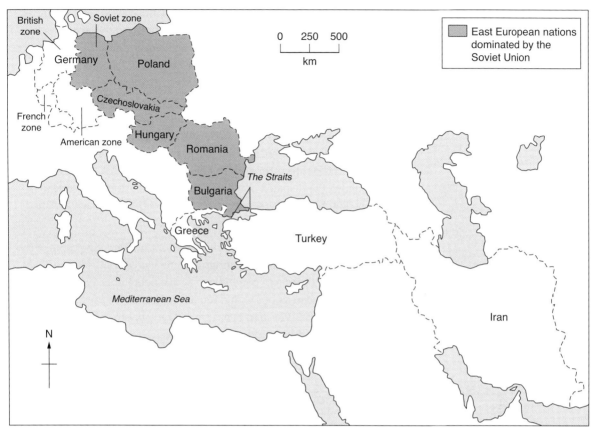

Figure 1.3 Areas of Soviet–American tension in 1946.

- the Sovietisation of Eastern Europe that began when its troops marched across the region *en route* to Berlin in 1944–5
- US secrecy over the atomic bomb, which signalled American mistrust of, and superiority over, its Soviet ally.

Both sides believed the other to be the aggressor in the Cold War, but the historian Martin McCauley was surely right in saying that both were expansionist powers, determined to encourage or force others to accept their domination and/or political system. This led to post-war conflict over particular areas, such as Iran, Greece, Turkey and Germany.

Greece and Turkey

The Truman administration wrongly believed that Stalin was behind the Greek Communist Party's opposition to the conservative Greek government and this, combined with disagreements over Turkey, caused acute problems in Soviet–American relations.

During the war, Churchill and Roosevelt had sympathised with Stalin over Soviet access from the Black Sea to the Mediterranean through the Straits (see Figure 1.3), but Stalin's post-war pressure on Turkey over this led Truman to send an American fleet to the Straits in August 1946.

Germany

During the war, the Soviets agreed to send raw materials from their German zone (see Figure 1.3 on page 15) in exchange for reparations from the other zones. However, during 1945–6, the Soviets plundered their zone, received the reparations from the Western zones, but sent nothing in return. In May 1946, America suspended the dispatch of reparations from the American zone to the Soviet zone and blamed the Soviets (and the French) for the lack of Allied agreement on Germany.

The Allied Control Council (ACC) comprised the four military governors of the occupied zones of Germany. ACC meetings became increasingly bitter during 1946. This prompted Byrnes (see page 14) to say at a September 1946 speech in Stuttgart that American troops would remain in Europe for the foreseeable future, and that the West's German zones should be economically and politically independent. When the British and American zones were combined in 1947 (the French joined in 1949), it was clear that the economic and political divisions of Germany and indeed of Europe were hardening.

Developments in the different German zones demonstrated how each power sought to create and/or support countries in their own image. Within the Soviet zone, the Communist Party was dominant, while in the Western zones there were free elections in which multiple parties participated.

The Council of Foreign Ministers again failed to reach agreement on German and Austrian peace treaties in their Moscow meeting in March 1947. When President Truman made his 'Truman Doctrine' speech in March 1947, it constituted a final and unequivocal American declaration of what was about to become commonly known as the Cold War.

The Truman Doctrine

Using the pseudonym 'Mr X', US diplomat George Kennan (see page 13) expanded on his idea of containment in his article in *Foreign Affairs* magazine, in July 1947. Kennan said the United States should oppose the Soviets 'with unalterable counter-force at every point where they show signs of encroaching upon the interests of a peaceful and stable world'. President Truman elucidated and advocated Kennan's containment doctrine in a speech to Congress on 12 March 1947. Truman said Greece and Turkey were threatened by Communist aggression and asked for $400 million to help them. Congress granted him the money.

SOURCE A

From Truman's 12 March 1947 speech to Congress, explaining the Truman Doctrine (available from http://avalon.law.yale.edu/20th_century/trudoc.asp).

The very existence of the Greek state is today threatened by … Communists … Greece must have assistance if it is to become a self-supporting and self-respecting democracy. The United States must supply that assistance. There is no other country to which Greece can turn. At the present moment in world history nearly every nation must choose between alternative ways of life. The choice is too often not a free one. One way of life is based upon the will of the majority and is distinguished by free institutions, representative government, free elections, guarantees of individual liberty, freedom of speech and religion and freedom from political oppression. The second way of life is based upon the will of a minority forcibly imposed upon the majority. It relies upon terror and oppression, a controlled press and radio, fixed elections and the suppression of personal freedoms. I believe that it must be the policy of the United States to support free peoples who are resisting attempted subjugation by armed minorities or by outside pressures… I believe that our help should be primarily through economic and financial aid.

What reasons does Truman give in Source A to support his request for aid to Greece?

The significance of the Truman Doctrine

The Truman Doctrine was highly significant. It affected and dominated US foreign policy for nearly half a century. It was one of the declarations of Cold War, the point at which the Truman administration and Congress made public the decision that Communism was a great threat that must be opposed. It did not represent a sudden departure in US foreign policy, but the culmination of much anxiety about and discussion of crises such as Iran, Greece, Turkey and Germany. Some contemporaries expressed doubts. Republican Senator Taft criticised the simplistic division of the world into two. Kennan himself said it was too sweeping because it failed to ask whether a threatened state was worth supporting and whether it was within US capabilities to support it. Journalist Walter Lippmann, who never thought much of Truman, approved aid to Greece but disliked Truman's tone: 'A vague global policy, which sounds like the tocsin [alarm bell] of an ideological crusade, has no limits. It cannot be controlled. Its effects cannot be predicted.' It certainly demonstrated the drawbacks of conducting foreign policy in a democracy, in that Truman knew that winning over the public necessitated that issues be painted in black and white, as good versus evil: a characterisation that left little room for manoeuvre in US foreign policy.

The Marshall Plan

Truman's Secretary of State, **George Marshall**, feared that the post-war devastation might make Western Europe vulnerable to Communist insurgency and the **Red Army**, especially as there were strong Communist parties in

 KEY FIGURE

George Marshall (1880–1959)
Army Chief of Staff in the Second World War, Marshall was Truman's Secretary of State (1947–9) and Secretary of Defence (1950–1). His Marshall Plan played a big part in the post-war revitalisation of Western Europe and in increased Cold War tensions.

 KEY TERM

Red Army The Soviet Union's army (the Soviet/Communist flag was red).

France and Italy in particular. West European countries were important trading partners and potential allies for the United States, so Truman decided to pump $13 billion into the restoration of their economies. When Marshall announced his plan in June 1947, he did not specify that the aid would be confined to Western Europe. The Soviets and the Eastern European states considered accepting Marshall Aid. However, the Soviets did not want to give full details of their economic devastation to the Americans, so they rejected the offer of aid and ensured that the East Europeans did so too (had the Soviets accepted the offer, it is doubtful that Congress would have financed Marshall Aid).

SOURCE B

From Secretary of State George Marshall's address at Harvard University, 5 June 1947, in which he advocated US aid to help Europe's post-war recovery (available from www.oecd.org/general/ themarshallplanspeechatharvarduniversity5june1947.htm).

Aside from the demoralizing effect on the world at large and the possibilities of disturbances arising as a result of the desperation of the [Europeans] …, the consequences to the economy of the United States should be apparent to all. It is logical that the United States should do whatever it is able to do to assist in the return of normal economic health in the world, without which there can be no political stability and no assured peace. Our policy is directed not against any country or doctrine but against hunger, poverty, desperation, and chaos. Its purpose should be the revival of the working economy in the world so as to permit the emergence of political and social conditions in which free institutions can exist … It is already evident that before the United States Government can proceed much further in its efforts to alleviate the situation and help start the European world on its way to recovery, there must be some agreement among the countries of Europe as to the requirements of the situation and the part those countries themselves will take in order to give a proper effect to whatever actions might be undertaken by this Government … The initiative, I think, must come from Europe … The program should be a joint one, agreed to by a number, if not all, European nations.

? Find evidence in Source B that might suggest (a) that the Soviets could have Marshall Aid and (b) that Marshall Aid was not intended for the Soviets.

The significance of the Marshall Plan

The Marshall Plan helped to seal the division of Europe into two antagonistic blocs. In response to American aid to Western Europe, the USSR tightened its hold over Eastern Europe, establishing full Communist Party domination in Hungary, Bulgaria, Romania and Poland, then last of all, in Czechoslovakia in spring 1948. From autumn 1947, the Soviets ordered the West European Communist parties to do all they could to bring down their national governments.

Within the United States itself, Marshall Aid demonstrated the **bipartisan** approach to the Cold War. In March 1948, Truman asked Congress to finance the Marshall Plan and to introduce universal military training and the **draft**.

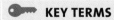

KEY TERMS

Bipartisan When Republicans and Democrats forgo political partisanship and co-operate on an issue.

Draft The US equivalent of British conscription; compulsory service in the nation's armed forces.

He said these measures were necessary because Soviet domination of Eastern Europe might be followed by a Soviet takeover of Western Europe too. In April 1948, the Republican-controlled Congress granted the Democrat Truman the money he requested even as the presidential election approached. However, they rejected his proposals for universal military training and the draft.

> ### The Truman Plan
>
> Congressional aide Clark Clifford had suggested that the Marshall Plan be called the Truman Plan, but Truman said, 'Anything that is sent up to the Senate and House with my name on it will quiver a couple of times and die.'

The Berlin Blockade

Amidst all this tension in and over Europe, it was not surprising that a great crisis arose, and that it occurred in the place where the Soviets and Americans came into closest contact – Germany. When Stalin blocked Western access to the Western zones of Berlin in June 1948 (see Figure 1.4, page 20), there could be no doubt that the Cold War was well and truly underway.

Truman had three options. He could surrender and get out of Berlin, but that would be humiliating and make the United States appear an unreliable ally. He could send military convoys down the *autobahns* to West Berlin, but even the feisty Truman considered that too aggressive and likely to lead to war. Truman chose a third option: millions of tons of supplies were airlifted by the Americans and the British into West Berlin until Stalin ended the blockade a year later in May 1949.

The significance of the Berlin Blockade

The Berlin Blockade was highly significant in two ways. First, it demonstrated how far each side was willing to go in the Cold War. Truman's choice of the third option and Stalin's passivity in face of the airlift suggested that neither wanted to risk war. Second, whatever Stalin's motives, the blockade was a failure. Whether he aimed to get the Western allies out of Berlin, or to halt the development of a West German state closely tied both politically and militarily to the Western bloc, or to test Western determination and unity, he failed spectacularly. The Western powers remained in West Berlin and demonstrated great unity, and the blockade precipitated the development of the North Atlantic Treaty Organisation (NATO) and a strongly pro-American West German state.

The development of two German states

The Truman administration had already been considering the establishment of a West German state and the blockade seemed to confirm the wisdom of the idea. In May 1949, a constitution was drawn up for the new West German state. In October 1949, the Soviets set up an East German state. The East Germans began to fence, mine and patrol their 850-mile frontier with West Germany.

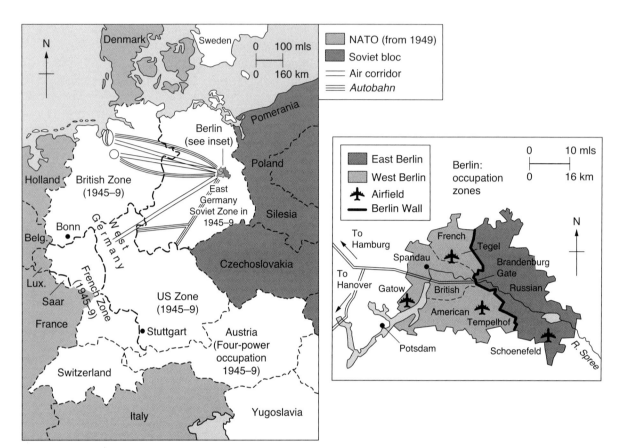

Figure 1.4 Cold War Germany.

NATO

The deterioration in relations with the Soviets confirmed the belief of Truman and the West Europeans that they needed to organise themselves into a defensive association lest the Red Army pour into Western Europe. A Communist coup in Czechoslovakia in spring 1948 represented the completion of the Iron Curtain and, combined with the Berlin Blockade, convinced Congress to agree to a massive increase in defence expenditure and to US membership of **NATO**.

NATO was significant in that:

- It completed the division of Western Europe and Eastern Europe. At first the division had been primarily political and economic. Now it was military.
- In 1955, West Germany's admission to NATO encouraged the Soviets to respond with the Warsaw Pact, the military alliance for the **Soviet bloc**.
- It could be argued that the establishment of NATO stabilised Europe. Both sides now knew where they stood. After the establishment of NATO and the fall of China to Communism, Asia became the great Cold War arena.

The Cold War and 'containment' in Asia

After the Second World War ended, the United States had given $2 billion aid to Chiang Kai-shek (see page 12), but American observers soon concluded that he was a hopeless case. In late 1949, **Mao Zedong**'s Communist forces defeated Chiang Kai-shek's Nationalist forces and the Chinese Civil War came to an end. Chiang and his followers fled to Taiwan. Truman now became a victim of his own doctrine. Many Americans thought that if Communism were such a threat, Truman should not have allowed China to become Communist. The Republicans blamed the Democrats for the 'loss' of China. It was soon commonly believed that China had been 'lost' because of Roosevelt's 'betrayal' of Chiang Kai-shek at Yalta (see page 11), insufficient US aid to Chiang, and treachery within Truman's State Department, which contained Communist sympathisers. However, as Truman and his State Department recognised, America could have done nothing short of total war to ensure the defeat of Mao Zedong and his Communist forces.

The Chinese Nationalist representative at the UN (Chiang Kai-shek's Taiwan, rather than Mao's People's Republic of China, held the China seat at the UN until 1971) warned that events in China could cause revolts and successes by Communist parties throughout Asia. Events in Korea in the summer of 1950 caused Truman and many Americans to believe that he was right.

The response to the rise of Communism in Asia

Truman responded to the rise of Communism in Asia by attempting to contain what he perceived to be Communist aggression in **French Indochina** (he offered the French financial aid in their struggle against Communist insurgents in Vietnam in spring 1950) and in Korea.

The course of events in the Korean War

On 25 June 1950, Communist North Korea attacked non-Communist and pro-American South Korea. With near-unanimous backing from Congress, the press and the public, President Truman sent air and naval assistance to South Korea and the US 7th Fleet to the Taiwan Straits. The US-dominated UN agreed that UN forces should be sent to Korea. Truman told reporters that this was not a US war but a UN 'police action'. However, although other members of the Western alliance (notably Canada and Britain) sent forces, the 'UN' force that fought alongside the South Koreans was primarily American. Truman's initial war aim was to drive the North Korean Communist forces out of South Korea.

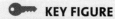

KEY FIGURE

Mao Zedong (1893–1976)

Mao led the Chinese Communist Party to victory over Chang Kai-shek's Chinese Nationalists in the Chinese Civil War (1945–9). He governed China, the first Asian Communist nation, until his death in 1976.

KEY TERM

French Indochina
Cambodia, Laos and Vietnam were French colonies from the late nineteenth century to 1954, when they gained their independence and 'French Indochina' ceased to exist.

> ## A grassroots president
>
> An Illinois Republican wrote to Truman, expressing approval of his stand over Korea: 'You may be a whiskey guzzling, poker playing buzzard as some say, but by damn, for the first time since old Teddy [Roosevelt] left there ... the United States has a grassroots AMERICAN in the White House.'

Douglas MacArthur (1880–1964)

A partisan Republican, MacArthur was a career soldier who led the US/UN forces in the Korean War. Initially successful there, he totally miscalculated over Chinese intervention in the war. When he publicly criticised Truman's policies, Truman sacked him. This was highly unpopular with the American people at first, until the army top brass gave Truman their support. Subsequently, Truman was praised for confirming civilian control over the military.

Rollback Republican policy, much talked about in the 1952 presidential election; it suggested the Democrat Truman's 'containment' was insufficiently dynamic, and that Communist expansion should not be simply stopped, but reversed.

38th parallel The line of latitude that formed the border between North and South Korea prior to the Korean War.

Armistice Agreement to stop fighting, usually a prelude to a peace treaty.

Status quo The current state of affairs.

With the advantage of preparation and surprise, the North Koreans made great advances. A US infantryman recalled how, 'Guys, sweat soaked, shitting in their pants, not even dropping them, moved like zombies' in retreat, while the casualty rate hit 30 per cent. However, US General **Douglas MacArthur**, the UN commander in Korea, turned the war around with a brilliant amphibious assault on Inchon in September 1950. This forced a North Korean retreat and at this point, Truman's war aims changed. The United States now sought the destruction of North Korea's forces and the reunification of Korea. This was no longer containment. This was what the Republicans called the '**rollback**' of Communism. Most Americans supported the change of aim. They believed that North Korean aggression should be punished and that South Korean morale would suffer if nothing were done. MacArthur, long an enthusiastic supporter of Chiang, wanted to invade China.

In October 1950, the Chinese warned that if American troops crossed into North Korea, China would enter the Korean War. MacArthur had assured Truman the Chinese would never intervene, but they did. US, UN and South Korean troops were driven back below the **38th parallel**. However, the situation was stabilised by April 1951 thanks to US General Matt Ridgway. In June 1951, China proposed an **armistice** which was finally agreed in July 1953 (Truman contributed to the prolongation of the war by insisting that Chinese prisoners of war should not be returned to China). The pre-war *status quo* was restored.

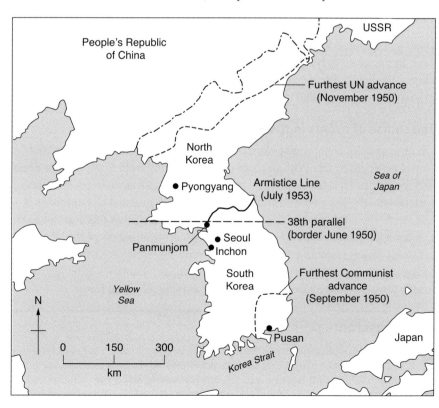

Figure 1.5 The Korean War.

Why did the United States fight in the Korean War?

During the Second World War, the Americans and Soviets agreed that when the war ended, American forces would take the Japanese surrender in the southern part of Korea and Soviet forces would take it in the north. Not surprisingly, the Soviets promoted Communism in the north of Korea and the Americans promoted an anti-Communist regime in the south. Two Korean states were created. Both the North Korean leader Kim Il Sung and the South Korean leader Syngman Rhee dreamt of reuniting and ruling the Korea peninsula. Both endorsed cross-border raids, but in June 1950 North Korea launched a full-scale attack on South Korea. Truman felt he had to respond because of foreign and domestic considerations. The foreign policy considerations were:

- An April 1950 National Security Council (**NSC**) planning paper (NSC 68) warned Truman that the Soviets had a 'fanatic faith' and aimed at total domination of Europe and Asia.
- The combination of the fall of Czechoslovakia, the Berlin Blockade and the North Korean attack convinced Truman that the Soviets were increasingly and ominously active and Truman considered Kim a Soviet (and Chinese) puppet.
- It seemed as if the world balance of power was tilting in favour of Communism – in 1949 the Soviets had exploded their first atomic bomb, and China had been 'lost' to Communism.
- South Korea was an anti-Communist state that the United States had helped create.
- Truman was concerned about the safety of Japan, which was close to Korea and lay within what Secretary of State Dean Acheson called the American defence perimeter.
- Truman felt that North Korea was testing the UN. He believed that failure to support the UN could encourage aggressors and lead to a third world war.
- American allies such as Britain and France were supportive, because they had problems with Communist insurgents in their Southeast Asian colonies.
- The United States dominated the UN and it was relatively easy to get UN support against the North Koreans.

The domestic considerations were:

- Cold War anxieties had grown in early 1950: Klaus Fuchs, who had worked on the atomic bomb, was revealed to be a Soviet spy; State Department official Alger Hiss was found guilty of lying about passing secret documents to the Soviet Union; Senator **Joseph McCarthy** had declared that Truman's State Department contained many Communists.
- The Republicans had bitterly attacked Truman over the 'loss' of China and he did not want to be accused of losing South Korea, especially as there were congressional elections in November 1950.

 **KEY TERM**

NSC The National Security Council advised the President on foreign policy.

 KEY FIGURE

Joseph McCarthy (1908–57)
McCarthy was an obscure, unimpressive senator from Wisconsin until he gained national fame by claiming that there were Communists in the Truman State Department. From 1950 to 1953, he was one of the most influential people in the USA.

The significance of the Korean War

Truman's response to the rise of Communism in Asia had been to take the nation into a bloody war that dramatically affected US foreign and domestic policies. The Korean War was significant in that:

- 36,914 Americans had died before President Eisenhower ended the war in 1953 (see page 75).
- Truman's initial war aim was achieved: South Korea was 'saved' for the United States and the Western alliance. It could be said that containment worked.
- The US attempt to reunify the peninsula failed.
- Asia replaced Europe as the central Cold War arena.
- It inspired Truman to give further support to French colonialism in Indochina and to the dictatorial regimes of Syngman Rhee in South Korea and Chiang Kai-shek in Taiwan.
- The United States dramatically increased military expenditure and massively increased its armed forces (as did the Soviet Union).
- It greatly embittered Chinese–American relations.
- It exacerbated Cold War tensions and intensified American anti-Communist hysteria (see page 36).
- It suggested that neither the United States, the Soviet Union nor China was willing to risk a third world war: Truman rejected MacArthur's suggestion that America use atomic bombs, the Chinese only intervened after several warnings and requested an armistice in spring 1951, and the Soviets left North Korea and China to do the fighting.

The Korean War also demonstrated the difficulties in conducting foreign policy and waging war in a democracy: Truman entered the war partly because he feared Republican attacks for 'losing' Korea and because he was anxious about the **congressional mid-term elections**; his change of war aims after Inchon owed much to popular demand for revenge against North Korean aggression; General MacArthur made many mistakes after Inchon, but Truman did not replace him until April 1951 because the general was so popular with the American people.

The Korean War and the powers of the presidency

As president, Truman was commander-in-chief of the US armed forces and he decided to deploy them in Korea from the start. He consulted congressional leaders and they agreed that South Korea must be assisted. The American Constitution gave Congress alone the power to declare war, but congressional leaders said there was no need for a congressional declaration of war. However, when the war became unpopular, it was commonly known as 'Truman's war', and rendered him virtually powerless to control Congress or to lead the country effectively.

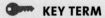

KEY TERM

Congressional mid-term elections Congressional elections are held every two years, so some are held along with the president's election, some are held in the middle of the president's term.

Summary diagram: The USA as a superpower

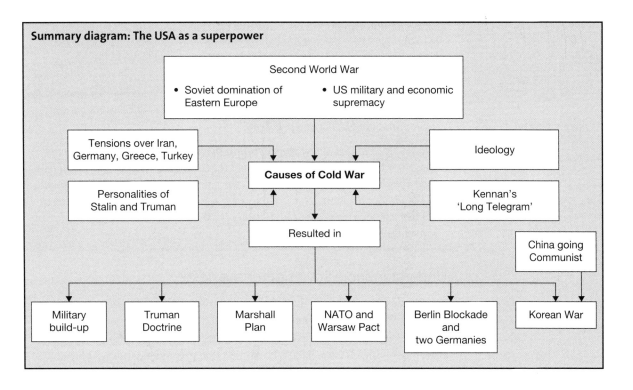

3 Key debate

▶ *Which side was to blame for the Cold War?*

Historians writing about the Cold War inevitably discuss why it began. This process invariably requires the historian to explore who bore responsibility for the conflict.

A war of Soviet aggression?

The majority of Western historians writing during the Cold War blamed the Soviets. This was not surprising, as many contemporaries viewed the Soviets as a threat to Western security.

EXTRACT I

From Malcolm Pearce and Geoffrey Stewart, *British Political History 1867–2001*, Routledge, 2002, p. 618.

[Those West Europeans who sought the establishment of NATO were] helped in this by Soviet behaviour. In February 1948 democracy in Czechoslovakia was snuffed out … then the crisis over Berlin kept tension high. In June 1948 the Soviet Union blocked road access by the Allies to Berlin, a breach of all previous agreements. The USA with enthusiastic support from Britain airlifted

between 5000 and 8000 tons a day of food as well as medical supplies into beleaguered Berlin for 324 days. It was made clear to the Soviet Union that interference with this airlift would mean war. Ominously, B-29 long-range bombers arrived in East Anglia. The USA had a monopoly of atomic weapons, a fact which the Soviets could not forget. At the same time America resolved to join the West European defence arrangements … The result was the formal inauguration of NATO in April 1949.

The USSR conceded defeat over Berlin in the next two months and the same year West Germany was created. Soviet intransigence, whether the result of wide-ranging aggression or merely … the bouncy behaviour of an ill trained pup, had been disastrous for her interests. A prosperous and armed Western Europe was in existence and in 40 years it was to destroy the Soviet Empire by peacefully, yet firmly, eye-balling her.

Understandable Soviet defensiveness?

As early as 1950, American historian William Appleman Williams rejected the orthodox Western interpretation and blamed his own country's aggression for the Cold War. There is sympathy for this view in this extract, along with some agreement with the historians who argued that misunderstandings played an important part in the origins of the Cold War.

EXTRACT 2

From Michael Lynch, *Stalin and Khrushchev: The USSR 1924–64*, Hodder, 1990.

Many commentators have emphasised Stalin's refusal to consider German reunification, or to give up the USSR's wartime gains in Eastern Europe, as a major factor in creating the Cold War. It has frequently been suggested that Stalin never fully understood the Western position. However, the misunderstanding was two-way. There was a Soviet perspective that the West never genuinely appreciated. Despite its victory over Germany and the emergence of Stalin as an outstanding world statesman, the Soviet Union felt more vulnerable than at any time since the Revolution. It was a matter of economics. The strain of total war from 1941–45 had exhausted the Russian economy; this was one reason why Stalin had been so adamant at Yalta on the issue of German reparations. The fear that he had always had of the West's being able to swamp the USSR was intensified by his knowledge of the USA's capacity, as witnessed by its prodigious war effort and the construction of the atomic bomb.

Were both sides equally culpable?

Historians such as the Soviet specialist Martin McCauley argued that both sides were wedded to expansionist ideologies and therefore equally to blame for the Cold War.

EXTRACT 3

From Martin McCauley, *Russia, America and the Cold War, 1949–91*, Longman, 2004, pp. 112–13.

*Russia and America competed with each other as systems. The systems can be perceived as communism and capitalism, freedom and tyranny, the command economy versus the market economy, individualism and collectivism, and the 'red' world versus the free world. Both dominant ideologies were utopian … [The Soviets believed] the Soviet Union would one day be the leading world power and America, which appeared so powerful and threatening, would become **Socialist**. America also had a utopian ideology … born of the conviction that America had the right and duty to enlighten the world … To become rich, happy and free, other nations had just to copy the United States. It was almost inevitable that Russia and America, given their utopianism, would construct empires. The number of countries in the[ir] respective zone[s] of imperial influence would be used as a benchmark to determine which was gaining the upper hand.*

In analysing Extracts 1, 2 and 3, is there evidence of pro-Western vocabulary or attitudes?

 KEY TERMS

Socialist Believer in a political philosophy that favours a more equal distribution of wealth than is attained under pure capitalism.

McCarthyism Anti-Communist hysteria triggered by Senator McCarthy.

④ Truman and post-war reconstruction

▶ *How successful were Truman's domestic policies?*

Truman's was a presidency characterised by crises and clashes at home and abroad. The anti-Communist hysteria and **McCarthyism** constituted the greatest domestic crisis, but Truman also clashed with the labour unions and with Congress. The first great domestic problem the new president faced was the economy.

The economy

After the Japanese surrender in 1945, many Americans feared another depression as factories laid off workers and as 12 million demobilised veterans returned home.

The employment of 12 million veterans

In 1945, Truman presented Congress with a bill that committed the government to ensuring full employment. However, when it passed the Employment Act, Congress would only empower the federal government 'to use all practical means' to foster 'maximum employment'.

Despite Truman's fears, most returning servicemen quickly found employment. Manufacturing industries boomed as factories reverted to peacetime production and struggled to meet the demand of the returned servicemen and their families. Their pent-up consumer enthusiasm generated many jobs. Many servicemen benefited from Roosevelt's GI Bill of Rights (1944), which gave returning veterans 52 weeks' unemployment pay and loans for education, housing, farms or businesses. It distributed $20 billion to 7.8 million veterans between 1945 and 1955.

Inflation and labour unions

The federal government **budget deficits**, the withdrawal of wartime price controls, and shortages of consumer goods as factories struggled to readjust, combined to produce the inflation that hit 25 per cent during 1945–6. In 1946, Truman sought to combat it through continued use of Roosevelt's Office of Price Administration (OPA), which had controlled prices during the war. Conservative Democrats and the Republicans sought the restoration of free market forces and weakened the OPA so much that prices rose spectacularly. This led to tensions with employers, who wanted to raise prices but keep wages down, and with unions, who wanted pay rises to cope with the inflation. Truman grew impatient with both groups, as both higher prices and higher wages would lead to more inflation.

Strikes

Union power increased in the Roosevelt years thanks to the **Wagner Act** (1935) and the wartime demand for **labour**. In 1945, 15 million workers were unionised – around 36 per cent of the non-agricultural workforce. When employers rejected demands for pay rises, labour responded with widespread strikes in 1946: 800,000 steelworkers walked out in January, 400,000 miners in April. When the railroad workers threatened to strike in May, Truman tried to mediate between labour and management. When the union leaders were uncooperative, a Truman aide told them that they could not simply say no to a president. In an interesting illustration of the powers of the presidency, they replied that nobody paid much attention to this president. Inundated with telegrams urging him to get tough, Truman said he would conscript the railroad workers and have the army run the railroads. Just as he informed Congress of his intent, the railroad workers called off their strike. The House of Representatives nevertheless agreed he should have the authority to conscript workers, but the Senate rejected the proposal as an unconstitutional expansion of presidential authority. In November 1946, the United Mine Workers started another strike, but the Truman administration took the union leader to court and won. This was a rare triumph in Truman's battles with the unions, which, in combination with continuing inflation, led many Americans to consider him an unimpressive leader in 1946.

The Taft–Hartley Act

During 1946 there were 4985 strikes involving 4.6 million workers. Altogether, 116 million working days were lost: three times the previous record high. The public, Republicans and conservative Democrats were tired of strikes. In 1947, the Republican-controlled Congress passed the Taft–Hartley Act to curtail union power. It said that:

- Unions were liable for breach of contract.
- Unions could not insist that all workers join a union as a condition of employment.
- The president could order an 80-day 'cooling-off' period before strikes.

Labour was furious at this curtailment of union power. Truman had vetoed the **bill**, but Congress overrode his veto.

Steel mills and presidential power

Steel profits had soared, but steelworkers had not had a pay rise since 1950. In April 1952, they threatened to strike. Steel was vital for the large quantities of munitions required during the Korean War (1950–3), so after his legal advisers and the Chief Justice told him he had the requisite power, Truman seized control of the steel mills under Executive Order No. 10340. 'The president has the power to keep the country from going to hell,' Truman assured staff who feared he was exceeding his authority.

There was much criticism and accusations that he was another Hitler. The *Washington Post* said it was one of the most high-handed acts by any president. When a journalist asked him if he could also seize the newspapers and radio stations if he desired, Truman, who had no intention of doing so, unwisely answered, 'Under similar circumstances, the president of the United States has to act for whatever is best for the country.'

The owners did not want federal government control of their mills, so they appealed to the law courts. The Supreme Court justices were liberals, appointed by Roosevelt and Truman himself, but they ruled that the president had exceeded his executive authority. Truman had overreached and humiliated himself.

The strike went ahead. It lasted several months and military output for 1952 was cut by a third. It was eventually settled, on the same terms as Truman had suggested months before.

On the whole, most Americans thought Truman mishandled the unions and inflation. He had tried but failed to persuade Congress to maintain price controls. He had tried to steer a middle course between what he considered to be both employer and union selfishness, but ended up pleasing no one. Nevertheless, by 1948, the economy was booming. Demand was high thanks to the GI Bill of Rights, soldiers' saved-up wartime wages and the post-war

KEY TERM

Bill Suggested legislation is passed to Congress in the form of a bill. When passed by both the Senate and the president, the bill becomes an Act or law. The president can veto a bill, but if there are sufficient votes, Congress can override his veto.

baby boom. Manufacturers and consumers had never had it so good. At the very least, it could be said that Truman had not damaged the nation's economy.

Anti-Truman jokes

Anti-Truman jokes were common in the media and in Washington during his presidency:

- 'Truman's got stiff joints from putting his foot in his mouth.'
- 'To err is Truman' (a variation on 'To err is human').
- 'I'm just mild about Harry' (a popular contemporary song was 'I'm Just Wild About Harry').
- 'If we're going to have a comedian in the White House, let's have a good one.'

Political divisions and domestic problems

Truman hoped to solve domestic problems by introducing the development of the welfare safety net introduced by Roosevelt's New Deal. His proposals included:

- freely available universal health care, to be funded by payroll deductions
- federally financed low-cost housing
- 'the redevelopment of large areas of the blighted and slum sections of our cities'
- increased Social Security payments and extended coverage
- a minimum wage rise from 40 cents per hour to 75 cents
- guaranteed prices and crop insurance for farmers
- public works programmes
- civil rights legislation.

These proposals exacerbated political divisions.

Congress and presidential power

While Congress rejected most of Truman's legislative proposals, he in turn vetoed 250 bills passed by Congress (Congress obtained the necessary two-thirds majority in each house to override twelve presidential vetoes). This was one of the worst periods of legislative conflict between a president and Congress in American history. Why?

Congressional resentment over the increase in the power of the presidency under Roosevelt and determination to regain the initiative poisoned relations with President Truman. Truman made it worse by asking Congress to pass reforming legislation in 1945: conservative members of Congress were tired of expensive New Deal-style policies and **House Minority Leader** Joseph Martin complained that 'not even President Roosevelt had asked for so much at one sitting.' Furthermore, Roosevelt had sought greater **executive powers** during a time of crisis, but there was no crisis now.

Naturally, the Republicans made Truman's presidency as difficult as possible. During the 1946 elections, the Republican slogan was 'HAD ENOUGH?' and for a short time it appeared that the answer was a resounding 'YES'. In the 1946 mid-term elections, the Republicans took control of Congress for the first time since 1928. Republicans interpreted this as a **mandate** for their policies of tax cuts, the restoration of the market economy and decreased federal government intervention in social welfare, although it was more of a voter reaction to rampant inflation and strikes (polls revealed that Americans considered strikes to be the nation's greatest problem).

Although Truman had a Democrat Congress for most of his presidency (apart from 1946–48), he still had few allies in Congress. Congressional Democrats were deeply divided: liberal Democrats often criticised him for failing to get more reforming New Deal-style legislation through Congress, while conservative Southern Democrats agreed with Republicans over unions and disagreed with Truman over civil rights. Prior to 1948, the Democrats were assured of the 'Solid South', where the predominantly white electorate hated the Republican Party (the party behind the North's defeat of the South in the Civil War, the freeing of the slaves and **Reconstruction**). However, when the Democrats began to take a more liberal stance on race (see page 44), the **Dixiecrats** left the party and selected Strom Thurmond as their presidential candidate in the 1948 presidential election. To the surprise of many, though, Truman was re-elected.

Truman's character and the 1948 presidential election

After their triumphs in the 1946 elections, the Republicans felt assured that Republican presidential candidate Thomas Dewey would defeat Truman in 1948. However, thanks in large part to his character and personality, Truman won. He embarked on a barnstorming 33-day, 30,000-mile (50,000 km) whistle-stop tour of the nation, defending his record and attacking the Republican 'do-nothing Congress'. He loved addressing the people, and they turned out in the hundreds of thousands to hear him. They had heard that he had said he would give the Republicans hell, and Paul Douglas, a Democrat candidate for the Senate in Indiana, wrote:

> *I was with Truman in the central part of the state. There was great applause, and there were constant shouts of 'Give em hell, Harry' … and he was at home with the crowd … he was simple, unaffected, and determined. We were proud of him.*

Truman always asked the crowd if they would like to meet the family, and they would cheer as wife Bess and daughter Margaret came out to wave at them. Voting results demonstrated the effectiveness of this very personal campaign: for example, Truman insisted on campaigning in Republican counties in Illinois, and he won them. Truman's favourite aide, Clark Clifford, said, 'It wasn't Harry Truman the politician who won, it was Harry Truman the man.' One Illinois woman said she voted for Truman because he was 'the common man's man'.

KEY TERMS

Mandate The authority to do something.

Reconstruction The process of rebuilding and reforming the eleven Southern states after their defeat in the Civil War.

Dixiecrats Southerners who broke away from the Democratic Party in 1948 because the Democrats were increasingly liberal on civil rights.

An Ohio voter said, 'Harry Truman, running around and yipping and falling all over his feet – I had the feeling he could understand the kind of fixes I got into.' 'You just have to take off your hat to a beaten man who refuses to stay licked,' said the deeply conservative New York *Sun*. The liberal *New Republic* said, 'It was fun to see the scrappy little cuss come out of his corner fighting.' While his joyous, feisty, determined and fiercely partisan character was probably the single most important reason for his victory, there were others:

- Some voters responded to his accusations that the Republican Congress had been a 'do-nothing Congress'. The Republican **platform** contained many measures that Truman had sought but Congress had refused to pass. When Truman challenged the Republicans to prove that they were serious about the social reform in their platform by passing legislation in a special session in July 1948, they did nothing.
- Many voters were benefiting from the booming economy.
- As an old farm boy himself, Truman knew what concerned farmers and he won their vote.
- Organised labour and blue-collar workers voted for him because he was better than a Republican.
- African-Americans voted for him because they approved of his stand on civil rights.
- Many voters approved of Truman's resistance to Communism, especially during the Berlin Blockade (see page 19). One aide wrote, 'There is considerable political advantage to the Administration in the battle with the Kremlin.'
- Dewey ran an overconfident and uninspired Republican campaign. He lacked Truman's warmth. 'Smile, Governor,' said one reporter. 'I thought I was,' answered Dewey. Crowds loved it when Truman asked them which word rhymed with '**hooey**'.

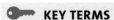

KEY TERMS

Platform Consists of the different policies or planks of a candidate or political party.

Hooey Nonsense.

Inauguration Day The president usually undergoes an elaborate inauguration ceremony on Capitol Hill, at which he is sworn into office.

African-Americans

The terms 'African-Americans' or 'black Americans' are used in this book to refer to Americans of African ancestry. African-Americans were commonly known as 'Negroes' until the mid-1960s. This term is now unacceptable.

In the election, Truman defeated Dewey by over 2 million votes, while the Democrats regained control of Congress. The Republicans had been so confident of victory that prior to the election, the Republican-controlled Congress had voted $80,000 to fund **Inauguration Day**. Truman and the Democrats gleefully spent it all on what turned out to be the most spectacular Inauguration Day to date.

SOURCE C

The conservative *Chicago Daily Tribune* newspaper was so certain that Dewey would beat Truman in the 1948 presidential election that it published somewhat prematurely. Here Truman holds up the paper.

What does Source C suggest to you about newspapers as sources for the historian?

Truman's Fair Deal

In January 1949, Truman introduced the phrase 'Fair Deal' to describe the social reforms he had repeatedly urged Congress to pass since 1945. His proposals resulted in some successes:

- Social Security was extended to an extra million Americans.
- The minimum wage was raised from 40 cents to 75 cents an hour.
- Farmers were assisted by measures for soil conservation, flood control and rural electrification.

Sometimes Truman had mixed success, as with the National Housing Act (1949).

Housing

The post-war housing shortage was the worst in American history (in Chicago, some people bought streetcars in which to live). The shortage was due to the wartime focus on the production of defence materiel and to the near 12 million men who returned from the war ready to start families. Truman constantly pressured Congress to alleviate the housing shortage. It eventually and reluctantly passed the Housing Act in 1949. The Act said that 810,000 federally subsidised public housing units should be built for low-income Americans.

Only 156,000 units were built by 1952 (356,000 by 1964) and some of what was built was poorly constructed, but it was better than nothing. It contributed to a construction boom that provided employment. The Act also included measures for slum clearance and urban renewal.

Congress totally rejected many of Truman's other Fair Deal proposals, including measures for federal health care and education.

Health insurance and education

Truman proposed a national health-insurance scheme based on a tax of 4 per cent on the first $6300 of a person's income. Congress attacked it as a tax-raising measure and because they felt it was not the federal government's job to tell people how to arrange their own healthcare. The medical profession, represented by the American Medical Association, attacked the proposal as **'socialised medicine'**.

Little was managed in education, despite increased evidence of problems in American schools, because education was seen as a state rather than a federal issue. Truman did obtain a National School Lunch Act (1946) that enabled poorer schoolchildren to eat a free or low-cost lunch.

Failure?

Truman did not help his cause in that he was not tactful when dealing with Congress. He needed their help on Communist subversion and the Korean War, and to get it, he had to give up on his Fair Deal. However, it was unlikely that even with tact and without the Korean War he could have obtained his Fair Deal dreams. Many Americans simply felt that the New Deal (see page 2) had done enough. They did not want to do more. Truman's healthcare and low-cost housing proposals were simply too revolutionary. Furthermore, they wanted no more Roosevelts. In order to ensure no more repeatedly elected presidents such as Roosevelt, Congress passed the 22nd **amendment** in 1951. It set a maximum two-term limit on presidents. The states ratified the Amendment, demonstrating the widespread concern aroused by Roosevelt's presidency (Truman himself had opposed Roosevelt standing for a third term).

The rise of McCarthyism

The greatest domestic crisis of Truman's presidency was the **Red Scare**, the anti-Communist hysteria exacerbated by Senator Joseph McCarthy.

Most Americans regarded Communism as an alien ideology, godless, repressive, aggressive and socialistic. This ideological aversion combined with the fear of Soviet military strength helped to generate the Red Scare of 1946–53, which was fuelled by **HUAC** (see below) and Republican Party ambitions, by Communist successes and by Truman himself.

KEY TERMS

Socialised medicine Conservative Americans opposed giving medical assistance to the poor, claiming that it smacked of socialism and Communism.

Amendment The Founding Fathers wrote out rules by which the United States was to be governed in the Constitution. New rules or amendments can be added.

Red Scare Periods of hysterical anti-Communism in the USA; the first was after the Russian Revolution, the second in the late 1940s to early 1950s.

HUAC The House (of Representatives) Un-American Committee investigated suspected Communists within the USA.

HUAC

The House of Representatives Committee on Un-American Activities (HUAC) was set up during the Great Depression to investigate left-wingers. In 1945, Congressman John Rankin suggested HUAC be made permanent and given broader powers to deal with domestic subversion (he was convinced it was a Communist plot when he discovered that the Red Cross did not label blood according to race).

In 1947, the Republicans dominated Congress and HUAC. They began investigating a supposed Hollywood-centred Communist conspiracy to overthrow the government. The 'Hollywood 10', a group of writers and directors who had been or were members of the American Communist Party, were convicted of contempt of Congress and given one-year prison sentences. The hysterical pursuit of suspects then moved to Broadway (New York City's theatre district) and to federal government employees.

Truman's responsibility for the new Red Scare

In March 1947, Truman contributed to the Red Scare. First, when Republican Senator Vandenberg advised him to 'scare the hell' out of the American people, in order to gain their support in his 'Truman Doctrine' speech (see page 17), he did so. It worked – perhaps too well. Second, he issued Executive Order No. 9835, which ordered an investigation into the loyalty of federal employees. He did this, an aide said, to steal the Republicans' thunder.

Sometimes, Truman let it be known that he thought the hunt for Communists had gone too far. In 1950, Congress passed the Internal Security Act (also known as the McCarran Act). It said that members of Communist-affiliated organisations had to register with the federal government or face prison or fines. Those who registered could be denied passports or deported. Truman was torn between trying to defend his administration from charges that it was lax on security and the desire to defend civil liberties. 'In a free country we punish men for the crimes they commit, but never for the opinions they have,' he said. He vetoed the act, but Congress overrode his veto.

Truman did not stop the Justice Department and the **FBI** working hard to hunt out Communists. FBI chief J. Edgar Hoover ordered his men to follow up all leads on supposed subversives, however trivial (he was especially interested to hear about the sexual activities of those being investigated). Estimates of the numbers affected vary, but it has been suggested that between 1947 and 1952 there were over 3 million investigations, several thousand resignations proffered in order to pre-empt investigations, and over 1000 dismissals. White House aide Clark Clifford recalled that Truman thought the Communist scare 'was a load of **baloney**. But political pressures were such that he had to recognize it.' Privately, Truman compared Hoover and the FBI to the *Gestapo*.

🔑 KEY TERMS

FBI The Federal Bureau of Investigation was set up in 1924 to help deal with crime.

Baloney Nonsense.

Gestapo Infamous Nazi secret police force.

Communist successes 1949–50

Americans grew even more anxious about Communism in 1949 when the Soviets exploded their first atomic bomb and China became Communist, and after there were several high-profile spy scandals in early February 1950. Klaus Fuchs, who had worked on the development of the atomic bomb, was arrested in Britain for betraying atomic secrets to the Soviets and State Department official Alger Hiss and Ethel and Julius Rosenberg were arrested in the United States.

The Communist Rosenbergs were the only American citizens executed for espionage in the Cold War. They were 'shopped' by Ethel's brother David. Like Julius, David was a Soviet spy. In 1996, David confessed that he had lied about his sister being a spy in exchange for the freedom of his wife (also a spy). Julius died after the first series of electrocutions, but when the attendants removed Ethel's strapping and other equipment after the normal course of electrocutions, it was found that her heart was still beating. Three more courses of electrocution were applied, after which smoke rose from Ethel's head. Doctors then attested that she was dead. No relatives would adopt the Rosenbergs' two orphaned sons, but a Jewish songwriter did so. It has been suggested that prejudice against Jewish-Americans played a part in the fate of the Rosenbergs.

Republican Party ambitions

Democrats had occupied the White House since 1933, so the Republicans needed issues with which to beat the Democrats. Patriotism demanded unity in opposition to the Soviet threat, so the best the Republicans could do was to attack the Democrats for waging the Cold War with insufficient vigour. Beginning with the Republican successes in the 1946 congressional elections, the strategy worked. A spring 1948 poll found that 73 per cent of Americans considered Truman too soft on the Soviets. In this already paranoid atmosphere, Republican Senator Joseph McCarthy convinced many Americans that the Truman administration contained Communists. The Red Scare was not McCarthy's fault, but it peaked under his influence.

McCarthy and McCarthyism

Born to a poor Irish farming family in central Wisconsin, Joseph McCarthy survived serious criticisms of his performance and behaviour as a county judge. His successful 1946 campaign for the Senate owed much to his lies about his war record (he claimed that his limp was due to a war wound, but it was the result of falling downstairs at a party).

In 1949, a poll of Washington correspondents voted McCarthy the worst US senator. Needing some good publicity, McCarthy presented himself as a diligent patriot, making a series of speeches in early 1950 in which he said there were card-carrying Communists in the State Department (the numbers he said he could name varied from speech to speech). The Senate then established a special committee under Millard Tydings, a conservative Democrat from Maryland, to investigate McCarthy's charges. The Tydings Committee quickly reported that McCarthy's lies were 'a fraud and a hoax', but McCarthy supporters in Maryland retaliated by circulating a fake photograph showing Tydings conversing animatedly with US Communist Party leader Earl Browder. Tydings failed to get re-elected in November 1950.

Investigations during the McCarthy hysteria

In 1952, McCarthy headed congressional committees that investigated Communist subversives in the United States. By 1953, these congressional investigations covered the media, the entertainment industry, colleges and universities. State legislatures joined in the witch-hunt and around 500 state and local government employees, 600 schoolteachers and 150 college professors lost their jobs. McCarthyites attacked US Information Agency libraries because they had exhibited the work of 'radicals' such as Mark Twain (1835–1910), creator of two of the most loved characters in American fiction, Huckleberry Finn and Tom Sawyer. The nation that considered itself to be the world's leading democracy was now stifling freedom of speech and censoring books.

McCarthy and the presidential election in 1952

In 1952, McCarthy helped ensure the defeat of many Democrats (he christened them 'Commie-crats'), including presidential candidate **Adlai Stevenson**. Future president Richard Nixon had made his name in anti-Communist investigations. He defeated Helen Gahagan Douglas in the 1950 California Senate race, mostly by accusing her of being a Communist (see page 64). In 1952, Nixon mocked 'Adlai the appeaser', graduate of the Truman administration's 'cowardly College of Communist Containment'. This anti-Stevenson feeling owed much to class hatred (McCarthy and Nixon came from poor backgrounds). Newspapers with working-class and/or right-wing editorship and readership were particularly hard on Stevenson. The New York *Daily News* called Adlai 'Adelaide' and said he 'trilled' his speeches in a 'fruity' voice. In a homophobic age, it was quite usual to smear establishment figures who had supposed Communist sympathies with suggestions of homosexuality.

How did McCarthy get away with it?

McCarthy terrorised many Americans with his untrue accusations. He got away with his lies because of:

- fear of Communist expansionism, as in China in 1949 and the North Korean attack of June 1950
- hysterical anti-Communism
- spy scares
- Republican ambitions to regain control of the presidency and Congress ('twenty years of treason')

KEY FIGURE

Adlai Stevenson (1900–65)

The Democratic presidential candidate in 1952 and 1956. The Democrats chose John F. Kennedy over Stevenson in 1960. Kennedy appointed him ambassador to the UN.

- Democrat fears that they dare not defend the accused lest they draw down McCarthy's fire on their own heads and be called Communist sympathisers (senators who did stand up to McCarthy suffered defeat in the 1952 congressional elections)
- McCarthy's good relationship with the press
- Republican reluctance to challenge him, particularly Truman's Republican successor, Dwight D. Eisenhower (see Chapter 2)
- the mindless, timid conformity that Harvard sociologist David Riesman said characterised Cold War Americans.

Much of the paranoia and persecution that affected Cold War America was due to McCarthy, who also influenced US foreign policy and defence policy. Along with the Truman Doctrine and containment, McCarthy played an important part in getting America involved in the Korean War. When Stalin died in 1953 and the new Soviet regime sought a relaxation of tensions, there was little serious attempt at US negotiations with the Soviet Union or China, and this was probably due to McCarthy.

The Cold War had a massive impact on American society and culture. The anti-Communist hysteria, which owed so much to McCarthy, damaged the American ideals of freedom of thought and freedom of expression. Thousands of innocent people suffered: several thousand lost their jobs, several hundred were jailed and over 150 were deported in a period when one's American identity demanded ideological conformity.

Summary diagram: Truman and post-war reconstruction

Problems	Imagined contemporary scores for Truman out of 10
Inflation	2
Unions	2
Employers	2
Housing shortage	4
Fair Deal	4
Relations with Congress	3
Relations with conservative Democrats	2
Winning the 1948 election	6

5 African-Americans in the North and the South

> ▶ *How far did the situation of African-Americans improve between 1945 and 1952?*

Black slaves were transported from Africa to North America in the seventeenth and eighteenth centuries. In the American Civil War (1861–5), the North defeated the slave-owning South and slavery was abolished under President Lincoln. However, Southern whites established a new system of race control in the late nineteenth century with the **Jim Crow** laws, which introduced *de jure* **segregation** of blacks and whites. In 1945, the 14 million African-Americans in the United States constituted 10 per cent of the population.

The South in 1945

In 1945, African-Americans had inferior social, economic, political and legal status in the South.

Social status

In 1945, after several years in an all-black school, a teenage Martin Luther King Jr was studying at all-black Morehouse College in Atlanta, Georgia. It was not only his college that was segregated. He had to sit at the back in the black section of a bus, or in a segregated carriage on a train. He could only drink from a 'colored' water fountain and use a 'colored' restroom. He could not sit at a Woolworth's lunch counter to eat a hot dog and drink a soda, but a white drugstore might serve him ice cream through a side window. It would be in a paper cup so no white person would ever have to eat off something used by a black person. King recalled that this segregation made him 'determined to hate every white person'.

Economic status

Many African-Americans in the South worked in agriculture, usually as sharecroppers. Those in the towns invariably held menial jobs such as domestics or **bell hops**. While jobs on the railroad were considered highly prestigious, it was church ministers, such as Martin Luther King Snr, who stood at the apex of Southern black society. Ministers could afford to send their children to college, but many African-Americans worked at tasks that left their potential unfulfilled. Rosa Parks and Fannie Lou Hamer subsequently played important parts in the **civil rights movement**: both were intelligent but undereducated women. In 1945, Parks worked as a part-time seamstress in a Montgomery, Alabama, department store and as a cleaner for a white family, while Hamer was an impoverished sharecropper. It was hard for African-Americans to escape the poverty trap in the South because their segregated educational institutions were far inferior to those of whites.

 **KEY TERMS**

Jim Crow An early 1830s' comic, black-faced, minstrel character developed by a white performing artist that proved popular with white audiences. Southern state laws that legalised segregation in the late nineteenth century were known as 'Jim Crow laws'.

***De jure* segregation** Racial segregation by law.

Bell hops Hotel porters.

Civil rights movement The predominantly black movement for equal rights for African-Americans.

SOURCE D

? What does Source D
suggest about US society
in 1948?

George McLaurin at Oklahoma State University in 1948. African-Americans in
the South had to use segregated facilities such as this.

Political status

Few Southern black people could vote in 1945, although the number was slowly
rising (3 per cent in 1940, 12 per cent in 1947). White registrars made it difficult
for black people to register to vote. Rosa Parks 'failed' the literacy test set by the
white registrar when she tried to register in 1943. Registrars asked impossible
questions, such as, 'What does Section 3, paragraph 1 of the state constitution
say?' or, 'How many bubbles are there in a bar of soap?' One straight-faced
African-American told the registrar he did not know but would like to be
told as he did not wish to remain ignorant forever. If attempted registration
was successful, would-be voters had to pay the **poll tax**. When Parks finally
registered in 1945, she had to pay $16.50 – a large sum for a seamstress.

Legal status

African-Americans had little or no protection from white police officers or
from the white justices and juries of the law courts. President Truman told how
returning black servicemen had been attacked with impunity in the South in
1945–6.

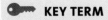 **KEY TERM**

Poll tax A tax levied on
would-be voters, which
made it harder for African-
Americans (who were usually
poorer) to vote.

SOURCE E

President Truman's replies in 1948 to letters from (1) an old army colleague and (2) Southern Democrats who disapproved of his stance on civil rights.

1. My very stomach turned over when I learned that Negro soldiers, just back from overseas, were being dumped out of army trucks in Mississippi and beaten. Whatever my inclinations as a native of Missouri might have been, as President I know this is bad. I shall fight to end evils like this … I am not asking for social equality, because no such things exist, but I am asking for equality of opportunity for all human beings …

2. When a Mayor and a City Marshal can take a Negro Sergeant off a bus in South Carolina, beat him up and put out one of his eyes, and nothing is done about it by the State Authorities, something is radically wrong with the system.

> What does Source E suggest about the situation of black Americans in 1941–8? **?**

Black Americans in the North in 1945

Life was better in the North, so millions of African-Americans migrated there from the South in the first half of the twentieth century in what became known as the **Great Migration**. Although forced to live in *de facto* **segregated** housing, they could sit where they liked on public transportation. Although many were impoverished, there were more well-paid jobs available, for example, at Ford car plants in Detroit, Michigan. African-Americans could vote in the North, and in 1945 two black congressmen sat in the US House of Representatives: William Dawson represented a Chicago **ghetto**, and Adam Clayton Powell represented New York City's **Harlem** ghetto (at this time, few white people would vote for a black person to represent them).

The impact of the Second World War

The Second World War had a dramatic impact on black Americans through migration, service in the armed forces, close proximity to whites, and increased activism and opportunities.

Migration

Many African-Americans migrated from the South to jobs in the defence industries in the North and in West Coast cities such as Oakland. There, the denser concentration of population in urban areas contributed to greater political power and to greater community consciousness and assertiveness.

Servicemen

When black soldiers accustomed to the greater freedom of the North found themselves stationed in the South, they frequently defied Jim Crow laws. Many black servicemen felt they deserved greater respect. For example, in 1943, a New

> 🔑 **KEY TERMS**
>
> **Great Migration**
> The Northward movement of Southern African-Americans during the twentieth century.
>
> ***De facto* segregated**
> Black and white people segregated in residential areas and some other public places in practice if not in law.
>
> **Ghetto** Area inhabited mostly or solely by (usually poor) members of a particular ethnicity or nationality.
>
> **Harlem** New York City's African-American ghetto.

Orleans bus driver ordered a black soldier to the rear of the bus. When he refused, all 24 black passengers supported him. They ended up in prison, but had demonstrated that attitudes were changing.

Hundreds of thousands of black servicemen returned from fighting German or Japanese fascism prepared to fight racism in the USA. An ex-corporal from Alabama said, 'I'm hanged if I'm going to let the Alabama version of the Germans kick me around … I went into the army a nigger; I'm comin' out a man.' During the late 1940s, Congressman Lyndon Johnson said:

> *The Negro fought in the war, and … he's not gonna keep taking the shit we're dishing out. We are in a race with time. If we don't act, we're gonna have blood in the streets.*

Many black veterans benefited from the GI Bill of Rights (see page 28): record numbers attended college, which improved their employment opportunities and made them more articulate in demanding equality.

Close proximity to whites

Under the pressure of war, blacks and whites worked together more than before and this caused tensions. For example, when the Alabama Dry Dock Company employed black workers, jealousy over the best jobs and white opposition to black males working alongside white females led to violent clashes. There were similar tensions where blacks and whites found themselves living and moving in closer proximity than ever before, in crowded wartime cities. This stirred greater black consciousness and activism.

Increased activism and opportunities

The National Association for the Advancement of Colored People (**NAACP**) was established in the early twentieth century to campaign for racial equality. The impact of the Second World War on black activism was clearly illustrated by the wartime rise in NAACP membership from 50,000 to 450,000. Wartime propaganda about fighting for democracy contributed to greater black assertiveness. Rosa Parks (see page 83) resented the fact that her brother was expected to fight for a country in which he was not allowed to vote. She joined the NAACP in 1942 because, she said, it 'was about empowerment through the ballot box. With a vote would come economic improvements.'

The war improved black American bargaining power. Black labour leader **A. Philip Randolph** threatened to bring Washington to a standstill unless there was equality within the armed forces and the workplace. President Roosevelt needed black workers, so he responded with the establishment of the Fair Employment Practices Commission (FEPC) to promote equality in the defence industries in which 2 million African-Americans were employed.

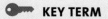

KEY TERM

NAACP The National Association for the Advancement of Colored People was the oldest and most respected black civil rights organisation.

KEY FIGURE

A. Philip Randolph (1890–1979)

In 1925, Randolph established the first black labour union, the Brotherhood of Sleeping Car Porters. His pressure forced Roosevelt to establish the FEPC, and contributed to Truman's desegregation of the armed forces in 1948. In 1963, Randolph masterminded the March on Washington. Randolph was important in the development of black recognition that mass, non-violent protest could evoke federal government aid.

Campaigns for civil rights

Black organisations stepped up their campaigns for equality during and after the war. In 1942, Christian Socialist James Farmer established the Congress of Racial Equality (CORE). CORE organised wartime **sit-ins** in segregated Chicago restaurants and a 1947 'Journey of Reconciliation', in which CORE activists rode buses across the South as an integrated group to test whether the Supreme Court's 1946 *Morgan* v. *Virginia* ruling against segregation on interstate transport was being followed.

The NAACP used a variety of tactics. These included economic boycotts. For example, in New Orleans in 1947, NAACP activists picketed stores that would not allow black women to try on hats. Most important of all though, was NAACP's litigation strategy. Back in 1896, the Supreme Court had ruled (*Plessy* v. *Ferguson*) that 'separate but equal' facilities were unconstitutional. The NAACP worked through the law courts to prove that segregated facilities were never equal and won three important victories in the Supreme Court in 1950:

- Segregation on railroad dining cars was illegal (*Henderson* v. *United States*).
- A black student could not be physically separated from white students in the University of Oklahoma (*McLaurin* v. *Oklahoma State Regents*).
- A separate black Texan law school was not equal to the all-white University of Texas law school, to which the petitioner had therefore to be admitted (*Sweatt* v. *Painter*).

These rulings virtually overturned *Plessy*, a process that would be completed with the 1954 *Brown* ruling (see page 86) against segregated education.

In the decade after the war, there was a dramatic upsurge in black activism in **Deep South** states such as Mississippi, Louisiana and Georgia. Roughly one-fifth of the adult black population voted in Georgia's **gubernatorial** election in 1946 and activists were particularly effective in Georgia's leading cities, Atlanta and Savannah. The power of the growing black vote bought change, as when Mayor Hartsfield of Savannah appointed six black police officers. Although resurgent white supremacy halted the black activism in Georgia from 1948, local black activism continued to flourish in Louisiana and Mississippi. For example, the Mississippi Progressive Voters' League attracted 5000 members within the first year of its existence (1947).

The main aim of the civil rights campaigns was to elicit action by the federal and state authorities to provide for political, social and economic equality. They had some successes.

KEY TERMS

Sit-ins When protestors sat in the 'wrong' seats in restaurants and refused to move, causing the establishment to lose custom and then, hopefully, desegregate.

Deep South States such as Mississippi, Alabama and Georgia, where segregation and racism were most deeply entrenched.

Gubernatorial Pertaining to being a state governor in the USA.

The responses of the federal and state authorities

During the Truman years, the Supreme Court led the way in promoting racial equality, but the president also provided a moral lead.

President Truman

The executive branch of the federal government had done little for African-Americans since the Civil War era. Truman himself had been typically racist in his younger days, telling his sweetheart Bess that one man was as good as another, 'so long as he is honest and decent and not a nigger or a Chinaman'. However, Truman changed. While a senator in the late 1930s, he supported legislation against the poll tax and **lynching**, and his good record on civil rights was one reason why Roosevelt chose him as his running mate in 1944. As president, Truman tried to help African-Americans through pressure on Congress and executive actions.

 **KEY TERM**

Lynching Unlawful killing (usually by hanging) of African-Americans.

Requests to Congress

Truman repeatedly sought, but never obtained, civil rights legislation through Congress. In 1945–6, he failed to get congressional approval for the continuation of the FEPC (see page 42). In 1946, he established a committee of liberals to investigate the attacks on returning black servicemen. The committee produced a liberal report entitled *To Secure These Rights* (1949). It called for the United States to live up to its claim to lead the free world by treating black Americans as equal. It advocated the elimination of segregation from American life through the use of federal power. It called for:

- anti-lynching legislation
- abolition of the poll tax
- voting rights laws
- a permanent FEPC
- an end to discrimination in interstate travel
- an end to discrimination in the armed forces
- a civil rights division in the Justice Department
- administration support for civil rights suits in the federal courts
- the establishment of the United States Commission on Civil Rights.

These were revolutionary recommendations and when Truman asked Congress to act on them, he was ignored. However, for the first time in nearly a century, a president had put civil rights firmly on the legislative agenda and given a moral lead to those who sought change.

Executive orders

In 1948, Truman issued executive orders to end discrimination in the armed forces and guarantee fair employment in the federal bureaucracy. The army top brass resisted as long as they could, until the pressures of the Korean War forced them to implement Truman's orders.

Truman's Executive Order No. 10308 established the Committee on Government Contract Compliance (CGCC), which put pressure on companies with federal contracts to end discrimination.

Truman's motivation

Was Truman simply after the black vote? Advisers told him that many believed 'the Northern Negro vote today holds the balance of power in presidential elections' because African-Americans voted as a bloc and were geographically concentrated in large, closely contested and electorally pivotal states such as New York, Illinois and Michigan. However, his stance alienated voters in the formerly Solid South and led to Thurmond's Dixiecrat challenge in 1948 (see page 31), so it seems more likely that Truman was motivated by his sense of fairness.

The Supreme Court and Congress

The judicial branch of the federal government was particularly helpful to African-Americans, with rulings that eroded the constitutional foundations

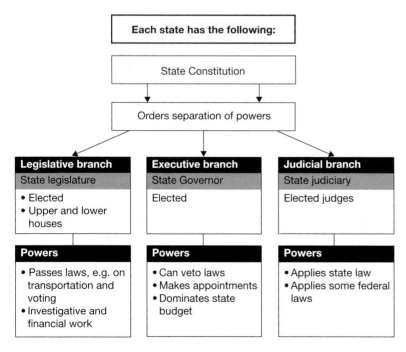

Figure 1.6 The structure of state government in the USA.

for Jim Crow (see page 43). However, the Supreme Court had no powers of enforcement. It relied on the president and Congress to enforce its rulings, and Congress did nothing to help black Americans in the Truman years. Due to seniority rules, conservative Southern Democrats dominated congressional committees, and they were steadfast opponents of racial equality.

State and local government

State and local government often proved helpful to African-Americans. By 1952, only five states retained the poll tax, eleven states and twenty cities had fair employment laws, and nineteen states had legislation against some form of racial discrimination. The interplay of local forces was always important, as when black parental pressure, a state court ruling and an enlightened school board combined to lead a single school in Delaware, Clayton High School, to admit black children. However, white politicians in the Deep South remained determined to obstruct black progress towards equality. State governments had control of voting, education and transportation within the state, and Southern states remained pro-segregation.

Summary diagram: African-Americans in the North and the South

North		South
North		**South**
Better employment opportunities but still disproportionately poor	**Economic status**	Mostly sharecropping and menial jobs, e.g. domestics
De facto segregation in housing and some public places indicated inferiority, but better than the South. Police officers often racist. Congress unhelpful over housing and discrimination. Schools in poor areas usually inferior quality	**Social status**	*De jure* segregation enshrined their inferior status in law. NAACP litigation elicited helpful Supreme Court rulings against segregation. Second World War increased consciousness and activism. No protection from local law enforcement/courts
Could vote, and where the black population was concentrated, black officials/representatives could be elected. National politicians increasingly aware of black vote	**Political status**	Few allowed to vote. Southern states dominated by politicians and officials determined to maintain white supremacy

---

6 Truman and post-war America: conclusions

▶ *Was Truman a successful president?*

'The general trend,' Truman wrote to his wife about what was being written about him in early 1950, 'is that I am a very small man in a very large place.' It is difficult to argue that Truman's domestic policies were successful. He had not managed as much as he had hoped over public housing and civil rights, although he had given an admirable moral lead over both. He failed to establish his medical insurance programme and most people thought he handled the unions and inflation badly. However, many Americans were better off by the end of his presidency. A 1952 census report showed unprecedented improvements in income, standards of living, education and housing in the Truman years, to which the president had made some contribution. In his final **State of the Union** message to Congress in January 1953, Truman said that his domestic record was a source of pride:

- 62 million Americans had jobs (11 million more than in 1946)
- unemployment was virtually nil
- farm and corporate income stood at an all-time high
- no insured bank had failed in nine years
- 8 million veterans had been to college
- Social Security benefits had doubled
- the minimum wage had been increased
- there had been progress on slum clearance
- millions of government-financed homes had been built
- incomes had risen more than prices.

As far as foreign policy was concerned, a few people then and since argued that there might not have been a Cold War had Roosevelt lived. Some say that the post-war Soviet Union was devastated and not the threat that Truman claimed it to be. However, it was two years before Truman made his declaration of Cold War in the Truman Doctrine and by that time most members of his administration had concluded that the Soviet Union needed to be opposed. Truman told advisers that he was proudest of his aid to Greece and Turkey, the Marshall Plan, NATO, the Berlin airlift and Korea, through all of which, he said, he had successfully contained Communism.

KEY TERM

State of the Union
Annual speech by the president, usually boasting of his achievements and setting out his future plans.

SOURCE F

? How far do you agree with Source F? What would you add to or subtract from this brief extract as your verdict on Truman's presidency?

Historian Henry Steele Commager's 1952 article on Truman's presidency in *Look* magazine was so controversially pro-Truman that the editors of the magazine stated that they totally disagreed with it. Quoted from David McCullough, *Truman*, Simon & Schuster, 1992, p. 916.

We cannot know what verdict history will pronounce upon it, but we can make a pretty good guess. It will perhaps record the curious paradox that a man charged with being 'soft' on communism has done more than any other leader in the Western world, with the exception of Churchill, to contain communism; that a man charged with mediocrity has launched a whole series of far-sighted plans for world reconstruction; that a man accused of being an enemy to private enterprise has been head of the Government during the greatest period of greatest prosperity for private enterprise; that a man accused of betraying the New Deal has fought one Congress after another for progressive legislation.

Chapter summary

After the Second World War, the United States was the wealthiest and most powerful nation in the world. However, it had its problems, including sharp divisions between rich and poor, black and white, and North and South, and the deteriorating relationship with the Soviet Union. Truman attempted to contain Communism in Europe by Marshall Aid and NATO and in Asia by US entry into the Korean War.

Truman wanted to introduce social reforms to address the divisions, but Congress resented the increase in the powers of the presidency under Roosevelt and was obstructive. Truman's presidency was characterised by exceptionally bitter political partisanship, notably Republican Senator Joseph McCarthy's accusations that the Democrat administration was 'soft on Communism' and full of traitors.

African-Americans suffered social, economic and political inequality, especially in the South. African-American activism increased after the Second World War and Truman and the Supreme Court were sympathetic, but Congress and the Southern states were not.

Refresher questions

Use these questions to remind yourself of the key material covered in this chapter.

1 How and why had President Roosevelt greatly changed the United States?

2 Why was the United States the most prosperous nation in the world after the Second World War?

3 In what ways and over what issues were Americans divided in 1945?

4 How and why did the Cold War start soon after the Second World War?

5 Why did Americans fight in the Korean War?

6 How successful was President Truman in waging the Cold War?

7 How well did President Truman handle domestic problems?

8 Why was Truman victorious in the 1948 presidential election?

9 Why and with what results did America experience the second Red Scare?

10 What was life like for African-Americans in 1945?

11 What was the impact of the Second World War on African-Americans?

12 How and with what results did African-Americans campaign for civil rights in the Truman years?

13 In what ways did the federal, state and local governments respond to the problems of black Americans?

 Question practice

ESSAY QUESTIONS

1 'President Truman had good reasons for leading the United States into the Korean War in 1950.' Explain why you agree or disagree with this view.

2 'The Second World War was a turning point for African-Americans.' Explain why you agree or disagree with this view.

3 'The power of the presidency declined under President Truman.' Assess the validity of this view.

4 'Inflation was the greatest domestic problem faced by President Truman.' Assess the validity of this view.

SOURCE ANALYSIS QUESTIONS

1 With reference to Sources 1 and 2, and your understanding of the historical context, which of these two sources is more valuable in explaining the impact of Senator McCarthy and his accusations after February 1950?

2 With reference to Sources 3, 4 and 5, and your understanding of the historical context, assess the value of these three sources to a historian studying the origins of the Cold War.

SOURCE 1

From an article by former Socialist turned militant anti-Communist Max Eastman, published in *The Freeman*, 1 June 1953.

Red Baiting – in the sense of reasoned, documented exposure of Communist and pro-Communist infiltration of government departments and private agencies of information and communication – is absolutely necessary. We are not dealing with honest fanatics of a new idea, willing to give testimony for their faith straightforwardly, regardless of the cost. We are dealing with conspirators who try to sneak in the Moscow-inspired propaganda by stealth and double talk, who run for shelter to the Fifth Amendment* when they are not only permitted but invited and urged by Congressional committee to state what they believe. I myself, after struggling for years to get this fact recognized, give McCarthy the major credit for implanting it in the mind of the whole nation.

* The right not to incriminate oneself.

SOURCE 2

From an article by former President Harry Truman, published in the *New York Times*, 17 November 1953.

It is now evident that the present [Republican] Administration has fully embraced, for political advantage, McCarthyism. I am not referring to the Senator from Wisconsin. He is only important in that his name has taken on the dictionary meaning of the word. It is the corruption of truth, the abandonment of the due process law. It is the use of the big lie and the unfounded accusation against any citizen in the name of Americanism or security. It is the rise to power of the demagogue who lives on untruth; it is the spreading of fear and the destruction of faith in every level of society.

SOURCE 3

From Truman's March 1948 speech to Congress (available from http://trumanlibrary.org/publicpapers/index.php?pid=1417).

Since the close of hostilities, the Soviet Union and its agents have destroyed the independence and democratic character of a whole series of nations in Eastern and Central Europe.

It is this ruthless course of action, and the clear design to extend it to the remaining free nations in Europe, that have brought about the critical situation in Europe today … I believe that we have reached the point at which the position of the United States should be made unmistakably clear … There are times in world history when it is far wiser to act than to hesitate … We must be prepared to pay the price for peace, or assuredly we shall pay the price of war.

SOURCE 4

From a statement by Stalin to a *Pravda* correspondent, published in *Pravda*, 13 March 1946, in response to Churchill's 'Iron Curtain' speech of 5 March 1946 (available from www.marxists.org/reference/archive/stalin/works/1946/03/x01.htm). *Pravda* was the official Soviet newspaper.

The Germans made their invasion of the USSR through Finland, Poland, Romania, Bulgaria and Hungary. The Germans were able to make their invasions through these countries because at the time governments hostile to the Soviet Union existed in these countries … The Soviet Union's loss of life has been several times greater than that of Britain and the United States put together. Possibly in some quarters an inclination is felt to forget about the colossal sacrifices of the Soviet people which secured the liberation of Europe from the Hitlerite yoke. But the Soviet people cannot forget about them. And so what can there be surprising about the fact that the Soviet Union, anxious for its future safety, is trying to see to it that governments loyal in their attitude to the Soviet Union should exist in these countries? How can anyone who has not taken leave of his wits describe these peaceful aspirations of the Soviet Union as expansionist tendencies on the part of our state?

SOURCE 5

From an article in *Pionerskaya Pravda*, a newspaper for young Soviets, August 1947, quoted in a 21 November 1949 article in the Ottawa *Evening Citizen*.

President Truman has announced the following principles of American foreign policy: the United States will everywhere support with weapons and money reactionaries, fascists who are hateful to their own people but who … are ready to place their country under American control. Two countries suitable for this were found at once: Greece and Turkey. But Greece and Turkey are too small and American appetites are great. American expansionists are dreaming of all Europe, or at least Western Europe. And so the 'Marshall Plan' emerges in America. It was announced that the United States wanted 'to help' the European countries to reconstruct their war-destroyed economies. Many believed this. But it was soon evident that the 'Marshall Plan' was simply a cunning way of subjecting all Europe to American capital.

CHAPTER 2

Eisenhower: tranquillity and crisis 1953–60

Eisenhower described his presidency as being characterised by peace, progress and prosperity. The USA was certainly prosperous, but multiple international crises rendered the 'peace' uneasy. While many Americans enjoyed unprecedented economic progress, some groups did not. African-Americans in particular protested their inequality. Peace, prosperity and progress are covered in the following themes:

★ The growth of the US economy in the 1950s and the impact of the 'consumer society'

★ Eisenhower's presidency

★ The USA and the Cold War

★ African-Americans in the North and the South

★ Assessing the Eisenhower years

Key dates

1952	Nov.	Eisenhower elected president	1955	July	Geneva summit and 'Open Skies'
1953	Jan.	Eisenhower inaugurated as president	1956	Nov.	Suez crisis
	July	Korean War ended			Hungarian revolution
1954	April	Army–McCarthy hearings			Eisenhower re-elected
	May	Brown	1957	Sept.	Civil Rights Act
		Dien Bien Phu			Little Rock crisis began
	June	CIA-supported coup in Guatemala		Oct.	Sputnik
	Sept.	Quemoy–Matsu crisis began	1958	Nov.	Berlin crisis began
1955	Feb.	SEATO established	1960	May	U-2 crisis

The growth of the American economy in the 1950s and the impact of the 'consumer society'

▶ *Was Eisenhower's America characterised by economic prosperity and progress?*

For many Americans during the 1950s, the American Dream was a reality. The booming economy led to a sharp rise in **consumerism**. The typical American family bought consumer goods that made the US lifestyle envied by many throughout the world.

The American economy

During the 1950s the American economy experienced unprecedented growth:

- The **GNP** rose in constant 1958 dollars from $355.3 billion in 1950 to $487.76 billion in 1960.
- By 1960, the median family income ($5620) gave a family 30 per cent more purchasing power than in 1950.
- In 1953–7, the cost of living rose by 2.8 per cent but factory wages by 8.6 per cent.
- Inflation and unemployment were low.

Why the American economy grew

Several factors explain American economic growth. First, the United States had emerged from the Second World War in far better economic shape than potential rivals (the European and Japanese economies suffered great wartime damage). Second, American industry and transportation benefited from cheap oil. Third, ever-increasing investment in research and development led to scientific and technological advances that increased productivity. Fourth, the population rose from 151.7 million in 1950 to 180.7 million in 1960 and this 'baby boom' encouraged the purchase of homes and children's clothes and toys.

The greatest growth industries in the 1950s (advertising, aeroplanes and airlines, cars, chemicals including plastics, construction, defence, electronics, food processing, pharmaceuticals, soft drinks and tobacco), helped transform American lifestyles, as illustrated by the construction, car and **service industries**.

Construction

The housing shortage that existed during Truman's presidency (see page 33) continued. Of 13 million new homes constructed to meet the demand between 1948 and 1958, 11 million were built in the suburbs. This construction boom provided employment and fulfilled the American Dream for the many who

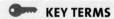

🔑 KEY TERMS

Consumerism
Great interest in acquiring consumer goods such as cars and kitchen gadgets.

GNP A country's gross national product is the aggregate value of goods and services produced in that country.

Service industries
Businesses that serve customers but are not involved in manufacturing, for example restaurants, motels and petrol stations.

KEY TERM

White flight The post-Second World War exodus of white Americans from inner-city areas, which were then left to minorities such as African-Americans.

loved and aspired to suburban life. Suburban growth owed much to the phenomenon of '**white flight**', when white Americans sought to escape cities with high taxes, crowded accommodation and growing ghettos.

The most famous suburban builders were the Levitt brothers. They began construction on their first 'Levittown' in Hempstead, Long Island, in 1947. Built primarily for young veterans, Hempstead had 17,000 homes, 80,000 residents, seven village greens and shopping centres, nine swimming pools and two bowling alleys. Residents were expected to conform to rules stipulating weekly lawn mowing, no fences and no washing hung out at weekends.

Levittown homes were very popular. When they went on sale, people queued to buy them. Priced at around $8000 (only two and a half times the average family income), the Hempstead homes were well constructed with central heating and built-in wardrobes on building plots twice the normal size. Most suburban Americans loved their spacious homes with modern bathrooms, gadget-filled kitchens and attached garages.

Cars

The automobile industry employed tens of thousands of Americans. When thousands of wives of the Association of Automobile Dealers attended an event at the White House in 1956, President Eisenhower's wife Mamie told her husband, 'That is one crowd that is prospering! I never saw so many furs and diamonds.'

Most of the cars on American roads in the 1950s were manufactured in Detroit by the so-called Big Three: General Motors, Ford and Chrysler. Their products – long, multi-coloured and decorated with large quantities of chrome and ostentatious tail-fins – reflected American self-confidence and affluence. Automobile manufacturers and the desire to demonstrate one's social status combined to convince consumers that they should buy a new car as often as possible. In 1955 alone, 7.9 million new cars were manufactured. An average 4.5 million cars were scrapped each year in the 1950s.

Growing car ownership changed American lifestyles in the 1950s. Spacious new cars with automatic transmission, power steering, powerful engines, radios, heaters and air conditioning gave an easy and luxurious drive, demonstrated one's status, and made lives easier and more varied. Americans could get to places faster and more comfortably. Cars freed them to live in spacious suburban homes within an easy drive of work. They could eat fast food, watch films and even attend church from the comfort of their car.

When Americans became exceptionally mobile, their new on-the-road culture necessitated cheap accommodation and fast food. In 1952, the modern American motel chain was born when the first Holiday Inn opened near Memphis. By 1960, there were 228 McDonald's. The landscape changed: large areas of rural America became covered by roads and adjacent motels, restaurants, stores, huge

SOURCE A

This 1958 Cadillac was a typical 1950s' automobile.

parking lots, neon signs and advertisements (some considered this as a negative development).

The increased mobility that cars offered contributed to the dramatic growth of the service industries and the changing nature of the American workforce.

Service industries

The growing use of cars led to the proliferation of motels, fast food outlets and out-of-town shopping malls. This contributed to increased numbers of service workers, such as waitresses, petrol station attendants, domestics and caretakers. However, not all of them could live the American Dream as many service industry jobs were poorly paid.

By 1960, the 7.6 million service workers and 21.2 million workers not engaged in manual labour (white-collar workers) outnumbered the 25.6 million manual workers (blue-collar workers). Growing automation decreased the need for heavy manual labour in factories and mines in the 1950s, and the proportion of industrial workers fell from 39 per cent to 36 per cent of the workforce. Although these blue-collar workers remained important, the consumer society helped make the economy more dependent on service industry and office-based work.

The impact of the 'consumer society'

The United States was a 'land of plenty' for many in the 1950s. This economic prosperity encouraged the development of a consumer society that generated social and cultural change.

> What do cars like the one in Source A suggest about America and Americans in the 1950s?

Many people were pleased by the 'consumer society'. Ever-increasing purchasing power enabled suburban Americans in particular to buy cars, labour-saving devices and anything else considered essential and/or fashionable. Washing machines, freezers and dishwashers made housewives' lives easier and became an essential part of the American Dream. The mass media (magazines, radio, and especially television) spread this message in advertisements, news stories, celebrity profiles and television shows.

Some intellectuals hated the impact of the consumer culture on American society. Harvard University economist John Kenneth Galbraith's *The Affluent Society* (1958) argued that his contemporaries were grossly materialistic and cared little about the less fortunate. Sociologist David Riesman feared that consumerism and runaway **materialism** were becoming central to the nation's identity and undermining 'traditional American values' such as hard work and careful money management. The historian and sociologist Lewis Mumford believed the consumer society contributed to the standardisation and conformity that characterised suburbia, where everyone had to keep up with their neighbours and have all the latest household gadgets and the new car. Many intellectuals blamed increasing conformity and consumerism on television and advertisements.

> **KEY TERM**
>
> **Materialism** Excessive preoccupation with material goods and consumerism.

> **?** How does Mumford use language to make his point about conformity in Source B?

SOURCE B

From Lewis Mumford's prize-winning book *The City in History*, Harcourt, Brace & World, 1961, pp. 486 and 509–12.

In the mass movement into suburban areas a new kind of community was produced … a multitude of uniform, unidentifiable houses, lined up inflexibly, at uniform distances, on uniform roads, in a treeless communal waste, inhabited by people of the same class, the same income, the same age group, witnessing the same television performances, eating the same tasteless pre-fabricated foods, from the same freezers, conforming in every outward and inward respect to a common mold … Thus the ultimate effect of the suburban escape in our time is, ironically, a low-grade uniform environment from which escape is impossible …

Television, advertising and conformity

In the consumer society, televisions were a must-have. By 1960, 90 per cent of US homes had at least one. Polls revealed television as the favourite leisure activity for over 50 per cent of Americans.

Television was frequently criticised for promoting:

- *Conformity*: 1950s' family sitcoms such as *Father Knows Best* (which ran from 1954 to 1960) and *The Adventures of Ozzie and Harriet* (1952–66) promoted conformity when they portrayed the domestic bliss of white, middle-class suburban families with mothers who invariably stayed at home as the ideal.

- *Consumerism*: non-stop advertisements and programme content suggested must-have products. In *I Remember Mama* (1949–56), young family members taught their immigrant parents that consumerism was good.

Advertisements were similarly criticised for promoting conformity and consumerism. In 1950, $5.7 billion was spent on advertising but $11.9 billion in 1960, mostly due to the rise of television. The advertising industry spent more on advertisements than the state and federal governments spent on education.

In 1954, Yale University historian David Potter claimed that advertising was as socially influential as education and religion, because it dominated the media, shaped popular standards and exercised social control. The power of the advertising industry inevitably elicited criticism. In his influential book, *The Hidden Persuaders* (1957), journalist Vance Packard described how advertisements psychologically manipulated consumers: candy advertisements targeted bored children at the supermarket checkout and cinema screens flashed images of Coca-Cola too fast to be seen consciously, yet sufficient to remind moviegoers to buy it in the intervals.

Liberals who disliked the consumerism, conformity and smug self-satisfaction that characterised 1950s' America, felt that President Eisenhower was the right man to lead the nation: they talked of 'the bland leading the bland'.

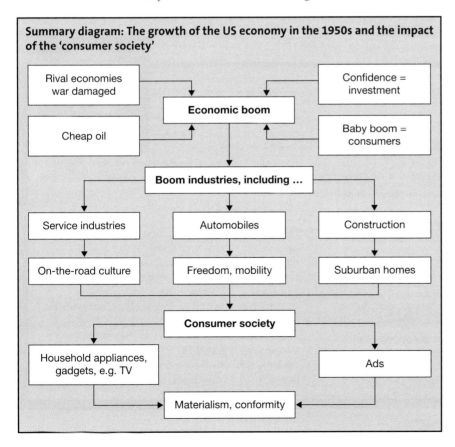

Summary diagram: The growth of the US economy in the 1950s and the impact of the 'consumer society'

Rival economies war damaged → Economic boom ← Confidence = investment

Cheap oil → Economic boom ← Baby boom = consumers

Boom industries, including ...
- Service industries
- Automobiles
- Construction

On-the-road culture · Freedom, mobility · Suburban homes

Consumer society

Household appliances, gadgets, e.g. TV · Ads

Materialism, conformity

② Eisenhower's presidency

▶ *Was Eisenhower a 'do-nothing' president?*

In his memoirs, Eisenhower (known as 'Ike' to his friends) recalled his parents telling him of the American Dream:

> *I have found out in later years we were very poor, but the glory of America is that we didn't know it then. All that we knew was that our parents – of great courage – could say to us, 'Opportunity is all about you. Reach out and take it.'*

Young Ike went ahead to live the Dream: the poor farm boy from Kansas became president of the United States.

The shaping of Eisenhower's personality and policies

Eisenhower's personality and politics were shaped by his boyhood. He grew up in a small, Midwestern town when there were few taxes to pay to the federal government because it did little for the American people. Local authorities provided schools, but families took care of their own sick, poor or elderly. 'Self-sufficiency was the watchword,' said Eisenhower's brother, Milton. Ike's conservative family and most of Abilene's 4000 population voted Republican.

Dwight D. Eisenhower

1890	Born in Texas, raised in Abilene, Kansas
1911–15	Attended West Point military academy (for officer training)
1916	Married Mamie Doud
1942–5	Commanded American forces in Europe
1945	Army Chief of Staff
1950	NATO commander
1953–61	President
1969	Died

General Dwight D. Eisenhower commanded the victorious Allied forces in Europe in the Second World War. This, coupled with his engaging smile and personality, made him exceptionally popular and was key to his election to the presidency in 1952 and his re-election in 1956.

Although Eisenhower disliked federal government activism in domestic affairs, he introduced the interstate highway system. The continued economic boom under him owed something to his determination to balance the federal budget, refusal to lower taxes and reluctance to spend even more on defence, but his civil rights record is generally considered unimpressive.

Eisenhower hoped to maintain peace and, after he extracted the troops from Korea, American forces saw no more combat for the next seven and a half years of his presidency. However, relations with the Soviet Union and China remained tense and there were dramatic crises over Quemoy and Matsu, Berlin and the U-2 spy plane. He established the 'independent' state of South Vietnam, which led his successors into the Vietnam War. He contributed reluctantly but greatly to the arms race with the Soviet Union (most Americans urged him to do even more).

Seeking a free college education, Eisenhower sat and passed the exam for West Point in 1910. His military career would further shape his personality and politics.

Leadership skills

After graduation from West Point, Eisenhower married wealthy Mamie Doud. The army quickly decided that he had great leadership skills. He:

- was an excellent and inspirational organiser
- mastered detail but did not get bogged down in it
- reacted well to pressure
- was a good team player
- empathised with his men
- was praised by General MacArthur (see page 22) as 'the best officer in the army' in the early 1930s.

After the United States entered the Second World War, Army Chief of Staff General George Marshall gave Eisenhower command of the American forces in Europe. General Eisenhower proved brilliant at public relations and at getting Anglo-American forces to work as one – an unprecedented task.

Supreme commander in Europe

General Eisenhower's military leadership was sometimes unimpressive, but his ability to foster teamwork and confidence was great. Britain's Field Marshal Montgomery said Eisenhower drew 'the hearts of men towards him' like a magnet: 'He merely has to smile at you, and you trust him at once.' In 1943, Eisenhower was given command of the Allied landings in France in 1944.

Subsequent Cold War struggles (see page 13) caused criticism of Eisenhower's rejection of Churchill's insistence that Allied forces do everything possible to beat the Soviets to Berlin. In an interesting example of how writing during the Cold War affected memoirs, Eisenhower gave different and not very truthful versions of his failure to take Berlin in *Crusade in Europe* (1948) and *At Ease* (1967). After Eisenhower's death, his colleague General Omar Bradley highlighted the self-serving and distorted accounts in Eisenhower's memoirs. Bradley explained Eisenhower's insistence on advancing towards Germany in a broad front rather than using pursuit without pause: 'It would give Monty [Field Marshal Montgomery] too large a role in the ground command, in effect upstaging and obscuring Ike. It was a time of extreme jingoism; the American public demanded its own epic-size war heroes, and it wanted them in command at the kill.' In 1943, Eisenhower's close friend General George Patton said, 'Ike wants to be president so badly you can taste it.'

Eisenhower emerged from the war with supreme self-confidence, even arrogance. This increased during his presidency, but was only expressed privately: in 1957 he read Field Marshal Montgomery's memoirs and noted that Monty 'doesn't want to say I was responsible for winning the war.'

**Robert Taft
(1889–1953)**

Senator Taft (1939–53), led the Senate opposition to Roosevelt's New Deal, convinced Congress to override Truman's veto of the anti-labour Taft–Hartley Act, and by 1950 was the generally acknowledged leader of the Republican conservatives. He lost the Republican presidential nomination to the moderate Thomas Dewey in 1940, 1948 and 1952. An isolationist, he opposed US membership of NATO and involvement in the Korean War.

Old Guard Conservative Republicans such as Senator Robert Taft.

States' rights Belief that the states have certain rights that the federal government in Washington should never diminish.

Presidential potential

After victory in Europe, Eisenhower was so popular that many experienced politicians were convinced he could win the presidency, but Eisenhower insisted that he found political activity 'distasteful' and that he did not have either political ambition or the 'slightest interest' in politics. He probably would not have won the Republican presidential nomination in 1948, so he accepted the post of president of Columbia University. In 1950 he welcomed President Truman's offer to head NATO.

In 1952, Eisenhower was anxious about the prospect of US foreign and defence policy in the hands of either the isolationist Republican Senator **Robert Taft** (in 1951, Eisenhower told a reporter that Taft was 'a very stupid man') or the Democrat Truman. With Truman submitting a budget with a $14 billion deficit to Congress, and Taft calling for the return of all US troops from Europe, Eisenhower concluded that it was his duty to run.

How and why Eisenhower won the 1952 presidential election

First, Eisenhower had to defeat Taft, the **Old Guard** favourite, for the Republican nomination. It was a narrow victory, but Eisenhower managed to appease the Old Guard by selecting Richard Nixon as his running mate. Nixon's militant anti-Communism appealed to the Old Guard, while his internationalism and relative liberalism on domestic policy made him acceptable to moderates. Nixon was a good foil to Eisenhower in that he was relatively young, an energetic campaigner, and able to hit the Democrats hard while Eisenhower maintained a more dignified stance.

Conservative voters liked Eisenhower's opposition to federal budget deficits ('A bankrupt America is a defenceless America'), high taxes, government bureaucracy and socialised medicine. They agreed with his support for **states' rights** and for McCarthy's assertion that the Democrats 'have shielded traitors to the Nation in high places' (see page 34). Although Eisenhower disliked McCarthy, he sounded just like him when he was campaigning in McCarthy's home state, Wisconsin.

Most importantly of all, Eisenhower was a war hero whom most voters felt could be trusted with the nation's security. He:

- criticised Democrat failures at Yalta (see page 11)
- dishonestly asserted that the decision to let the Soviets reach Berlin first had nothing to do with him
- said that Truman had 'lost' China (see page 21) and was soft on Communism abroad ('if we had been less soft and weak, there probably would have been no war in Korea')
- criticised containment ('negative, futile and immoral … [it] abandons countless human beings to despotism and godless terrorism'), and looked forward to East European nations regaining independence
- promised if elected to go to Korea and, by implication, end the war.

Ultimately, Eisenhower won 55 per cent of the vote to the Democrat Adlai Stevenson's 45 per cent. Eisenhower even managed to take five Southern states and his popularity helped make Congress Republican again.

Eisenhower's cabinet

When the president-elect chose his cabinet, *The New Republic* commented, 'Eisenhower has picked a cabinet of eight millionaires and one plumber' (Secretary of Labour, Martin Durkin, was formerly head of the plumbers' union and the only Democrat in the cabinet). The eight were businessmen or lawyers. Eisenhower said of Secretary of State **John Foster Dulles**, 'There is only one man I know who has seen more of the world and talked with more people and knows more than he does – and that's *me*'. His Chief of Staff was Sherman Adams, known as Eisenhower's 'Abominable No Man', because he fiercely controlled access to the president.

The policies of 'dynamic conservatism'

Eisenhower disapproved of the New Deal (see page 2) because he believed in self-sufficiency, but felt it would be political suicide to try to dismantle it. He called himself a 'liberal' or 'progressive' Republican. He said his was a 'dynamic conservatism' or 'modern Republicanism', which he explained as 'conservative when it comes to money, liberal when it comes to people.'

Conservative when it comes to money

Eisenhower was horrified that defence expenditure had rocketed by 300 per cent in Truman's final 30 months. Eisenhower

- felt it necessary to control defence expenditure in order to balance the budget (he worked hard and often successfully to avoid a deficit)
- believed there was no security without a sound economy
- knew that excessive expenditure on defence was money that could be spent on social improvements (Source C).

 **KEY FIGURE**

John Foster Dulles (1888–1959)

Eisenhower's loyal and much valued Secretary of State. Dulles was more of a Cold Warrior than Eisenhower – he wanted to spend more on defence and frequently advocated the use of nuclear weapons. Dulles was somewhat sanctimonious and long-winded (the then British Prime Minister Anthony Eden famously quipped, 'dull, duller, Dulles').

SOURCE C

Eisenhower's 'The Chance for Peace' speech to newspaper editors, April 1953 (available from www.presidency.ucsb.edu/ws/?pid=9819).

Every gun that is made, every warship launched, every rocket fired signifies, in the final sense, a theft from those who hunger and are not fed, those who are cold and are not clothed. This world in arms is not spending money alone. It is spending the sweat of its laborers, the genius of its scientists, the hopes of its children. The cost of one modern heavy bomber is this: a modern brick school in more than 30 cities. It is two electric power plants, each serving a town of 60,000 population. It is two fine, fully equipped hospitals. It is some 50 miles of concrete highway. We pay for a single fighter plane with a half million bushels of wheat. We pay for a single destroyer with new homes that could have housed

 Does Source C confirm Eisenhower's claim that his was a 'dynamic conservatism'?

more than 8,000 people. This, I repeat, is the best way of life to be found on the road the world has been taking. This is not a way of life at all, in any true sense. Under the cloud of threatening war, it is humanity hanging from a cross of iron.

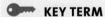

KEY TERM

Military–industrial complex Influential figures in the armed forces and defence industry, who profited from war.

Eisenhower's defence cuts antagonised both Republicans and Democrats. They and the press were particularly critical after the Soviets took the lead in the space race (see page 73), and Eisenhower was openly accused of leaving the United States defensively vulnerable. What Eisenhower called 'the **military–industrial complex**' pressed him to spend more on defence throughout his presidency. The political pressure was such that he spent far more on defence than he considered necessary, although this was far less than many other Americans wanted.

Liberal when it comes to people

Eisenhower persuaded the Republican-controlled Congress to pass legislation that:

- increased Social Security benefits and added 10 million to its coverage in 1954
- raised the minimum wage from 75 cents to $1 per hour in 1955
- gave federal aid to education
- established the interstate highway system.

Education

Eisenhower often said that education was as important as defence – possibly more so. There was an acute shortage of school buildings and schoolteachers in the United States in the 1950s, and one critic said that what Eisenhower's dynamic conservatism meant in practice was that he would 'strongly recommend the building of a great many schools, but not provide the money'. That was unfair. From 1955, Eisenhower proposed legislation to help finance school construction in poorer states, but Congress rejected the proposal because it would have benefited the segregated South. Then, frightened by *Sputnik* (see page 73), Congress passed the 1958 National Defence Education Act. It gave low-cost loans to college students and it gave federal funds to the states in order to improve courses in science, mathematics and foreign languages, subjects considered important for the Cold War struggle. This legislation was revolutionary in that it introduced the principle of direct federal aid to education. Eisenhower also continued the free lunch programme that Truman had introduced for poor schoolchildren (see page 34).

Employment

Partly because Eisenhower refused to overspend, there was little inflation or unemployment during his presidency, although there were several recessions. Secretary of Defence Charles Wilson epitomised unsympathetic conservative Republicanism when he suggested that unemployed car workers in Detroit should go looking for work instead of waiting for handouts. Eisenhower's more moderate Republicanism was demonstrated when he promoted the largest public works project in American history. Eisenhower's construction of the interstate highway system – a massive project for one often criticised as a 'do-nothing' leader – employed millions.

Interstate highways

Eisenhower revolutionised American roads. Why?

- In 1919, Eisenhower led a military convoy across the nation and saw that the poor quality of American roads endangered military transportation. Good roads were important for national defence.
- The number of cars on American roads was increasing, so more and better roads were needed.
- The economy faced trouble after the Korean War ended (see page 21) and defence expenditure decreased. Road construction would create employment and help economic growth.
- The poor roads were mostly due to federal–state disagreements over funding. Eisenhower thought that it could only be the federal government that undertook an interstate highway system, because the federal government alone had the requisite national overview.

Another great construction project was the St Lawrence Seaway, which opened the Great Lakes to ocean traffic.

Liberal on squirrels?

By the end of Eisenhower's presidency, critics claimed he had been a 'do-nothing president' who had spent too much time playing golf. The American Public Golf Association built a putting green on the White House lawn for Eisenhower. Truman had fed the squirrels there so much that they were almost tame: Eisenhower wanted them shot because they buried nuts on his greens, but the Secret Service trapped them and took them to another park.

The Department of Health, Education and Welfare (HEW)

Eisenhower established a new government department, HEW, headed by Texan Democrat Oveta Culp Hobby, the second woman to hold a cabinet post (Roosevelt had appointed the first). In 1955, her department oversaw the distribution of the new polio vaccine. Polio had crippled Roosevelt (see page 3) and over 57,000 Americans contracted the disease in the 1952 epidemic.

Another development beneficial to health was legislation in 1956 that added 500,000 acres to the national park system, along with visitor centres and other amenities.

Richard Nixon as vice president

Richard Nixon became one of the most hated politicians in US history (see Chapter 5). Why did the loved and respected Eisenhower choose and retain him as vice president, and how successful was Nixon's vice presidency?

Nixon's background

Born into a struggling family in a small, shabby house in Yorba Linda, California, Nixon's childhood was dominated by the death of one brother and the chronic sickness of another. An exceptionally clever and hard-working youth, he won a place at Yale University but could not afford to take it up. After attending a local college, he won a scholarship to the prestigious Duke University Law School. His legal career was halted for service in the Second World War. He married pretty, popular schoolteacher Pat Ryan in 1940. In these early years he had a reputation for honesty.

Nixon was elected to the House of Representatives in 1946 and like many other Republicans suggested that his Democrat rival had Communist sympathies. Privately he acknowledged this was untrue. 'I had to win.' he said, 'That's the thing you don't understand. The important thing is to win.' Running for the Senate in 1950, he called his opponent Helen Gahagan Douglas, a '**Pink** Lady' who 'follows the Communist Party line' and was 'pink right down to her underwear'. Douglas nicknamed him 'Tricky Dick'.

Nixon gained national fame through his election campaigns and his prominence in the House Un-American Activities Committee pursuit of Communists (see page 35). The comfortably partisan Nixon was a good foil to the more moderate Eisenhower, about whom the Old Guard had their doubts.

Nixon's work as vice president 1953–61

Vice President Nixon served Eisenhower well. He frequently disagreed with the president's policies, but was loyal and co-operative. Their disagreements focused on the battle against Communism at home (Nixon wanted a more aggressive pursuit of supposed Communists in the government) and abroad (for example, Nixon wanted to continue fighting in Korea in 1953). Eisenhower entrusted Nixon with partisan campaigning, liaising with the Old Guard, civil rights advocacy and goodwill trips abroad.

Partisan campaigner

Eisenhower used Nixon to attack the Democrats, explaining, 'He can sometimes take positions which are more political than it would be expected that I take.' Sometimes Eisenhower praised his attacks, sometimes not. In 1953, Eisenhower told Nixon to tone down partisan attacks on the Democrats, because Southern Democrats were as economically and socially conservative as Republicans and gave the administration vital votes in Congress. In his campaign for the Republican Party in 1958, Nixon said that Truman's foreign policy had led to war

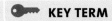

KEY TERM

Pink Having Communist sympathies.

while Eisenhower's had led to peace. Eisenhower publicly rebuked him, saying 'foreign policy ought to be kept out of partisan debate'. As a *New York Times* journalist said, 'Like most politicians, Mr Nixon talks in hyperboles, makes sweeping generalizations of sometimes dubious validity, and is adept at planting the dark and ominous inference. But he does it with extraordinary finesse.' Perhaps Nixon was simply the perfected product of an imperfect political system.

Liaison with Congress

As the only member of the Eisenhower administration with congressional experience, Nixon was full of helpful suggestions about how to deal with Congress and the press. He worked hard to smooth out differences between the White House and the Old Guard and to prevent his friend McCarthy from damaging the administration. (Adlai Stevenson labelled Nixon 'McCarthy in a white collar'.) Nixon got McCarthy onside several times during 1953 over some Eisenhower nominees, but mostly failed to restrain him.

Civil rights advocate

Nixon's stance on civil rights was exceptionally liberal by contemporary standards. Some felt that he simply sought black votes for the Republican Party, but his speeches against discrimination and inequality make one wonder whether this was a decent man corrupted by the American political system and/ or his own ambitions.

Goodwill ambassador

Eisenhower used Nixon as no vice president had been used before, as a goodwill ambassador to foreign nations. Nixon responded well. He worked hard to understand each of the many countries seemed visited. Sometimes he contributed to continuing good relations with the leaders he met; other times he seemed more concerned with the press these trips gave him back home.

American identity abroad: Nixon in Venezuela

In 1958, Nixon made a goodwill tour of several Latin American nations. Many Latin Americans resented US economic dominance and support for dictatorial anti-Communist leaders. When the Nixons arrived at Caracas airport, a large, mostly teenage crowd shouted obscenities and 'Go home Nixon' and threw fruit and other objects. Then their motorcade got stuck at a roadblock in a rough area. A yelling mob of over 4000 shouted 'Kill Nixon', shattered his limousine windows with rocks and fists, then rocked it to overturn it. Nixon restrained those around him who wanted to start shooting at the students. Finally, Venezuelan soldiers cleared a path and the limousine sped off, its windscreen wipers going full pelt to clear off tobacco-stained spit.

When Eisenhower heard his vice president was in danger of his life, he launched 'Operation Poor Richard' (a title Nixon loathed). US troops and the fleet were put on standby near Venezuela, but the Venezuelan army restored order.

Nixon arrived back in Washington airport to a hero's welcome, greeted by the president, the cabinet and half of Congress.

A heartbeat from the presidency

By the time the 1956 presidential election approached, Eisenhower was beginning to see himself as indispensable. When John Foster Dulles told him that he was the most trusted leader in the world and the greatest force for world peace, Eisenhower said that assessment was 'substantially correct'. Although he had a heart attack in September 1955, he feared that Americans might elect a president who did not understand when and where defence cuts could be safely made, and ran again, on his record of 'peace and prosperity'.

Eisenhower's heart attack made his choice of running mate for 1956 particularly important. Adlai Stevenson called the vice presidency 'this nation's life-insurance policy' (he lost quite a few votes in 1956 when he said that Eisenhower would probably die during a second term).

KEY TERM

Politicking Focusing on elections.

Eisenhower was unsure about retaining Nixon in 1956. In spring, he told a friend that Nixon lacked 'presidential timber'. He considered Nixon immature, probably because Nixon always thought in terms of **politicking** rather than of governing. He also worried that, as he said, 'People don't like him.' He suggested Nixon take a cabinet post and obtain some essential executive experience. Although sensible from the viewpoint of the development of leadership skills, Nixon knew it would be interpreted as a presidential vote of no confidence. Eisenhower left the choice to Nixon, who chose to stay on the ticket, supported by the 180 out of 203 House Republicans who said 'stick with Dick'. Nixon then toned down his partisanship and made unusually positive speeches, emphasising Eisenhower's achievements rather than Democrat disasters. Eisenhower's ambivalence continued: in 1960, he frequently discussed other possible candidates for the Republican nomination.

> ### Death of a president
>
> Journalist Tom Wicker was scolded by his editor's wife for raising money for Adlai Stevenson in 1956: 'But Mrs Hoyt, don't you realise that Eisenhower has had a heart attack?'
>
> 'Young man, I would vote for Eisenhower if he were dead.'

When Eisenhower had a heart attack in 1955, a stomach operation in 1956 and a stroke in 1957, Nixon conducted himself admirably. He made no unseemly grab for power but exuded confidence and calmness. After his stroke, Eisenhower demonstrated great confidence in Nixon taking over the presidency should he be incapacitated again. In private, Eisenhower was notoriously critical of the capacity of others and he seems to have considered Nixon the next best Republican presidential candidate – the best of a bad bunch.

The Republican Party

The Republicans were deeply divided between conservatives and moderates. Eisenhower was moderate and on the left of the party (his brother Edgar deplored his progressiveness). On the right were the conservative Old Guard, led by Senator Robert Taft until his death in July 1953, and then by Senator William Knowland of California.

Relations between the Eisenhower White House and congressional Republicans were tense from the start. On Eisenhower's second day as president, Senator McCarthy delayed Eisenhower's nomination for Under Secretary of State. Dulles complained that the ten investigations that Republican congressional committees were conducting into his State Department (they sought dirt on the Democrats) made it difficult for his department to do meaningful work. 'Republican senators are having a hard time getting through their heads that they now belong to a team that includes rather than opposes the White House,' lamented Eisenhower.

The problem was that the Old Guard were never really convinced that Eisenhower was one of them. He, in turn, was sometimes contemptuous of and exasperated with them. When Taft died, it was even harder for Eisenhower to gain their co-operation. Of his replacement, Senator William Knowland, Eisenhower wrote in his diary, 'There seems to be no final answer to the question, "How stupid can you get?"' He feared for the future of the party, writing in his diary that 'the Republican Party must be known as a progressive organization or it is sunk'. He frequently fantasised about leaving it and setting up 'an intelligent group of independents'. Although the Republicans narrowly gained control of Congress in 1952, they lost it in 1954 ('just too many turkeys running on the Republican ticket,' said Nixon). Eisenhower was always far more popular than his party, and although he won the presidency in 1956, the party did badly. That depressed Eisenhower, who said to Nixon, 'I think that what we need is a new party.' He told other Republicans that his victory was a victory for 'Modern Republicanism'.

In 1958, the Republicans suffered their worst defeat since the depression in 1958 because:

- there was an economic recession
- Republican candidates seemed relatively unimpressive
- Eisenhower seemed old and tired
- the Democrats had waged an aggressive campaign, criticising 'six years of leaderless vacillation' and weakened national defences.

Republican Party divisions were demonstrated in tensions over domestic and foreign policy.

Foreign policy

Eisenhower had disagreed with leading Republicans over foreign policy since 1949, when Senator Taft and what Eisenhower called 'blind, stupid isolationists' had voted against NATO (see page 20). Eisenhower felt that Taft was 'playing politics', primarily interested 'in cutting the President [Truman], or the Presidency, down to size.' As president, Eisenhower and conservative Republicans disagreed over several foreign policy issues (see Table 2.1).

Table 2.1 Republican foreign policy divisions

Eisenhower	Old Guard
Foreign aid was a good Cold War investment	Opposed foreign aid
Supported NATO, a 'Europe-firster'	Some opposed NATO and were 'Asia-firsters'
Considered peace in Korea his greatest achievement	Along with Dulles and Nixon, opposed the peace terms
Criticised Democrats for giving away Chinese territory and Eastern Europe at Yalta, but refused to repudiate the Yalta agreements because they included those on US access to Berlin	Wanted Eisenhower to repudiate Yalta
Sought to improve Soviet–American relations	Felt his attendance at the 1955 Geneva summit signalled recognition of the Soviet East European empire and were furious when he invited Soviet Premier Khrushchev to visit the United States in 1959
Considered the Bricker Amendment 'senseless'	45 out of 48 Republican senators supported the 1953 Bricker Amendment, which would have restricted the president's constitutional power to make treaties with foreign nations. It was narrowly defeated thanks to the Democrats, especially Senator Lyndon Johnson

Domestic policy

Eisenhower often gained more support from congressional Democrats than from his own party, for example, over farming subsidies and the extension of Social Security. Eisenhower got on well with leading Democrats, especially Lyndon Johnson, who dominated the Senate. Johnson said, 'Eisenhower was so popular, whoever was supporting him would be on the popular side'. Eisenhower disagreed with conservative Republicans over:

- tax cuts (he agreed to a large tax cut in 1954 but rejected their demands for more, because that would damage the prospects of a balanced budget)
- New Deal legislation (the Old Guard were disappointed that he did not dismantle it)
- investigating Communists in the government (the Old Guard considered him lax on the issue).

McCarthy was perhaps the greatest problem that the Republican Party and domestic politics posed for Eisenhower.

The end of McCarthyism

Eisenhower disliked and disapproved of Senator McCarthy, describing him privately as 'a pimple on the path of progress' and 'an embarrassment for the administration'. Eisenhower's refusal to take on McCarthy worried some of his friends, some journalists and most Democrats. Some criticised Eisenhower for failing to exercise political leadership.

Why did Eisenhower allow McCarthy to continue his intemperate crusade?

- McCarthy had considerable popular support. An August 1954 poll showed that 50 per cent of Americans and 62 per cent of Republicans still admired him. Eisenhower did not want to destroy the Republican Party and he needed McCarthy's support in the Senate.
- Eisenhower said it 'would have made the Presidency ridiculous' to 'get into a pissing contest with that skunk … I really believe that nothing will be so effective in combating his particular kind of trouble making as to ignore him. This he cannot stand.'
- Eisenhower believed that McCarthy would ultimately destroy himself.

Unhampered by the new president, McCarthy continued his search for supposed traitors. Eisenhower did nothing when McCarthy's lieutenants hounded **Voice of America** for having subversive books in overseas libraries. Some books were burned. Dulles sacked 830 Voice of America employees.

As Eisenhower anticipated, McCarthy's extremism eventually lost him support. The final straw was the 'Army–McCarthy' hearings of April–June 1954.

The Army–McCarthy hearings

McCarthy led a congressional investigation into supposed subversives on New Jersey army bases. After McCarthy gave the Secretary of the Army a difficult time, newspapers said that McCarthy was defeating the Eisenhower administration. Eisenhower then denied McCarthy access to administration personnel and records. In the Cold War, much was done that Eisenhower thought best kept secret for reasons of national security. He pointed out that executive branch employees had to be able to be 'completely candid' when discussing policy options. Despite considerable dismay in Congress at this unprecedented expansion of executive powers, it helped bring about McCarthy's downfall. Without the **subpoena** power, McCarthy could obtain no concrete evidence or sensational disclosures, so the hearings seemed meaningless. McCarthy appeared drunk and was reduced to bullying bluster that alienated television audiences (Lyndon Johnson had cleverly arranged the hearings to be televised). Eisenhower joked, 'It's no longer McCarthyism. It's McCarthywasm.'

 **KEY TERMS**

Voice of America US government's broadcasting vehicle targeted at foreign nations since 1942.

Subpoena Order to appear before a court as a witness.

McCarthy's poll ratings slumped. In March 1955, the Senate finally censured him. He had been highly significant. He

- made it difficult for Eisenhower to decrease Cold War tensions
- unfairly inflicted misery on tens of thousands of innocent Americans
- endangered the principle of free speech
- damaged the Republican Party.

In 1954, Adlai Stevenson said, 'A political party divided against itself, half McCarthy and half Eisenhower, cannot produce national unity'.

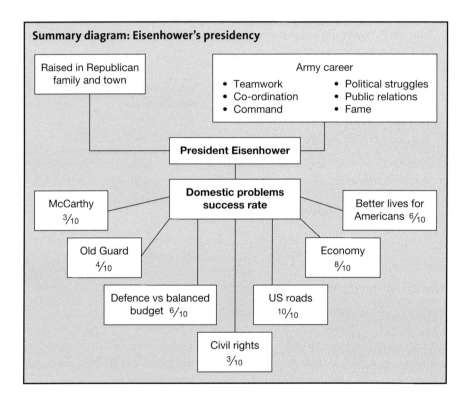

During 1945, General Eisenhower worked well with the Soviets on the Allied Control Council (see page 16). He was shocked by the devastation he observed in the Soviet Union, and convinced that there was no possibility of a Soviet–American war. He noted how insecure the US atomic bomb made the Soviets feel, but in 1946 assured Truman that the Soviets were insufficiently strong to attempt an offensive: 'I don't believe the Reds want a war. What can they gain? They've gained about all they can assimilate.'

3 The USA and the Cold War

▶ *How successfully did Eisenhower manage the Cold War?*

However, by mid-1947, Eisenhower was convinced of Soviet aggression and he agreed with Truman that Communism must be contained, otherwise 'we will find ourselves an isolated democracy in a world controlled by enemies … we face a battle to extinction between the two systems.' In October 1950, he accepted Truman's offer to command NATO. It was his fears for the nation's defence in the hands of either Truman ('a fine man who, in the middle of a stormy lake, knows nothing of swimming') or Taft (who sought the return of all American troops from Europe) that made Eisenhower decide to run for president in 1952.

Superpower rivalry and conflict with the USSR

Eisenhower prioritised foreign and defence policy: his first inauguration speech was totally focused on the dangers of aggressive Communism and war. In 1953, he gave Taft 'the essentials of our global strategy':

- Western Europe must not go Communist, so the United States needed to strengthen it.
- The Middle East had half the world's oil, so the Soviets must not be allowed to control it.
- Southeast Asia was critical, so the French must be supported in Vietnam.
- America must stay strong, yet not weaken itself by overspending on defence.

Defence and expenditure

Ironically, Eisenhower was the Cold War president most devoted to slashing the military budget, perhaps because only a trusted former general could dare to attempt this. Eisenhower believed that continued military expenditure at the Truman administration's level ($50 billion a year) would lead to inflation and economic ruin. 'We must not go broke,' he said. He did not want a deficit in the federal budget, or an economy dependent on 'the military–industrial complex'. From the start, he clashed with Congress over his planned defence cuts, but he usually got what he wanted. Eisenhower described the US nuclear arsenal as 'fantastic', 'crazy' and 'unconscionable', but he could not always resist Defence Department demands for more weapons.

In an attempt to reconcile the conflicting demands of the military, which wanted to spend more money, with those of the Treasury, which wanted to spend less, Eisenhower initiated a 'New Look' defence policy.

Eisenhower's 'New Look' defence policy

Under Eisenhower's 'New Look', the United States would have fewer conventional forces and rely instead on nuclear weapons: he wanted '**more bang for a buck**'. In 1954, Secretary of State Dulles said America would use 'massive retaliatory power' to halt aggression, explaining that 'massive retaliation' meant being 'willing and able to respond vigorously at places and with the means of [our] own choosing.'

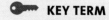 **KEY TERM**

More bang for a buck
Eisenhower administration policy emphasising reliance upon nuclear weapons rather than excessive expenditure on conventional forces.

Massive retaliation generated doubts: the *New York Times* criticised **brinkmanship** and Army Chief of Staff Matt Ridgway said it was inflexible and left the USA with only one option in a crisis. However, supporters claimed that the threat of massive retaliation would prevent crises by stopping Communist aggression and expansionism. Eisenhower said that the beauty of massive retaliation was that it confused the enemy, which could never be sure what the United States would do.

Despite all the talk of massive retaliation, Eisenhower told his advisers to forget about using the bomb ('You boys must be crazy. We can't use those awful things against Asians for the second time in less than ten years. My God'). He maintained peace through the American nuclear arsenal and his military reputation, calmness in crises and gestures towards a Cold War thaw.

Cold War thaw

When Stalin died in spring 1953, a new Soviet leader, Georgi Malenkov, talked of peace and 'mutual understanding'. Eisenhower responded with his 'Chance for Peace' speech (see page 61). First, he said, Russia would have to agree to several conditions, including a free, united Germany and the independence of the East European nations. The Soviets inevitably rejected those demands, which would have damaged the Soviet security system won at the cost of an estimated 30 million lives during the Second World War. Possibly, Eisenhower missed a great opportunity here. Soon he had to deal with another Soviet leader **Nikita Khrushchev**, whose volatility made peaceful coexistence unlikely.

Still, there was something of a thaw, signalled by the first meeting of Soviet–American leaders since Potsdam. There were no meaningful agreements at the 1955 Geneva summit, but the Cold War was a little less cold that year. However, the nuclear arms race continued apace.

The nuclear arms race

The United States first produced atomic bombs in 1945, the Soviets in 1949. The Americans exploded their first hydrogen bomb in 1952, the Soviets in 1953. In his 'Chance for Peace' speech, Eisenhower warned about the dangers of this nuclear arms race and subsequently made several suggestions designed to decrease the tensions:

- *December 1953*: in his 'Atoms for Peace' speech at the UN, Eisenhower proposed pooling nuclear resources to co-operate on the development of the peaceful use of atomic power. However, the Soviets were unwilling to give up any of their **fissionable** materials as the Americans had stockpiled more.
- *July 1955*: at the Geneva summit, Eisenhower suggested 'open skies' in which both sides could fly over the other's territory to monitor any great military build-up. Although open skies were about to become a reality through the development of satellites, Khrushchev rejected the proposal as Eisenhower's 'transparent espionage device'.

- *October 1958*: Soviet–American talks on a nuclear bomb test ban treaty began at Geneva but got nowhere. As always, the secretive Soviets rejected Eisenhower's repeated suggestions of a simultaneous halt to nuclear testing, because it would necessitate inspection systems. Khrushchev and Eisenhower agreed that they did not want war but failed to agree on anything else.

The United States had 1500 nuclear weapons in 1953 but around 6000 by 1961. Although Eisenhower told Republican leaders he 'just didn't know how many times you could kill the same man', the political pressure upon him to continue to stockpile nuclear weapons and to stay ahead of the Soviets was demonstrated during the *Sputnik* crisis.

Sputnik and the space race

In October 1957, the Soviets launched the first satellite (*Sputnik*) into space. Many Americans reacted hysterically, believing that the Soviets could now send nuclear warheads across the oceans. Although Eisenhower assured them of the difference between launching a satellite and firing an intercontinental ballistic missile or ICBM (in January 1959 the USA was the first to test an ICBM), the hysteria continued. One scientist said *Sputnik* was a greater defeat than Pearl Harbor. The press was unusually antagonistic towards Eisenhower. Despite open accusations that he was neglecting national security, Eisenhower refused to overreact: there would be no fallout shelter programme, nor any great build-up in the armed or nuclear forces.

In January 1958, the United States put a small satellite into orbit, but in May, the Soviet Union launched *Sputnik II*, which was nearly 300 times heavier than the first satellite. The continued hysteria prompted Eisenhower to ask Congress to establish the National Aeronautic and Space Administration (NASA).

Faced with frequent and increasing accusations that he neglected defence, Eisenhower could not reassure Americans by telling them how much he was using covert warfare.

The U-2 crisis and covert warfare

One method of covert warfare was the use of the **CIA** to engineer the overthrow of governments unacceptable to the USA. This was done in Iran (1953) and Guatemala (1954), and was planned for Cuba (see page 108).

A second covert warfare method was spying, whether through individuals on the ground or through planes such as the U-2, a reconnaissance plane from which the enemy could be photographed. Eisenhower had doubts about U-2 flights, but the CIA assured him that there would be no problems: pilots were under orders to press the self-destruct button if the plane was in trouble. After four years of successful U-2 spy flights over the Soviet Union, pilot Gary Powers and his U-2 spy plane were shot down by the Soviets in 1960. When the Soviets triumphantly announced that they had shot down a U-2, Eisenhower assumed

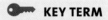

KEY TERM

CIA The Central Intelligence Agency was set up in 1947 to monitor Communist threats early in the Cold War.

there would be no surviving evidence. The Eisenhower administration claimed that the plane had been engaged on a meteorological mission. When the Soviets produced both pilot and plane intact, the administration then claimed that Powers lacked authorisation to fly over the Soviet Union. A humiliated Eisenhower finally admitted responsibility for the spy flight and, a few days later, prepared to meet Khrushchev at the Paris summit.

Khrushchev waited until Eisenhower was in Paris before setting out unacceptable conditions (such as an apology from Eisenhower) for the summit to continue. Khrushchev shouted anti-American abuse for 45 minutes. The summit and the prospects for improved relations were ruined. Eisenhower bore considerable responsibility, for he had authorised the U-2 flights.

Responses to developments in Western and Eastern Europe

When Eisenhower became president, Western Europe was securely in the American camp and Eastern Europe was part of the Soviet Empire. During 1953, Eisenhower pressed the West Europeans for the closest possible European military and political integration to strengthen the West against the Soviet threat, and to save America money. In December 1954, he finally persuaded the French to agree to German rearmament, which strengthened NATO and was a considerable achievement on Eisenhower's part.

Despite Republican campaign promises in 1952 about the rollback of Communism, nothing had been done: Eastern Europe remained within the Soviet bloc. Eisenhower knew that conservative Republican demands for rollback were unrealistic and wanted the 1956 platform to 'make it clear that we advocate liberation by all peaceful means', rather than by war. Events in Hungary demonstrated that the commitment to rollback was a sham.

Hungary

In 1956, Hungarian anti-Soviet demonstrations developed into a revolt. When the Soviets sent in tanks and 250,000 soldiers, the Hungarian rebels expected American aid because of promises of rollback. However, Eisenhower pointed out that landlocked Hungary was 'as inaccessible to us as Tibet'. Furthermore, there was a concurrent crisis in the Middle East (see page 79), which Eisenhower considered more important. So, the Iron Curtain (see page 14) remained impenetrable – apart from West Berlin.

Berlin

Khrushchev was anxious about Germany. First, since the establishment of two German states (see page 19), the West had refused to give East Germany diplomatic recognition on the grounds that it lacked legitimacy. Second, West Berlin was a disruptive enclave within the Soviet bloc, a centre of Western espionage and a magnet for skilled East German workers. In November 1958, Khrushchev demanded that West Berlin become a 'free city' and threatened to turn the **access routes** (see page 20) to Berlin over to East Germany (that would force Western recognition of East Germany). Eisenhower did not respond.

The Democrats, press, Defence Department and arms industry accused Eisenhower of failing to take the Berlin crisis sufficiently seriously. One journalist asked him about the general belief that his administration 'puts a balanced budget ahead of national security'. Eisenhower responded that anyone who had read Lenin knew 'the Communist objective is to make us spend ourselves into bankruptcy', and asked the reporters, 'What would you do with more ground forces in Europe? Would you start a ground war?'

Eisenhower made it clear that the United States would always support West Berlin, but denied that there was a Berlin crisis. That gave Khrushchev room to retreat and the crisis passed.

Reactions to the rise of Communism in Asia

When Eisenhower became president, the United States was involved in a war against Communism in Korea (see page 21) and most Americans believed that Moscow and Beijing (Stalin and Mao had signed the **Sino-Soviet alliance** in 1950) were behind Communist activity in the Philippines, Malaya and Indochina.

Ending the war in Korea, 1953

After his election in November 1952, Eisenhower flew to Korea. He saw that the Communists were well established and concluded that the United States should exit the stalemate. Many significant figures disagreed and wanted an offensive, including Syngman Rhee (see page 23), Dulles, Nixon and the US commander in Korea. Eisenhower nevertheless pressed the Chinese to agree to peace in Korea by refusing to deny that he might use nuclear weapons. Exhausted and fearful that the new Soviet regime would be unsupportive, China signed the armistice.

Vietnam

After the Second World War, the Vietnamese nationalist and Communist **Ho Chi Minh** led the fight for independence against French colonialism. Seeing France as a bulwark against Communist expansionism in Asia and Europe, and anxious not to 'lose' Vietnam, Truman had given over $2 billion to sustain the French war effort. Eisenhower continued Truman's policy.

In 1954, the French begged Eisenhower for an American air strike to help them in their battle against the Communists at Dien Bien Phu. Nixon and Dulles both advocated supporting the French. The arguments for intervention were that Eisenhower

- considered a co-operative, strong, anti-Communist France important to the Western alliance

KEY TERMS

Access routes Land routes that crossed East Germany *en route* to West Berlin.

Sino-Soviet alliance Alliance between Communist China and the USSR, dating from 1950 treaty.

KEY FIGURE

Ho Chi Minh (1890–1969)

Vietnamese nationalist and Communist who led the Vietnamese in their struggle for independence against the French (1945–55). After the Americans set up South Vietnam in 1955, he led North Vietnam's struggle to reunify the nation.

- had advocated rollback in 1952 but had not 'liberated' a single soul from Communism
- did not want accusations that he 'lost' Vietnam
- was told by his National Security Council that Vietnam was 'vital to the security of the United States' because its loss to Communism would affect the global balance of power.

In an April 1954 press conference, Eisenhower explained his **domino theory**: if America allowed Vietnam to fall to Communism, other Southeast Asian countries would follow. He said this was undesirable because Southeast Asia had valuable resources and because millions would be lost to a Communist dictatorship. However, there were persuasive arguments against intervention:

- Some advisers doubted whether the loss of one small country to Communism would trigger the loss of others.
- Others felt that US intervention in Vietnam would be pointless, a 'serious diversion of limited US capabilities', and could snowball.
- Eisenhower had just gained massive popularity by getting American troops out of Korea and did not want to send them into Southeast Asia again (while heading NATO he had said 'no military victory is possible in that kind of theater').
- The 'New Look' (see page 71) meant that few American troops were readily available.
- Eisenhower doubted the wisdom of being too closely entangled with the French in Indochina, because he considered them 'a hopeless, helpless mass of protoplasm' and because he felt that the American tradition of anti-colonialism would be damaged by involvement with French colonialism.
- Neither the British nor Congress supported American military intervention at Dien Bien Phu.

When Eisenhower opted against intervention, the French were defeated at Dien Bien Phu and decided to leave Vietnam.

The Geneva conference 1954

It was agreed at Geneva that the French would exit, Vietnam would be temporarily divided into a Communist North and a non-Communist South, and there would be nationwide elections and reunification in 1956. However, Eisenhower refused to sign these Geneva Accords and created, then sustained, the new 'state' of South Vietnam under the leadership of **Ngo Dinh Diem**. By 1961, Eisenhower had given Diem $7 billion in aid and nearly 1000 American advisers, and had established **SEATO** to protect South Vietnam. However, the Communists were increasingly active and effective in disrupting South Vietnam.

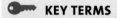

KEY TERMS

Domino theory President Eisenhower's belief that if one country fell to Communism, neighbouring countries would fall soon after.

SEATO Southeast Asia Treaty Organisation established in 1954 and consisting of Australia, France, New Zealand, Pakistan, Philippines, Thailand, the UK and the USA.

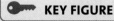

KEY FIGURE

Ngo Dinh Diem (1901–63)

Led the anti-Communist South Vietnamese state created by the Americans from 1955 to 1963.

Vice President Nixon said the problem was that the South Vietnamese simply 'lacked the ability to conduct a war by themselves or govern themselves', but the real problem was that Eisenhower (who privately admitted that Ho Chi Minh would win 80 per cent of the popular vote in any nationwide elections in Vietnam) had committed the United States to an unimpressive leader in a state that was not viable.

Given the subsequent dramatic escalation of the American commitment to Vietnam, Eisenhower is often praised for keeping American troops out. However, he missed the opportunity for the United States to exit with the French, at which stage it would have been the French who 'lost' Vietnam to Communism. Instead, Eisenhower staked American prestige on the continued existence of the South Vietnamese state he had created. Although his actions were understandable given the domestic Cold War pressures, he bears massive responsibility for the future Vietnam War.

China

American antagonism towards Communist China was increased by the Korean War (see page 24) and by the 1954 Quemoy and Matsu crisis.

Quemoy and Matsu were small islands situated in the Taiwan Strait, which separated Mao Zedong's Communist China from Chiang Kai-shek's Taiwan. Quemoy and Matsu were nearer to mainland China than Taiwan, but Chiang Kai-shek controlled them. Soon after the establishment of SEATO, the Chinese

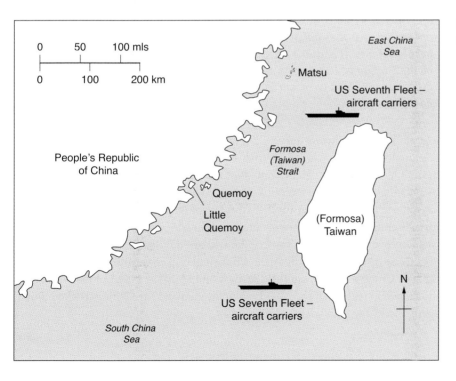

Figure 2.1 The Quemoy and Matsu crisis.

KEY TERM

JCS The Joint Chiefs of Staff were the heads of the army, navy and air force.

? What evaluative words would you use to describe Eisenhower's comments in Source D?

bombarded them (September 1954). The **JCS** pressed Eisenhower to intervene. He responded that the United States had no treaty with Chiang Kai-shek, and that he did not want to risk war with China and the USSR over two small islands: 'Those dammed little offshore islands. Sometimes I wish they'd sink,' he said.

Amidst Chinese talk of 'liberating' Taiwan, American anti-Chinese sentiment increased when China contravened the Korea armistice provisions (see page 22) and imprisoned American pilots shot down over China in the Korean War. Under even greater pressure to act, Eisenhower signed a treaty with Chiang Kai-shek (see page 12), committing the United States to the defence of Taiwan.

SOURCE D

From Eisenhower's response to questions about the possibilities of a pre-emptive strike against the Chinese, at a November 1954 press conference. Quoted in Stephen Ambrose, *Eisenhower: Soldier and President*, Simon & Schuster, 2003, pp. 393–4.

A president experiences exactly the same resentments, the same anger, the same kind of sense of frustration almost, when things like this occur to other Americans, and his impulse is to lash out … [This would be the easy course: Americans would automatically unite and the president would have a simple task, to win the war.] *There is a real fervor developed throughout the nation that you can feel everywhere you go. There is practically an exhilaration about the affair. In the intellectual and spiritual contest of matching wits and getting along to see if you can win, there comes about something … an atmosphere is created … an attitude is created to which I am not totally unfamiliar … It is well that war is so terrible; if it were not so, we would grow too fond of it … [I had] the job of writing letters of condolence by the hundreds, by the thousands, to bereaved mothers and wives. That is a very sobering experience … Don't go to war in response to emotions of anger and resentment; do it prayerfully.*

In early 1955, Eisenhower asked Congress for authorisation enabling him to react in defence of Taiwan and 'closely related localities' (no one knew if that meant Quemoy and Matsu). Congress granted it. Eisenhower's public suggestion that he might use tactical atomic weapons led to Democrat accusations of irresponsibility and risking another world war for two little islands. As tensions rose, Eisenhower was deliberately incomprehensible on the issue of using atomic weapons over Taiwan ('Don't worry,' he told one adviser, 'if that question comes up, I'll just confuse them'). By April, China had backed down. There was another flurry of Chinese activity against Quemoy and Matsu in 1958, but Eisenhower threatened to respond if the islands were invaded and the Chinese backed down again. Eisenhower had defused both crises.

Responses to crises in the Middle East

Asia, Africa and the Middle East contained many nations that had struggled or were struggling for independence from colonialism. Both the United States and the Soviet Union were keen to 'win' these **Third World** nations.

The Middle East was desirable to both superpowers due to its oil and the strategic importance of the Suez Canal, which linked the Mediterranean and the Indian Ocean. Eisenhower faced three great crises in the Middle East, over Iran, the Suez Canal and Arab nationalism.

Iran

In 1951, Iran's democratically elected Prime Minister Mohammad Mossadegh seized the British-owned Anglo-Persian Oil Company. British and American oil companies and the CIA assured Eisenhower that Iran might turn Communist. Eisenhower used the CIA to encourage an Iranian coup in 1953 that restored the authority of the dictatorial, pro-American Shah (Emperor), who gave US oil companies 40 per cent of Iranian oil.

Egypt and the Suez Canal crisis

The Americans tried to persuade the Arab states that the Soviet Union was their great enemy, but Arab hostility focused on Israel. Why?

After a near 2000-year absence from the Middle East, Jews had returned in the twentieth century to land that had by now long been inhabited by native Palestinians. The UN recommended two separate Palestinian states, one Arab, one Jewish, but in May 1948 the Jews proclaimed the establishment of the state of Israel. The neighbouring Arab states were infuriated by the Israeli dispossession of Palestinian land and by Israeli treatment of the Palestinians within Israel.

Eisenhower sought to keep out of the Arab–Israeli tensions. He refused to sell arms to either side, but hoped to win Arab friends through economic aid.

Nasser and Egypt

Eisenhower promised Egypt financial and technical aid to build the Aswan Dam. However, Egypt's leader Colonel Nasser bought Soviet-supplied arms from the Czechs, recognised China and seemed to be trying to create a neutral bloc in the Cold War. With Eisenhower hospitalised with an intestinal obstruction, Dulles withdrew the aid offer in July 1956. Nasser then nationalised the Anglo-French-owned Suez Canal, saying its revenues would finance the dam. Britain and France resented the loss of their investments and wanted to ensure continued access to the Canal. The British sought American support for military action against Nasser, but Eisenhower said this would 'antagonize the American people' and that 'Nasser was within his rights'. Britain, France and Israel (which resented Nasser's organisation of an Arab anti-Israeli coalition) then secretly prepared for action.

KEY TERM

Third World The term used for less-developed nations during the Cold War, when America and its allies constituted the first world, the Communists the second world, and the non-aligned and less developed nations were the third group of countries.

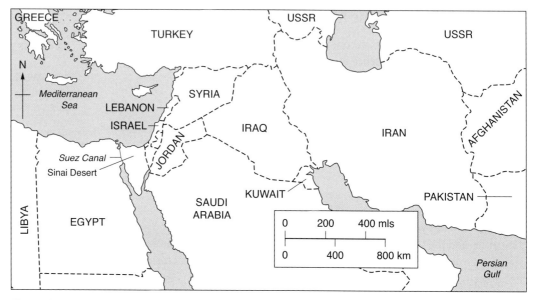

Figure 2.2 The Middle East in 1956.

The Suez Crisis or Tripartite Aggression took place in late October 1956. Israel attacked Egypt and took the Sinai desert, then Britain and France moved in to safeguard the Suez Canal. The global reaction was hostile and Eisenhower's pressure forced Britain and France to withdraw. The British had expected American sympathy for their actions because Eisenhower disliked Nasser, but Eisenhower wanted to

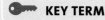 **KEY TERM**

Neo-colonialism The use of political and economic (rather than military) pressure to force a weaker country to do what the more powerful country desires.

- keep in with the Arab nations for their oil and their friendship against the Communist bloc
- avoid alienating Muslims across the world
- avoid association with Anglo French **neo-colonialism** lest it make Third World countries ally with the Soviet Union
- teach Britain, France and Israel never to act without keeping him informed ('nothing justifies double-crossing us')
- keep the Soviets out of the Middle East – when Khrushchev proposed joint Soviet–American action against Britain and France, Eisenhower warned him not to put troops into the Middle East.

Eisenhower received international acclaim, but Nasser and the Soviets continued to pose problems.

Arab nationalism

By 1958, Saudi Arabia, Iraq, Jordan and Lebanon were buying military equipment from the United States, while Syria and Egypt were supplied by the Soviets and Israel by France. Another force for instability was Nasser, who aroused the Arab nationalism that contributed to the July 1958 overthrow of the pro-Western Iraqi monarchy. This worried the Lebanese government, which appealed for American aid.

Eisenhower felt compelled to do something 'to stop the trend toward chaos'. For the only time in his presidency, he sent the US military into another country – Lebanon. American troops landed on the Lebanese beaches amidst sunbathers, never fired a shot, and exited within the month. The Lebanese regime was secured and Nasser adopted a lower profile.

There was no Communist threat in Lebanon, so what had motivated Eisenhower?

- The Lebanese leader had sought US intervention.
- There was no chance of a Soviet–American clash.
- It disproved Democrat charges that his New Look was inflexible.
- It showed that Eisenhower was not too old and weak to respond to threats.
- It was a display of American strength and determination that served as a warning to Nasser and a reassurance to allies such as Saudi Arabia.

Eisenhower and the Cold War: conclusions

Eisenhower aimed to make the world more peaceful, but it is difficult to claim that he succeeded. The Soviets and Americans were now willing to attend summits, but the Geneva summit produced nothing concrete and the Paris summit collapsed. The escalation of the arms race, while not as much as many Americans wanted, demonstrated that superpower rivalry and conflict continued.

Eisenhower strengthened Western Europe and defused a Berlin crisis. However, his inactivity over Eastern Europe demonstrated the impact of political manoeuvres upon the Cold War. Republican advocacy of rollback had owed much to Republican desire to get at the Democrats, but it encouraged a Hungarian revolt in which 3000 Hungarians died.

For the most part, Eisenhower continued Truman's policy of containment. He deserves praise for going against the advice of most of his advisers to be more warlike during 1953–4 over Korea, Dien Bien Phu, possible Chinese intervention in Vietnam, Quemoy and Matsu, and Chinese treatment of shot-down pilots. He restored peace and the pre-war *status quo* in Korea. His treaty with Chiang and hints about the use of nuclear weapons ensured that Quemoy and Matsu remained in Chiang's hands without any US military action against China. The northern part of Vietnam was lost to Communism, but an anti-Communist state was set up under American auspices in South Vietnam. There, Eisenhower's response to the rising threat of Communist expansion could be considered his sole example of rollback. However, it would cause great problems for Eisenhower's successors.

Eisenhower defused crises in the Middle East, where he showed both the Soviets and Arab nationalists that the United States was a force to be reckoned with.

Eisenhower made covert warfare an essential part of US foreign policy. It led to the support of dubious regimes in Iran and Guatemala, but it could be argued that covert rather than open warfare helped save American lives. Indeed, overall, the former soldier demonstrated admirable restraint over military activity and over defence expenditure.

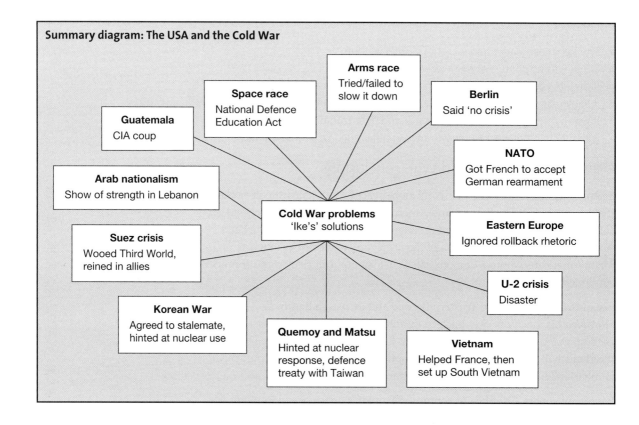

Summary diagram: The USA and the Cold War

- **Arms race** — Tried/failed to slow it down
- **Space race** — National Defence Education Act
- **Berlin** — Said 'no crisis'
- **Guatemala** — CIA coup
- **NATO** — Got French to accept German rearmament
- **Arab nationalism** — Show of strength in Lebanon
- **Cold War problems** — 'Ike's' solutions
- **Eastern Europe** — Ignored rollback rhetoric
- **Suez crisis** — Wooed Third World, reined in allies
- **U-2 crisis** — Disaster
- **Korean War** — Agreed to stalemate, hinted at nuclear use
- **Quemoy and Matsu** — Hinted at nuclear response, defence treaty with Taiwan
- **Vietnam** — Helped France, then set up South Vietnam

4 African-Americans in the North and the South

▶ *Was there a successful civil rights movement in the Eisenhower years?*

President Truman put civil rights firmly on the national political agenda (see page 44). This encouraged the emergence of what some historians consider to be a civil rights movement in the Eisenhower years.

The emergence of the civil rights movement

Prior to Eisenhower's presidency, black labour leader A. Philip Randolph (see page 42) and the NAACP led the struggle for civil rights. NAACP litigation won several helpful Supreme Court rulings (see page 43), notably the 1954 *Brown* ruling against segregated education (see page 87). However, the Supreme Court lacked powers of enforcement. Sustained black community protest in Montgomery, Alabama, in 1956 demonstrated an alternative method of black activism.

The Montgomery bus boycott

The Montgomery bus boycott is usually seen as the start of the modern civil rights movement. The underlying cause was Montgomery's segregated buses and the behaviour of white bus drivers. For example, in 1955, a black mother put her two babies on the front 'white' seats to free her hands to pay her fare, the driver yelled, 'Take the dirty black brats off the seats' and hit the accelerator. The babies fell into the aisle. Many in Montgomery's black community had had enough of such behaviour.

Rosa Parks

1913	Born in Montgomery, Alabama, of mixed race descent
1931	Married Raymond Parks, a founder member of Montgomery's NAACP
1942	Joined NAACP
1945	Registered to vote
1946	Attended NAACP leadership training seminar
1955	Arrested for refusing to give up her seat on a bus to a white man
1957	Moved to Detroit
2005	Died

As a child, Rosa went to bed fully clothed each night, ready to flee if the Ku Klux Klan attacked the family home. During the Second World War, she joined NAACP, which she said 'was about empowerment through the ballot box'. She considered moving North to Detroit where, she said, 'you could get a seat anywhere on a bus'. However, Detroit's race riots in 1943 made her realise that 'racism was almost as widespread in Detroit as in Montgomery'. An enthusiastic and active member of NAACP, she attended an NAACP leadership training seminar in 1946. She was inspired by the 1954 *Brown* ruling, recalling, 'You can't imagine the rejoicing among black people, and some white people.' It readied her to make a public stand against white oppression: 'Every day in the early 1950s we were looking for ways to challenge Jim Crow laws.'

After her arrest in December 1955, Rosa Parks lost her job as a seamstress in a Montgomery department store, her husband Raymond Parks was forced out of his job at a US Army base, their white landlord raised their rent, and they received countless death threats. The Parks were now branded 'troublemakers' and unemployable. Furthermore, many black Montgomery activists were jealous of her fame. So, she and Raymond moved to Detroit. During the 1960s, Parks admired many aspects of Malcolm X and the black power movement (see page 165).

Women had long played an important part in black campaigns for equality, especially because whites were reluctant to use physical force against them. Accounts of Rosa Parks often depict her as a tired old lady, probably because that makes for a more dramatic story than being a 42-year-old trained and committed activist.

Martin Luther King Jr

1929	Born in Atlanta, Georgia
1956	Prominent in the Montgomery bus boycott
1957	Established SCLC
1961–2	Unproductive involvement in Albany Freedom Movement
1963	Organised Birmingham campaign. 'I have a dream' speech during the March on Washington
1965	Selma campaign
1966	Chicago ghetto campaign
1968	Assassinated by a white racist

King was born into a well-educated and relatively prosperous family. His grandfather and father were Baptist pastors and NAACP activists. Young Martin received a poor education in Atlanta's segregated schools and faced further prejudice when he went North to college in Boston. In 1954, he became pastor of Dexter Avenue Baptist church in Montgomery, Alabama.

King gained national attention during the Montgomery bus boycott of 1956 and was soon regarded by many as the leading spokesman for black Americans. He and his SCLC were very important in the civil rights movement, especially in the campaigns in Birmingham (1963) and Selma (1965). In 1966, he turned his attention to the ghettos of the North, but made little impact on the dreadful conditions there (see page 168).

King brilliantly manipulated white officials whom he knew would use such violence against peaceful black protesters that the media would become interested. His use of this tactic in Birmingham (coupled with his remarkable oratory in the March on Washington) contributed to the passage of the Civil Rights Act (1964). His use of this tactic in Selma was vital to the passage of the Voting Rights Act (1965). Those two acts ended *de jure* segregation in the South and enabled African-Americans there to vote.

There had long been talk of a bus boycott to force the white bus company owners to reconsider their policies. The local NAACP branch wanted a 'test case' to put this in action. When branch secretary Rosa Parks was arrested in December 1955 for refusing to stand to give a white man her seat on the bus, NAACP organised a boycott of the buses, assisted by the local black college and the black churches. The black community sought integrated buses and the employment of black drivers. A 26-year-old Baptist minister, Martin Luther King Jr, was chosen to lead the boycott. It lasted for a year and most of Montgomery's 50,000 black population participated.

 KEY TERMS

Citizens' Councils
Southern organisations set up in protest after the *Brown* ruling.

Mass direct action
Large-scale protest movements, for example the Montgomery bus boycott.

Results and significance of the Montgomery bus boycott

- The white Montgomery **Citizens' Council** organised the opposition to the boycott, using arrests and intimidation to frighten leaders such as King. That attracted favourable nationwide attention to the black community's efforts.
- The boycott demonstrated the potential power of a new mode of activism, **mass direct action**, but it was NAACP litigation that ensured the desegregation of Montgomery's buses through the Supreme Court's *Browder* v. *Gayle* ruling (November 1956).
- It was only Montgomery's buses that were desegregated.

- A major new black leader had emerged. King and his inspirational oratory gained national attention and in 1957 he established the Southern Christian Leadership Conference (SCLC) to continue the fight against segregation.

After the Montgomery bus boycott, civil rights protestors gained little national attention for several years, which is why one might hesitate to talk of the civil rights movement at this time. However, in 1960, black college students, who were educated and more impatient with inequality than their parents, triggered a sustained civil rights movement.

Student sit-ins

In February 1960, four black college students in Greensboro, North Carolina, spontaneously refused to leave the all-white Woolworth's cafeteria when asked. Other students took up and retained the seats, day after day. The cafeteria had to close.

As many as 70,000 students participated in sit-ins across the South. The sit-ins were highly significant:

- They helped to erode Jim Crow: loss of business made Woolworth's desegregate all its lunch counters by the end of 1961 and 150 cities began to desegregate public places.
- Black students had been mobilised, although when they set up the Student Non-Violent Coordinating Committee (SNCC), inter-organisational strife increased. NAACP lawyer Thurgood Marshall refused to represent 'a bunch of crazy colored students', while SNCC opposed King's 'top-down' leadership, preferring to empower ordinary black citizens at grassroots level, as in the SNCC voter registration campaign in the Mississippi Delta (1961–4).
- The sit-ins shifted the focus of black activism from litigation to mass direct action, a method King would perfect in Birmingham and Selma (see pages 117 and 160).

The policies and attitudes of the main political parties

The race policies and attitudes of the Democrats and Republicans were for the most part shaped by electoral considerations.

Democrats

Although most Southern Democrats opposed civil rights for black Americans (see page 4), others in the Democratic Party had become increasingly liberal on race because of:

- basic human decency
- awareness of the increasing importance of the black vote outside the South
- increased black consciousness and unwillingness to accept inequality
- recognition that racism helped keep the South the poorest region in America.

From 1948, Democrat policy was to promote the civil rights programme advocated by Truman (see page 44). In 1952 and 1956, the party platform said, 'The Democratic Party is committed to support and advance the individual rights and liberties of all Americans.'

Republicans

The Republican Party disliked large-scale federal interventionism on any great issue and, like many Democrats, respected states' rights and hesitated to impose change on the South. Nevertheless, the party platform in 1952 and 1956 claimed commitment to racial equality and in 1956 it dropped the 1952 commitment to states' rights.

Like the Democratic Party, the Republican Party contained some who were relatively liberal on race, such as Supreme Court Chief Justice Earl Warren and Vice President Nixon. However, most Republicans remained conservative. Eisenhower had one African-American on his staff, ex-NAACP worker E. Frederic Morrow. Morrow considered this Republican administration ignorant of civil rights issues and black feelings.

Republicans were aware of the increasing importance of the black vote in the North, but because most black Northerners voted Democrat anyway, and because Republicans hoped to profit from Southern white disillusionment with increasing Democrat liberalism on race, Republican support for civil rights was muted.

Overall, the policies and attitudes of the main political parties were apparently changing for the better, although electoral calculations probably played the biggest part in this slow change.

The responses of the state and federal authorities

The three branches of the federal government responded in varying degrees of enthusiasm and effectiveness to the growing civil rights movement, but white-dominated Deep South state governments remained opposed to racial equality.

The response of the Supreme Court

The Supreme Court was the branch of the federal government most responsive to black problems before the 1960s. Important rulings in the Eisenhower years included *Browder* v. *Gayle* (see page 84), *Cooper* v. *Aaron* (see page 90) and, most important of all, the *Brown* ruling of 1954.

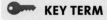
KEY TERM

Border state States such as Kansas and Missouri, situated on the edge of the American South and sharing similar characteristics.

Church minister Oliver Brown lived in Kansas, one of seventeen states where schools were legally segregated. He could not send his daughter to the whites-only school five blocks away from where they lived. Instead, she had to cross railroad tracks to get to the all-black school twenty blocks away. Brown therefore challenged this in the law courts. The NAACP decided to support him, hoping that the case might succeed because Kansas was a **border state**.

In *Brown* v. *The Board of Education, Topeka, Kansas*, the Supreme Court adjudged that even if facilities were equal (black schools always received less funding, so they never were equal), separate education was psychologically harmful to black children.

The *Brown* ruling was highly significant:

- Rosa Parks said that *Brown* inspired African-Americans to further activism.
- *Brown* removed all constitutional sanction for segregation, but was not a total victory for the NAACP because the Supreme Court gave no date by which desegregation had to be achieved and said nothing about *de facto* segregation outside the South.
- Although the NAACP gained the *Brown II* (1955) ruling that integration be accomplished 'with all deliberate speed', the Supreme Court's lack of enforcement powers meant that implementation of the ruling varied. In the peripheral and urban South, desegregation was introduced quite quickly: 70 per cent of school districts in Washington DC and the border states of Delaware, Kentucky, Maryland, Missouri, Oklahoma and West Virginia all desegregated schools within a year. However, schools remained segregated in Deep South states (Georgia, South Carolina, Alabama, Mississippi and Louisiana).
- *Brown* engendered a white backlash. From 1956 to 1959, Virginia whites staged a 'massive resistance' campaign, closing some schools rather than desegregate (Virginia labour unions financed segregated schools when the public schools were closed). White opposition to desegregated schools was most famously demonstrated in Little Rock (see page 90). Most Southern politicians signed the Southern Manifesto, in which they pledged to oppose *Brown*. White Citizens' Councils were formed throughout the South to defend segregation. By 1956, they boasted roughly 250,000 members, many of whom were highly respected members of their local community. Even more ominously, the Ku Klux Klan was revitalised.

Ku Klux Klan (KKK)

The Ku Klux Klan was an armed white racist group established after the South's defeat in the Civil War but soon quashed by the federal government. It revived in 1915 and gained members across the USA, especially in the cities of the North and Midwest to which black Americans had gravitated during the early twentieth century. *Brown* revitalised the Klan, but the Montgomery bus boycott suggested it had lost some of its impact: when Montgomery's buses were desegregated, the Klan sent 40 carloads of robed, hooded members through Montgomery's black community, which instead of the usual retreat behind closed doors, emerged to wave at them. The Klan nevertheless persisted in activities such as the bombing of King's motel room during the Birmingham campaign (see page 117). During the 1970s, Klan membership tripled and violence increased.

The response of the executive

In his first State of the Union address, in February 1953, Eisenhower called for a combination of publicity, persuasion and conscience to help end racial discrimination. He worked against discrimination in federal facilities in Washington and federal hiring, but his President's Committee on Government Contracts lacked teeth. Some people defend Eisenhower's civil rights record because he appointed Chief Justice Warren, who was vitally important in the *Brown* ruling, and also other moderate Republicans who made liberal rulings on segregation in the lower federal courts in Louisiana and Georgia.

Although sometimes helpful, Eisenhower was less inclined than Truman to propel America towards racial equality because:

- Eisenhower often reminded people that he was born in an all-white town in the South and spent much of his life in Southern states and in the segregated armed forces.
- Eisenhower was uneasy in the presence of African-Americans. He only met black leaders once and assured his speechwriter that his public calls for equality of opportunity did not mean that black and white had 'to mingle socially – or that a Negro could court my daughter'.
- Eisenhower was ideologically opposed to large-scale federal intervention in the states and sympathetic to states' rights. After attempted desegregation by school officials in Clinton, Tennessee, and Mansfield, Texas, led to mob violence, a reporter asked Eisenhower whether the federal government would intervene. Eisenhower said that it was a local issue – 'under the law the federal government cannot … move into a state until the state is not able to handle the matter'.
- The Republican Party had done unusually well in the Southern states as a result of Democrat divisions over civil rights, and could only lose by adopting a firm civil rights policy.
- Eisenhower frequently highlighted the 'great emotional strains' and possible 'social disintegration' that would arise in the South from school desegregation. He said it was 'difficult … to change a man's heart' by legislation or force.

Eisenhower and inaction

Eisenhower's preferred mode on civil rights violations seemed to be inactivity, as shown in the high-profile cases of Emmett Till and Autherine Lucy in 1955–6.

Southern whites used violence and intimidation to maintain their supremacy and there was little protection for African-Americans in the law courts. For example, when 14-year-old Chicagoan Emmett Till visited Southern relations in 1955, he spoke to or flirted with (some say wolf-whistled at) a white woman. His mutilated body was dragged out of a Mississippi river soon after. His murderers boasted of what they had done but went unpunished.

SOURCE E

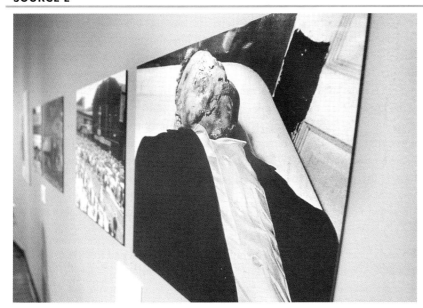

The famous 1955 photo of Emmett Till in his coffin, on display at the Chicago Historical Society's 'Without Sanctuary' exhibition.

Why do you suppose Emmett Till's mother wanted his coffin open, as seen in Source E?

SOURCE F

From journalist William Bradford Huie's article on Emmett Till's murder for *Look* magazine in 1956. Huie paid Till's killers for their story. Here, one of the murderers explains his motivation (available from **www.pbs.org/wgbh/amex/till/sfeature/sf_look_confession.html**).

Well, what else could we do? He was hopeless. I'm no bully; I never hurt a nigger in my life. I like niggers – in their place – I know how to work 'em. But I just decided it was time a few people got put on notice. As long as I live and can do anything about it, niggers are gonna stay in their place. Niggers ain't gonna vote where I live. If they did, they'd control the government. They ain't gonna go to school with my kids. And when a nigger gets close to mentioning sex with a white woman … I'm likely to kill him. Me and my folks fought for this country, and we got some rights. I stood there … and listened to that nigger throw that poison at me, and I just made up my mind. 'Chicago boy,' I said, 'I'm tired of 'em sending your kind down here to stir up trouble. Goddam you, I'm going to make an example of you' …

What can you infer from Source F about the ways in which African-Americans lacked equality in the USA in 1955?

Eisenhower said nothing about the murder of Till or about Autherine Lucy. In 1955, Lucy had successfully taken the University of Alabama to a federal court to obtain admission as its first black student, but she was quickly expelled in 1956. Although Eisenhower had said he would always support federal court orders, he did nothing. However, he was finally forced into action at Little Rock in 1957.

The response of the state authorities

The impact of the *Brown* ruling illustrates the tensions between the authorities in a federal system of government. President Eisenhower had urged Chief Justice Warren to avoid ruling in favour of desegregated schools in *Brown*, assuring him that Southerners were not 'bad people … All they are concerned about is to see that their sweet little girls are not required to sit in school alongside some big overgrown Negroes.' Warren ignored Eisenhower and masterminded the Supreme Court's *Brown* ruling. Then the state authorities in the South did all they could to resist the desegregation of schools (and universities). In February 1956, four Southern state legislatures passed **interposition resolutions** that said that the *Brown* ruling had no effect in their states. Conservative Democrat Governor Allan Shivers of Texas, an Eisenhower supporter, sent law enforcement officers to defy a court order on desegregation, saying, 'I defy the federal government.'

Although Eisenhower said that Supreme Court decisions had to be accepted and that US marshals would enforce a federal court order if a federal court cited someone for contempt, he failed to use federal power in response to actions such as those of Shivers – until the Little Rock crisis in Arkansas.

The Little Rock crisis

The city of Little Rock planned to comply with the *Brown* ruling by 1963. Central High School was to be the first integrated school and, encouraged by NAACP, nine African-American students attempted to enter it in September 1957. Keen to exploit racism to gain re-election, Arkansas Governor Orval Faubus ordered the Arkansas **National Guard** to keep the students out. An abusive white mob surrounded the students as they tried to enter the school.

Riots in Little Rock made Eisenhower fear the breakdown of law and order. He reluctantly sent in federal forces to protect the 'Little Rock Nine'. Little Rock was highly significant for the civil rights movement:

- Although the Supreme Court ploughed ahead, ruling that any law that sought to keep public schools segregated was unconstitutional (*Cooper* v. *Aaron*, 1958), Little Rock demonstrated how Supreme Court rulings met tremendous resistance in practice. The 'Little Rock Nine' suffered violent attacks when they attended Central High. They were pushed down the stairs and had chemicals and wads of burning paper thrown at them. As Eisenhower had feared, Faubus closed all Little Rock's high schools during 1958 and 1959 rather than integrate (he got re-elected). Central High School was finally integrated in 1960, other Little Rock schools by 1972.
- Faubus's use of the National Guard demonstrated how white-dominated law enforcement in the South gave no protection to African-Americans.
- There was much congressional criticism of Eisenhower's intervention in Arkansas, for example, from Democrat Senators Lyndon Johnson and John Kennedy.

KEY TERMS

Interposition resolutions
Assertions of states' right to oppose federal government actions deemed unconstitutional.

National Guard
State reserves that can be federalised by the president during an emergency.

- Eisenhower demonstrated no clear moral leadership on civil rights. He had been forced into action, but said in a television statement that he had intervened because of the breakdown of law and order and therefore, by implication, not in support of desegregation. Warren thought that a word of approval from the president on *Brown* would have helped stop the mob violence that kept African-Americans out of white schools throughout the South. Eisenhower's speechwriter Arthur Larsen said that the 'inescapable conclusion' was that the president 'was neither emotionally nor intellectually in favor of combating segregation'.
- In his television statement, Eisenhower did point out that 'our enemies are gloating' over Little Rock: a reminder that Cold War imperatives sometimes made Americans take a more liberal stance on race to substantiate national claims about equality of opportunity in the pursuit of the American Dream.
- The power of television was demonstrated at Little Rock, where on-the-spot reporting was pioneered. Images of black children being spat at by aggressive white adults shocked many Americans.
- Many black activists decided that Supreme Court rulings were insufficient and that other forms of activism were required.

The response of the legislature

Two Civil Rights Acts were passed during Eisenhower's presidency. They demonstrate the response of the executive and legislature to the black situation.

1957 Civil Rights Act

Inspired by a desire to win the black vote in the 1956 election year, the Eisenhower administration drew up a civil rights bill that aimed to ensure black voting rights. Around 80 per cent of Southern African-Americans were not yet registered, including some college professors. Eisenhower publicly praised the bill, expressing 'shock' that only 7000 of Mississippi's 900,000 black population were registered to vote and that registrars set impossible questions (see page 40) for those trying to register.

As Southern Democrats worked to weaken the bill, Eisenhower cravenly claimed that he did not really know what was in it ('there were certain phrases I did not completely understand') and did not fight to keep it intact.

The bill passed as a much weakened act that did little to help African-Americans (any public official indicted for obstructing a black voter would be tried by a white jury that would invariably rule in the official's favour). Many considered it a nauseating sham, but some black leaders were pleased: it was the first such act since 1875. As King said, 'The present bill is far better than no bill at all.'

1960 Civil Rights Act

In May 1958, Eisenhower was concerned about bombings of black schools and churches in the South. He introduced what he considered a moderate civil rights bill, but Southern Democrats diluted its provisions again. It finally passed because both parties sought the black vote. It made the obstruction of court-ordered school desegregation a federal crime, and established penalties for the obstruction of black voting.

Together, Eisenhower's Civil Rights Acts added only 3 per cent of black voters to the electoral rolls during 1960. However, they constituted an acknowledgement of federal responsibilities and encouraged civil rights activists to work for more legislation.

Summary diagram: African-Americans in the North and the South

Significant events	Responses
1954 NAACP won *Brown* ruling	• Eisenhower disapproved • Supreme Court sympathetic • Southern whites established Citizens' Councils • Ku Klux Klan revitalised • Some states and cities desegregated schools • Inspired further black activism • Southern politicians declared opposition
1955 Murder of Emmett Till	• White jury found killers not guilty • No federal government response
1955 University of Alabama excluded Autherine Lucy	• No Eisenhower response, despite Supreme Court ruling that she should be admitted • Black students continued to press for admission to white universities, but slow progress
1956 Montgomery bus boycott	• Citizens' Council and Klan tried intimidation • Southern businesses increasingly sensitive to black economic power • Supreme Court helpful • Encouraged further black activism
1957 Little Rock	• Governor Faubus and Little Rock whites determinedly opposed desegregation • Eisenhower reluctantly intervened • Supreme Court helpful • Desegregation slow to occur
1957 and 1960 Civil Rights Acts	• Southern Democrats diluted them • Eisenhower introduced but did not push the bills • Only a few more black voters so some black criticism, but some felt it breached the dam

Assessing the Eisenhower years

▶ *Was Eisenhower a great president?*

Popular contemporary slogans included 'Trust Ike' and 'I like Ike', and most of the time, most Americans did. He received a record average 64 per cent approval rating over his two terms. Most people attributed the self-confidence of 1950s' America to the grandfatherly, self-confident Eisenhower. Was it all Ike? He inherited US military supremacy, and the economic boom would surely have happened regardless of who was president, and although he certainly had many successes, he also had failures.

Assessments of Eisenhower's achievements should take into account that he aimed to:

- *Restore the dignity of the presidency* because he believed that Truman's character and behaviour had demeaned it. Eisenhower was certainly dignified and respected.
- *Balance the budget.* He usually succeeded (he ended the fiscal year 1960 with a billion-dollar surplus). His fiscal policies and his refusal to cut taxes or to ramp up defence spending combined to control inflation and contributed to the unprecedented prosperity.
- *Improve the nation's transportation system* and thereby increase national unity and prosperity. His interstate highway system did just that.
- *Bring the Old Guard into the mainstream of the party* in order to make it more electable. He failed.
- *Demonstrate American moral superiority over the Soviet Union.* He exercised no moral leadership on civil rights, although it could be argued that his hands-off attitude helped keep the South relatively calm, that he had sponsored the first civil rights bill in a century and that he did finally intervene in Little Rock.
- *Contain Communist aggression.* He did so during the Quemoy and Matsu (1955) and Berlin (1959) crises.
- *Improve relations with the Soviet Union.* There was a slight relaxation of tensions.
- *Slow down the arms race.* He barely succeeded.
- *Keep American troops out of action.* This he did after he withdrew them from Korea. He said, 'The United States never lost a soldier or a foot of ground in my administration. We kept the peace. People asked how it happened – by God, it didn't just happen, I'll tell you that.'

KEY TERM

Missile gap Used in the USA for the perceived superiority of the number and power of the USSR's missiles in comparison with its own.

- *Maintain the nation's defences.* Critics, including the chiefs of staff, publicly accused him of neglect and allowing the Soviets to take the lead in missiles and the space race. He defended himself to the press, saying, 'I've spent my life in this, and I know more about it than almost anybody.' He was probably right. There was no '**missile gap**' (see page 97), he strengthened NATO and overall the nation was as safe as it could be. He stood alone in holding back a tidal wave of military build-up.

There were things that he did not aim to do and perhaps should have. For example, he left it to McCarthy to destroy himself. Some Republicans were disappointed that he failed to dismantle the New Deal. Indeed, the number covered by Social Security doubled, benefits rose, the New Deal regulatory commissions continued, and public works were expanded even more than under Roosevelt and Truman. From the point of view of those in his party who had talked a great deal of rollback, he had failed. Under him, the United States 'lost' North Korea, North Vietnam and Cuba, and perhaps missed an opportunity in Eastern Europe. Some have said that he kept the United States out of Vietnam, others have claimed that he was the one who got the United States into Vietnam.

Chapter summary

In the years 1953–60, the American economy boomed and many consumers could afford to buy the homes and consumer goods that they desired. Some believed consumerism was changing American society for the worse, making Americans more materialistic and conformist.

With the exception of interstate highway construction, President Eisenhower's domestic policies achieved little of note. It was left to Senator McCarthy to bring about his own downfall and to African-Americans to push the federal government into change. While the president and Congress were lukewarm in support of what some believe was an emerging civil rights movement (as demonstrated in the Montgomery bus boycott), the Supreme Court gave enthusiastic support to civil rights.

Eisenhower preferred to focus on foreign policy. He ended the war in Korea and steered the nation through several further Cold War crises without sending US forces into military action again or using nuclear weapons. He felt that American security depended on balancing the budget and tried to put a brake on excessive expenditure on defence, but was only partially successful.

Refresher questions

Use these questions to remind yourself of the key material covered in this chapter.

1 Which American industries did particularly well in the 1950s and why?

2 In what ways did the consumer society change American lives?

3 Why did the McCarthyite hysteria eventually end?

4 Why and with what results did Eisenhower choose Richard Nixon as his vice president?

5 What were Eisenhower's domestic achievements?

6 Explain the differences between Old Guard Republicans and moderate Republicans.

7 What motivated Eisenhower's Middle East policies?

8 How, why and with what results did Eisenhower seek to contain Communist China?

9 How far did Eisenhower improve relations with the Soviets?

10 Why did the civil rights movement emerge during the Eisenhower years?

11 Describe and explain a) Republican and b) Democrat policies and attitudes towards African-Americans in the Eisenhower years.

12 How, why and to what extent did the a) Supreme Court, b) Congress, c) Eisenhower and d) state governments help African-Americans?

 Question practice

ESSAY QUESTIONS

1 'President Truman did more for African-Americans than President Eisenhower.' Explain why you agree or disagree with this view.

2 'Eisenhower's America was blessed with peace, prosperity and progress.' Explain why you agree or disagree with this view.

3 'Eisenhower's foreign policy was generally successful.' Assess the validity of this view.

4 'Senator McCarthy has been unfairly blamed for the Cold War hysteria of the Truman and Eisenhower years.' Assess the validity of this view.

SOURCE ANALYSIS QUESTIONS

1 With reference to Source E of Chapter 1 (page 41) and Source F of this chapter (page 89), and your understanding of the historical context, which of these two sources is more valuable in explaining white attitudes to African-Americans in the years 1945–55?

2 With reference to Source E of Chapter 1 (page 41) and Sources C (page 61) and F (page 89) of this chapter, and your understanding of the historical context, assess the value of these three sources to a historian studying whether the American Dream was a reality in the Eisenhower years.

CHAPTER 3

Kennedy and the 'New Frontier' 1961–3

When John Fitzgerald Kennedy accepted the Democrat nomination for the presidency in July 1960, he introduced his 'New Frontier' idea. The New Frontier offered Americans a set of challenges involving science and space, peace and war, ignorance and prejudice, and poverty and surplus. Kennedy said that if these challenges were met they would bring about a version of the American Dream that emphasised 'the public interest' rather than 'the private comfort', as during the Eisenhower years. This chapter explores whether Kennedy and Americans realised his new American Dream, through sections on:

★ The New Frontier

★ Challenges to American power

★ African-Americans in the North and the South

★ The United States by late 1963

The key debate on *page 132* of this chapter asks the question: Was Kennedy a successful president?

Key dates

1960	July	Kennedy introduced 'New Frontier' idea
	Nov.	Kennedy defeated Nixon in presidential election
1961	Jan.	Kennedy inaugurated as president
	March	Peace Corps established
	April	Bay of Pigs fiasco
	May	First American in space
	May	Freedom Rides
	June	Vienna summit
	Aug.	Alliance for Progress

1961	Aug.	Berlin Wall erected
1962	Oct.	Cuban missile crisis
1963	Feb.	*The Feminine Mystique* published
	April	Birmingham campaign began
	July	Kennedy proposed civil rights legislation
	Aug.	March on Washington
	Oct.	Nuclear Test Ban Treaty
	Nov.	Diem assassinated
	Nov.	Kennedy assassinated

The New Frontier

▶ *Were Kennedy's domestic policies new and successful?*

Kennedy had promised much with his 'New Frontier' speech, but amidst all the subsequent hype there are those who have questioned the extent of his achievements. What is beyond doubt is that John Kennedy ran an impressive campaign in 1960.

The presidential election of 1960 and reasons for Kennedy's victory

Kennedy won the Democrat nomination in July 1960, then narrowly defeated Republican Vice President Richard Nixon in the November 1960 election. This defeat owed much to errors made by Eisenhower and Nixon, but also something to Kennedy himself.

Eisenhower's errors

Eisenhower was not particularly helpful to Nixon's presidential campaign. Perhaps he remained ambivalent about Nixon and his abilities (see page 66), or perhaps he was a tired, tetchy old man, prone to errors.

Instead of promoting Nixon's candidacy, Eisenhower was preoccupied with defending his presidential record against Kennedy's attacks on his policies on defence and poverty (when Kennedy claimed that 17 million Americans went to bed hungry each night, Eisenhower said snidely, 'They must all be dieting').

Eisenhower made two policy decisions that he considered right for the nation but were damaging to Nixon's candidacy:

- After the 1959 budget deficit of nearly $13 billion, Eisenhower and Congress agreed on huge spending cuts to ensure a surplus in 1960. Eisenhower ignored Nixon's warning that this, coupled with the **Federal Reserve** keeping money tight, would lead to a recession and damage Nixon's campaign. Nixon was proved right.
- Eisenhower refused to refute Kennedy's (inaccurate) accusation that there was a 'missile gap' in the Soviets' favour, lest it prompt Khrushchev (see page 72) into a further arms build-up. This left Nixon looking weak on defence.

Nixon made his experience of governing central to his campaign, but when a reporter asked Eisenhower for an example of a 'major idea' of Nixon's that he had adopted, Eisenhower answered: 'If you give me a week, I might think of one.' This remark greatly damaged Nixon's claim to governmental experience.

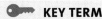

KEY TERM

Federal Reserve The US central bank.

John Fitzgerald Kennedy

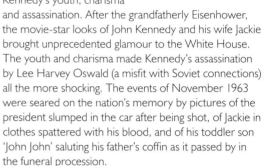

1917	Born in Boston, Massachusetts
1940	Graduated from Harvard University; wrote the bestseller *Why England Slept*
1943	Decorated for wartime service in the Pacific
1947–53	Served in the House of Representatives; criticised Truman administration for 'losing' China
1953	Ambivalent about family friend Senator Joseph McCarthy: 'Half my people in Massachusetts look upon McCarthy as a hero'
1954	Wrote *Profiles in Courage*
1953–60	Senator; served on Senate Foreign Relations Committee; advocated aid to emerging Third World nations; said France should grant independence to Algeria
1960	Elected president
1961–3	President
1963	Assassinated

John 'Jack' Kennedy was born into a wealthy, ambitious Irish-American family. After an undistinguished career in Congress, he narrowly defeated the Republican candidate Richard Nixon in the 1960 presidential election.

Many people have long been fascinated and attracted by Kennedy's youth, charisma and assassination. After the grandfatherly Eisenhower, the movie-star looks of John Kennedy and his wife Jackie brought unprecedented glamour to the White House. The youth and charisma made Kennedy's assassination by Lee Harvey Oswald (a misfit with Soviet connections) all the more shocking. The events of November 1963 were seared on the nation's memory by pictures of the president slumped in the car after being shot, of Jackie in clothes spattered with his blood, and of his toddler son 'John John' saluting his father's coffin as it passed by in the funeral procession.

The popular fascination with Kennedy has affected opinions of his performance as president. He prioritised foreign policy and his presidency was characterised by crises, for which he and/or Khrushchev clearly bore some blame. He bequeathed a greatly escalated involvement in Vietnam to his successor, President Lyndon Johnson, whose domestic achievements were far greater than Kennedy's but owed something to Kennedy's death.

Eisenhower had been very open about his health issues while president, and it is difficult to understand why he refused to allow Nixon to call for the candidates to make their health public. Although Kennedy looked fit, an aide followed him throughout the campaign with a black bag full of drugs for Kennedy's multiple ailments. When the bag was temporarily mislaid, Kennedy said 'it would be murder' if its contents became known.

Was Kennedy fit to be president?

Kennedy had Addison's disease (a life-threatening hormone imbalance), colitis (an inflammation of the colon), compression fractures of the spine and chronic prostatitis (inflammation of the prostate gland). These necessitated large quantities of medication, some of which was known to impact on personality and performance. Furthermore, Kennedy allowed a fashionable New York physician nicknamed 'Dr Feelgood' to inject him with painkillers and 'pep pills' (amphetamines). No reputable historian has concluded that Kennedy's daily ingestion of a cocktail of drugs affected his presidential performance, although his health was such that some have wondered whether he would have survived a second term.

Nixon's errors

Nixon contributed his fair share to his defeat. He did not let Eisenhower campaign for him until October 1960, which irritated Eisenhower. In his memoirs, Nixon claimed he was responding to Mamie's pleas over Eisenhower's health, but it was possibly a desire to prove he was his own man.

Nixon rejected Eisenhower's advice over televised debates with Kennedy. Eisenhower rightly pointed out that as Nixon was already well known, the debates would simply give Kennedy free advertising. Kennedy debated effectively and looked better on television:

- While Kennedy looked straight at the cameras, Nixon looked sideways at Kennedy and projected shiftiness.
- After a weekend at **Cape Cod**, Kennedy seemed relaxed and a picture of glowing health, but Nixon was tired and recovering from an infection. Sweat streaked Nixon's make-up, his eyes were hollow and black-ringed, and his jowls drooped. 'My God! They've embalmed him before he even died,' exclaimed Chicago's Democrat Mayor Daley.

Nixon's obvious exhaustion during the debates owed much to his foolish promise to campaign in all 50 states. Exhaustion perhaps explains his inaction over Martin Luther King Jr's arrest after participation in an Atlanta sit-in in October 1960. The Kennedy campaign made much of how Kennedy's call to Coretta King helped secure her husband's release. Eisenhower believed that the call gained Kennedy black votes that helped him win the election. Eisenhower and Nixon blamed Nixon's running mate, Henry Cabot Lodge, for losing Southern white votes by promising a black cabinet member. In contrast to Nixon and in defiance of his closest advisers, Kennedy chose a running mate who helped him win the South, Lyndon Baines Johnson.

Kennedy's performance

Kennedy began his presidential campaign disadvantaged by his unpopular father, and by his youth and Catholicism. He handled these problems well.

'Pop'

Kennedy's father, Joseph Kennedy, had supported **appeasement** of Nazi Germany in the 1930s and many openly asserted that he was trying to purchase the presidency for his son (he used his money and influence highly effectively in the 1960 campaign). Jack Kennedy disarmed reporters in 1958 when he joked that he had 'just received the following wire from my generous daddy – DEAR JACK – DON'T BUY A SINGLE VOTE MORE THAN IS NECESSARY – I'LL BE DAMMED IF I'M GOING TO PAY FOR A LANDSLIDE.' While Nixon had no rapport with journalists ('They are all against me'), Kennedy charmed them with wit and modesty.

 **KEY TERMS**

Cape Cod A seaside resort in northeast USA.

Appeasement Placating Nazi Germany.

'It's not the Pope I'm afraid of, it's the pop'
Truman was more frightened of John Kennedy's powerful father, noted for his advocacy of appeasement of Hitler, than of the possibility that the Roman Catholic Kennedy would put loyalty to the Pope before loyalty to America.

Anti-Catholicism
The influx of Catholic immigrants from Ireland and southern Europe in the nineteenth century generated great anti-Catholic prejudice in the USA.

In what ways is Source A dubious about Kennedy's political ambitions?

Pope

Although Harry Truman famously said, **'It's not the Pope I'm afraid of, it's the pop,'** Kennedy's religion was more of a problem than his father. **Anti-Catholicism** remained strong. Kennedy pointed out that no one had asked his religion when he fought in the Second World War, and assured voters that his first loyalty was to his country, not to Rome. The narrow margin of his victory in terms of the popular vote owed much to Protestant reluctance to vote for the first Catholic president of the United States.

Youth

In the face of much comment and anxiety about his youth, Kennedy helped turn it to his advantage. Unlike Nixon, Kennedy was an exceptionally personable candidate. Kennedy's film-star looks attracted people as he worked the crowds. One reporter said the campaign was 'just an effective presentation of a celebrity'.

SOURCE A

From *New York Post* columnist William Shannon, writing in 1957, quoted in Robert Caro, *The Passage of Power*, Random House, 2012, p. 52.

There is a growing tendency on the part of Americans to 'consume' political figures in much the same sense we consume entertainment personalities on television and in movies. Month after month, from the glossy pages of Life *to the multicolored cover of* Redbook, *Jack and Jackie smile out at millions of readers; he with his tousled hair and winning smile, she with her dark eyes and beautiful face. We hear of her pregnancy, of his wartime heroism, of their fondness for sailing. But what has all this to do with statesmanship?*

Kennedy's most effective use of his youthfulness lay in his telling exploitation of the contrast with the elderly Eisenhower (privately, Kennedy called Eisenhower 'that old asshole' and Eisenhower called Kennedy 'that young whippersnapper'). Kennedy encapsulated this campaign theme in his slogan, 'LET'S GET THE COUNTRY MOVING AGAIN', which suggested a dynamic contrast to Eisenhower and stagnation. Kennedy emphasised that not all Americans participated in the American Dream under Eisenhower, citing 7 per cent unemployment and underemployment: he presented a new version of the American Dream that offered something more than prosperity in his New Frontier speech.

SOURCE B

John F. Kennedy was a particularly photogenic politician. This photo shows him sailing with his fiancée Jackie Bouvier in 1953.

How does Source B help to explain Kennedy's popularity?

The ideas behind the New Frontier

Kennedy introduced and explained his New Frontier in his presidential nomination **acceptance speech** at the Democratic **National Convention** in July 1960.

 **KEY TERMS**

Acceptance speech
A candidate's speech accepting that he is his party's nominee for the presidency.

National Convention
A few weeks before the presidential election the Republicans and Democrats both hold National Conventions in which each party selects or confirms its candidate for the presidency.

What do you suppose some voters might find
a) appealing or
b) unappealing in
Source C?

SOURCE C

John Kennedy's acceptance speech, July 1960 (available from www.jfklibrary.org/Research/Research-Aids/JFK-Speeches/Democratic-Party-Nomination_19600715.aspx).

The New Deal and the Fair Deal were bold measures for their generations – but this is a new generation … Too many Americans have lost their way, their will, and their sense of historic purpose. It is a time, in short, for a new generation of leadership – new men to cope with new problems and opportunities … I stand tonight [in Los Angeles] facing west on what was once the last frontier. From the lands that stretched 3000 miles behind me, the pioneers of old gave up their safety, their comfort and sometimes their lives to build a new world here in the West … Their motto was not 'every man for himself' – but 'all for the common cause' … We stand today on the edge of a New Frontier – the frontier of the 1960s – a frontier of unknown opportunities and perils … The New Frontier of which I speak is not a set of promises – it is a set of challenges. It sums up not what I intend to OFFER the American people, but what I intend to ASK of them … Beyond that frontier are the uncharted areas of science and space, unsolved problems of peace and war, unconquered pockets of ignorance and prejudice, and unanswered questions of poverty and surplus … The choice our nation must make [is] … between the public interest and the private comfort.

An exploration of the ideas behind the New Frontier gives considerable insight into Kennedy's personality and policies.

'Poverty and surplus'

'Poverty and surplus' did not initially interest Kennedy. Born to a wealthy Boston-Irish family, he was thirteen when the Great Depression hit America but, as he said, 'I really did not learn about the depression until I read about it at Harvard.'

The Kennedys were very wealthy and not particularly liberal, but like most Irish-Americans they were Democrats. Assisted by family money and his own wartime heroism, Kennedy was elected in 1946 to the House of Representatives for a predominantly working-class Boston constituency. Kennedy supported legislation that would help his constituents, but as yet they were 'people about whose needs Kennedy knew or cared little', according to Alan Brinkley's 2012 biography. He was uninterested in the work of the House ('we were just worms'). His preoccupations were international affairs and gaining higher office. Aides assured him that the latter necessitated a greater emphasis on 'poverty and surplus'. Campaigning in impoverished West Virginia in 1960 apparently opened Kennedy's eyes to the issue (Source D). He promised that if elected he would not be indifferent to poverty as the Eisenhower administration had been. However, much of this rhetoric was specifically targeted at impoverished West Virginia and fellow Democrats who doubted his liberal credentials. Clearly, Kennedy was a flexible politician, quick to learn and eager and able to captivate.

SOURCE D

From Kennedy's speech in West Virginia, 25 April 1960, quoted in Robert Dallek, *John F. Kennedy: An Unfinished Life, 1917–1963*, **Penguin, 2003, pp. 254–5.**

I assure you that after five weeks living among you here in West Virginia, I shall never forget what I have seen. I have seen men, proud men, looking for work and cannot find it. I have seen people over 40 who were told that their services are no longer needed – too old. I have seen young people who want to live in the state, forced to leave the state for opportunities elsewhere … I have seen older people who seek medical care that is too expensive for them to afford. I have seen unemployed miners and their families eating a diet of dry rations.

How useful is Source D to a historian studying Kennedy's attitude to 'poverty and surplus'?

'Peace and war'

Kennedy had a lifelong fascination with 'peace and war'. He gave an early demonstration of his intelligent grasp of foreign policy issues in his book *Why England Slept* (1940), which investigated the difficulties inherent in mobilising a democracy to fight a totalitarian state. As both congressman (1947–52) and senator (1953–60), Kennedy focused on foreign issues, where he was always more interested and confident. Kennedy conducted **Cold Warrior** campaigns that emphasised how Democrats defended the nation against evil, expansionist Communism better than Republicans. In 1960, he suggested that the Eisenhower administration was stuck in a Cold War rut, but was not specific as to how he would effect change.

🔑 **KEY TERM**

Cold Warrior One who wanted the US to wage the Cold War with even more vigour.

'A new generation of leadership'

Kennedy was a master of rhetoric, thanks to highly effective writers and advisers. In keeping with his theme of change and dynamism, Kennedy needed to differentiate himself from the New Deal and Fair Deal (see pages 2 and 33), while also demonstrating his liberalism. This was brilliantly done through the New Frontier ideas, which tarnished the Eisenhower era as one of selfish complacency, and burnished the Kennedy charisma with an idealism and dynamism that captured the popular imagination forever after. However, there are questions over the extent to which Kennedy's New Frontier was successful.

The personalities of the Kennedy administration

The new president surrounded himself with able advisers:

- Theodore Sorensen was a superb writer of speeches and articles, whose skills Kennedy had long utilised (Sorensen wrote articles in Senator Kennedy's name and contributed a great deal to Kennedy's 1956 bestseller, *Profiles in Courage*). Sorensen always reminded Kennedy of the political importance of domestic policy.

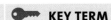

KEY FIGURE

**Robert Kennedy
(1925–68)**

Known in his youth as the 'runt' of the family, Harvard law graduate Bobby was legal assistant to Senator Joseph McCarthy, then Attorney General under his brother. He left the Johnson administration in 1964 and was elected senator for the state of New York (1965–8). He was assassinated during his 1968 presidential campaign, in which he came across as more liberal than his brother had ever been (some attribute that to grief over his brother's death).

KEY TERM

Attorney General Head of the Justice Department in the federal government.

- Other White House insiders included members of what was known as Kennedy's 'Irish Mafia', such as Lawrence O'Brien, who focused on legislative liaison, and appointments secretary Kenneth O'Donnell. The ultimate insider was the president's brother, **Robert 'Bobby' Kennedy**, who became **Attorney General**. Many were horrified by this nepotism. Vice President Johnson recorded that influential Senator Richard Russell 'thinks it's a disgrace for a kid who's never practiced law to be appointed. I agree with him.' Subsequently, Johnson would say, 'Don't kid anybody about who is the top adviser … Bobby is first in, and last out, and Bobby is the boy he listens to.'
- Kennedy surrounded himself with brilliant academics such as McGeorge Bundy, a former Harvard dean who was Kennedy's national security adviser. Civil rights aide Harris Wofford, himself an academic, felt uneasy about the brilliant minds in the White House whom he considered 'too much like Kennedy – cool, skeptical, pragmatic'.
- Amidst the intellectuals, Vice President Johnson's Texas accent, comparatively poor education and earthy language (it was commonly said you could take a farm boy out of the farm but you could not take the farm out of the farm boy) were looked down upon. However, Johnson had a far better grasp of congressional politics than anyone else in the Kennedy administration.

Kennedy's cabinet

The only cabinet member who became a White House insider was dynamic, tough-talking, persuasive Robert McNamara, who had been a successful business executive (a Ford Motor Company 'whiz kid'). As Defence Secretary under Kennedy and Johnson, McNamara played such an important part in US policy-making over Vietnam that some have called the Vietnam War 'McNamara's War'. McNamara was a Republican, as was Treasury Secretary Douglas Dillon. Kennedy considered Defence and Treasury the most important cabinet appointments. He wanted personal control of foreign policy, so he pointed the self-effacing Dean Rusk as Secretary of State, describing him as 'a good errand boy'.

'The best and the brightest'

Overall, Kennedy's men had little experience in governing. Johnson was a legislative expert, but Kennedy did not want to be seen as reliant on his expertise. Whereas the Eisenhower White House was run with an army command-like structure, the Kennedy White House made rapid-fire decisions but was also somewhat chaotic, which worried Bobby (Source E).

SOURCE E

From Bobby Kennedy's letter to Jack Kennedy, 14 March 1963. Sorensen Papers, Kennedy Library, Latin American Folder, Subject Files 1961–1964.

I think there should be periodic meetings of a half a dozen or so top officials of the Government to consider Cuba [and South America] … I think this kind of effort should be applied to other policies as well. The best minds in government should be utilised in finding solutions to … any problems. They should be available in times other than deep crises and emergencies as is now the case. You talk to McNamara, but mostly on Defense matters, you talk to Dillon but primarily on financial questions … These men should be sitting down and thinking of some of the problems facing us in a broader [con]text. I think you could get a good deal more out of what is available in Government than we are at the present time.

> How much weight do you think a historian should give to Bobby's criticism of his brother John Kennedy's governmental style in Source E?

In 1972, the journalist David Halberstam referred to the academics, intellectuals and leaders of industry with whom Kennedy populated his White House as 'the best and the brightest'. Amidst some great errors, especially in foreign policy (Halberstam accused them of arrogantly foolish policies in Vietnam), they also had some successes at home and abroad.

Kennedy's domestic policies

In his New Frontier speech, Kennedy had spoken of the challenge of poverty. He asked Congress for legislation to meet that challenge and used his executive powers:

- The Area Redevelopment Act (1961) granted $394 million to extend employment opportunities in poorer states such as West Virginia. Although poorly funded by Congress, it created 26,000 jobs and training programmes that benefited 15,000 people. However, 5 million Americans remained unemployed and Congress refused to reauthorise the act in 1963 because Republicans resented the focus on key Democrat congressional districts and Southern Democrats were furious with Kennedy over civil rights (see page 123).
- The Manpower Development and Training Act (1962) aimed to train and retrain workers who were unemployed because of increased automation and technological change. By December 1962, the administration boasted 351 approved programmes for 12,600 trainees in 40 states. However, these programmes mainly subsidised officials and private interests who provided the training, rather than greatly decreasing the number of unemployed.
- The Social Security Amendments Act (1961) expanded benefits for elderly and disabled people.
- The Minimum Wage Act raised the minimum wage by 25 cents to $1.25 an hour. An additional 3.6 million workers were covered, although half a million of the poorest remained without coverage, including 150,000 laundry

workers, most of whom were black women (Republicans opposed the 25 cent raise and Southern Democrats had no desire to help black women).

- The interstate highway system (see page 63) was extended, providing jobs in the construction industry.
- The Food and Agriculture Act (1962) gave federal subsidies to farmers, but rural poverty persisted despite administration efforts.
- The Omnibus Housing Act (1961) granted $5 billion for the extension of existing programmes such as urban renewal and public housing, and authorised low-interest loans for struggling middle-income families. However, Congress aimed to get America out of recession rather than to alleviate poverty, so the act was designed to help developers, construction unions and Democrat candidates running for office in the cities more than the poor.
- Kennedy used his executive powers to focus federal purchasing power and construction projects on areas of high unemployment and to direct the Department of Agriculture to double food distributions to the poor and unemployed. Kennedy's pilot **food stamp programme** fed 240,000 people at a cost of $22 million annually. He also supported and extended Eisenhower's school lunch and milk programmes so that 700,000 more children could have a hot lunch, and 85,000 more schools, childcare centres and camps received fresh milk.

KEY TERM

Food stamp programme
First used during the Great Depression, revived by President Kennedy, made permanent by the Food Stamp Act (1964); impoverished individuals present stamps provided by the government for food.

Legislative failures

Most historians consider Kennedy's legislative record unimpressive. Kennedy's men did not liaise effectively with Congress and failed to get congressional support for his major legislative initiatives, which were:

- federal financial aid for elementary and secondary education (rejected in 1961)
- senior citizen health care to alleviate the poverty from which many elderly people suffered because of medical bills (rejected in 1963)
- a Department of Urban Affairs and Housing to co-ordinate programmes to halt urban decline (repeatedly rejected during 1961–2)
- a civil rights bill to end Jim Crow in the South (see page 39) that remained stuck in Congress at the time of Kennedy's death in 1963
- tax cuts to stimulate the economy (rejected in 1963).

No major new domestic legislation was passed during his presidency. Much of what Congress passed was not New Frontier legislation but extensions of existing programmes. However, it could be argued in Kennedy's defence that he faced uncooperative Republicans and conservative Southern Democrats in Congress, but had at least put 'poverty and surplus' firmly on the national legislative agenda.

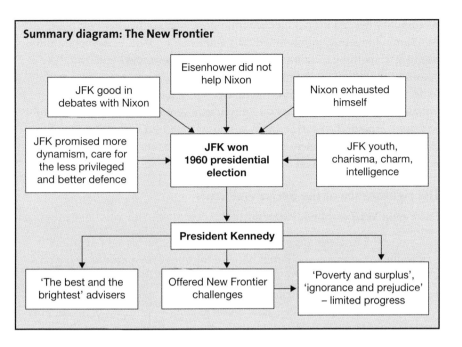

Summary diagram: The New Frontier

- Eisenhower did not help Nixon
- JFK good in debates with Nixon
- Nixon exhausted himself
- JFK promised more dynamism, care for the less privileged and better defence
- **JFK won 1960 presidential election**
- JFK youth, charisma, charm, intelligence

↓

President Kennedy

- 'The best and the brightest' advisers
- Offered New Frontier challenges → 'Poverty and surplus', 'ignorance and prejudice' – limited progress

 Challenges to American power

▶ *How successful was Kennedy's foreign policy?*

In his New Frontier speech, Kennedy spoke of the challenge of 'unsolved problems of peace and war'. He was fascinated by such issues. As he said to Richard Nixon after the Bay of Pigs disaster in spring 1961 (see page 109):

> *It really is true that foreign affairs is the only important issue for a president to handle, isn't it? I mean, who gives a shit if the minimum wage is $1.15 or $1.25, in comparison to something like this?*

Kennedy faced frequent Communist challenges to American power, especially in Berlin, Cuba and Vietnam.

The legacy of crises over Berlin and relations with Khrushchev

Khrushchev was struggling to stay in power, partly because of his failure to make progress on the Berlin problem (see page 74). Between 1949 and 1958, over 2 million East Germans fled to West Germany, usually via Berlin. The number of people escaping was growing. The East German government wanted Khrushchev to halt this public and persistent reminder of its unpopularity, while Khrushchev worried that West Berlin was a Western centre of espionage and propaganda (it was a glittering example of Western prosperity).

Khrushchev needed a foreign policy triumph. Berlin seemed the best place. At a summit meeting with Kennedy at Vienna in June 1961, Khrushchev told Kennedy something must be done about Berlin or he would hand over the access routes to East Germany (see page 75). Such summits were supposed to decrease tensions but Vienna increased them: soon after, Khrushchev announced increased defence expenditure and Kennedy followed suit. Then, without warning, the East Germans sealed off their hundred-mile frontier with West Berlin with wire fences on 13 August 1961, and four days later erected a 30-mile wall between West Berlin and East Berlin.

The significance of the Berlin Wall crisis

The **Berlin Wall** was highly significant:

- It stopped East Germans escaping East Germany and brought a certain stability to Germany and Berlin because the lines of demarcation were now clearly drawn.
- It increased West German antagonism and anxiety with regard to the Soviet bloc. Kennedy visited West Berlin to assure its citizens of his support. He wanted to tell them he felt like one of them – 'I am a Berliner' ('*Ich bin Berliner*'). He got his German wrong and said '*Ich bin ein Berliner*' ('I am a doughnut'), but the enthusiastic and welcoming West Berliners knew what he had meant to say.
- It increased Cold War tensions: soon after, both the USSR and the USA resumed nuclear testing.
- Western writers interpreted it as a triumph, because it demonstrated how East Germany needed to wall its people in, but Soviet bloc writers also claimed victory, because the West had been unable to stop its construction.
- Getting away with constructing the Wall might have encouraged Khrushchev's adventurism in Cuba.

The challenge of Castro

In January 1959, the left-wing **Fidel Castro** overthrew the pro-American Cuban dictator Fulgencio Batista. Castro increasingly criticised America's economic stranglehold over Cuba and threatened American property there, although in spring 1960 both the US ambassador to Cuba and the CIA concluded that he was *not* Communist. Eisenhower responded with economic sanctions on Cuba (July 1960). He approved the CIA build-up of a Cuban exile military force that would hopefully overthrow Castro.

Kennedy thus inherited increasingly tense US–Cuban relations, along with Eisenhower's plan for a CIA-supported invasion of Cuba by discontented Cuban exiles.

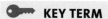

KEY TERM

Berlin Wall The wall divided Communist East Berlin from pro-Western West Berlin.

KEY FIGURE

Fidel Castro (1926–)

Castro led Cuba from 1959 to 2008. His criticisms of the USA and his close association with the USSR and with revolutionary movements in Africa in particular, made Cuba important in the Cold War.

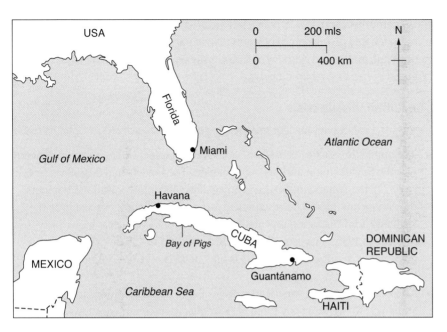

Figure 3.1 Cuba in the Cold War. (Guantánamo is a US naval base and a legacy of US domination of Cuba after the Spanish-American war of 1898.) Cuba lies only 90 miles south of Florida.

The Bay of Pigs fiasco

Kennedy received warnings against the invasion of Cuba from many quarters, including Truman's Secretary of State Dean Acheson and the British. He nevertheless went ahead with it because:

- He believed that Third World countries such as Cuba were the great new Cold War arena.
- The plan had been endorsed by a military-hero president and by the CIA, which was at the height of its prestige.
- He was a prisoner of his own militant anti-Communist rhetoric (in 1960 he promised that, if elected, he would not allow Cuba to become a Soviet base in the Caribbean).
- Using Cuban exiles seemed a cheap and easy way to get rid of Castro.

In April 1961, 1600 Cuban guerrillas landed at the Bay of Pigs. Their invasion was a disaster because:

- The Cuban exiles and US newspapers had forewarned Castro.
- The invaders landed miles away from the mountains to which they were supposed to flee if anything went wrong.
- Castro was very popular in Cuba, especially in the Bay of Pigs area, where he frequently holidayed.
- Kennedy always insisted that US aid be minimal.

The exiles were killed or captured. Kennedy suffered worldwide humiliation, but to his amazement received an 82 per cent approval rating from the American people. Unsurprisingly, Castro moved closer to the Soviets and announced that he was a Communist (he was essentially a pragmatist and had been driven to the Communist camp by US policies). Khrushchev concluded that Kennedy was a soft touch and proceeded to bully and bluster at the Vienna summit, erect the Berlin Wall, and install missiles in Cuba in the belief that Kennedy would either not react or mess up again if he did.

The Cuban missile crisis

In August 1962, Soviet nuclear missiles and technicians arrived in Cuba. Why?

- Although Khrushchev claimed his aim was to protect Cuba, his main concern was the Soviet Union and his own position. The Soviets had 50 ICBMs (see page 73), the Americans 304. The Soviets had 150 intercontinental bombers, the Americans 1200. These statistics worried Khrushchev, especially as the Kennedy administration repeatedly boasted about US nuclear superiority in autumn 1961. A massive Soviet ICBM build-up would be expensive, so it made sense to put existing **MRBMs** and **IRBMs** on Cuba, 90 miles from the US coast.
- Khrushchev resented American missiles being based in Turkey and pointed at the USSR: 'we must pay them back in their own coin … so they will know what it feels like to live in the sights of nuclear weapons.'
- Khrushchev wanted to impress his critics at home and in China.
- As Khrushchev had got away with building the Berlin Wall, he hoped he could get away with the installation of missiles in Cuba.

Kennedy's response

During September 1962, there were rumours in the American press that the Soviets had put offensive missiles in Cuba. Kennedy warned the Soviets that this would be intolerable but was confident that they would never station nuclear missiles outside their own territory. On 14 October, a U-2 spy plane photographed missile sites in Cuba. Two days later, Kennedy established his Executive Committee of the National Security Council (Ex Comm) to consider the options:

- Doing nothing was not an option because Kennedy feared it would endanger US national security if the nation looked weak in the face of Soviet missiles 90 miles off the Florida coast, and because he did not want Khrushchev to have another triumph.
- Using normal diplomatic channels such as the United Nations would be too slow.
- Unaware that the nuclear warheads were already in place in Cuba, some of the military preferred a '**surgical air strike**' or another invasion of Cuba, but Kennedy feared that would kill the Russians in Cuba and perhaps trigger a third world war.
- Some suggested the US withdraw missiles in Turkey in exchange for a Soviet withdrawal of missiles from Cuba, but Kennedy did not want to be seen backing down over Turkey.

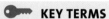

KEY TERMS

MRBMs Medium-range ballistic missiles.

IRBMs Intermediate-range ballistic missiles.

Surgical air strike Air strike on specified targets.

- A naval blockade would prevent Soviet vessels getting more men and materials to Cuba.

> ## State Department opposition to a surgical air strike
>
> Under Secretary of State George Ball opposed the surgical air strike option, having 'concluded from the records of Allied bombing in Europe that if the medical profession should ever adopt the air force definition of *surgical*, anyone undergoing an operation for appendicitis might lose his kidneys and lungs yet find the appendix intact.'

Kennedy chose the blockade option, but felt that the word blockade was too aggressive and instead spoke of a 'quarantine'. The advantage of a blockade was that it would give Khrushchev time to think again. The disadvantages were that it would give him time to complete the installation of the missiles, and a Soviet–American war might begin if the Soviets defied the blockade.

The Kennedy administration kept the Cuban missile crisis secret for over a week, but on 22 October Kennedy informed the American people of the missiles and the quarantine. The situation was unbelievably tense. The United States had B-52 bombers on red alert and 156 ICBMs primed and ready to go.

Initially, the blockade line around Cuba was 800 miles, then Kennedy decreased it to 500 miles to give Khrushchev more time to think. On 24 October, two Soviet ships and a Soviet submarine neared the 500-mile blockade line but then, with the world apparently on the verge of nuclear annihilation, Khrushchev halted the ships and the submarine.

On 26 October, while Kennedy prepared for a possible invasion of Cuba, Khrushchev offered to get the missiles out if Kennedy stopped the blockade and promised not to invade the island. The next day, Khrushchev added a further demand – the removal of American missiles from Turkey. Kennedy ignored the second offer and accepted the first, informing the Soviets that if they failed to reply, the United States would invade Cuba on the 29th.

In the end, Khrushchev backed down. Although Kennedy had publicly promised not to invade Cuba, he had secretly promised to withdraw American missiles from Turkey. In addition, Khrushchev realised that the United States had nuclear and naval superiority and was prepared for war.

The significance of the Cuban missile crisis

The West considered the crisis a triumph for Kennedy. Khrushchev's fall from power soon after (October 1964) suggests that the Soviets agreed. Both the USA and the USSR were frightened by the crisis, which led to something of a Cold War thaw:

- A hotline was installed between the Kremlin and the White House so that in future crises the Soviet and American leaders could communicate directly by telephone (June 1963).

- The Soviets and Americans signed the first treaty that attempted to put a brake on the nuclear arms race – the Partial Nuclear Test Ban Treaty (August 1963).

Despite the contemporary and subsequent praise for Kennedy's performance, he can be criticised over the Cuban missile crisis. His involvement in the Bay of Pigs invasion and subsequent CIA anti-Castro plots gave Castro and Khrushchev every reason to fear another invasion and take preventive steps. It has also been suggested that the outcome of the Cuban missile crisis contributed to American overconfidence and the increased involvement in Vietnam.

The deepening involvement in Vietnam

In a 1956 speech to the **American Friends of Vietnam**, Congressman John Kennedy declared 'the tiny nation for which we are in large measure responsible' to be very important to the United States. Clearly, President Kennedy would at the very least continue the commitment to South Vietnam because he believed in containment (see page 16), the domino theory (see page 76) and the importance of the Third World – especially Vietnam.

(see page 16), the domino theory (see page 76)

KEY TERM

American Friends of Vietnam US organisation that lobbied in favour of South Vietnam 1955–75.

? In what theory does Source F suggest Congressman Kennedy believed?

SOURCE F

From Congressman John Kennedy's 1956 speech to the American Friends of Vietnam, a pro-South Vietnamese organisation of which he was a member (available from www.jfklibrary.org/Research/Research-Aids/JFK-Speeches/Vietnam-Conference-Washington-DC_19560601.aspx).

Let us briefly consider exactly what is 'America's Stake in Vietnam': Vietnam represents the cornerstone of the free world in Southeast Asia, the keystone of the arch, the finger in the dike. Burma, Thailand, India, Japan, the Philippines, and obviously Laos and Cambodia … would be threatened if the red tide of Communism overflowed in Vietnam … Her economy is essential to the economy of Southeast Asia; and her political liberty is an inspiration to those seeking to obtain or maintain their liberty in all parts of … the world … [Vietnam is] a proving ground for democracy in Asia … [and] a test of American responsibility and determination in Asia … [where we must stop] the relentless pressure of the Chinese Communists … No other challenge is more deserving of our effort and energy … Our security may be lost piece by piece, country by country.

Kennedy did not want to be accused of 'losing' Vietnam, and was also sensitive about his youth and inexperience. A journalist told him at a White House luncheon in autumn 1961:

We can annihilate Russia and should make that clear to the Soviet government … you and your Administration are weak sisters … [America needs] a man on horseback … Many people in Texas and the Southwest think that you are riding [your daughter] Caroline's tricycle.

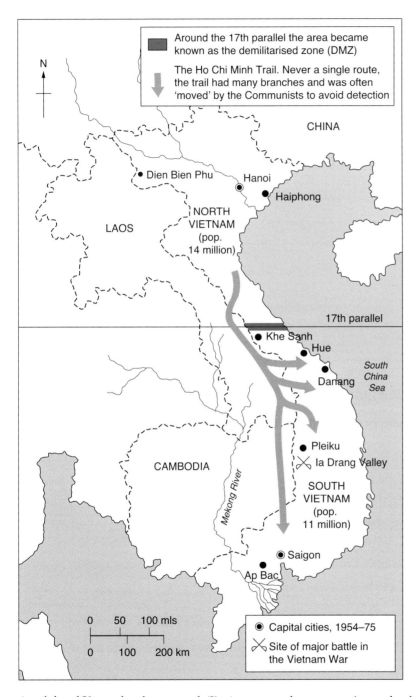

Figure 3.2 Important places in Vietnam during the American involvement. The Ho Chi Minh Trail was a vital supply route for men and materials coming from North Vietnam to South Vietnam. US bombing failed to destroy it.

Within the map:

Around the 17th parallel the area became known as the demilitarised zone (DMZ)

The Ho Chi Minh Trail. Never a single route, the trail had many branches and was often 'moved' by the Communists to avoid detection

CHINA

N

Dien Bien Phu

Hanoi

Haiphong

NORTH VIETNAM (pop. 14 million)

LAOS

17th parallel

Khe Sanh

Hue

Danang

South China Sea

Pleiku

Ia Drang Valley

CAMBODIA

Mekong River

SOUTH VIETNAM (pop. 11 million)

Saigon

Ap Bac

0   50   100 mls

0   100   200 km

⊙ Capital cities, 1954–75

✕ Site of major battle in the Vietnam War

A red-faced Kennedy who retorted, 'I'm just as tough as you are', was clearly a president who thought he had much to prove.

Kennedy's military and civilian advisers urged him to continue the involvement: Rusk and McNamara told him that a US departure would 'undermine the credibility of American commitments everywhere'. After the Bay of Pigs fiasco, Kennedy told a friend, 'We just can't have another defeat in Vietnam.'

Escalation in Vietnam

When Kennedy became president in January 1961 there were under 1000 American advisers in Vietnam. At his death in November 1963 there were nearly 17,000, many of whom were involved in combat, for example, at the battle of **Ap Bac** in 1963. Kennedy greatly escalated the US involvement because Diem (see page 76) seemed incapable of defeating the Communists in South Vietnam, and because the administration, particularly McNamara, kept hoping that more advisers and war materiel might stabilise the situation.

As the Communists grew stronger in South Vietnam, Kennedy had several options. Withdrawal was not one of them because he would be accused of 'losing' Vietnam.

The reform option

The Kennedy administration urged Diem to introduce social, economic and political reforms that would make his regime more popular. When Diem rejected this reform option, the American press grew increasingly critical of him. David Halberstam of the *New York Times* was particularly hostile, and Diem's influential sister-in-law Madame Nhu told American reporters that he 'should be barbecued and I would be glad to supply the fluid and the match'.

The American ground troops option

Even as he increased the number of American 'advisers' in South Vietnam to nearly 17,000, Kennedy knew that sending in US **ground troops** was not the solution and rejected the advice of his military to do so:

> *The troops will march in, the bands will play; the crowds will cheer, and in four days everyone will have forgotten. Then we will be told we have to send in more troops. It's like taking a drink. The effect wears off, and you have to take another.*

By spring 1963, Kennedy was disheartened, telling a journalist friend:

> *… we don't have a prayer of staying in Vietnam … These people hate us. They are going to throw our asses out … But I can't give up a piece of territory like that to the Communists and then get the American people to re-elect me.*

Events in Vietnam in spring 1963 convinced him that the best option was to replace Diem.

The replacement of Diem option

In spring 1963, amidst further references to barbecues by Madame Nhu, Buddhist monks burned themselves to death in protest against the Catholic Diem's religious policies. Despite having sent over 10,000 Americans to Vietnam

KEY TERMS

Ap Bac Battle between Vietnamese Communist guerrillas and the army of South Vietnam, which was assisted by US 'advisers' (1963).

Ground troops In March 1965, President Johnson sent the first few thousand regular soldiers (rather than just 'advisers') to Vietnam.

by this time, Kennedy asked, 'Who are these people? Why didn't we know about them before?' If he really did not know that most South Vietnamese were Buddhist, his administration was incredibly ill informed. Perhaps he was simply trying to deflect blame from himself.

The Buddhist protests in Vietnam demonstrated Diem's unpopularity. Some historians have suggested that Kennedy should have taken this opportunity to exit Vietnam, using the argument that Diem repeatedly rejected American advice to introduce reforms. His brother had floated the idea that perhaps 'now was the time to get out of Vietnam entirely', but Kennedy feared 'loss of Vietnam' accusations at home and loss of face abroad.

Kennedy knew that an effective South Vietnamese regime was essential, saying in a September 1963 interview:

> We can help them, we can give them equipment, we can send our men … as advisers, but they have to win it – the people of Vietnam – against the Communists.

He nevertheless concluded the interview by saying, 'I think we should stay'. So, the administration decided that the best option was to work towards a better South Vietnamese government, and colluded in the overthrow (and inevitable assassination) of Diem by South Vietnamese army generals in November 1963. Vice President Johnson said that collusion increased the US commitment. As the US commander in Vietnam, General William Westmoreland, said, it 'morally locked us in Vietnam'. Trapped by domestic and international Cold War politics, Kennedy had massively escalated the US involvement in Vietnam.

Covert warfare and assassination

Many find it difficult to believe that Kennedy approved the assassination of Diem, but it is significant that the CIA had several plans to deal with Fidel Castro that included assassination.

After the Bay of Pigs humiliation, the Kennedys urged the CIA to gain revenge on Cuba. A CIA memorandum of 1961 boasted 800 sabotage operations, 150 arson attacks, and bombs placed at power and railway stations in Cuba. The Mafia were keen to re-establish their lucrative prostitution, gambling and drugs operations in Havana, so the CIA approached them about assassinating Castro. A disgruntled ex-girlfriend (she said Castro had made her abort their child) claimed she was promised $80 million to kill Castro with a toxic shellfish pill. However, when they met, she recorded that 'love proved stronger', and she flushed the pill down the bidet. Other CIA suggestions included poisoning Castro's cigars, offering him a pen with a poisoned tip, contaminating his diving suit with tuberculosis, and exploding clamshells in the area where he dived to blow his legs off. Convinced that Castro's beard was an essential component of his charisma, the CIA also considered dropping depilatory powder into his shoes to make it fall out. 'We believe,' said Castro, 'that the Central Intelligence Agency has absolutely no intelligence at all.'

Summary diagram: Challenges to American power

Challenge	Communist victory?	US victory?	Draw?
Cuba – Bay of Pigs	✓		
Cuba – missile crisis		✓	
Berlin			✓
Vietnam	✓		

③ African-Americans in the North and the South

▶ *How successful was the civil rights movement in the years 1961–3?*

In 1960, Malcolm X (see page 165) drew attention to the problems of the black ghettos in the big cities outside the South, but it was still Southern segregation that repeatedly hit the headlines during Kennedy's presidency.

The rise of the civil rights movement

The sit-ins (see page 85) confirmed the shifting focus of black activism from litigation to mass direct action (see page 84). They were quickly followed by the first 'Freedom Ride' (May 1961), which was masterminded by CORE (see page 43): a small, integrated group travelled the South to test Supreme Court rulings against segregation on interstate transport (*Morgan* v. *Virginia*, 1946) and on interstate bus facilities (*Boynton* v. *Virginia*, 1960). CORE's director James Farmer explained:

> *We planned the Freedom Ride with the specific intention of creating a crisis. We were counting on the bigots in the South to do our work for us. We figured that the government would have to respond if we created a situation that was headline news all over the world, and affected the nation's image abroad.*

Farmer proved correct. Alabama racists attacked the passengers with clubs and chains and burned their buses. Attorney General Bobby Kennedy responded by working to enforce the Supreme Court rulings.

Unlike the 1950s, there was non-stop, highly publicised and large-scale black activism in the early 1960s, so that there could be little doubt now that there was a civil rights movement (see page 82). Many people considered Martin Luther King Jr to be its leader.

The role of Martin Luther King Jr

For seven years after his contribution to the Montgomery bus boycott (see page 83), King and his SCLC achieved little of note. King participated in an Atlanta sit-in 1960 but refused to join the Freedom Rides because he feared arrest. His involvement in the Albany campaign (1961–2) was unproductive because of black divisions:

- SNCC (see page 85) resented SCLC involvement.
- Some members of the black community were paid informants of Albany's white city leadership.
- Local black leaders resented 'outsiders'.
- Violence by some members of Albany's black community achieved bad publicity, while local police chief Laurie Pritchett carefully avoided violence and unfavourable media attention.

However, King did far better in his Birmingham campaign in 1963.

Events in Birmingham: spring 1963

King chose Birmingham, Alabama, for a big SCLC campaign against segregation and unequal opportunities for several reasons:

- SCLC needed a success and rival black organisations were relatively inactive there.
- King said Birmingham was 'by far' America's 'worst big-city' for racism. Impatient with the Kennedy administration's inactivity, King said, 'To cure injustices, you must expose them before the light of human conscience and the bar of public opinion.'
- White divisions in Birmingham looked promising. White businessmen believed racism held the city back, while white extremists had recently castrated an African-American, prohibited the sale of a book that featured black and white rabbits, and campaigned to stop 'Negro music' being played on white radio stations.
- Most promising of all, the Public Safety Commissioner 'Bull' Connor was a determined segregationist with a notoriously short fuse. When the Freedom Riders were attacked by a racist mob in Birmingham, Connor sent his policemen home because it was Mother's Day.

King admitted 'tremendous resistance' to his planned demonstrations amongst Birmingham's black community, many of whom felt that Connor's imminent retirement made action unnecessary. However, as expected, Connor's behaviour attracted media attention. His police and dogs turned on the few black demonstrators and King defied an injunction and marched, knowing that his arrest would gain national attention. Kept in solitary confinement and refused private meetings with his lawyer, King used prison toilet paper on which to write an inspirational and widely published 'Letter from Birmingham Jail'. Coretta called President Kennedy, who obtained King's release.

The marches still lacked black support and King became discouraged 'You know, we've got to get something going. The press is leaving.' Despite his doubts about the morality of the policy, King enlisted black schoolchildren, some as young as six, in the protests. It proved a highly successful strategy. Birmingham hit the national headlines as Connor's high-pressure water hoses tore clothes off students' backs. Five hundred young marchers were soon in custody and SCLC succeeded in its aim of 'filling the jails' with 2000 protesters.

As blacks and whites resorted to violence, Birmingham degenerated into chaos, which President Kennedy said was 'damaging the reputation' of America. Race relations in Birmingham deteriorated, but the campaign had national significance.

SOURCE G

? How could events in Source G be seen as 'damaging the reputation' of America?

A black demonstrator being attacked by one of Bull Connor's police dogs in Birmingham, Alabama, 1963. An SCLC worker said the demonstrator was trying to stop other demonstrators responding to police violence.

The significance of Birmingham

Birmingham was a media triumph for SCLC: as one leading staffer said, 'There never was any more skilful manipulation of the news media than there was in Birmingham.' SCLC had exposed the evils of Southern segregation to the nation and the world. The Kennedy administration admitted that Birmingham was crucial in persuading it to push the bill that eventually became the 1964 Civil Rights Act. Birmingham inspired protests throughout the South in the summer of 1963: 'We are on the threshold of a significant breakthrough, and the greatest weapon is the mass demonstration,' said King.

The March on Washington: August 1963

Marches were a favourite tactic of civil rights activists, and the nation's capital was a favourite location. The March on Washington aimed to encourage passage of Kennedy's civil rights bill and executive action to increase black employment. The moving force behind the March was A. Philip Randolph (see page 42). King believed the March would advertise the effectiveness of non-violent protest at a time when non-violence was losing its popularity among African-Americans impatient at the slow pace of change.

The March was a great success. A quarter of the predominantly middle-class crowd of around 250,000 were white. King's memorable 'I have a dream' speech was an exceptionally powerful appeal to white America. He said that his dream of equality was 'deeply rooted in the American Dream'. He challenged Americans to live up to their much vaunted reverence for the Declaration of Independence (which said that 'all men are created equal') and for the Bible. Although the *New York Times* opined that the televised March left Congress unmoved, it surely played a part in the eventual passage of the 1964 Civil Rights Act, because so many contemporaries were impressed by the well-behaved crowd and King's inspirational rhetoric.

The opponents of civil rights

There was much opposition to African-American demands for civil rights from the general public, especially in the South, and from law enforcement officials and politicians.

Congress and public opinion

Most Southern whites remained vehemently opposed to black equality. Many leading citizens belonged to Citizens' Councils (see page 84) and some even joined the Ku Klux Klan (see page 87). Southern white businessmen were divided: in 1963, many in Birmingham felt that segregation damaged business, but were aware that if they took the lead in integration they risked a white customer backlash. For example, after Martin Luther King Jr's campaign in St Augustine, Florida, in spring 1964, some white businessmen reluctantly desegregated, but when their premises were picketed and firebombed by the

Ku Klux Klan, they resegregated. In addition, Southern whites who supported civil rights were likely to be ostracised by the rest of the white community. For example, Mississippi newspaper owner Hazel Brannon Smith recorded how 'my newspapers were boycotted, bombed and burned … my life was threatened and my husband lost his job', as a result of her pro-civil rights editorials. White juries were unwilling to convict fellow whites who murdered African-Americans. For example, NAACP official Medgar Evers was murdered in Mississippi in 1963. Byron De La Beckwith, who belonged to both the Citizens' Council and the Ku Klux Klan, was arrested. However, two juries failed to find him guilty (he was eventually found guilty and imprisoned – in 1994).

There was also popular opposition to civil rights outside the South. Racism and respect for states' rights (see page 60) help explain the opinion polls that showed that most American voters believed integration should evolve gradually rather than through federal enforcement. One poll in the Kennedy years showed that civil rights were at the bottom of the list of voter concerns. Many whites outside the South considered the black protests dangerously provocative. For example, a 1961 poll revealed that 63 per cent of Americans opposed the Freedom Rides.

Naturally, Congress responded to the wishes of the electorate and Republicans combined with Southern Democrats to block or weaken civil rights legislation. Congress diluted Eisenhower's civil rights bills in 1957 and 1960, and blocked Kennedy's civil rights bill in 1963.

Southern politicians and law enforcement officials

Discrimination against African-Americans by Northern law enforcement officials played an important part in provoking the black ghetto riots of 1964–8 (see page 169). However, Southern law enforcement officials were far worse. Many, such as Bull Connor, were both willing and determined to maintain segregation, although not all of those who went along with segregation were racists. After the disastrous campaign in Albany (see page 117), Martin Luther King Jr said, 'I sincerely believe that Chief Pritchett is a nice man, a basically decent man, but he's so caught up in a system that he ends up saying one thing to us behind closed doors and then we open the newspaper and he's said something else to the press.'

Most Southern politicians were Democrats. While Northern Democrats were relatively liberal on race, Southern Democrat politicians constituted the most conservative group within the party. As so many African-Americans remained unable to vote, Southern politicians from both major parties responded to a predominantly white electorate that sought to retain the Jim Crow laws on segregation. Indeed, a politician who failed to support segregation might not get elected. Governor George Wallace in Alabama is a good example.

George Wallace

Prior to 1958, the Democrat George Wallace was a moderate on race. In his 1958 gubernatorial campaign he was supported by the NAACP and he criticised the Ku Klux Klan, which endorsed his opponent, John Patterson. White Alabamans had voted for moderates such as Wallace before, but the Montgomery bus boycott frightened many white voters and made them more extreme. Patterson defeated Wallace easily, prompting Wallace to tell an aide, 'I was out-niggered by John Patterson. And I'll tell you here and now, I will never be out-niggered again.'

In 1962, Wallace ran for Governor again, this time as a racist. He declared his opposition to black voter registration, blamed integration for increasing crime and unemployment, and worked closely with the Ku Klux Klan. As a result, he won the election by the biggest margin ever. In his **inaugural address** in January 1963, he declared his support for states' rights ('I draw the line in the dust and toss the gauntlet before the feet of [federal government] tyranny'). His call for 'segregation now, segregation tomorrow, segregation forever' gained him nationwide recognition.

Alabama was the last state to integrate its universities. When Kennedy federalised the National Guard to ensure the integration of the University of Alabama in 1963, Wallace advertised his racist credentials to white voters by standing defiantly on the university's steps. Wallace ran for president in 1968, and won 13.5 per cent of the popular vote (the Republican candidate Richard Nixon won 43.4 per cent, the Democrat Hubert Humphrey won 42.7 per cent). All of Wallace's votes came from Deep South states.

KEY TERM

Inaugural address Speech made by the president or a state governor after he has been inaugurated.

Opposition to activists' methods

Some Americans sympathised with the aims of the civil rights movement but disliked the methods and counselled patience. Among them were the Kennedys. In 1961, Bobby Kennedy condemned white attacks on SNCC workers attempting to register black voters in Mississippi, but said:

> *Mississippi is going to work itself out. Maybe it's going to take a decade and maybe a lot of people are going to be killed in the meantime … But in the long run I think it's for the health of the country and the stability of the system.*

President Kennedy considered SNCC unnecessarily provocative 'sons of bitches'. 'SNCC has got an investment in violence,' he said.

Kennedy's policies in response to the pressures for change

When Kennedy was 12 years old, his wealthy Boston-Irish family moved to New York to escape snubs from upper-class Bostonians of Anglo-Saxon ancestry. Despite the family's own experience of WASP discrimination (see page 9), Robert Kennedy admitted that before 1961, 'I didn't lose much sleep about Negroes, I didn't think about them much. I didn't know about all the injustice.'

While a senator, Kennedy opposed Eisenhower's civil rights bill (see page 91), but as civil rights became a more prominent national issue, Kennedy's interest increased proportionately. In his 1960 election, he promised to help African-Americans if elected and said that racism was immoral and damaged America's international image.

Despite his campaign assurances, President Kennedy did not attempt to get civil rights legislation from Congress during 1961–2 because:

- his electoral victory had been very narrow
- polls showed voters were unenthusiastic about civil rights
- alienating the Southerners in Congress would damage the rest of his legislative programme.

However, he tried to help in other ways.

Executive actions

Kennedy responded to the pressures for change through appointments, litigation and symbolic gestures to help African-Americans.

Employment

Kennedy was shocked to learn how few African-Americans were employed in important positions in the federal government: for example, only 48 of the FBI's 13,649 employees were black, and most of them were chauffeurs. Kennedy therefore made an unprecedented number of black appointments to the federal bureaucracy and appointed 40 African-Americans to top posts such as associate White House press secretary. He appointed five black federal judges, including **Thurgood Marshall**. However, 20 per cent of his Deep South judicial appointments were segregationists.

Kennedy used his executive powers to create the **Equal Employment Opportunity Commission (EEOC)**, which aimed to ensure equal employment opportunities for federal employees and in companies with contracts with the federal government. EEOC had some successes, such as the integration and promotion of African-Americans at the Lockheed aircraft plant in Georgia. In typical Kennedy fashion, his EEOC exaggerated its successes, boasting a rise from one to two black employees as a 100 per cent increase in black employment. It was difficult: employers frequently complained that they were simply complying with demands from their workers for segregated facilities.

Voting rights

The Kennedy Justice Department brought 57 legal cases against illegal violations of black voting rights in the South. When Bobby Kennedy threatened Louisiana officials with contempt of court sentences, for denying funds to

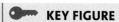

KEY FIGURE

Thurgood Marshall (1908–93)

An NAACP lawyer from 1935, Marshall won legal victories against segregated schools and universities and for equal pay for black teachers. His arguments in the *Brown* case (1954) were particularly impressive. He won 29 out of the 32 cases he contested before the Supreme Court. In 1962, President Kennedy appointed him to the US Court of Appeals in New York. President Johnson appointed him US solicitor-general in 1965, then made him the Supreme Court's first black justice in 1967.

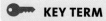

KEY TERM

Equal Employment Opportunities Commission (EEOC)
A federal agency established to deal with unequal employment opportunities for ethnic minorities.

newly desegregated schools in New Orleans, it hastened desegregation in New Orleans, Atlanta and Memphis. However, in 1963, the administration retreated on voting rights in Mississippi when influential Democrat senators protested.

Symbolic gestures

Symbolic gestures were an easy and politically painless way for President Kennedy to suggest commitment to racial equality. For example, he invited more black guests to the White House than any previous president. Although he rejected their requests for legislation, NAACP leader Roy Wilkins said, 'Everyone went out of there absolutely charmed by the manner in which they had been turned down.'

The Kennedys were not keen to respond to activism. For example, they refused to help SNCC workers attacked by whites in Mississippi (see page 85). However, civil rights activists frequently forced a response.

Reacting to protests

President Kennedy did not want to respond to the Freedom Riders: he said they were unpatriotic in exposing American domestic problems during the Cold War. However, the Freedom Riders' persistent pressure forced Attorney General Robert Kennedy to get an Interstate Commerce Commission ruling supporting the Supreme Court rulings that terminals and interstate bus seating be integrated.

James Meredith and the University of Mississippi

James Meredith, the 28-year-old grandson of a slave and son of a sharecropper, served in the US Air Force for a decade. He wanted a university education, but his local black college had poorly qualified teachers. Meredith therefore applied to the white University of Mississippi, which rejected him. When Meredith obtained legal aid from the NAACP and a Supreme Court decision in his favour, Bobby Kennedy sent 500 marshals to help him enrol. The ill-equipped marshals clashed with a white racist mob: two people were shot and one-third of the marshals were injured. President Kennedy then sent in the Mississippi National Guard and US Army regulars, and Meredith enrolled. Kennedy also sent the National Guard to implement the desegregation of the University of Alabama (see page 121).

Birmingham and the March on Washington

President Kennedy said the television pictures of Bull Connor's treatment of black protesters in Birmingham sickened him and that he could 'well understand' black exasperation. Robert Kennedy sent Justice Department representatives to Birmingham. They helped prepare both sides for eventual desegregation. Birmingham, coupled with the March on Washington, encouraged Kennedy to promote the civil rights bill, even though he knew it would be hard to get congressional co-operation: 'A good many programmes

I care about may go down the drain as a result of this – we may all go down the drain.' The bill was stuck in Congress at his death, partly because liberals tried to push it too far for Republicans. Ironically, Kennedy's assassination greatly contributed to the passage of the bill in 1964.

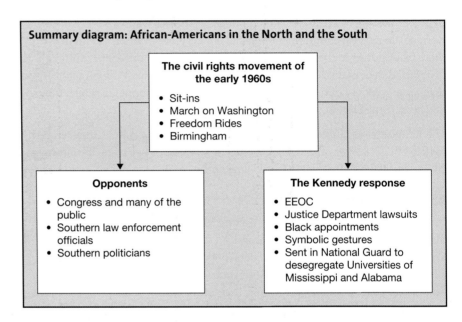

Summary diagram: African-Americans in the North and the South

The civil rights movement of the early 1960s
- Sit-ins
- March on Washington
- Freedom Rides
- Birmingham

Opponents
- Congress and many of the public
- Southern law enforcement officials
- Southern politicians

The Kennedy response
- EEOC
- Justice Department lawsuits
- Black appointments
- Symbolic gestures
- Sent in National Guard to desegregate Universities of Mississippi and Alabama

④ The United States by 1963

▶ *Was the American Dream a reality in 1963?*

The US position as a world power

In 1963, the United States was by far the most powerful country in the world. The Soviet Union was the next most powerful, but the United States possessed far more missiles, a superior navy and, as Khrushchev pointed out in his memoirs, 'the Americans have already surrounded the Soviet Union with a ring of their military bases'. These bases were situated in the many nations with which the United States had created alliances.

The United States had masterminded:

- defensive organisations such as NATO (1949), SEATO (1954) and **CENTO** (1959)
- treaties with countries such as Australia, New Zealand, the Philippines and Japan (all 1951), South Korea (1953) and Taiwan (1954) (contemporaries had joked about the **'pactomania'** of Secretary John Foster Dulles (see page 61) with good reason).

KEY TERMS

CENTO Anti-Soviet organisation, formerly known as the Baghdad Pact, but reconstituted as the Central Treaty Organisation in 1959. Its members included Turkey, Pakistan, Iran, Britain and the USA.

'Pactomania' Eisenhower's Secretary of State John Dulles made so many treaties with other anti-Communist foreign nations that contemporaries joked about his obsession with pacts.

In contrast, the Soviets were short of committed friends and allies. Events in Hungary in 1956 demonstrated the unpopularity of the Soviet domination of Eastern Europe (see page 74). Despite the Sino-Soviet alliance of 1950 (see page 75), the relationship between the two Communist giants had greatly deteriorated by late 1963. The Kennedy administration was aware of this but still viewed China as a great threat, especially in Vietnam.

Had Kennedy improved America's international position?

Kennedy's record on 'unsolved problems of peace and war' was mixed. Despite its nuclear arsenal and treaties, Americans still felt insecure during Kennedy's presidency. This was primarily because the USSR still possessed the nuclear capacity to destroy the United States many times over. Ironically, Kennedy's triumph in the Cuban missile crisis was about to increase that insecurity in two ways. First, Soviet determination that naval and nuclear inferiority would never again force them to back down prompted a Soviet build-up that resulted in Soviet–American nuclear and naval parity by the end of the decade. Second, America greatly worried its allies during the crisis. France's President de Gaulle complained furiously that the United States had informed, rather than consulted him, and responded by removing French troops from NATO in 1966.

On the other hand, Kennedy had signed the first treaty that attempted to slow the nuclear arms race (see page 112). Furthermore, he was deeply conscious of American identity abroad. While continuing the American imperialist tradition in Cuba in 1961 and in South Vietnam in 1961–3, he simultaneously worked to improve the nation's image in the Peace Corps and in space.

Kennedy's Peace Corps

In 1961, Kennedy established his Peace Corps. He described it as an organisation that allowed Americans to fulfil their responsibilities to 'world development' and 'world peace' by means of young volunteers sent to help poorer nations to help themselves through teaching and technical aid. Although he insisted that the Peace Corps was not an instrument of 'propaganda or ideological conflict', he privately expressed the hope that it would counter Soviet propaganda that depicted the United States as selfishly exploiting weaker nations and would show that American national values were superior to Soviet values.

Kennedy's inspired choice to head the Peace Corps was his brother-in-law Sargent Shriver, a tireless, idealistic, charismatic, well-travelled businessman who attracted quality staff. Thousands volunteered and those who completed the tough training programme (22 per cent failed) went off to live and work alongside the nationals of the country to which they were allocated. Between 1961 and 1963, the Peace Corps sent volunteers to 44 developing countries that requested aid.

The success of Kennedy's Peace Corps was attested by frequent Soviet criticism. Although cynical American critics derided 'Kennedy's Kiddie Korps' bouncing around the world in Bermuda shorts, 71 per cent of Americans approved of the Peace Corps, tens of thousands volunteered, and both political parties attested to their success when they voted to finance it for the next 50 years. Many volunteers impressed their host nations and improved the American image there. This was certainly a 'New Frontier' in the Cold War.

Kennedy and the space race

In May 1961, Kennedy was convinced that something had to be done about a series of American humiliations in space:

- After *Sputnik* in October 1957 (see page 73), the Soviets boasted incessantly about their lead in achievements in space.
- A US satellite launch failure in November 1957 caused worldwide embarrassment (British newspaper headlines included 'Oh, What a Flopnik').
- In April 1961, the Soviet Yuri Gagarin orbited the earth. American journalists reminded Kennedy that he had pledged to energise the US space programme and asked why the Soviets were the first to send a human into space.

Kennedy needed a success in space to help restore faith in America's international primacy and in his leadership after the Bay of Pigs fiasco. In May 1961, he told Congress that he wanted to land a man on the moon before the end of the decade. He said it would demonstrate American superiority and bring valuable international prestige, especially in the 'battles for minds and souls' in the new Cold War arena of the Third World. Kennedy spent a great deal of time justifying the $40 billion cost of a moon landing ($225 for each American). In a 1962 speech, he echoed his July 1960 New Frontier speech about the challenge of 'uncharted areas of science and space', saying that such difficult goals tested and measured a nation's greatness. However, his real preoccupation was a Cold War triumph. Privately, he told NASA (see page 73) chief James Webb he was not interested in space – only in beating the Soviets.

Despite considerable opposition to the moon programme, it could be argued that Kennedy eventually won the argument. By 1965, 58 per cent of Americans favoured 'the moon project' and in 1969 the United States proudly landed the first man on the moon to international acclaim. By achieving this, Kennedy opened another New Frontier in the Cold War.

Economic prosperity

In 1963, the United States remained by far the world's most prosperous nation. During Kennedy's presidency, the GNP expanded by 20 per cent and industrial production by 22 per cent, while personal income rose by 15 per cent. However, there were problems. The boom years of 1946–57 (fuelled by the pent-up demand of the war years) were over and there were frequent slowdowns in economic growth, as in 1961 and late 1962. Kennedy was concerned about the nation's international balance of payments deficit (he joked that he should keep his father and extravagant wife at home to decrease it). In a spring 1963 poll, Americans put inflation and unemployment (which averaged 1.2 per cent and 5 to 7 per cent, respectively, between 1961 and 1963) on their list of major concerns. Nevertheless, the prosperity of the majority of Americans was the envy of the rest of the world.

The Other America

Kennedy was well aware of the problem of poverty in the United States. While he liked to emphasise his own failure to understand economics, he employed and/or talked with leading academics such as John Kenneth Galbraith, and read:

- Galbraith's *The Affluent Society* (1958), which emphasised the poverty of a permanent American underclass
- Michael Harrington's *The Other America*, which described the poverty-stricken existence of 40–60 million Americans
- Dwight Macdonald's *New Yorker* essay-review on the invisible poor.

Such reading encouraged Kennedy's plans to make poverty a major issue in what he hoped would be a second presidential term.

Although there were impoverished white Americans, as Kennedy had seen in West Virginia in 1960, the 20 per cent of the American population in poverty was disproportionately from three ethnic minorities: African-Americans, Hispanic-Americans and Native Americans.

Racial and ethnic poverty

In the South, the majority of African-Americans were employed in sharecropping or as domestics, as illustrated by two of the most impressive female participants in the civil rights movement: Rosa Parks had been a seamstress and a cleaner before the Montgomery bus boycott, and Fannie Lou Hamer was a sharecropper before gaining national prominence at the Democratic National Convention in 1964. As Lyndon Johnson frequently pointed out, this constituted large-scale unused potential.

In the North, the combination of:

- government policies (the federal government gave generous help to white war veterans seeking to buy suburban homes)
- 'white flight' to the suburbs (see page 54)
- the African-American Great Migration northwards to escape Jim Crow (see page 41)

had changed the nature of big American cities. They became increasingly characterised by large ghettos in which African-Americans were crowded into low-quality housing, without access to good schools or amenities. White flight, much fuelled by the desire to get away from African-Americans, deprived cities of their tax base and so their decreased revenues left them struggling to deal with urban decay. While New York City's Harlem ghetto and Chicago's South Side ghetto were notable examples of urban decay, Southern cities such as Atlanta also experienced white flight and ghettoisation. As city councils and developers in cities such as Chicago tore down black neighbourhoods and replaced them with commercial buildings and expensive housing for whites, African-Americans said bitterly, 'urban renewal equals Negro removal'. Although Truman and Kennedy tried to alleviate the black housing shortage, it was difficult to gain funding from Congress: only 325,203 federal housing units were built between 1945 and 1965. Poor schools, poverty, white unwillingness to live alongside African-Americans, and discriminatory financial practices (see page 127) made it difficult to escape the ghettos, especially as increased automation decreased the number of reasonably paid jobs for the unskilled.

Poverty, poor education and poor housing also characterised Mexican-American lives in urban ghettos or rural squalor in Arizona, California, New Mexico and Texas. Native Americans also suffered discrimination and poverty, whether on reservations or in urban ghettos (notably Minneapolis–St Paul).

The growing pressures for social change from women and youth

Although contemporary critics characterised Americans in the Eisenhower years as complacent, some groups did not share the self-satisfaction. Along with African-Americans, Hispanic-Americans and Native Americans, some women and young people were dissatisfied with the American Dream. By 1963, some of them were expressing that dissatisfaction.

Women and change

Women's activism grew dramatically in the 1960s because of persistent inequality and the influence of Betty Friedan and other protest movements.

Inequality

Women lacked economic equality in 1963. Increasing numbers of women worked after the Second World War, but in 1963 most remained in low-paid jobs such as waitresses, cleaners, shop assistants or secretaries. Educated women were expected to choose 'female occupations' such as nursing and teaching, which conformed to traditional stereotypes of women as nurturers and carers. Many employers were sexist. In the mid-1960s, Congresswoman Martha Griffiths scolded an airline that had fired stewardesses when they married or reached the age of 32, saying, 'You are asking … that a stewardess be young, attractive and single. What are you running, an airline or a whorehouse?'

Statistics demonstrated inequality in employment opportunities in the early 1960s: for example, women constituted 80 per cent of teachers but only 10 per cent of principals, and only 7 per cent of doctors and 3 per cent of lawyers.

Gender inequality was often enshrined in law and practice. Eighteen states refused to allow female jurors, six said women could not enter into financial agreements without a male co-signatory. Schools expelled pregnant students and fired pregnant teachers. Some states prohibited married women from accessing contraception. Daniel Patrick Moynihan, a leading figure in President Nixon's administration, admitted that 'male dominance is so deeply a part of American life the males don't even notice it'.

The activist tradition among women

The women's movement did not appear out of the blue in the 1960s. Established in 1916, the National Women's Party was still active, particularly in demanding an **Equal Rights Amendment (ERA)** to the Constitution in order to guarantee gender equality. Labour movement activists had long been influential in the Democratic Party and they helped persuade President Kennedy to establish his Commission on the Status of Women. Although Kennedy's commission called for equal pay, it also suggested special training for marriage and motherhood and rejected **feminist** demands for the ERA.

 **KEY TERMS**

Equal Rights Amendment (ERA) Congress passed the ERA in 1972. Designed to help women and minorities in employment and education, it was never ratified by sufficient states.

Feminist Advocate of equal political, social, economic and legal rights for women.

Not surprisingly, increasing numbers of middle-class women agitated for equal pay, equal work, equal opportunities and equal respect in the 1960s.

Betty Friedan and domesticity

Women's magazines, films and advertisements in the 1950s frequently promoted domesticity as the norm and the ideal. Many girls were encouraged to play with dolls, to emphasise their femininity, and to play down their intellectual capacity. Some women took refuge in tranquillisers (the quantity taken doubled between 1958 and 1959) or alcohol as a result of this.

Betty Friedan was a Smith College graduate and suburban housewife in her forties. In 1963, she drew attention to the dissatisfaction of many middle-class housewives. In *The Feminine Mystique* (1963) she wrote about what she described as 'the problem that has no name'. She said that women were imprisoned in a 'comfortable concentration camp', taught that 'they could desire no greater destiny than to glory in their own femininity'. That destiny required focusing on the needs of their children and husband rather than on their own needs. Friedan urged women to break out of the 'camp' and fulfil their potential through education and work. Her bestselling book tapped a reservoir of discontent, especially among college students.

SOURCE H

From Betty Friedan's *The Feminine Mystique* (1963), Penguin Classics reprint, 2010, p. 1.

The problem lay buried, unspoken, for many years … It was a strange stirring, a sense of dissatisfaction, a yearning that women suffered in the … [mid-] twentieth century … Each suburban wife struggled with it alone. As she made the beds, shopped for groceries, matched slipcover material, … chauffeured Cub Scouts and Brownies, lay beside her husband at night – she was afraid to ask even of herself the silent question – 'Is this all?'

Study Source H. What are the limitations in Betty Friedan's *The Feminine Mystique* as a source for the historian investigating American women in 1963?

... There was no word of this yearning in the millions of words written about women, for women, in all the columns, books, and articles by experts telling women their role was to seek fulfilment as wives and mothers ...

The proportion of women attending college in comparison with men dropped from 47% in 1920 to 35% in 1958. A century earlier, women had fought for higher education; and now girls went to college to get a husband. By the mid-fifties, 60% dropped out of college to marry, or because they were afraid too much education would be a marriage bar ...

American girls began getting married in high school ... Girls started going steady at 12 ... an advertisement for a child's dress ... in the New York Times in ... 1960, said: 'She Too Can Join the Man-Trap Set.'

KEY FIGURE

Stokely Carmichael (1941–98)

Born in the West Indies, brought up in Harlem and educated at segregated Howard University, Carmichael participated in CORE's Freedom Rides then joined the SNCC and participated in SNCC's voter registration campaigns in Mississippi. Charismatic, handsome and a good organiser, he was elected leader of SNCC when its members became more militant. He brought the phrase 'Black Power' to prominence in the Meredith March and became such a celebrity that egalitarian SNCC members christened him 'Stokely Starmichael'. He tried to engineer a merger between SNCC and the Black Panthers (see page 172), but both organisations repudiated him in 1968. This, coupled with a total of 36 arrests, encouraged him to leave America and spend the remainder of his life in Africa.

The impact of other protest movements

Other protest movements encouraged women's activism in the 1960s in two ways:

- Protests such as the sit-ins and Freedom Rides showed that activists could help persuade businesses and the federal government to bring about beneficial change.
- Women encountered discrimination and sexual harassment in civil rights organisations such as the SNCC and in SDS (see below).

SNCC leader **Stokely Carmichael** supposedly said that the best position for women in the movement was horizontal, while one SDS male confessed, 'Women made peanut butter, waited on table, cleaned up and got laid. That was their role.' In 1964, women constituted 33 per cent of SDS members but only 6 per cent of the leadership. Although SDS approved a pro-women's rights resolution, the accompanying debate was characterised by male ridicule of and contempt for gender equality. Having been politicised by organisations such as SNCC and SDS, some disillusioned women moved on to campaign for women's rights.

Youth and change

There was unprecedented student unrest during the 1960s. In his inaugural address in 1961, Kennedy said, 'Ask not what your country can do for you; ask what you can do for your country.' For many of the young, change and improvement seemed possible in their optimistic, affluent society led by this charismatic and idealistic young president.

One of the earliest and most influential student organisations was the Students for a Democratic Society (SDS).

The SDS and the New Left

SDS was established in 1960 by Tom Hayden and other University of Michigan students. They were inspired by the socialists of the 1930s, the **beat generation** and student participation in the civil rights movement (see page 85).

In 1962, representatives of SDS, SNCC, CORE and the **Student Peace Union** met at Port Huron, Michigan. They called on students to:

- change the political and social system
- liberate the poor, racial minorities, and all enslaved by conformity
- support a peaceful foreign policy.

SDS emphasised the potential of the individual (currently stifled by the impersonal nature of the big universities, bureaucracy and the centralisation of all power) and called for 'participatory democracy' and a '**New Left** … consisting of younger people' to awaken Americans from 'national apathy'. While SDS did not come to national attention until its involvement in anti-Vietnam War protests in 1965, the Port Huron Statement (Source J) suggests that for some Americans in the Kennedy years, the American Dream was an illusion.

SOURCE I

From the 1962 Port Huron Statement, which set out the ideas espoused by Tom Hayden and the Students for a Democratic Society (SDS) (available from www.h-net.org/-hst306/documents/huron.html).

We are people of this generation, bred in at least modest comfort, housed now in universities, looking uncomfortably to the world we inherit … We begin to see complicated and disturbing paradoxes in our surrounding America. The declaration 'all men are created equal …' rang hollow before the facts of Negro life in the South and the big cities of the North. The proclaimed peaceful intentions of the United States contradicted its economic and military investments in this Cold War status quo … While two thirds of mankind suffers undernourishment, our own upper classes revel amidst superfluous abundance.

KEY TERMS

Beat generation
Participated in, or supported, a countercultural movement of the late 1950s, characterised by spontaneity, free love and general defiance of authority and convention; famous published figures included the poet Allen Ginsberg and the novelist Jack Kerouac.

Student Peace Union
National student organisation, active from 1959 to 1964.

New Left Student group of the early 1960s, who wanted greater racial and economic equality and an end to social conformity.

What can you infer about the American Dream from Source I?

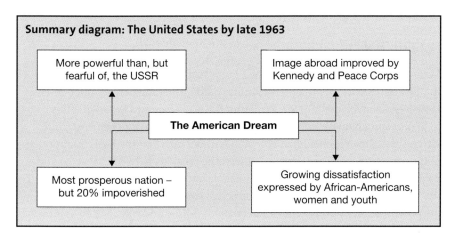

Summary diagram: The United States by late 1963

- More powerful than, but fearful of, the USSR
- Image abroad improved by Kennedy and Peace Corps
- **The American Dream**
- Most prosperous nation – but 20% impoverished
- Growing dissatisfaction expressed by African-Americans, women and youth

5 Key debate

▶ *Was Kennedy a successful president?*

While Americans consistently rate John Kennedy among the five greatest American presidents, a 1988 gathering of 75 historians and journalists described him as 'the most overrated public figure in American history'.

Despite the difficulties presented by his charisma, the brevity of his presidency and the circumstances of his death, most historians give both positives and negatives in their assessments.

Domestic policies

Most historians remain unimpressed by Kennedy's domestic achievements, particularly with regard to his legislative agenda. Historian James Giglio (1991) stated, 'One is hard pressed to give Kennedy high marks in the legislative arena.' However, many historians are tempted by the 'what if' scenario – one example is Robert Dallek.

EXTRACT I

From Robert Dallek, *John F. Kennedy: An Unfinished Life 1917–1963*, Penguin, 2003, pp. 708–10.

None of Kennedy's major reforming initiatives – the tax cut, federal aid to education, Medicare,* and civil rights – became law during his time in office. Yet all his significant reform proposals, including plans for a housing department and a major assault on poverty, which he had discussed in 1961 and 1963, respectively, came to fruition under Lyndon Johnson. Johnson, of course, deserves considerable credit for these reforms … Johnson's enactment of Kennedy's reform agenda testifies to their shared wisdom about the national well-being … No one should deny Johnson credit in winning passage of so many Great Society bills … Nevertheless, it is arguable that Kennedy would have made similar gains in a second term …

* Federal medical insurance.

Foreign policy

Many historians believe Kennedy had great successes with the Peace Corps, the Test Ban Treaty, Berlin and the military strengthening of the United States. However, some blame him for escalating the arms race and for an inability to look at the Cold War with fresh eyes. The historian George Herring (2008) wrote, 'The New Frontiersmen accepted without question the basic assumptions of the containment policy. They perceived the tensions between Moscow and Beijing, but they still viewed Communism as monolithic and a mortal threat to the United States.' Giglio felt that 'Kennedy never did develop a coherent and purposeful strategy and oscillated between hardline and conciliatory approaches [to the Soviet Union] with little apparent rationale.' Historian James Patterson praised Kennedy for being 'less of a hard-line Cold Warrior' than some of his rhetoric suggested and for prudence over **Laos, Congo and Indonesia**. However, overall, Patterson was critical of Kennedy's unimaginative foreign policy.

KEY TERM

Laos, Congo and Indonesia During Kennedy's presidency, Laos was bitterly divided between Communists and non-Communists; the Congo had a civil war after one province seceded; President Sukarno of Indonesia pursued aggressive policies towards neighbouring countries.

EXTRACT 2

From James Patterson, *Grand Expectations: The United States, 1945–1974*, Oxford University Press, 1996, pp. 516–17.

Although he knew there was no missile gap, he eagerly increased defence spending and helped to escalate the arms race. Despite the Bay of Pigs debacle, he persisted in plans to harass and frighten Castro, thereby accentuating the provocative behaviour of Khrushchev. Ignoring evidence to the contrary, he held fast to cliches – especially in public – such as the domino theory and the existence of a monolithic 'international' Communism. He persisted in celebrating … military moves [for example in Cuba and Vietnam] to solve deeper social and political problems … Contrary to the claims of his acolytes, he did not grow very much on the job.

Vietnam

It seems possible to see in Dallek a preference for Kennedy over Johnson. While Dallek says Kennedy would probably have achieved what Johnson achieved in domestic reforming legislation, he also says Kennedy would not have got America deeper into Vietnam as Johnson did: 'No one can prove, of course, what Kennedy would have done about Vietnam between 1964 and 1968. His actions and statements, however, are suggestive of a carefully managed stand-down from the sort of involvement that occurred under LBJ [Johnson].'

Cuba

Most historians praise Kennedy for his handling of crises, particularly the Cuban missile crisis. George Herring is more negative.

EXTRACT 3

From George Herring, *From Colony to Superpower: US Foreign Relations since 1776*, Oxford University Press, 2008, pp. 689–726.

The missile crisis was the defining moment of the Kennedy presidency, and many observers have given him high marks. He was firm but restrained in responding to this most critical challenge, it is argued. He sought advice from different quarters. He left Khrushchev room for retreat. He did not gloat in the apparent US victory. The October confrontation is also the most studied of Cold War crises, and as more has been learned, the praise for Kennedy has been tempered. To be sure, Khrushchev bears primary responsibility for the confrontation. He deluded himself into thinking that he could get away with an *incredibly rash move. But Kennedy's obsession with Cuba and the hostile actions carried out in Mongoose* provided the occasion and rationale for Khrushchev's actions, a connection totally lost on US officials at the time. Even while he rejected the more risky alternatives, Kennedy's initial response pushed the two nations to the verge of war. He did hold the hawks at bay and displayed skill in crisis management. But he would have been the first to admit that luck and chance helped determine the outcome. The United States came within hours of an invasion that could have had horrific consequences. The number of Soviet troops in Cuba far exceeded US estimates, and they were armed with tactical nuclear weapons. An invasion could have triggered nuclear war.*

* Operation Mongoose was the covert operations of the CIA against Fidel Castro.

> **?** Which of Extracts 1, 2 or 3 do you consider most unfavourable and what pro-Kennedy arguments could you give in opposition to it?

Chapter summary

In 1960, Kennedy defeated Nixon in the presidential election because he was a more personable candidate (witty, self-effacing, charming and charismatic) who made fewer errors during the campaign. He was desperate to offer a contrast to Eisenhower and a new kind of liberalism – hence his New Frontier idea. Kennedy was an intelligent, pragmatic politician and his White House contained 'the best and the brightest', but despite some measures to help the poor, their legislative record was unimpressive, perhaps because of Kennedy's style of governing. Kennedy's most important adviser was his brother Bobby, although Robert McNamara was a highly influential Defence Secretary.

In terms of foreign policy, both the Americans and the Soviets perceived the construction of the Berlin Wall as a triumph for their side in the Cold War. Kennedy had one clear disaster (the Bay of Pigs) over Cuba, and one generally acknowledged success (the Cuban missile crisis). He also greatly increased the US commitment to Vietnam. Regarding civil rights, Kennedy's support was muted and mostly symbolic, although the sit-ins, Freedom Rides, Birmingham campaign and March on Washington kept black inequality on the national political agenda. White Southerners strongly opposed black equality and Northern whites were frequently unsympathetic. The civil rights bill was stuck in Congress at Kennedy's death, in 1963.

The USA remained the world's wealthiest nation in 1963, but roughly 20 per cent of the population were poor and the economy was increasingly prone to recessions and trade deficits. Americans witnessed how inequality could be overcome by protest and some women demanded change because of their economic inequality and/or unfulfilled suburban lives and/or the impact of the civil rights movement. Additionally, some groups of young people, especially students, became deeply critical of American values and behaviour.

Refresher questions

Use these questions to remind yourself of the key material covered in this chapter.

1 Give five reasons why Kennedy defeated Nixon in the 1960 presidential election.

2 Choose five important individuals in the Kennedy administration and give their job title, functions and influence.

3 Explain the ideas behind Kennedy's New Frontier speech in 1960.

4 Why was Khrushchev anxious about Berlin?

5 What was the significance of the Berlin Wall?

6 Why and with what results did Kennedy back the Cuban exiles' invasion at the Bay of Pigs?

7 What was the significance of the Cuban missile crisis?

8 To what extent had Kennedy committed the United States in Vietnam?

9 Why and with what results did Martin Luther King Jr campaign in Birmingham in 1963?

10 How did Kennedy promote the desegregation of universities in the South?

11 Why did Kennedy struggle to get his civil rights bill through Congress?

12 Give arguments for the propositions that a) America had nothing to fear from the Soviet Union and b) America had a great deal to fear from the Soviet Union.

13 What was SDS's version of the American Dream?

14 Why did *The Feminine Mystique* sell so well?

15 What economic problems did the United States face in 1963?

 Question practice

ESSAY QUESTIONS

1 'Kennedy defeated Nixon in the 1960 presidential election because of the televised debates.' Explain why you agree with or disagree with this view.

2 'Kennedy's New Frontier ideas failed to result in anything significant.' Explain why you agree with or disagree with this view.

3 'Kennedy met the Communist challenge more successfully than Eisenhower.' Assess the validity of this view.

4 'Betty Friedan was the most important factor behind the increased pressure for change from women.' Assess the validity of this view.

SOURCE ANALYSIS QUESTIONS

1 With reference to Sources H (page 129) and I (page 131), and your understanding of the historical context, which of these two sources is more valuable in explaining the growing pressures for social change by 1963?

2 With reference to Sources C (page 102), H (page 129) and I (page 131), and your understanding of the historical context, assess the value of these three sources to a historian studying the extent to which the American Dream was a reality during Kennedy's presidency.

CHAPTER 4

The Johnson presidency 1963–9

President Lyndon Johnson's 'Great Society' offered Americans the most idealistic version of the American Dream yet, but many considered his dream illusory. Some African-Americans participated in protests against continuing poverty and discrimination, while some young people protested against what was perhaps unfairly termed 'Johnson's war' in Vietnam. The war did great damage to Johnson and his presidency, to many of those who fought there, to the economy and to perceptions of American identity abroad. This chapter explores the reality and disillusion involved in the American Dream through sections on:

★ Johnson as president

★ Maintaining American world power

★ African-Americans in the North and the South

★ Social divisions and protest movements

Key dates

1963	Nov.	Kennedy assassinated; Johnson became president	1965	April	Watts riots
1964–8		Annual summer riots in black ghettos		Aug.	Voting Rights Act
1964	July	Civil Rights Act	1966	Jan.	Chicago Freedom Movement began
	Autumn	Berkeley Free Speech Movement began		June	Meredith March
				June	National Organisation of Women established
1965	Feb.	Rolling Thunder began			
	March	First ground troops in Vietnam		Oct.	Black Panthers established
	March	Selma	1968	Jan.	Tet Offensive
	April	Medicare and Medicaid; Education Act		April	Martin Luther King Jr assassinated

 Johnson as president

▶ *Did Johnson realise his Great Society dream?*

After Kennedy's assassination in November 1963, Vice President Lyndon Johnson became president. Johnson's great interest was domestic policy, but his escalation of the Vietnam War consumed the later years of his presidency and made him one of America's most unpopular presidents. Some believe Johnson was nothing more than an unprincipled politician, but his presidency indicates that he was an idealist who wanted to make the United States a better and fairer place for its inhabitants. His early life and career offers useful insights into his personality and future policies.

Personality and policies

Johnson's father's service in the Texas state legislature gave young Lyndon a lifelong fascination with politics. After he left school, Lyndon attended Texas State Teachers College. His contemporaries were convinced he 'was going somewhere'. They found him amusing, liked his warmth and genuine interest in them, but disliked his bragging, '**brown nosing**' and how 'he would just interrupt you' and dominate any conversation. The family could not afford college fees, so Lyndon took a teaching job in 1928.

 **KEY TERM**

Brown nosing Flattering and kowtowing to someone in order to gain favour.

Pre-presidential career

Johnson taught in a segregated school in what he described as 'one of the crummiest little towns in Texas'. He recalled his 28 Mexican-American pupils as 'mired in the slums', 'lashed by prejudice' and 'buried half-alive in illiteracy'. Believing education would be their escape route, Johnson bribed, bullied, cajoled and encouraged them. They adored him. There was much truth in his subsequent claim that, 'I wanted power to give things to people … especially the poor and the blacks.'

Political power provided more opportunities than teaching to 'give things to people', and Johnson jumped at the opportunity to become an aide to Texan Congressman Richard Kleberg in 1931. Johnson thoroughly enjoyed Washington life and in 1934 wooed Claudia Taylor (nicknamed 'Lady Bird') with the whirlwind energy and determination that characterised all his efforts.

In 1935, Johnson was appointed Texas state director for the National Youth Administration (NYA), a Roosevelt New Deal agency. He was the youngest and, the NYA national head adjudged, the best state director. As always, he was totally committed to the task at hand. He helped over 28,000 young Texans gain employment on government projects such as the construction of roadside parks all over Texas. Washington ordered him to have a black leader as a close adviser, but Johnson said he would be 'run out of Texas' if he did. He explained that 'long established' and 'deep-rooted' racial customs 'cannot be upset overnight'. However, he worked hard to alleviate black unemployment (nearly 50 per cent in 1932). Although he privately referred to African-Americans as 'niggers', they thought him unusually helpful. He sometimes slept at black colleges to see how the New Deal was working.

Congressman

In 1937, Johnson was elected to Congress. He demonstrated great talent for getting on with the powerful, including President Roosevelt, who called him

Lyndon Baines Johnson

1908	Born in Texas
1934	Married 'Lady Bird'
1937–61	Congressman then senator
1961–3	Vice president
1963	Became president after Kennedy's assassination
1964	Elected president
1968	Did not run for re-election
1969	Retired to Texas
1973	Died

Lyndon Baines Johnson ('LBJ') spent his life in public service: teacher (1929), congressional aide (1931–5), Texas state director for President Roosevelt's National Youth Administration (1935–7), congressman (1937–49), senator (1949–61), vice president (1961–3) and president (1963–9). He loved power, not only for its own sake but also for what it enabled him to do for others.

Johnson proved himself a master of the American legislative process while in the Senate, then obtained an unprecedented quantity of social reform legislation as president. Not all his **'Great Society'** programmes were successful, but his civil rights legislation and Medicare in particular improved many lives. From 1965 he was increasingly focused on the Vietnam War. He greatly escalated the US involvement and consequently became (and remains) exceptionally unpopular, but it could be argued that he was a victim of what historians have called the 'commitment trap' set by his predecessors.

Johnson's presidency was accompanied by unprecedented protests, sexual liberalisation and countercultural movements, all of which were given ample media coverage. Voters associated much of this tumult with Johnson and his policies. In the socially and politically conservative backlash that followed his presidency, some of his reforms were discredited, although some proved highly valued and popular.

 **KEY TERM**

'Great Society' President Johnson said he wanted to create an American society free from the racism and poverty which were particularly prevalent in the urban ghettos.

'the most remarkable young man'. One Roosevelt aide said the new young congressman 'got more projects and more money from his district than anybody else. He was the best congressman for a district that ever was.' Johnson strongly supported Truman's foreign policy, but was conservative on domestic issues. Along with his fellow Southern Democrats, he voted against civil rights measures that aimed to prevent lynching, eliminate poll taxes and deny federal funding to segregated schools.

Racist or idealist?

Although Johnson's Texas was 15 per cent black and 12 per cent Hispanic, anyone who sought elected office had to appeal to white segregationist voters. Johnson's opposition to Truman's civil rights programme (see page 44) disgusted black Texans. While they were not admirable, his explanations were valid within the contemporary Southern political context. He said:

- the bills would never have passed anyway
- he could only 'go so far in Texas'
- he was not anti-black but pro-states' rights
- civil rights legislation that tried 'to force people to do what they are not ready to do of their own free will and accord' would lead to a 'wave of riots' across the South
- civil rights legislation would not help blacks and Hispanics as much as better housing, schooling and healthcare would.

Nevertheless, when, in 1949 a segregated Texas cemetery refused to bury a Mexican-American war hero, Johnson arranged a burial in Arlington National Cemetery, which won him front-page praise in the *New York Times*. Some white Texans interpreted this as an attempt to win minority votes, or as a cynical publicity stunt by a politician with national ambitions who sought to look free from sectional prejudices. However, it took courage to make gestures such as this when most Texan voters were white. Furthermore, Johnson worked quietly to get black farmers and black schoolchildren equal treatment in his congressional district. In 1938, he obtained federal funding for housing in Austin, Texas, which benefited poor Mexican-Americans, African-Americans and whites. He helped pre-empt white opposition by appealing to white self-interest: he told the press that America would not have to worry about the appeal of ideologies such as Communism if it gave everyone good housing and a job. Clearly, Johnson appeared inconsistent on race because of the combination of the need to keep in with voters of all colours and his own ambition and idealism.

SOURCE A

From the mid-1940s, African-American Robert Parker worked for Johnson as a part-time servant at private dinner parties in Washington. In 1986, Parker recalled that it was sometimes a 'painful experience'. Quoted in Robert Dallek, *Lone Star Rising*, Oxford University Press, 1991, pp. 276–7.

[I feared] the pain and humiliation he could inflict at a moment's notice … In front of his guests Johnson would often 'nigger' at me. He especially liked to put on a show for [Mississippi] Senator Bilbo, who used to lecture: 'the only way to treat a nigger is to kick him' … I used to dread being around Johnson when Bilbo was present, because I knew it meant that Johnson would play racist. That was the LBJ I hated. Privately, he was a different man as long as I didn't do anything to make him angry. He'd call me 'boy' almost affectionately. Sometimes I felt that he was treating me almost as an equal … Although I never heard him speak publicly about black men without saying 'nigger', I never heard him say 'nigger woman'. In fact, he always used to call his black cook, Zephyr Wright, a college graduate who couldn't find any other work, 'Miss Wright' or 'sweetheart'.

Judging from Parker's comments in Source A, would you conclude that Johnson was a racist?

Senator

After a narrow defeat in a 1941 campaign for the Senate in which his opponent falsified voting figures, Johnson won his next Senate race in 1948 by doing the same. (Johnson obtained 1028 votes in one precinct in Jim Wells County, where only 600 people were registered to vote.)

In 1955, Johnson became **Senate Majority Leader**. He knew each senator's weaknesses, prejudices and ambitions, and played on them to become the most successful legislative master ever. In what became known as 'the Johnson treatment', he would stand nose to nose with other senators, invading their personal space, clutching their arms, and bullying, cajoling and persuading them into voting as he wished.

 **KEY TERM**

Senate Majority Leader
Leader of the majority party in the Senate.

SOURCE B

? What does Source B suggest about how Johnson applied 'the treatment'?

As both senator and president, Johnson (left) gave other politicians 'the treatment'. Here, his old mentor Senator Richard Russell (right), gets the treatment because of his opposition to the civil rights bill, December 1963.

When Johnson ensured that Eisenhower's 1957 civil rights bill obtained sufficient Democrat votes to pass, the *Washington Post* called it 'Johnson's Masterpiece'. Although he contributed to the bill's dilution (see page 91), Johnson had persuaded Congress to agree in principle that African-Americans deserved the vote.

Johnson's changing position on civil rights

One of the few Southern politicians who supported the Supreme Court's *Brown* decision (see page 86), Johnson nevertheless remained careful to appease Southern racists. In 1956, he killed a civil rights bill in Congress, but then he orchestrated the passage of two Civil Rights Acts (1957 and 1960) that, although diluted, helped prepare the way for further civil rights legislation.

Johnson changed his position on civil rights because he believed:

- the South had to accept desegregation in order to make economic advances (racial tensions made the South unattractive to investors)
- America was 'just throwing aside one of our greatest [economic] assets' by racism, which was 'un-American' and damaged the nation's reputation
- it was important to uphold the Constitution and the place of the Supreme Court within it: 'However we may question the [*Brown*] judgment,' it 'cannot be overruled now'
- he could not be seen to be too narrowly Southern if he wanted to fulfil his presidential ambitions (he was one of the three Southern senators who refused to sign the Southern Manifesto against *Brown*)
- he needed some dramatic legislative achievement such as a Civil Rights Act to demonstrate his talent for creating consensus

- the Democrats were in danger of losing Northern black voters to the Republicans
- *Brown* and the Montgomery bus boycott (see page 83) had shown that change was inevitable and it made sense to go along with it: he said, 'The Negro fought in the [Second World] war, and … he's not gonna keep taking the shit we're dishing out. We're in a race with time. If we don't act, we're gonna have blood in the streets.'

As always, Johnson's motivation was controversial. While one senator described his support of *Brown* as 'one of the most courageous acts of political valour I have ever seen', **Hubert Humphrey** said that Johnson used his stance on *Brown* for political gain, hoping to win Northern black and white voters. Humphrey was surely wrong: many of those close to Johnson said he had a genuine sympathy for greater racial equality, despite his use of racist language in order to ingratiate himself with other white Southerners.

Vice president

In 1960, Johnson hoped to be the Democrat candidate for the presidency, but was soundly defeated by Kennedy during a debate. Such Kennedy performances, coupled with the two men's disparity in wealth and education, left Johnson regarding Kennedy with a mixture of resentment and admiration.

When Kennedy chose Johnson as his running mate, both Democrat liberals and conservative Southern Democrats were aghast. A Dallas mob threatened Johnson and Lady Bird, carrying placards saying 'LBJ SOLD OUT TO YANKEE SOCIALISTS'. Kennedy chose Johnson to help him win the South, which Johnson did, but the stress of doing so made him very unpleasant (one old friend resigned, missing 'the sweet and kind and attractive Lyndon I used to know … the morale of your staff is awful').

EEOC

Kennedy had asked Johnson to chair his Equal Employment Opportunity Commission (EEOC) (see page 122). Johnson told Kennedy he did not want the job because the EEOC lacked the necessary money and power, but when Kennedy insisted, Johnson did his best. CORE's James Farmer considered Johnson's motivation genuine, not political. Farmer and NAACP leader Roy Wilkins both rated him higher than President Kennedy on civil rights issues. However, the EEOC made little progress. Johnson could not push contractors too far and too fast on equal employment, lest it damage him and the administration. Federal jobs held by African-Americans increased by 17 per cent in 1962 and 22 per cent in 1963, but black activists remained dissatisfied.

President

The death of President Kennedy made Vice President Johnson president. Johnson came to the presidency in 1963 with great legislative experience and admirable ambitions for a better America. The combination of that experience

KEY FIGURE

Hubert Humphrey (1911–78)

Mayor of Minneapolis (1945–8), Minnesota senator (1949–64), then Johnson's vice president (1965–9). He had long been one of the most liberal members of the Democratic Party, but by 1968 was tainted by his association with the Johnson administration and its escalation in Vietnam. Defeated in the 1968 presidential election by the Republican Richard Nixon, he returned to the Senate 1971–8.

SOURCE C

? Study Source C. Why do you suppose everyone, including Jackie Kennedy, thought she should be alongside Johnson when he was sworn in?

Lyndon B. Johnson taking the oath of office aboard Air Force One (the presidential aeroplane) at Love Field Airport, two hours and eight minutes after the assassination of John F. Kennedy in Dallas, Texas. Jackie Kennedy (right), still in her blood-soaked clothes, looks on.

and ambition, his exceptionally forceful personality, and the emotions aroused by the assassination of President Kennedy, gave him the opportunity to try to bring about his version of the American Dream: the 'Great Society'.

The impact of the Kennedy legacy

The death of the youthful, charismatic President Kennedy traumatised the nation. Many of Kennedy's White House insiders, particularly Bobby Kennedy, looked on Johnson as something of a usurper, not to be trusted with the Kennedy legacy, although Johnson himself subsequently said that when he became president, 'I became the custodian of his will … the custodian of the Kennedy dream.' Jackie Kennedy burnished the legend and helped create a mythical legacy by likening the Kennedy White House to the court of Camelot, full of noble knights. But what exactly was the Kennedy legacy?

- Kennedy's death generated a feeling in Congress and the nation that there should be some legislative tribute and that the nation must somehow change and improve. Johnson brilliantly used this desire to memorialise Kennedy to obtain anti-poverty legislation and the civil rights bill. Johnson introduced bills with emotive references to Kennedy, for example, by saying, 'Let us here highly resolve that John Kennedy did not live – or die – in vain' and 'And now the ideas and the ideals which [Kennedy] so nobly represented must and will be translated into effective actions.'

- The national mourning for Kennedy translated into sympathy for Johnson and Kennedy's party that contributed to the Democrat triumphs in the 1964 elections.
- Kennedy had greatly increased the US involvement in Vietnam, and Johnson would escalate it further – citing as one explanation for the escalation that he felt he must continue Kennedy's policies. It was here that the Kennedy legacy proved fatal (see page 152).

There is considerable disagreement over the Kennedy legacy, over whether or not Kennedy would have got out of Vietnam, over whether Kennedy could have got the civil rights bill through Congress, and over whether Johnson's 'War on Poverty' (see below) was simply a continuation of Kennedy's policies. However, it is certain that Johnson's 'Great Society' dream was far more radical a vision than Kennedy would have espoused.

President Johnson's pursuit of the 'Great Society'

For most people, the American Dream consisted of ever-increasing affluence. In a May 1964 speech, President Johnson offered a new version of the American Dream, in which the federal government would engineer a Great Society characterised by:

- racial equality (see page 160)
- the end of poverty (see below)
- educational reform (see page 145)
- modern housing (see page 145)
- the end of urban decay (see page 145)
- peace with other nations.

Americans had already demonstrated readiness to respond to an idealistic president who repudiated the selfishness and complacency of the 1950s. Amidst the gloom over Kennedy's assassination, many welcomed Johnson's optimism and positivity about what America could achieve. With a 75 per cent approval rating in the polls that owed much to Kennedy's death, and the feeling that the nation should rally around his chosen successor, Johnson persuaded Congress to enact an exceptional quantity of reforming legislation that impacted on millions of lives.

The war on poverty

Johnson considered ending poverty the most important element of his Great Society. In January 1964, he declared 'unconditional war on poverty' and persuaded Congress to pass an Economic Opportunity Act (EOA). Johnson boasted that 'for the first time in all the history of the human race, a great nation … is willing to make a commitment to eradicate poverty among … the forgotten fifth.' The EOA established an Office of Economic Opportunity (OEO) to co-ordinate the war on poverty and in February 1965, Johnson proudly informed Congress of its progress:

- 44 states had anti-poverty programmes, with six more states to follow.
- 53 Job Corps centres providing job training were receiving thousands of applications daily.
- Members of 25,000 families on welfare were receiving work training.
- 35,000 college students were on work-study programmes, under which poorer students could earn federal funding through part-time work.
- 35,000 adults were learning to read and write.
- 90,000 adults were enrolled in basic education programmes.
- Neighbourhood Youth Corps in 49 cities and eleven rural communities were giving young people jobs to help them stay in education or receive training.
- 8000 Volunteers in Service to America (VISTA) were assisting groups such as needy children, Native Americans and migratory workers.
- Over 4 million were receiving AFDC benefits (Aid to Families with Dependent Children).
- Loans were being given for small businesses and rural development. For example, $17 million was distributed in rural loans in 1968.

Poverty and health

The elderly had always constituted a large proportion of America's poor, partly because health care was a great expense for them. Democrats such as Johnson had long advocated federal financial support for health care, but conservative Americans insisted that subsidised or free healthcare smacked of Communism. With Democrat majorities in both houses of Congress and Johnson's legendary powers of persuasion (some said bullying), Congress established **Medicare** and **Medicaid** in the Social Security Act of 1965.

Johnson rightly boasted that he had produced 'a healthcare revolution'. Medicare lifted millions of elderly Americans out of poverty. Along with Medicaid, it helped 19 million Americans in 1966 and, within a decade, Medicare became so popular that no president dared to oppose it lest he alienate the powerful 'grey vote'. However, there were problems:

- There were gaps in coverage in Medicare and Medicaid (for example, spectacles).
- Medicare and Medicaid both proved far more expensive than the Johnson administration anticipated, mostly because the legislation allowed hospitals and doctors to set the fees. Medicaid increased the amount spent by the federal and state governments on health care for poorer citizens from $1.3 billion in 1965 to over $2 billion in 1966. In that year, a House of Representatives committee estimated that the cost of Medicare would rise to $12 billion by 1990, but that turned out to be $98 billion.
- Although one-fifth of the population benefited from Medicare and Medicaid by 1976, the problem of reasonably priced care for all Americans remained.

 **KEY TERMS**

Medicare Introduced under President Johnson in 1965; provided federally funded health insurance for over-65s and those with disabilities, regardless of their income or existing medical conditions.

Medicaid Introduced under President Johnson in 1968; the federal government gave financial assistance to states to help them provide medical treatment to impoverished residents who could not afford essential medical services.

Poverty and education

Johnson's Great Society promised improvements in education: 'nothing matters more to the future of our country,' he said. In 1964, he highlighted the problems:

- 54 million Americans had never finished high school.
- 8 million had under five years of schooling.
- 100,000 high-school graduates with proven ability could not afford to enter college.
- Schools were overcrowded, run down and short of good teachers.

Presidents rarely obtained funds for education because Congress felt it should be under local control. However, emphasising that the United States spent 'seven times as much on a youth that is gone bad' as on one who stayed in school, Johnson obtained congressional agreement that federal expenditure on education be doubled to $8 billion in order to solve the problems he had highlighted. Two important acts in 1965 channelled the money towards the poorest states and the poorest children: the Elementary and Secondary Education Act (ESEA) and the Higher Education Act (HEA).

By the end of Johnson's presidency, over 13 million children had benefited from federal aid to education; the percentage of those with a high-school diploma rose; the shortage of teachers had been ended; new buildings had been constructed; and the accessibility of a college education increased (by 1970, 25 per cent of college students received some financial aid from the HEA). Johnson's biographer Robert Dallek concluded, 'If his educational reforms did not lead to a Great Society, they have at least made for a better society. It is an achievement for which Johnson deserves the country's continuing regard.'

Poverty and urban problems

American inner cities were characterised by poverty and poor schools and housing. Envisaging a Great Society without urban decay and urban housing problems, Johnson suggested legislation and Congress responded with varying degrees of enthusiasm and effectiveness.

Despite the legislation of 1965–6, the ghettos continued in their dire state. Housing was a major cause of ghetto discontent. Four-fifths of the Detroit ghetto rioters arrested in 1967 (see page 169) had jobs paying over $120 weekly, suggesting that it was housing and alienation rather than poverty that caused their dissatisfaction. However, white taxpayers did not want to fund large-scale improvements and the majority opposed integrated housing.

In 1968, Johnson focused on obtaining an end to discrimination in housing. This would cost taxpayers nothing but hopefully alleviate ghetto overcrowding. Congress responded with the Fair Housing Act, but it proved unsuccessful because of white opposition (see page 163).

Table 4.1 President Johnson's suggested legislation and the congressional response 1965–6

Johnson's suggestions	The congressional response
A new government department – Housing and Urban Development (HUD) – to co-ordinate the various programmes to combat housing shortages and decay in the cities in which over two-thirds of Americans lived	Congress agreed to HUD (1965)
Chicago, Detroit, Houston, Los Angeles, Philadelphia and Washington DC to be designated 'demonstration cities' or 'model cities', in which the local community and all levels of government would work on affordable housing and transportation, recreational facilities and slum clearance	Congress passed the Demonstration Cities Act (1966), but at $1.2 billion the programme was underfunded. Johnson estimated the total cost at $2.4 billion, but the *New York Times* said New York City alone needed $6 billion. The newspaper claimed that the Model Cities failed because members of Congress demanded something for themselves, so that the six cities became 150 cities and the money was spread too thinly to be effective
Cheaper and desegregated housing	Congress passed the Omnibus Housing Act (1965), which financed rent supplements and $8 billion of low- and moderate-income housing, and the Fair Housing Act (1968). The latter was ineffective in the face of White opposition. Also, through federal loans and his famed powers of persuasion, Johnson persuaded builders to construct reasonably priced housing

SOURCE D

From President Johnson's 19 February 1968 message to Congress urging passage of the Fair Housing Act (available from http://mondale.law.umn.edu/pdf14/v.114_pt.3_p.3358-3361.pdf).

[This bill] seeks to ensure that every American has the opportunity to provide a decent home for his family. Segregation in housing – the product of long-standing discriminatory real estate practices – has compounded the Nation's urban problem. Minorities have been artificially compressed into ghettos where unemployment and ignorance are rampant, where human tragedies and crime abound, and where city administrations are burdened with rising social costs and falling tax revenues. Fair housing practices, backed by meaningful federal laws that apply to every section of the country – are essential if we are to relieve the crisis in our cities.

In Source D, what does Johnson mean by 'the Nation's urban problem'?

Did Johnson win the war on poverty?

Contemporary assessments of the success of the War on Poverty varied, usually according to the political stance of the assessor. Statistics that suggest success include:

- 19 million Americans benefited from Medicare and Medicaid in 1966
- over 13 million children and young people benefited from Johnson's education legislation
- a million children benefited from his **Head Start** programme and 50,000 students from his **Upward Bound** programme
- the percentage of the American population in poverty fell from 17 per cent in 1965 to 11 per cent in the early 1970s
- the 3.9 per cent unemployment rate in 1967 was a 13-year low
- the minimum wage rose by 35 cents
- federal expenditure on the poor rose from $13 billion in 1963 to $20 billion in 1966.

However, statistics that suggested improvement to some were criticised by others. Conservative critics attacked this level of federal expenditure on the poor as unsustainable (they enjoyed pointing out that it cost more to put a ghetto youth in the Job Corps than in Harvard University), while liberal critics unrealistically demanded even more expenditure.

Johnson failed to eradicate poverty. For example, a third of non-white families still lived below the **poverty line**, with **infant mortality** and unemployment rates nearly twice those of whites. He deserves credit for drawing attention to poverty and for his efforts to combat it, but also criticism for making politically unrealistic promises, and for weaknesses in the planning and implementation of his anti-poverty programmes (see below).

The decline of Johnson's American Dream

Johnson found himself torn between 'the woman I really loved – the Great Society' and the 'bitch of a war' against Communism in Vietnam (see page 151).

In his January 1966 State of the Union address, Johnson said America could afford both the Great Society and the war, but his War on Poverty became a casualty of the war in Vietnam. By 1966, there was a growing belief that his Great Society had run out of steam.

Why the Great Society ran out of steam

- President Kennedy's brother-in-law Sargent Shriver (see page 125) claimed, 'Vietnam took it all away, every Goddammed dollar. That's what killed the war on poverty. It wasn't public opinion.' Between 1965 and 1973, $15.5 billion was spent on the Great Society, $120 billion on Vietnam.

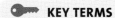 **KEY TERMS**

Head Start A federal government programme to help economically disadvantaged pre-schoolers, providing educational, health, social and other services.

Upward Bound Federal government-financed programme linking higher education institutions to poor students with college potential; established by President Johnson.

Poverty line An amount set by the US government; those whose annual family income is below this are legally defined as 'poor', which is important for federal aid entitlements.

Infant mortality The proportion of infants who die before a certain age is taken as an indication of a nation or group's health and well-being.

- The war precipitated inflation and tax rises that made the Great Society unpopular. In 1967, Missouri's governor told Johnson there was 'no great public support for your Great Society programmes'. Congress made Johnson agree to cuts in the programmes.
- Some said the Great Society was an unrealistic dream: Richard Nixon described the War on Poverty as a 'cruel hoax'. Taxpayers were never going to grant unlimited funds to help the poor.
- There were unforeseen consequences, as when programmes to help the urban poor were hijacked by black radicals (see page 172), which worried Johnson and the Democrats.

Assessing Johnson's Great Society

Johnson's own aides and allies admitted to problems with the Great Society, and yet celebrated Johnson's achievements:

- Top aide Joseph Califano warned Johnson that 'extravagant rhetoric' unsupported by adequate funding would lead to unrealistic expectations and disillusionment, but also said, 'All of us knew that we'd been part of a monumental social revolution.'
- Senate Majority Leader Mike Mansfield warned about the proliferation and efficiency of programmes, yet said that Johnson had done more than Franklin Roosevelt 'ever did or thought of doing'.

Assessments of Johnson's Great Society achievements vary according to the political stance of the American making the judgement: when Johnson greatly increased the role and expenditure of the federal government in areas such as education and welfare, conservatives lamented that his social welfare programmes increased dependency, while liberals lamented that the War on Poverty failed to end poverty, and had little impact on American cities and even less on rural areas.

For many of the poor, elderly, sick and unemployed, Johnson made a considerable difference. Although the *Boston Globe* said that the great Newark ghetto riots of July 1967 (see page 169) demonstrated that the civil rights and anti-poverty legislation had done little to help African-Americans, Johnson helped make a massive difference for many, especially in the South. Critics say that his broken promises led to disillusionment with government and politics and damaged liberalism, while supporters are awed by aspirations and efforts that went far beyond what any other president conceived and attempted, with the possible exception of Johnson's hero Franklin D. Roosevelt. Johnson certainly never managed to do as much as he had hoped, repeatedly saying: 'So little have I done, so much have I yet to do.'

Personality, popularity and policies

President Truman's Secretary of State Dean Acheson once said to Johnson, 'Let's face it, Mr President, you just aren't a likeable man.' After he became president, Johnson often seemed mean and bullying when he failed to get what he wanted. Many are shocked that he made aides continue to work with him while he defecated in the bathroom, although it could be argued that presidential time was too precious to be wasted. And yet, for all his many faults and errors, he genuinely sought to make America and the world a better place.

Economic developments

In many ways it seemed as if the American post-war economic boom would never end. For example, under Eisenhower there had been a 19 per cent growth in GNP, but under Kennedy and Johnson it was 39 per cent. Perhaps unsurprisingly, 96 per cent of Americans in the first half of the 1960s believed their standard of living would continue to improve, and during most of his presidency Lyndon Johnson rightly boasted that the economy was booming. However, the Vietnam War had a dramatic and adverse effect on the American economy because of the inflationary pressures that resulted from federal government overspending.

1964

Johnson boasted about:

- 43 months of unbroken business expansion (the longest such period since the Second World War)
- limited inflation
- low unemployment
- pleasing GNP growth.

1965

There were signs that the booming economy was overheating. In August, Johnson tried to persuade labour and industry to prevent inflation by following wage and price guidelines. He persuaded steel workers and bosses to co-operate and in December approved an interest rate rise designed to cool the economy down.

1966

In his speeches, Johnson rightly claimed that Americans were 'a people who live in abundance unmatched on this globe.' He pointed out that in the past five years:

- after-tax wages had risen by 35 per cent
- corporate earnings had risen by over 65 per cent
- farm income had risen by nearly 40 per cent
- unemployment was at 13-year low.

Johnson assured Americans that the nation could afford the Great Society and the Vietnam War. However, with inflation at its highest for 10 years, many people doubted that it could. While Johnson hoped funding for the war would come from a growing economy free of strikes and inflation, and from streamlined government rather than from politically unpopular tax rises, the doubters were proved right. The pressure to raise prices and wages mounted and in late 1966 the dam broke. Many workers and employers agreed on inflationary rises.

1967

Johnson's advisers had been pressing him to call for a tax hike. The prospective budget deficit of over $10 billion finally persuaded him to seek a tax increase in his January 1967 budget message. He told Americans how affluent they were but admitted that there had been a 4.5 per cent rise in consumer prices in the previous 18 months and that interest rates were rising. He could have added that there was a slowdown in capital investment, less residential construction, flat-lining industrial production, depressed retail sales, lower corporate profits, and that the GNP's performance in the first quarter of 1967 was the worst since the 1960 recession.

During the summer and autumn there was a 4.5 per cent increase in the GNP and a fall in unemployment to 3.8 per cent, but problems remained with an increasing federal budget deficit, inflation and rising consumer prices. In October, 60 per cent of Americans saw the high cost of living as their number one problem (only 5 per cent named Vietnam).

1968

By early 1968, the nation's economic problems were great:

- The federal budget deficit for 1968 was an estimated $19.8 billion.
- Although the United States had a trade deficit in seventeen out of the previous eighteen years, the 1967 trade deficit of nearly $4 billion was three times that of 1966.
- America's problems with inflation and trade and federal budget deficits were frightening financial markets everywhere. The trade deficit was made up by sending gold abroad, so that by 1965 US gold supplies had decreased by 40 per cent since 1945. This caused a run on the dollar: when reserves dropped to $12.4 billion (the lowest since 1937), the dollar was greatly weakened.

Conclusion

Johnson admitted the problems when he told Congress in 1967 that it was unwise to reject his proposed further tax rises 'while the storm clouds of inflation gather, while interest rates begin to soar, while international money markets are disrupted, while uncertainty hangs over our economy'.

SOURCE E

The words of Johnson's old friend, Senator Richard Russell of Georgia, to the Georgia assembly in January 1967. Quoted in Robert Dallek, *Flawed Giant: Lyndon Johnson and His Times, 1961–1973*, Oxford University Press, 1998, p. 307.

[I am] one of those who has questioned whether this nation, for all its wealth and resources, can fight a war of the magnitude of Vietnam and carry on a broad range of domestic spending – without a tax increase or a dangerous deficit. The President apparently believes that we can. For the sake of the country and the soundness of the dollar, I hope and pray that he is right.

Were Russell's doubts in Source E proved right?

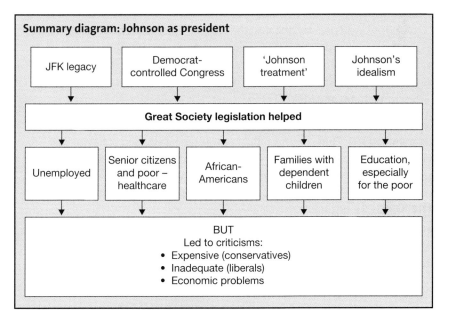

Summary diagram: Johnson as president

JFK legacy → Democrat-controlled Congress → 'Johnson treatment' → Johnson's idealism →

Great Society legislation helped

→ Unemployed → Senior citizens and poor – healthcare → African-Americans → Families with dependent children → Education, especially for the poor →

BUT
Led to criticisms:
• Expensive (conservatives)
• Inadequate (liberals)
• Economic problems

② Maintaining American world power

▶ *Why and with what results did Johnson escalate the war in Vietnam?*

When Lyndon Johnson became president in November 1963, the US-sponsored anti-Communist state of South Vietnam was protected by the US-created SEATO (see page 76) and governed by the US-supported General Minh, who had around 17,000 American 'advisers'. By 1968, America had 535,000 American ground troops in South Vietnam but was no nearer to defeating the Communist forces of North Vietnam and their many supporters and soldiers within South Vietnam itself.

Why Johnson continued the US involvement in Vietnam

There is no question that Johnson greatly escalated the war in Vietnam, although that is not to say that it was 'Johnson's war'. Within the contemporary context, Johnson arguably had little choice but to continue the war because of the nation's Cold War convictions, the Kennedy legacy and the failings of the **Saigon regime**.

Cold War convictions

Johnson was typical of his contemporaries in believing

- that Communist nations were aggressive dictatorships, appeasement of which would probably lead to war (Johnson said, 'If you let a bully come into your front yard one day, the next day he'll be up on your porch, and the day after that he'll rape your wife in your own bed')
- in containment and the domino theory (see pages 14 and 76)
- that it was a question of national honour to continue the commitment to South Vietnam and SEATO.

Like many Democrats, Johnson never forgot Republican accusations that Truman had lost China. Johnson did not want to be accused of having lost Vietnam, and repeatedly said he did not want to be the first president to lose a war.

The Kennedy legacy

Johnson knew a long war would probably lose popular and congressional support, and that the Saigon government was weak and unpopular. However, the Kennedy legacy left him little room for manoeuvre for several reasons:

- The Kennedy administration had colluded in the assassination of Diem, which as Johnson and General Westmoreland (the US Commander in Vietnam), said had morally locked the United States into Vietnam.
- Johnson felt constitutionally and emotionally obliged to continue the assassinated president's policies. 'I swore to myself that I would carry on. I would continue for my partner who had gone down ahead of me … When I took over, I often felt as if President Kennedy were sitting there in the room looking at me.' Two days after Kennedy's assassination, Johnson told Ambassador Lodge in Vietnam that he was not going to 'lose Vietnam … Tell those generals in Saigon that Lyndon Johnson intends to stand by our word.' 'My first major decision on Vietnam had been to reaffirm President Kennedy's policies,' Johnson said later.
- Johnson naturally retained Kennedy's Secretary of Defence Robert McNamara and Secretary of State Dean Rusk. This meant that no new ideas emerged on Vietnam. The Kennedy men did not want to admit past errors in increasing the involvement. They believed an American withdrawal would make the United States appear on unreliable ally and a faint-hearted enemy.

McNamara subsequently admitted that Johnson's civilian and military advisers never asked the appropriate searching and relevant questions about the war and were sadly ignorant about Vietnam.

The failings of the Saigon regime

Soon after Diem's assassination it became clear that General Minh and his successors were even less capable. In March 1964, McNamara visited Saigon and described the situation under the new leadership of General Khanh as 'very disturbing': the South Vietnamese were generally apathetic and unwilling to fight. Like Kennedy, Johnson was pressed by his military and civilian advisers to escalate and to take the war to North Vietnam itself.

Why Johnson escalated the war

In August 1964, the Johnson administration was informed of what Americans perceived as unprovoked North Vietnamese attacks on US ships on espionage missions in North Vietnamese coastal waters (blinded by what Senator Fulbright of Arkansas called 'the arrogance of power', few Americans considered that such missions along the enemy's coast might be seen as inviting attacks). Congress gave Johnson the power to 'take all necessary steps' to help South Vietnam in the **Gulf of Tonkin resolution**.

Johnson's role in the passing of that resolution has been much criticised:

- It has been said that he sought the resolution because he was planning escalation. However, it could be argued that it was his job as commander-in-chief to be prepared for any eventuality.
- It has been claimed that he deceived Congress and the people about the espionage missions and the attacks. In his defence, it could be said it was his responsibility to respond – and quickly – if US ships were under attack.
- Johnson has been accused of political calculation: his Republican opponent in the 1964 presidential election had declared Johnson 'soft on Communism', so Johnson had to appear tough. He certainly did, and when he bombed North Vietnam for the first time in late summer 1964, his approval rating rocketed from 42 to 72 per cent.

An exploration of the reasons why he escalated the war helps clarify whether or not he always intended to do so. He escalated because of the continuing incompetence and unpopularity of the Saigon government, the Working Group's recommendations and the need to defend American personnel in Vietnam.

The incompetence and unpopularity of the Saigon government

Successive South Vietnamese governments proved incapable of winning the war. Essentially, they were unpopular and unwilling to reform, while Ho Chi Minh and the Communists had introduced popular land reforms and received considerable Soviet and Chinese aid. In late 1964, Dean Rusk guessed that 'a pervasive intrusion of Americans' into South Vietnamese affairs was needed.

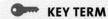 **KEY TERM**

Gulf of Tonkin resolution
1964 congressional authorisation for the president to do as he saw fit in South Vietnam.

The Working Group

In 1964, Johnson ordered representatives of the State Department, the Defence Department, the CIA and the JCS to study Vietnam and make recommendations. In November 1964, this Working Group:

- said that an independent, anti-Communist South Vietnam was vital to America
- reiterated the domino theory
- said that American 'national prestige, credibility and honour' were at stake
- emphasised that escalation was necessary due to the weak Saigon government, which was 'close to a standstill' and 'plagued by confusion, apathy, and poor morale'
- suggested heavier bombing, to be halted only if North Vietnam would accept the continued existence of a non-Communist South Vietnamese government.

These recommendations do not suggest that this was simply Johnson's war.

The first great escalatory step: Rolling Thunder

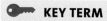

KEY TERM

Viet Cong Vietnamese Communist guerrillas.

Johnson took his first great escalatory step in early 1965, when he began large-scale and continuous bombing of Vietnam in 1965, in response to concerns about the security of US bomber bases and personnel. For example, in February 1965, the **Viet Cong** attacked a huge American camp near Pleiku, killing eight Americans and wounding 100. Johnson said, 'I've had enough of this', and his advisers all urged retaliation. Johnson began the bombing of North Vietnam that became known as 'Rolling Thunder'. Polls revealed that 67 per cent of Americans approved his actions. The aims of Rolling Thunder were to:

- secure American positions in South Vietnam
- decrease Communist infiltration from North Vietnam (see page 113)
- demoralise the North Vietnamese government
- encourage the South Vietnamese government.

The *New York Times* said that the United States was 'in an undeclared and unexplained war', but Johnson refused to declare war, lest Cold Warriors made him go all out and invite large-scale Soviet or Chinese intervention: 'Think about 200 million Chinese coming down these trails,' said Johnson. 'No Sir! I don't want to fight them.' Also, he feared that a declaration of war would cause Congress to cut funding for his Great Society.

The second great escalatory step: ground troops

In spring 1965, Johnson took his second great escalatory step when he sent in American ground troops in response to General Westmoreland's request for greater protection for the US bomber bases at Danang.

In an April 1965 speech, Johnson summed up the reasons for escalation:

- The United States needed to fight if it wanted to live securely in a free world.
- North Vietnam had aggressively attacked South Vietnam and should be opposed.
- North Vietnam was a puppet of expansionist Communist powers (the USSR and China) who wanted to conquer all of Asia.
- Eisenhower and Kennedy had helped to build and defend South Vietnam: abandoning it would be dishonourable and would cause all US allies to doubt America's word and credibility.
- Appeasement could lead to a third world war.

At this stage, polls and White House mail revealed:

- 70 per cent of the nation was behind Johnson
- 80 per cent believed in the domino theory
- 80 per cent favoured sending American soldiers to stop South Vietnam falling
- 47 per cent wanted Johnson to send in even more troops.

Table 4.2 Number of American ground troops in South Vietnam 1965–7

Date	Number of troops
March 1965	3500
December 1965	200,000
December 1966	385,000
December 1967	535,000

Even as Johnson sent in more and more troops, the United States was no nearer to victory, as demonstrated during the **Tet Offensive**.

The Tet Offensive and the media's role in the Vietnam War

In January 1968, North Vietnam launched an unprecedented offensive against South Vietnam. Tens of thousands of Communist soldiers attacked cities and military installations in the South. The Americans and South Vietnamese were preoccupied with the **Tet festival** and did not expect the Communists to break the traditional holiday truce. The Communists demonstrated that they could move freely and effectively throughout the South, including Saigon and the American embassy grounds (the US ambassador had to flee the embassy in his pyjamas). It took 11,000 American and South Vietnamese troops three weeks to clear Hue of enemy forces. The Tet Offensive cost a great many lives and caused incredible damage: 3895 Americans, 4954 South Vietnamese military, 14,300 South Vietnamese civilians and 58,373 Communist soldiers died. Over half the houses in historic Hue were totally destroyed, and nearly a quarter were seriously damaged.

The dramatic scenes in Saigon in particular were headline news in the United States, where media coverage of Tet (and other events in Vietnam) increasingly challenged the government's position and veracity. Many people believe that the media turned the public against the war.

 **KEY TERMS**

Tet Offensive Great Communist offensive in South Vietnam in early 1968.

Tet festival Vietnamese New Year, celebrating the arrival of spring.

Before Tet, the government had been publicly optimistic about the war and the media had been generally supportive. However, when the media showed Communists overrunning the South Vietnamese capital during Tet, America's most trusted television reporter, Walter Cronkite, felt he had been misled: 'What the hell is going on? I thought we were winning the war.' Johnson said, 'If I've lost Cronkite, I've lost America.'

Did the media snatch defeat from the jaws of victory?

In many ways, the Tet Offensive could be seen as a Communist defeat: it took North Vietnam several years to get over it. Contrary to North Vietnamese hopes, the South Vietnamese people had not risen up to help the Communists, which damaged the Communist claim to be a liberation force.

On the other hand, the Tet Offensive could be seen as an American defeat. Although American and South Vietnamese forces regained control of the South Vietnamese cities, the Communist position in rural areas was strengthened because of the Communist performance in Tet. Furthermore, South Vietnam's population had not rallied to the unpopular Saigon regime. The offensive seemed to show that although the United States could stop the overthrow of the Saigon government, it had failed to make it viable in the face of Communist determination to overthrow it.

Whether or not the US forces had been defeated, the media images made it seem that they had. American television viewers saw Communist forces in the grounds of the American embassy. American newspaper readers saw a photo of a Saigon general shooting a bound captive in the head, which damaged Americans' faith in their side as the 'good guys' (later it was discovered that the captive was a Viet Cong death squad member who had just shot a relation of the general). An anti-war television reporter made many Americans question what was being done in Vietnam when he repeated a soldier's unforgettable words about one South Vietnamese village: 'We had to destroy the town to save it.'

If the media had turned the public against the war, it was only because the media demonstrated the reality: the United States had supported its South Vietnamese creation since 1955, but even after three years of greatly escalated US involvement, South Vietnam remained unable to cope with the Communist challenge.

The end of escalation

After Tet, Johnson rejected repeated JCS requests for more troops. This has led many to conclude that Tet, and popular reaction to media coverage of it, was responsible for the start of the slow US withdrawal from Vietnam. However, it had been obvious to the Johnson administration before Tet that the United States simply could not win in South Vietnam. In early 1967, McNamara told Johnson:

> *The picture of the world's greatest superpower killing or seriously injuring 1,000 noncombatants a week, while trying to pound a tiny, backward nation into submission on an issue whose merits are hotly disputed, is not a pretty one.*

Knowing the war could not be won, McNamara resigned in autumn 1967, and, in a last tearful White House conference, condemned:

> *the goddammed Air Force and its goddammed bombing campaign that had dropped more bombs on Vietnam than on Europe in the whole of World War II and we hadn't gotten a goddammed thing for it.*

McNamara's successor as secretary of defence, Clark Clifford, doubted the domino theory and the wisdom of US involvement. Tet simply confirmed what Clifford and Johnson already knew. The United States had to get out. The war was unwinnable, a significant proportion of Americans opposed it (see page 177); and the American economy (see page 149) and national image were suffering.

Relations between the USA and its Western allies

When he became president, Johnson aimed to strengthen the Atlantic community through the modernisation of NATO, greater European integration and improved East–West relations. However, the Vietnam War damaged relations between the USA and its Western allies, and the Soviets took advantage of the American preoccupation with Southeast Asia to engage in a great nuclear and naval build-up.

Like many Americans, Johnson believed his country was a beacon of democracy and had always fought for freedom. In 1964 he said, 'Our cause has been the cause of mankind.' He believed that if the Communists could be defeated in Vietnam, the United States could then help transform that nation: 'I want to leave the footprints of Americans there,' he said, and spoke of constructing a **Tennessee Valley Authority** in Vietnam's Mekong Delta (see the map on page 113). However, the Vietnam War did more to damage America's image abroad than any previous event.

Critical allies

Of the 40 nations allied to the United States, only Australia, New Zealand, South Korea and Thailand sent troops to Vietnam, and South Korea and Thailand had to be bribed to do so. Japan criticised the escalation and sold supplies to both sides, while in April 1965 Canadian Prime Minister Lester Pearson made a critical speech in Philadelphia (he received a particularly unpleasant version of the 'Johnson treatment' at **Camp David**). However, the greatest and most effective critic was French President Charles de Gaulle.

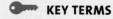 **KEY TERMS**

Tennessee Valley Authority New Deal programme that modernised the Tennessee Valley through electrification.

Camp David Presidential retreat in the rural hills of Maryland.

President Charles de Gaulle

A State Department memorandum of December 1963 considered de Gaulle a problem, but not a major one. However, as the Vietnam involvement increased, de Gaulle greatly damaged the United States:

- De Gaulle repeatedly told representatives of other nations that the United States could not be counted on if the Soviets invaded Europe, a contention that grew more persuasive as America became increasingly bogged down in Vietnam.
- De Gaulle criticised the 'bombing of a very small people by a very large one' in an 'unjust … detestable war'.
- De Gaulle took advantage of the American preoccupation with Southeast Asia to assume the leadership of Western Europe. He promoted the influence of France and undermined that of the United States.
- De Gaulle tried to wean West Germany from the Western Alliance, but West Germany valued the US nuclear shield and remained within NATO. However, along with West Germany's Willy Brandt, de Gaulle established economic and cultural ties with the Eastern bloc despite US opposition.
- France withdrew from NATO in 1966. The enforced removal of the NATO headquarters and 26,000 American troops from France is the clearest illustration of how Vietnam helped divide and weaken the Western Alliance.
- While the United States was keen for Britain to join the European Economic Community (EEC), de Gaulle vetoed it in 1967, saying Britain would be an American Trojan horse within the EEC.
- Finally, in the mid-1960s de Gaulle demanded that the US Treasury redeem several hundred million dollars in gold, which set off a wave of speculation against the dollar.

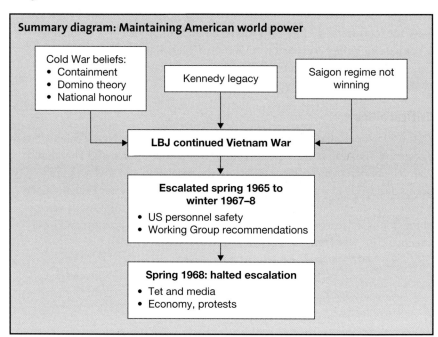

Summary diagram: Maintaining American world power

Cold War beliefs:
- Containment
- Domino theory
- National honour

Kennedy legacy

Saigon regime not winning

LBJ continued Vietnam War

Escalated spring 1965 to winter 1967–8
- US personnel safety
- Working Group recommendations

Spring 1968: halted escalation
- Tet and media
- Economy, protests

3 African-Americans in the North and the South

▶ *How successful was the civil rights movement during Johnson's presidency?*

One aspect of the Great Society of which President Johnson dreamt was racial equality. He said that discrimination was morally wrong, and described how, when his black cook drove to Texas, she could not use the whites-only facilities in a petrol station:

> *When they had to go to the bathroom, they would all … pull off on a side road, and Zephyr Wright, the cook of the vice-president of the United States, would squat in the road to pee. That's wrong. And there ought to be something to change that.*

Johnson believed reform would help the economic, political and spiritual reintegration of the South within the nation and felt duty-bound to see the late President Kennedy's bill through. He told the NAACP leader Roy Wilkins that as president he was now 'free at last' from his Texas constituency and able to help African-Americans. Wilkins considered him 'absolutely sincere', and Martin Luther King Jr's associate Andrew Young praised him for promoting the bill even though 'he knew it was not politically expedient'.

Johnson's role in passing civil rights legislation

The civil rights bill faced considerable opposition in Congress, including the longest **filibuster** in Senate history. However, it finally became an act because:

- Black activists drew the attention of the nation and its legislators to injustices.
- The NAACP, trade unionists and churches lobbied Congress incessantly.
- Kennedy had won over the Republican **Minority Leader** before his death.
- Important congressional leaders such as the Democrat Hubert Humphrey worked hard on the bill.
- One Johnson aide gave the credit for the passage of the bill to Johnson himself. The president devoted a staggering amount of his time, energy and political capital to breaking the Senate filibuster and ensuring the passage of the act. He made emotive appeals to national traditions and ideals and to Kennedy's memory, insisting that the best way to honour the slain president was to pass his bill. Like all skilled politicians, Johnson always adjusted what he said in order to appeal to his audience, so he won over some Southerners by appealing to their self-interest. He emphasised how the bill would help to get African-Americans and Hispanic Americans working:

> *I'm gonna try to teach these nigras that don't know anything how to work for themselves instead of just breedin'; I'm gonna try to teach these Mexicans who can't talk English to learn it so they can work for themselves … and get off of our taxpayer's back.*

KEY TERMS

Filibuster Tactic prolonging congressional debates to stop bills being voted on.

Minority Leader Leader of the minority party in the House of Representatives or the Senate.

- The bill had gained increasing national support: by January 1964, 68 per cent of Americans favoured it. After Birmingham (see page 117), national religious organisations had increasingly supported the measure. Congress could not afford to ignore this marked swing in public opinion.

The Civil Rights Act (1964)

Johnson's 1964 Civil Rights Act gave the federal government the legal tools to end *de jure* segregation in the South. It prohibited discrimination in public places, furthered school desegregation and established an Equal Employment Commission. However, there were problems:

- African-Americans felt the act had not gone far enough. Most still suffered from poverty and discrimination. As a result, in the weeks following the act's passage, there were riots in the black ghettos of many East Coast cities.
- The act did little to facilitate black voting. It took Martin Luther King Jr's Selma campaign to ensure the black right to vote.

Selma and the Voting Rights Act (1965)

King explained his campaign in Selma, Alabama, saying Selma 'has become a symbol of bitter-end resistance to the civil rights movement in the Deep South.' Around 50 per cent of Selma's 29,000 population was African-American, but despite an SNCC campaign only 23 people were registered to vote. Lawsuits initiated by Robert Kennedy's Justice Department remained bogged down in the courts. The Civil Rights Act of 1964 had not brought any great improvements. King knew that Selma's Sheriff Jim Clark could be trusted to react as brutally as Bull Connor had at Birmingham, which would bring national publicity and revitalise SCLC and the civil rights movement.

Events in Selma

King led would-be voters to register at Selma County Courthouse, but despite a federal judge's ruling, they were unsuccessful. Several incidents made headlines. A trooper shot a black youth shielding his mother from a beating. Whites threw venomous snakes at African-Americans trying to register. Clark clubbed a black woman (keen for the media to show brutality, King held back men attempting to stop him). King wanted to be arrested to publicise the fact that Selma blacks were not allowed to register to vote, and his effective letter was published in the *New York Times*:

> This is Selma, Alabama. There are more Negroes in jail with me than there are on the voting rolls.

However, Selma had not proved as explosive as King had hoped, so the SCLC and SNCC organised a march from Selma to Montgomery (Alabama's capital) to publicise the need for a Voting Rights Act. Eighty Alabama whites joined the march. On what was christened 'Bloody Sunday', state troopers attacked the marchers with clubs and used tear gas. King considered the national criticism of Selma's whites that this aroused 'a shining moment in the conscience of man'. 'Let us therefore continue our triumphant march to the realization of the American Dream,' he said, as sympathetic interracial marches took place in cities such as Chicago, Detroit, New York and Boston. Although Johnson had been asking Congress for voting rights legislation for months, Congress might well have failed to deliver the Voting Rights Act without Selma.

The Voting Rights Act (1965)

The Voting Rights Act was passed because:

- King's Selma campaign had drawn national and international attention to the continuing disfranchisement of black Americans in the South
- the United States claimed to be the leader of the free world, and Communist propaganda emphasised the inequality demonstrated at Selma
- Johnson used his famous powers of persuasion, for example, in an impressive speech to Congress in March 1965.

SOURCE F

From President Johnson's speech to Congress in support of the voting rights bill (March 1965) (available from www.lbjlib.utexas.edu/johnson/archives.hom/ speeches.hom/650315.asp).

Rarely are we met with a challenge … to the values and the purposes and the meaning of our beloved Nation. The issue of equal rights for American Negroes is such an issue … The command of the Constitution is plain … It is wrong – deadly wrong – to deny any of your fellow Americans the right to vote in this country … A century has passed, more than 100 years, since the Negro was freed. And he is not fully free tonight … A century has passed, more than 100 years, since equality was promised. And yet the Negro is not equal … The real hero of this struggle is the American Negro. His actions and protests, his courage to risk safety and even to risk his life, have awakened the conscience of this Nation … He has called upon us to make good the promise of America. And who among us can say that we would have made the same progress were it not for his persistent bravery, and his faith in American democracy?

Look up King's 'I have a dream' speech in Washington in 1963. Can you find any similarities and/or differences between that speech and Source F?

Johnson's Voting Rights Act disallowed literacy tests and questions on state constitutions (see page 40), and replaced racist Southern white registrars with federal registrars.

The impact of change on the South

The end of *de jure* segregation and the black enfranchisement effected by Johnson's Civil Rights Act and Voting Rights Act revolutionised the South. By late 1966, only four Deep South states, including Alabama and Mississippi, had fewer than 50 per cent of their eligible black voters registered (see map on page 8) and by 1968 even Mississippi was up to 59 per cent. By 1980, the proportion of African-Americans registered to vote was only 7 per cent less than the proportion of whites. The numbers elected to office in the South increased sixfold from 1965 to 1969, then doubled between 1969 and 1980. In 1960 there had been no black officials in Mississippi; by 1980 there were over 300.

In 1980, King's old friend Bayard Rustin recorded that he found the South transformed 'from a reactionary bastion into a region moderate in racial outlook and more enlightened in social and economic policy'. Johnson's Education Acts (see page 145) speeded up school desegregation and helped black colleges. His civil rights legislation opened the way for a larger and richer black middle class. His Great Society contributed to decreases in black unemployment (down 34 per cent) and in the percentage of blacks living below the poverty line (down 25 per cent) in the South and across the nation. However, many African-Americans continued to suffer poor housing, poor schools, poor job opportunities and an inability to get out of the poverty trap. Doctors reported to a 1969 congressional hearing that a considerable number of black children in Mississippi were so hungry that they ate tree bark.

Limitations on Johnson's role in passing civil rights legislation

Johnson had done more for African-Americans than any previous president, but found it hard to progress further after 1965. The underlying reason was the change in white opinion that resulted from black violence (see below) and the cost of the Vietnam War. That change impacted on Congress and local officials.

Congress

After 1965, Congress responded to decreased white sympathy for civil rights legislation:

- In 1966, Congress rejected an administration civil rights bill, one aim of which was to prohibit housing discrimination. Polls showed that 70 per cent of white voters opposed large numbers of black neighbours.
- Johnson found it hard to sustain support for his war on poverty. In response to his 1968 request for legislation to help African-American children suffering from rat bites in rundown ghetto accommodation, members of Congress joked that he should send in a federal cat army to deal with his 'civil rats bill'.

Local officials

Johnson had to rely on state and local authorities, officials and employees to carry out his programmes. They were sometimes reluctant to co-operate. For example, although the 1964 Civil Rights Act said federal funding should not be given to segregated schools, Chicago's Mayor Daley was a valuable political ally, so he got his funds and kept his *de facto* segregated schools. This pattern was repeated in other Northern cities.

Urban riots, Black Power and the white backlash

Successive summers of rioting in black ghettos from 1964 until 1968 caused a white backlash. After the riots in Los Angeles' Watts ghetto in 1965 (see page 169) the exasperated Los Angeles' police chief asked what else anyone could expect, 'when you keep telling [black] people they are unfairly treated and teach them disrespect for the law'. As television showed black youths shouting 'burn, burn, burn', gun sales to suburban whites soared. Tired of being blamed for the black predicament, whites were turning against Johnson's reform programme. Johnson was amazed, disappointed and hurt by what he called 'that crazy rioting' in Watts: 'How is it possible, after all we've accomplished?'

The riots helped ensure that Johnson could do little more to help African-Americans after the 1965 Voting Rights Act. A 1965 poll showed that 88 per cent of whites advocated black self-improvement, more education and harder work, rather than government help. A 1966 poll showed that 90 per cent opposed new civil rights legislation. In a 1967 poll, 52 per cent said Johnson was going 'too fast' on integration, and only 10 per cent said 'not fast enough'. Black militants also fuelled the white backlash. When the **Black Panthers** (see page 172) advocated self-defence and **Black Power**, they frightened and alienated whites.

The Vietnam War and rising taxes

The expense and distraction of the Vietnam War (see page 157) stopped Johnson introducing all the social reforms he desired. The war was the main reason why the **federal government deficit** rose from $1.6 billion in 1965 to $25.3 billion by 1968. The deficit forced Johnson to ask Congress for tax rises. White voters attributed these higher taxes to the near 50 per cent increase in federal expenditure on the poor. As a result, Johnson's social reform programme grew increasingly unpopular. White Americans were tired of paying out for America's oppressed minorities. Polls recorded 'racial problems' as the nation's most important domestic issue and many believed that Johnson's reforms encouraged riots and Black Power militancy (see page 172).

Johnson's 'open housing law'

While Johnson supported integrated housing, arguing that 'imprisoning the Negro in the slums' was immoral and exacerbated racial tensions, whites opposed integrated housing, sometimes because of racism, mostly because black movement into white neighbourhoods made property values fall. Johnson received his worst-ever hate mail over his plea for integrated housing, and Congress repeatedly rejected his appeals for legislation until King's assassination in 1968 made Congress feel it had to respond with a legislative tribute. The 1968 Fair Housing Act prohibited discrimination in the sale or rental of housing, but proved difficult to enforce in the face of determined white opposition.

 **KEY TERMS**

Black Panthers A group of militant black activists who used revolutionary rhetoric, ostentatiously carried guns, monitored police brutality and distributed free meals to the ghetto poor.

Black Power A vaguely defined black movement with aims including separatism, and greater economic, political, social and legal equality for African–Americans.

Federal government deficit When the federal government is spending more than it is receiving in taxes.

Too far, too fast

'We have come too far too fast during your administration,' a leading Democrat told Johnson. Johnson recognised that he could not work miracles. In June 1966, he told a White House conference on black problems that:

> The dilemma that you deal with is too deeply rooted in pride and prejudice, too profound and too complex, and too critical to our future for any one man or any one administration to ever resolve.

He knew there was a limit to the amount of legislation that any administration could pass: 'It's a little like whiskey,' said Johnson. 'It is good. But if you drink too much it comes up on you.'

Nevertheless, Johnson's achievements were great. His Civil Rights Act and Voting Rights Act transformed his beloved South. Another important Johnson legacy was his Executive Order of 1965, which required any institution receiving federal funding to employ more non-whites. This accelerated the spread of **affirmative action**, which liberals praised as greatly helping minorities in education and employment, and conservatives criticised as discriminating against whites and demeaning blacks.

Although the situation of many black Americans remained dire, Johnson had helped improve their social, political and economic status through his civil rights legislation, affirmative action policies and War on Poverty. 'I think Johnson was the best we ever had,' said civil rights activist Bayard Rustin.

Developments in the civil rights movement

Civil rights organisations such as the NAACP, SCLC and CORE focused on the fight against *de jure* segregation and disfranchisement in the South between 1956 and 1965. After the 1964 Civil Rights Act and the 1965 Voting Rights Act, the movement's mission in the South seemed accomplished. Meanwhile, another strand of the civil rights movement was developing in the North, where the focus was upon ghetto deprivation. Public attention was first drawn to ghetto problems by Malcolm X and the **Nation of Islam (NOI)**. While the civil rights movement in the South sought integration with whites, Malcolm X and the NOI were part of the black separatist tradition.

Elijah Muhammad and the Nation of Islam

The NOI (a name suggesting a separate nation within the USA) was founded by Wallace Fard in Detroit in 1930, then led by Elijah Muhammad from 1934 to 1975. Although Elijah Muhammad said he was the prophet of Allah, the 'Messenger of Islam', his teachings differed from those of orthodox Islam. For example, he claimed that Allah originally created human beings with black skin, but then an evil scientist, Yakub, created other races. His last evil creation was the white race. Whites would rule the world for several thousand years, but then Allah would return and end their supremacy.

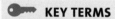

KEY TERMS

Affirmative action Giving disadvantaged minorities extra opportunities (even if others were better qualified) in education and employment in order to compensate for previous unfair treatment.

Nation of Islam (NOI) Black separatist religion that considered all whites evil. Also known as Black Muslims.

Malcolm X

1925   Born Malcolm Little in Omaha, Nebraska

1946–52 Joined the Nation of Islam while imprisoned

1959   National fame after being featured in a television documentary called *The Hate That Hate Produced*

1963   Criticised the March on Washington

1964   Split from the NOI, then rejected its teachings

1965   Assassinated by NOI gunmen

Malcolm Little's father believed in black separatism, and Malcolm attributed his death (1931) to white supremacists. Malcolm's impoverished, widowed mother could not cope and was placed in a mental hospital (1939). He subsequently claimed that a teacher told him his dream of becoming a lawyer was not a 'realistic goal for a nigger'. Full of resentment, he moved to Boston's black ghetto (1941). There, he took traditional black employment as a shoeshine boy and railroad waiter, then switched to drug dealing, pimping and burgling. In 1946, he was sentenced to ten years' imprisonment. In prison, he joined the NOI, which taught him 'the white man is the devil … a perfect echo … [of my] lifelong experience'. When released in 1952, he adopted the name Malcolm X (the X was in place of the African name taken from his enslaved ancestors).

He rose quickly within the NOI, recruiting thousands of new members in Detroit, Boston, Philadelphia and New York. He became Minister of Temple Number 7 in Harlem.

After the 1959 television programme *The Hate That Hate Produced*, Malcolm attracted national attention, particularly for saying that African-Americans should defend themselves 'by any means necessary'. He criticised King's 'non-violence', and mocked the March on Washington as the 'farce on Washington'. In 1963, Elijah Muhammad suspended Malcolm for making unpopular remarks about President Kennedy's assassination. He was disillusioned by Elijah Muhammad's romantic affairs and his refusal to allow him to join those risking their lives in Birmingham in 1963: 'We spout our militant revolutionary rhetoric,' said Malcolm, but 'when our own brothers are … killed, we do nothing'. In 1964, he left the NOI.

Malcolm was important as the harbinger of Black Power of the 1960s and as a role model, inspiration and icon for discontented ghetto residents. He also played a big part in the alienation of white America. 'Yes, I am an extremist,' he said. 'The black race in North America is in an extremely bad condition.'

The NOI aimed to

- provide African-Americans with an alternative to the white man's Christian religion (Malcolm X said Christianity was a religion 'designed to fill [black] hearts with the desire to be white … A white Jesus. A white virgin. White angels. White everything. But a black Devil of course')
- increase black self-esteem
- keep white and black Americans separate (Malcolm X mocked African-Americans such as King who dreamt of integration, saying, 'Imagine, you have the chance to go to the toilet with white folks!')
- encourage African-Americans to improve their economic situation.

From the 1930s, the NOI established temples in Northern black ghettos such as Detroit, New York and Chicago. In the 1950s, the NOI's most brilliant preacher, Malcolm X, attracted the attention and devotion of frustrated ghetto residents with his rejection of integration and his bitter attacks on white America. However, the movement gained little publicity until a 1959 television documentary called *The Hate that Hate Produced* brought the NOI national prominence and white hostility. Addressing 10,000 people in Washington DC in 1959, Elijah Muhammad attacked the 'turn the other cheek' philosophy of Martin Luther King Jr and Christianity as perpetuating enslavement. He advocated separatism and armed self-defence against white aggression.

Achievements of the NOI

The NOI attracted much criticism from both blacks and whites:

- Some of the NOI's solutions to black problems, such as a return to Africa or a separate black state in the Deep South, were unrealistic.
- NOI teachings exacerbated interracial divisions and antagonised other African-Americans (the NOI derided Martin Luther King Jr as an **Uncle Tom**, a 'fool' who humiliatingly begged for access to a white-dominated world and urged non-violence on his defenceless followers, while he described the NOI as a 'hate group').
- The NOI lost some credibility among African-Americans when Malcolm X and of two of Elijah Muhammad's sons left it and publicised the rampant materialism and hypocrisy among the movement's leadership (1964), and over NOI involvement in the assassination of Malcolm X (1965).
- Although the NOI and the Black Power movement both favoured separatism, cultural revival and self-help, Elijah Muhammad's dismissive attitude towards non-Muslim African culture alienated some Black Power activists. For example, in 1972, Elijah Muhammad – who hated what he called 'jungle styles', such as Afro haircuts or colourful African-style garments – said, 'I am already civilized and I am ready to civilize Africa'.

On the other hand, most Black Power advocates revered Elijah Muhammad and the NOI as forerunners of the new black nationalism, and there were many positive achievements. Estimates of NOI membership by 1969 ranged from 25,000 to 250,000. Numbers were inevitably limited because the NOI demanded much: members were expected to live a religious life and to reject adultery, alcohol, tobacco and flamboyant clothing. However, the NOI newspaper *Muhammad Speaks* had a weekly circulation of 600,000 by the mid-1970s, indicating that non-members found comfort in its message of separatism and self-defence. The NOI attracted and inspired ghetto inhabitants because of its self-confidence and emphasis on racial pride and economic self-help. Elijah Muhammad created many businesses, such as restaurants, bakeries and grocery stores, that symbolised black success and gave rare employment opportunities in the ghettos. The NOI established schools in cities such as Detroit and Chicago in which children were taught black history, which Malcolm X emphasised as very important: 'We are lost people. We don't know our names, language, homeland, God or religion.'

When Elijah Muhammad died in 1975, his obituaries in the white press were surprisingly favourable. *Newsweek* described him as 'a kind of prophetic voice in the flowering of black identity and pride', while the *Washington Post* said

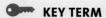
KEY TERM

Uncle Tom A black person who behaves in an overly subservient way to whites. Based on a character in Harriet Beecher Stowe's *Uncle Tom's Cabin*.

he inculcated 'pride in thousands of black derelicts, bums, and drug addicts, turning outlaws into useful, productive men and women'. The NOI continued to thrive after Elijah Muhammad's death.

The aims, methods and achievements of Malcolm X

Malcolm X aimed to improve the lives of black Americans. His main method was the use of sermons, speeches and writing to advertise and encourage critical thinking on race problems, and, some would argue, to encourage racial hatred and violence. Towards the end of his life, Malcolm claimed that he put forward the extremist position in order to make King's demands more acceptable to the white population. In Washington in 1964, Malcolm attended the debate on the civil rights bill, saying, 'I'm here to remind the white man of the alternative to Dr King.'

> ## Malcolm, Martin and the American Dream
>
> In 1962, Malcolm X said, 'What is looked upon as an American Dream for white people has long been an American nightmare for black people.' In his famous speech during the March on Washington in 1963, Martin Luther King Jr said the black dream of freedom was 'a dream deeply rooted in the American Dream'. Malcolm responded, 'While King was having a dream, the rest of us Negroes are having a nightmare.'

A changed Malcolm X

In March 1964, Malcolm left the NOI, and went on to establish the Organisation of Afro-American Unity (OAAU), which aimed to unite everyone of African descent and to promote black political, social and economic independence. The month after, while on pilgrimage to Mecca, Malcolm established good relations with white Muslims, and rejected the NOI's racist theology. The NOI harassed and intimidated him until his assassination in 1965 – by NOI members. Some historians consider Malcolm's development genuine, while others claim that his 'sudden realisation' of the 'true' Islam was a ploy to re-create his public image. Many people ignore the changed Malcolm, preferring to focus on his earlier, more extreme beliefs and actions.

Malcolm X's achievements have always been controversial. Thurgood Marshall (see page 122) was particularly critical of the NOI ('run by a bunch of thugs') and of Malcolm ('What did he achieve?'). Black baseball player Jackie Robinson pointed out that while King and others put their lives on the line in places like Birmingham, Malcolm stayed in safer places such as majority-black Harlem. Many considered him irresponsible and negative and blamed him for the increased black violence (in 1965, the Watts rioters had cried, 'Long live Malcolm X!'). While he criticised civil rights activists such as Martin Luther King Jr, he never established organisations as effective or long lasting as the NAACP or the SCLC. His suggestions that black people were frequently left with no alternative other than violence seemed negative, irresponsible and unhelpful. CORE's James Farmer called him a 'talented demagogue'.

On the other hand, Malcolm rightly drew early attention to dreadful ghetto conditions. He became a black icon and role model for black youth, particularly through his exploration of his feelings of rejection and his search for his identity in his 1965 *The Autobiography of Malcolm X*. One Harlem woman said, 'He taught me that I was more than a "Little Black Sambo" or "kinky hair" or "nigger".' Perhaps most important of all, Malcolm inspired the new generation of black leaders such as SNCC's Stokely Carmichael and CORE's Floyd McKissick and the Black Power movement in general. He was the first prominent advocate of separatism and what subsequently became known as Black Power.

The radicalisation of African-Americans

The radicalisation of African-Americans was demonstrated in the Black Power movement, the origins of which lay in the influence of Malcolm X, ghetto problems, and the disillusion experienced by SNCC and CORE amongst others.

Ghetto problems

Although the great civil rights movement of 1954–65 effected change in the South, it did nothing for the problems of the ghettos in the North, Midwest and West. That prompted King to switch his focus to the ghettos. He organised a campaign in Chicago in 1966, moving his family into a ghetto apartment for the duration. They found ghetto life soul-destroying. Accommodation was poor, amenities were few.

Those born in the ghetto found it hard to break out of the cycle of poverty. Only 32 per cent of ghetto pupils finished high school, compared to 56 per cent of white children. Ghetto schools did not provide a solid educational foundation for good jobs. Increased automation decreased the availability of unskilled employment in the 1950s and 1960s and contributed to disproportionate black unemployment. In the early 1960s, 46 per cent of unemployed Americans were black. Some ghettos, including Chicago's, had 50–70 per cent black youth unemployment.

The activities of the older civil rights organisations in the ghettos had little positive impact. King's Chicago campaign attracted a great deal of national attention, but whereas Northern whites often sympathised with African-Americans who suffered segregation and disfranchisement in the South, they were unsympathetic when King's Chicago campaign drew attention to the exclusion of African-Americans from Northern white working-class suburbs such as Cicero. King said, 'I have been in many demonstrations all across the South, but I have never seen in Alabama and Mississippi mobs as hostile and hate-filled as I have seen in Chicago.' Most Northern whites sympathised with Cicero's white residents and their belief that an influx of African-Americans would cause local schools to deteriorate and property values to plummet.

Unsurprisingly, ghetto residents took matters into their own hands and engaged in riots.

The impact of change: urban riots

During the five so-called 'long hot summers' of 1964–8, inner-city riots became an annual summer event. The first major race riot was in Watts (Los Angeles) in 1965. With 34 deaths, 1000 injuries, 3500 rioters and looters arrested, and over $40 million of damage to largely white-owned businesses, the Watts riots gained national attention. King told the press that it was 'a class revolt of underprivileged against privileged … the main issue is economic'. After the Watts riots, virtually every large US city outside the South had a race riot. For example, in July 1967, amid rumours of police brutality against a black taxi driver, Newark's black ghetto erupted. In six days of riots, 26 died, 1500 were injured, and much of the inner city was burned out. Then Detroit followed. Forty died, 2000 were injured, 5000 were arrested and 5000 were made homeless. Johnson had to send federal troops to settle Detroit. Many cities had several riots, for example, Oakland, California (1965 and 1966), Cleveland, Ohio (1966 and 1968), and Chicago, Illinois (1966 and 1968). One Johnson aide counted 225 'hostile outbursts' from 1964 to 1968, in which 191 were killed, 7942 wounded and 49,607 arrested.

> ### King and Watts
>
> Ghetto residents in Watts, Los Angeles, did not suffer from the *de jure* segregation on which Martin Luther King Jr focused, but from the poverty, *de facto* housing segregation and discrimination that characterised the ghettos of the North and West. As a result, one Watts resident said, 'King, and all his talk about non-violence, did not mean much. Watts had respect for King, but the talk about non-violence made us laugh. Watts wasn't suffering from segregation, or the lack of civil rights. You didn't have two drinking fountains … . When Johnson signed the civil rights bill in [19]64, nobody even thought about it in Watts … It had nothing to do with us.'
>
> 'How can you say you won, when 34 Negroes are dead, your community is destroyed, and whites are using the riots as an excuse for inaction?' King asked a group of Watts residents. 'We won because we made them pay attention to us,' they shouted back.

Causes of the urban riots

While there was certainly a 'copycat' element to the riots, the FBI blamed the misery of ghetto life, oppressive summer weather and Communist agitation. Johnson blamed poverty and despair. Whereas 8 per cent of whites lived below the poverty line, 30 per cent of blacks did so; 18 per cent of whites lived in substandard housing, compared to 50 per cent of non-whites. Between 1959 and 1965, the number of poor Americans decreased from 39 million to 33 million, but the percentage of poor African-Americans increased from 28 to 31 per cent. Black unemployment (at 7 per cent) was twice that of whites, but the riots could not just have been about unemployment because in Detroit, 80 per cent of those arrested had well-paid jobs. Johnson explained that it was more likely 'bad housing' and 'the hate and bitterness which has been developing over many years'.

Johnson's investigatory Kerner Commission (1967–8) blamed white racism above all, saying that African-Americans saw the police as 'the occupying army of white America, a hostile power'. The absence of black policemen fuelled ghetto tensions against white police 'outsiders'. A subsequent analysis of ghetto riots found that 40 per cent involved alleged police abuse or discrimination. The *Boston Globe* described the 1967 Newark riots as 'a revolution of black Americans against white Americans, a violent petition for the redress of long-standing grievances'. It said Johnson's legislation had effected little fundamental improvement.

As ghetto misery was long standing, it obviously cannot adequately explain the eruptions of 1964–8. Why were there unprecedented numbers of riots then?

- Some people suggest that Johnson's extravagant Great Society rhetoric raised hopes that were dashed and therefore played a part in provoking the riots.
- The assassination of Martin Luther King Jr by a white racist in April 1968 provoked major riots in 100 cities, with 46 dead, 3000 injured and 27,000 arrested. A total of 21,000 federal troops and 34,000 national guardsmen restored order following $45 million of damage to property.
- The impact of change in the South was perhaps the most important reason for the riots. African-Americans outside the South concluded that protests brought improvements and were resentful that although the South had changed, nothing had been done for the ghettos of the North and West.

Why whites did not want to help

Reports such as the Kerner Report recommended increased expenditure on the ghettos, but most whites did not want to pay extra taxes to improve the ghettos, particularly after the Vietnam War led to tax rises. Whites did not want to ease ghetto overcrowding by welcoming black residents to their neighbourhood: property prices would plummet and black children from a deprived background might hold back white children in school and damage their employment prospects.

While whites increasingly perceived blacks as seeking 'handouts', blacks increasingly perceived whites as uninterested and unsympathetic. Not surprisingly then, by the late 1960s a new generation of black radicals had emerged out of the impoverished ghettos and, especially through the Black Power movement, demanded change.

The radicalisation of SNCC and CORE

Many ghetto residents felt that organisations such as the NAACP and SCLC knew little about ghetto life and were unhelpful and ineffective. Many younger black activists criticised 'de great lawd' Martin Luther King Jr and his emphasis on the South, the 'white man's' Christian religion and non-violence – none of which seemed helpful to the ghettos. However, ghetto residents recognised that civil rights activism had led to improvements and were inspired to be active themselves. Some rioted (see above). Others looked to new leaders such as Malcolm X and Stokely Carmichael. Their advocacy of self-defence seemed a more appropriate response to white oppression than King's 'love thine enemy'.

SNCC members disillusioned over the slow progress toward racial equality and the lack of federal protection during SNCC's voter registration campaign in 1964 (the Mississippi Freedom Summer), elected Stokely Carmichael as SNCC leader (he replaced the less militant John Lewis). CORE also elected a more radical leader (Floyd McKissick replaced James Farmer). Both organisations excluded white members (SNCC from 1966, CORE from 1968) and declared non-violence inappropriate if black people needed to defend themselves.

The radicalisation of the younger generation of African-Americans was demonstrated in the Meredith 'March against Fear' in 1966.

The Meredith March

Famous as the University of Mississippi's first black student (see page 123), James Meredith planned a 220-mile walk from Memphis, Tennessee, to Jackson, Mississippi, to encourage African-Americans to vote. After he was shot by a white bigot and temporarily immobilised, black organisations declared that they would continue his walk. There were 400 marchers by the third day, including Martin Luther King Jr and the new SNCC leader, Stokely Carmichael.

Black divisions damaged the March. The NAACP wanted it to focus national attention on the new civil rights bill and withdrew when Carmichael criticised the bill. King welcomed white participants; SNCC rejected them. After Carmichael was arrested and white bystanders waved Confederate flags, shouted obscenities and threw things at the marchers, SNCC people sang:

> *Jingle bells, shotgun shells,*
> *Freedom all the way,*
> *Oh what fun it is to blast,*
> *A [white] trooper man away.*

When released, Carmichael urged the burning of 'every courthouse in Mississippi' and demanded 'Black Power'. Crowds took up the chant. King tried to encourage chants of 'freedom now' lest the words 'Black Power' alienate white sympathisers and encourage a white backlash. He urged non-violence and begged Johnson to send in federal troops to protect the marchers but, as in Selma, Johnson refused. Meanwhile, Meredith felt excluded and began a march of his own. Some SCLC leaders joined him to disguise the split. The 15,000 main marchers ended at Jackson with rival chants of 'Black Power' and 'freedom now'.

King despaired. 'I don't know what I'm going to do. The government has got to give me some victories if I'm going to keep people non-violent.' He felt he could no longer co-operate with the SNCC, telling the press, 'Because Stokely Carmichael chose the march as an arena for a debate over Black Power, we did not get to emphasize the evils of Mississippi and the need for the 1966 Civil Rights Act.' He admitted that African-Americans were 'very, very close' to a public split. The NAACP no longer wanted to co-operate with the SCLC or SNCC and it seemed that leadership of the civil rights movement was passing to the advocates of Black Power.

Black Power

Black Power meant different things to different people:

- For some it meant black supremacy or revolution. For example, in 1968, Elijah Muhammad said, 'Black Power means the black people will rule the white people on earth as the white people have ruled the black people for the past six thousand years.'
- SNCC's Floyd McKissick said 'Black Power is not hatred.' It 'did not mean black supremacy, did not mean exclusion of whites from the Negro revolution, and did not mean advocacy of violence and riots', but 'political power, economic power, and a new self-image for Negroes'.
- Conservative black Republican Nathan Wright equated Black Power with black capitalism and organised conferences in Newark in 1967 and Philadelphia in 1968. He won support from SCLC and from Republican presidential candidate Richard Nixon, who said Black Power meant, 'more black ownership, for from this can flow the rest – black pride, black jobs, black opportunity and yes, Black Power'.
- King called Black Power 'a slogan without a programme', but when people persisted in using the phrase, he tried to give it more positive connotations:

    The Negro is in dire need of a sense of dignity and a sense of pride, and I think Black Power is an attempt to develop pride. And there is no doubt about the need for power – he can't get into the mainstream of society without it … Black Power means instilling within the Negro a sense of belonging and appreciation of heritage, a racial pride … We must never be ashamed of being black.

One of the few areas of unanimity on Black Power was this emphasis on black pride and black culture. African-Americans frequently adopted 'Afro' hairstyles and African garb. Black college students successfully agitated for the introduction of black studies programmes.

Perhaps the most famous manifestation of Black Power was the Black Panthers.

The Black Panthers

The 'Black Panther Party for Self-Defense' was established in Oakland, California, in October 1966, by 24-year-old Huey Newton and 30-year-old

SOURCE G

Huey Newton, founder of the Black Panthers in his San Francisco, California headquarters in 1967.

What point do you suppose Newton was trying to make in the photograph in Source G?

Bobby Seale. The Black Panthers adopted a predominantly black paramilitary uniform, with berets and leather jackets, and held inspirational rallies characterised by cries of 'Power to the People' and 'The revolution has come, it's time to pick up the gun.' They had a radical and nationalistic manifesto that sought

- federal government compensation to black Americans for the enslavement of their ancestors
- freedom for incarcerated African-Americans, and black juries when black people were tried
- black exemption from military service

- a UN-supervised referendum of black Americans 'for the purpose of determining the will of black people as to their national destiny'
- no police brutality
- improvements in ghetto living conditions.

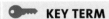

KEY TERM

Chapters Local branches of an association.

The Black Panthers never boasted more than 5000 members. Their 30 urban **chapters** were mostly in West Coast cities such as Oakland and Northern cities such as New York, Boston and Chicago. The Black Panthers won a great deal of respect in the ghettos, especially for their emphasis on self-help: they set up ghetto clinics to advise on health, welfare and legal rights, and ran lessons to educate young people in their beliefs. They provided childcare for working mothers and free food. For example, in 1970 the Southern California chapter of the Free Breakfast programme served up over 1700 meals weekly to the ghetto poor.

Citing the second amendment to the American Constitution (which said that citizens had the right to carry arms), armed Black Panthers followed police cars in the ghettos in order to expose police brutality. This led to some violent shoot-outs. In May 1967, Black Panthers surrounded and entered the California State Capital Building in Sacramento, accusing the legislature of considering repressive legislation. The Black Panthers routinely engaged in petty crime and sought confrontation with, and advocated the killing of, police officers. Not surprisingly, they were targeted and destroyed by the police and FBI during 1967–9.

A 1970 poll revealed that 64 per cent of black Americans took pride in the Black Panthers, although Newton's biographer Hugh Pearson claimed they were 'little more than a temporary media phenomenon'.

The decline of Black Power

Black Power 'peaked' in 1970, but this was followed by a swift decline because

- the movement was always relatively ill-defined, which contributed to poor organisation and disagreements over aims
- the movement never really produced a persuasive and effective blueprint for change (for example, talk of a separate black nation within the USA was unrealistic)
- when female supporters of Black Power found their role limited, they frequently turned to feminism instead
- when SNCC and CORE became more militant and expelled whites, they lost their invaluable white liberal funding (SNCC ceased to exist in 1973).

What had the Black Power movement achieved?

Groups such as the Black Panthers gave useful practical help to ghetto-dwellers. More importantly, there is no doubt that talk of and/or participation in the Black Power movement raised the morale of many black Americans. Perhaps the main legacy with regard to black pride was the establishment of courses on black history and culture in American educational institutions. It could also be said that Black Power activists, like civil rights activists, kept the ghetto problems on the political agenda and helped ensure the federal government's promotion of affirmative action (see page 164).

On the other hand, some have argued that Black Power contributed to the demise of what had been an effective civil rights movement. They claim that ghetto rioters and armed Black Panthers helped decrease the white sympathy that had been key to the progress of the non-violent civil rights activists. It could, of course, be argued that the civil rights movement would have lost momentum and effectiveness regardless because, as Black Power adherents found, the Northern ghetto problem proved insoluble.

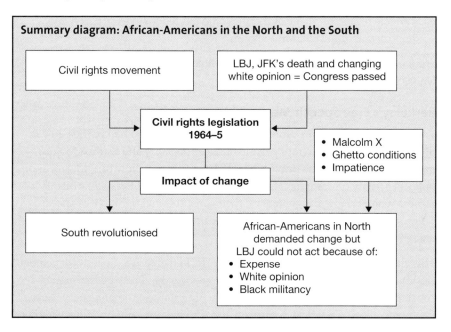

Summary diagram: African-Americans in the North and the South

Social divisions and protest movements

▶ *Did the 'decade of protest' change the USA?*

While the 1950s was a decade considered by many to be characterised by consensus, conformity and stagnation, the 1960s was a decade of change and protests from Americans who did not share in the American Dream and/or sought to revise it. The civil rights movement helped inspire the radicalisation of some African-Americans and also other protesters such as students, women and those opposed to the Vietnam War.

Education and youth

Unprecedented numbers of students protested in the 1960s for some or all of the following reasons:

- The rocketing student population decided it should and could protest without risk because everyone else seemed to be protesting, there was safety in numbers, and students had no jobs to lose or families to support.
- President Kennedy's New Frontier rhetoric had encouraged idealism on issues such as peace and prejudice. Many students took up his challenges and demanded peace in Vietnam and an end to prejudice against ethnic minorities.
- The civil rights movement gave practice and inspiration to many student protesters.
- Students resented college authorities who treated them as children and supported an unjust war in Vietnam.

Student radicalism first gained national attention in December 1964 at the University of California at Berkeley.

Berkeley's Free Speech Movement

The leader of the Berkeley protests was Mario Savio. Savio had participated in SNCC's black voter registration campaign (see page 85) and wanted to raise money for SNCC, but the university authorities did not allow fundraising and political activity on campus. This prompted thousands of Berkeley students to protest against this infringement on their constitutional right to free speech. They occupied the administration building until the police ejected them and made 800 arrests.

This student movement became known as the Berkeley Free Speech Movement (FSM). Its slogan was, 'You can't trust anyone over 30.' The students gained considerable support from the Berkeley teaching staff, so the university backed down and allowed political discussion and activities on campus. However, there was another flare-up in 1965 when a student was arrested for displaying the word 'fuck'.

FSM triggered nationwide student protest. Students criticised their universities as impersonal, bureaucratic and excessively regulatory (the **age of majority** was 21, so universities served *in loco parentis*), and demanded a say in university government. Anti-war students disliked universities undertaking (paid) research for government defence agencies. After Johnson sent the first American ground troops to Vietnam in 1965, the war became the greatest target of student protesters, although by 1969 many older Americans were also involved.

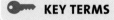

KEY TERMS

Age of majority Age at which an American legally became an adult (ranging from 18 to 21 years, depending on the US state).

In loco parentis In place of parents.

Anti-war movements

The Student Peace Union, established in 1959, had 3000 members by 1962, but tens of thousands more students became anti-war activists in response to the Vietnam War. Their motives varied:

- Some feared the draft.
- Some believed the Vietnamese should be left to decide on their form of government.
- Some were particularly opposed the American bombing that caused Vietnamese civilian casualties.

The first notable protest took place in May 1964, when 1000 Yale University students staged a protest march in New York City. During 1965, many universities held 'teach-ins' with anti-war lectures and debates: 20,000 participated in a Berkeley teach-in. The protests frequently led to disorder: in 1965, 8000 marchers (mostly from Berkeley) clashed with the Oakland police and vandalised cars and buildings.

The largest anti-war protest to date was staged by SDS in Washington DC in 1965. Possibly as many as 25,000 participated in a March that brought SDS national attention. SDS and the New Left (see page 131) established the National Mobilisation Committee to End the War (the Mobe) and organised a demonstration in Washington as part of the Stop the Draft Week in 1967. Over 100,000 attended the march, chanting 'Hell no, we won't go.'

Growing anti-war violence

During 'Stop the Draft' week, draft cards were publicly burned across America, and several thousand Berkeley radicals tried to close down the Oakland draft headquarters. The demonstrators faced 2000 police, who attacked them with clubs, so they retaliated with cans, bottles, smoke bombs and ball-bearings placed on the street to stop police horses. High on drugs, some vandalised cars, parking meters, newsstands and trees.

By 1968, many protests were violent: the main targets were the offices of the Reserve Officer Training Corps (ROTC) and campus administration buildings. Across the nation, many of these offices and buildings were burned or bombed. The trigger for many of the protests in 1968 was events at Columbia University in New York City, which demonstrated how anti-war sentiment often combined with other grievances to generate youth activism.

Columbia University protests

In 1968, Columbia University students had multiple grievances, including:

- The university's involvement in weapons research, which assisted the government and the Vietnam War effort.

- The relationship between the university and the black and Hispanic populations in adjacent Harlem. Since 1958, Columbia expansion programmes had led to the eviction of several thousand Harlem residents from properties owned by the university. In 1968, Columbia planned to construct a gym in a public park. The Harlem population would be able to access the gym, but through a separate door. Students interpreted this as a segregationist policy and opposed the construction of 'Gym Crow' (defenders said that the separate door was necessary because the gym was situated on a hill).

These grievances generated protests in which 1000 of Columbia's 17,000 students participated. Students seized five university buildings and covered the walls with pictures of Malcolm X and Communist heroes such as **Karl Marx** and **Che Guevara**. The police used clubs and made 692 arrests. Columbia shut down for that term, and abandoned the gym and many defence contracts. Hundreds of similar occupations followed across the nation.

Did student protests achieve anything?

Some protesters failed to achieve their aims, as with the ineffective opposition of SDS and the New Left to American materialism. Other protesters achieved their aims, as with the civil rights movement in the South and the behaviour of university authorities. Many people believe that the anti-war protests, in which the students constituted a majority, helped persuade Johnson to halt escalation and Nixon to end the war (see page 209). Others argue that Johnson and Nixon were motivated by their realisation that America could not win the war. Some say it was a combination of both.

While some people credit the student protesters with improving the quality of American life for ethnic minorities and with ensuring the US withdrawal from Vietnam, others believe that student protest promoted violence, offered little that was constructive and damaged the great American liberal tradition. Many contemporary Americans disliked protesters and the **counterculture**. This contributed to a conservative reaction that helped gain the Republican Richard Nixon the White House in the election of November 1968.

The youth counterculture

There is disagreement over the definition of the counterculture. Some define it as including all who protested against the dominant culture, such as feminists, anti-war activists, the Black Panthers (see page 172) and **hippies**. Some focus solely on hippies when they consider the counterculture. The hippies certainly seem to best illustrate a movement that adopted an alternative lifestyle to that of the dominant culture.

The roots of the hippie counterculture lay in the beat generation (see page 131). The hippie counterculture rejected American society's emphasis

KEY TERMS

Karl Marx First great theorist of Communism.

Che Guevara Argentine revolutionary, closely associated with Fidel Castro and Cuba.

Counterculture An alternative lifestyle to the dominant culture; in the case of 1960s' America, the 'drop-out' mentality, as compared to the dominant, materialistic, hard-working culture of the students' parents.

Hippies Young people (often students) who, in the 1960s, rejected the beliefs and fashions of the older generation, and favoured free love and drugs.

on individualism, competitiveness and materialism for communal living and harmony. In their uniform of faded blue jeans, they listened to music that reaffirmed their beliefs, singing Joan Baez's *We Shall Overcome*, the Beatles' *All You Need is Love*, and anti-war songs.

In the mid-1960s, a group of alienated young people moved into San Francisco's Haight-Ashbury area, wearing 'alternative' clothes such as Indian kaftans, attending '**happenings**', smoking and selling cannabis, adopting new names such as Coyote and Apache, and growing their hair. Perhaps as many as 100,000 hippies visited Haight-Ashbury, which became a centre of a bohemian lifestyle and was rechristened 'Hashbury' because of the popularity of **hash**. Two events in San Francisco in 1967 gained national attention. The first was the Human Be-in that took place in Golden Gate Park in January 1967. Thousands of young people marched to celebrate personal freedom, communal living and environmentalism. The second was the 'Summer of Love', which attracted tens of thousands of followers of the counterculture. *Time* magazine estimated that there might be 300,000 hippies, because every major city had 'hippie enclaves'.

Woodstock

The greatest counterculture happening was the Woodstock rock festival in New York State in 1969, which 400,000 attended. Their favourite slogan was 'Make love not war'. One enthusiastic participant recalled how 'everyone swam nude in the lake, [having sex] was easier than getting breakfast, and the pigs [police] just smiled and passed out the oats [drugs]'. The headline acts were Joan Baez, Jefferson Airplane and Jimi Hendrix. Hendrix's performance of the American national anthem, 'Star Spangled Banner', attracted criticism from those who interpreted his use of amplifier feedback and distortion to make a sound like exploding bombs as an anti-war statement.

The significance of the hippies

The hippie movement had faded by the mid-1970s, but it had influenced US society. Hippies drew attention to and popularised Eastern philosophy and religion, health foods and environmentalism, and contributed to the liberalisation of attitudes towards sex and drugs. They also helped trigger the conservative reaction that brought Richard Nixon to the White House. Overall, the impact and significance of the hippies was of less importance than that of those who protested against the Vietnam War and racial and gender inequality.

Feminism

In 1966, Betty Friedan (see page 129) and others formed the National Organisation for Women (NOW). NOW held its founding conference in Washington DC in October 1966 and issued a Statement of Purpose explaining why the organisation was needed (see Source H). The organisers were unhappy when the government's Equal Employment Opportunities Commission

KEY TERMS

Happenings 1960s' events such as rock concerts and festivals attended by hippies, among others.

Hash Also known as marijuana, cannabis or pot.

Title VII The anti-sex discrimination section of the 1964 Civil Rights Act.

Reproductive rights A woman's right to know about and have access to contraception and abortion.

❓ What can you infer from Source H about the class and background of the founder members of NOW?

(EEOC) refused to enforce **Title VII** of the 1964 Civil Rights Act, which banned discrimination in employment on the basis of sex as well as race. NOW aimed to monitor the enforcement of the legislation and to demand an amendment to the Constitution that affirmed women's right to equality in all areas.

SOURCE H

From the National Organisation of Women's Statement of Purpose (1966) (available from http://wps.prenhall.com/wps/media/objects/173/177769/29_nowst.HTM).

[NOW aims] to break through the silken curtain of prejudice and discrimination against women in government, industry, the professions, the churches, the political parties, the judiciary, the labor unions, in education, science, medicine, law, religion, and every other field of importance in American society. …

There is no civil rights movement to speak for women, as there has been for Negroes and other victims of discrimination. The National Organization of Women must therefore begin to speak.

NOW used a variety of tactics, including:

- Litigation. For example, NOW represented Lorena Weeks, who said that the Southern Bell company had contravened the 1964 Civil Rights Act when it denied her application for promotion to switchman (a railroad worker who changes the points on a track) because a woman would not be able to lift a weight of 30 pounds. Weeks and NOW lost the initial case in 1966, but were victorious in 1969 after several appeals. In 1968, NOW won a Pennsylvania Supreme Court ruling (*Commonwealth of Pennsylvania* v. *Daniel*) that overthrew Pennsylvania's Muncy Act, under which women convicted of crimes punishable by a prison term of three years or more had to receive the maximum possible sentence and could be jailed for twice as long as men for a similar crime.
- Political pressure. For example, NOW presented politicians with a Bill of Rights for Women (1968) that sought the enforcement of Title VII, equal access to education and employment, maternity leave, federally funded childcare to assist working mothers and **reproductive rights** (NOW was the first national organisation to endorse the legalisation of abortion).
- Public information campaigns. For example, in 1967 NOW helped gain national attention for the flight attendants' fight against sexist airline advertisements such as 'I'm Debbie, Fly Me'.
- Protests. For example, NOW organised a national strike for equality in 1970, with the slogan 'DON'T IRON WHILE THE STRIKE IS HOT'.

From women's rights to women's liberation

The women's rights movement in the early and mid-1960s sought equal rights and opportunities in work. The late 1960s saw the development of an overlapping women's liberation movement, in which radical feminists put a new emphasis on publicising and opposing sexist oppression and cultural practices that objectified women.

Among the leading radical feminists were Jo Freeman, Shulasmith Firestone and Ti-Grace Atkinson. Freeman illustrates the connection between the protest movements of the 1960s. She served on the FSM committee at Berkeley and worked on voter registration for SNCC in Mississippi and Alabama. In 1967, Freeman and Firestone attended a National Conference of New Politics in Chicago. The conference director, William Pepper, said that their resolution on gender equality did not merit floor discussion: 'Move on little girl. We have more important issues to talk about here than women's liberation.'

Consciousness-raising

Pepper inspired Freeman to produce a newsletter, *Voice of the Women's Liberation Movement*, which encouraged the formation of women's liberation groups nationwide. The first national meeting of women's liberation activists was held in Chicago, where Freeman lived. Freeman said the women's liberation movement was a 'younger branch' of the women's movement that 'prides itself on its lack of organization … Eschewing structure and damning the idea of leadership … thousands of sisters around the country are virtually independent of each other.' Support for 'women's lib' was generated through Freeman's newsletter and through '**consciousness-raising**' meetings in colleges and in the community that sought to raise awareness of gender inequality and to encourage activism to combat it. Awareness certainly increased: in 1960, one-quarter of women polled said they felt discriminated against; after consciousness-raising, it reached two-thirds by 1974.

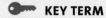 **KEY TERM**

Consciousness-raising
Procedure adopted by feminists to raise awareness of women's issues.

The experience at the National Conference of New Politics inspired Shulasmith Firestone to establish a women's liberation group in New York City, the New York Radical Feminists, which held consciousness-raising meetings focused upon the issue of male subordination of females, an issue that also concerned Ti-Grace Atkinson. Atkinson left NOW in 1968 because she considered it insufficiently radical. She set up a group called The Feminists in New York City. Atkinson argued that the sexual revolution had benefited men more than women as it had given them easier access to women's bodies. She criticised pornography and marriage, which she likened to slavery ('We can't destroy the inequities between women until we destroy marriage').

Disunity in the women's movement

Women activists frequently disagreed over tactics and issues:

- Some NOW members felt that the dramatic demonstrations by some supporters of 'women's lib' alienated public opinion. For example, in 1968, over 100 'women's libbers' disrupted the swim-suited parade at the Miss

America beauty pageant in Atlantic City with a stink bomb and crowned a live sheep 'Miss America'. They threw bras, girdles, curlers, false eyelashes, wigs and other 'women's garbage' into a 'freedom trash can', singing:

Atlantic City is a town without class,
they raise your morals and they judge your ass.

- Some women activists disagreed over the demand for legalised abortion ('the right of women to control their reproductive lives').
- Breakaway groups such as the Radicalesbians resented the lack of support from NOW for lesbian women.
- Some felt that the women's movement was dominated by white, middle-class concerns.

Despite the disunity, the women's movement would prove to be more lasting than most 1960s' protest movements. It was an effective movement, as demonstrated in 1967 when President Johnson responded to NOW lobbying with an executive order banning gender discrimination by federal contractors. NOW monitored enforcement, fighting over 1000 discrimination cases and winning $13 million compensation for women by 1971.

Sexual liberalisation

Exceptional changes in attitudes in the 1960s constituted a sexual revolution with increased acceptance of casual premarital sex, abortions and extramarital relations. These changes were rapid: for example, 74 per cent of women in 1969 said they believed premarital sex was wrong, only 53 per cent by 1973.

The origins of the sexual revolution lay in slowly changing attitudes after the Second World War, when sensationalist book covers and *Playboy* (first published in 1953) increasingly emerged on to the open shelves rather than from under the counter. The **Kinsey Reports** (1948 and 1953) on American sexual mores reflected and hastened the liberalisation of sexual behaviour. The pace of change speeded up even more after 1960, when the widespread availability of the first oral contraceptive for women ('the pill') liberated many women from fears of pregnancy and when many groups were demanding greater freedom and change.

Long-standing conservatism about birth control and abortion remained:

- It was 1965 before the Supreme Court ruled that married couples could not be refused contraception (*Griswold* v. *Connecticut*).
- It was 1974 before doctors could no longer refuse birth control to unmarried adults for 'moral reasons'.

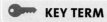

KEY TERM

Kinsey Reports
US academic Alfred Kinsey published widely read reports (1948, 1953) on the sexual mores of Americans.

- Abortion was illegal until 1973, so women sought backstreet practitioners, or used bleach douches or inserted coat hangers instead. Many women died from these unsafe, unregulated practices. In the early 1960s, one Chicago hospital treated over 5000 women for abortion-related complications.

While liberals saw the 1960s as characterised by an upward trajectory towards ever-greater freedom, conservatives bemoaned the 'permissive society' as contributing to the breakdown of the traditional family unit.

The role of the media

The media provided exhaustive coverage of the protest movements and counterculture of the 1960s. While the media might ridicule movements such as feminism, it gave them a national platform that helped change attitudes. This was clearly the case with the civil rights movement.

The news media and civil rights

Coverage of the civil rights movement helped its progress. For example, repeated showings of the violence of Bloody Sunday (see page 160) helped win Northern white support for the Voting Rights Act. However, media coverage of ghetto riots and radicalised African-Americans helped turn many against further aid for black Americans after 1965. Martin Luther King Jr had much positive media coverage in the North when he focused on the problems in the South, but received unfavourable coverage after his Chicago campaign (see page 168) and the development of his increasingly socialist convictions ('something is wrong with the economic system of our nation … with capitalism').

The media made much of the unusual and the extreme, such as the Black Panthers and hippies.

The news media and other protests

The media gave hippies coverage out of all proportion to the numbers involved: reporters and television cameras flocked to cover 'happenings' in San Francisco in 1967 and there was disproportionate coverage of the roughly 10,000 countercultural communes established between 1965 and 1975. In October 1967, the Diggers of San Francisco, who sought a social revolution and the end of capitalism, proclaimed the 'Death of Hippie' and rejected the counterculture because they said it had been taken over by the media. Media coverage of hippies elicited a backlash among the socially conservative.

Media coverage of the more radical African-Americans (especially the Black Panthers) and anti-war protesters was also out of all proportion to the numbers involved (see page 174).

Summary diagram: Social divisions and protest movements

Protesters, aided by media	Success?		
	Yes?	No?	Some?
Students vs university authorities			✓
Students vs racism			✓
Students and adults vs war			✓
Hippies vs dominant culture		✗	
NOW vs inequality in unemployment			✓
Women's libbers vs male domination in society			✓
African-American radicals			✓

Chapter summary

President Johnson was a complex personality, capable of eliciting affection and admiration but also intense dislike. His main interests were domestic politics and the promotion of a Great Society, free of inequality. He persuaded Congress to pass an unprecedented quantity of social reform legislation, which brought him both blame and acclaim. The Great Society, but more especially the Vietnam War, destabilised the American economy.

Johnson's exploitation of Kennedy's memory contributed to the passage of reforming legislation, but Kennedy left a pernicious legacy in the commitment to South Vietnam. Johnson escalated the war in Vietnam because he thought it was important to America's Cold War position and he did not want to be the first president to lose a war. The war generated protests and alienated allies.

Johnson's civil rights legislation ended segregation and enabled African-Americans to vote in the South, but the combination of increased black radicalism and cost left him unable to do much to improve the big city ghettos. The Black Power movement owed much to Malcolm X. It helped promote black self-esteem but the actions of groups such as the Black Panthers and ghetto rioters alienated white America.

American society seemed increasingly divided under Johnson, with protests against racial and gender inequality, university authorities and the war. Some young people 'dropped out' completely. Exhaustive media coverage of protests contributed to a growing socially conservative backlash.

Refresher questions

Use these questions to remind yourself of the key material covered in this chapter.

1 Why did Johnson continue then escalate the commitment in Vietnam?

2 How successful were Johnson's Great Society programmes?

3 What was the impact of the Kennedy legacy on Johnson?

4 From what economic problems did the United States suffer in the 1960s?

5 How did the Vietnam War impact on America's international image?

6 How and why did de Gaulle become a major problem to Johnson?

7 Why was civil rights legislation passed in 1964, 1965 and 1968?

8 Why did African-Americans become more radical in the mid-1960s?

9 In what ways did the media affect American politics and society in the 1960s?

10 How and why did the women's movement change during the Johnson years?

 Question practice

ESSAY QUESTIONS

1 'Johnson's legislative achievements were mostly due to the Kennedy legacy.' Assess the validity of this view.

2 'Vietnam was Johnson's war.' Assess the validity of this view.

3 'Johnson's Great Society dream failed.' Assess the validity of this view.

4 'In comparison with the more traditional civil rights movement, the Black Power movement achieved little.' Assess the validity of this view.

SOURCE ANALYSIS QUESTION

1 With reference to Sources 1, 2 and 3, and your understanding of the historical context, assess the value of these three sources to a historian studying the passage of civil rights legislation during Johnson's presidency.

SOURCE 1

From a 1966 account by two journalists, Rowland Evans and Robert Novak, *Lyndon B. Johnson: The Exercise of Power*, New American Library, 1966, p. 104.

The [Johnson] Treatment could last ten minutes or four hours. It came, enveloping its target, at the Johnson Ranch swimming pool, in one of Johnson's offices, in the Senate cloakroom, on the floor of the Senate itself – wherever Johnson might find a fellow Senator within his reach.

Its tone could be supplication, accusation, cajolery, exuberance, scorn, tears, complaint, and the hint of threat. It was all of these together. It ran the gamut of human emotions. Its velocity was breathtaking, and it was all in one direction. Interjections from the target were rare. Johnson anticipated them before they could be spoken. He moved in close, his face a scant millimeter from his target, his eyes widening and narrowing, his eyebrows rising and falling. From his pockets poured clippings, memos, statistics. Mimicry, humor, and the genius of analogy made The Treatment an almost hypnotic experience and rendered the target stunned and helpless.

SOURCE 2

From President Johnson's advice to Senator Hubert Humphrey concerning the importance of the leader of the Republicans in the Senate, Everett Dirksen of Illinois, to the administration's efforts to get the civil rights bill passed in 1964. Quoted in Randall Bennett Woods, *LBJ: Architect of American Ambition*, Harvard University Press, 2007, p. 474.

This bill can't pass unless you get Everett Dirksen. You and I are going to get Ev. It's going to take time. We're going to get him. You make up your mind now that you've got to spend time with Ev Dirksen. You've got to let him have a piece of the action. He's got to look good all the time. Don't let those [liberal] bomb throwers, now, talk you out of seeing Dirksen. You get in there to see Dirksen. You drink with Dirksen! You talk with Dirksen! You listen to Dirksen!

SOURCE 3

From President Johnson's speech before Congress in support of the voting rights bill (March 1965) (available from **www.lbjlib.utexas.edu/johnson/archives.hom/speeches.hom/650315.asp**).

Rarely are we met with a challenge ... to the values and the purposes and the meaning of our beloved Nation. The issue of equal rights for American Negroes is such an issue ... The command of the Constitution is plain ... It is wrong – deadly wrong – to deny any of your fellow Americans the right to vote in this country ... A century has passed, more than 100 years, since the Negro was freed. And he is not fully free tonight ... A century has passed, more than 100 years, since equality was promised. And yet the Negro is not equal ... The real hero of this struggle is the American Negro. His actions and protests, his courage to risk safety and even to risk his life, have awakened the conscience of this Nation ... He has called upon us to make good the promise of America. And who among us can say that we would have made the same progress were it not for his persistent bravery, and his faith in American democracy?

CHAPTER 5

Republican reaction: the Nixon presidency 1968–74

Richard Nixon is perhaps the most hated president in American history due to his prolongation of the Vietnam War and the political scandal known as 'Watergate'. However, he eventually took America out of Vietnam, improved relations with China and the Soviet Union and, despite his conservative rhetoric, tried to help the disadvantaged. The issue of whether he deserves his appalling reputation is explored in the following sections:

★ The presidential election of 1968 and the reasons for Nixon's victory

★ The domestic policies of the Nixon administration

★ The limits of US world power

★ The Watergate affair and its aftermath

Key dates

1969	Jan.	Nixon became president	1973	Feb.–Aug.	Senate investigated Watergate affair
	Oct.–Nov.	Anti-war protests		April	Haldeman, Ehrlichman and Dean resigned
1970	May	Kent State students killed			
1971	April	Supreme Court ruled pro-busing		July	Existence of White House taping system revealed
1972	Feb.	Nixon visited Communist China		Nov.	Seven White House tapes surrendered
	May	Soviet–American SALT treaty	1974	March	Seven Nixon aides indicted
	June	Attempted cover-up after Watergate break-in discovered		July	Supreme Court ordered release of tapes that proved Nixon ordered cover-up
	Nov.	Kissinger announced 'peace is at hand'; Nixon re-elected		Aug.	Nixon resigned
	Dec.	Draft ended		Sept.	President Ford pardoned Nixon
1973	Jan.	Watergate burglars convicted			

The presidential election of 1968 and the reasons for Nixon's victory

▶ *What explained Nixon's unexpected political comeback?*

Richard Nixon won the 1968 presidential election because of Democrat divisions and **Middle America**'s reaction against the changes and protests of the 1960s.

Divisions within the Democratic Party

In late 1967, Democrat liberals sought a Democrat candidate to challenge President Johnson for the Democrat nomination for the presidency in 1968. New York Senator Robert Kennedy (see page 104) had turned publicly against the Vietnam War in May 1965. A friend urged him to run for the presidency because of the 'moral imperative of stopping the war by dislodging Johnson', but Kennedy feared he would be accused of splitting the Democratic Party. Furthermore, the *New York Post* publisher told him he lacked sufficient support: 'Who is for you? … The young, the minorities, the Negroes, the Puerto Ricans.'

McCarthy versus Johnson

In January 1968, the liberals persuaded anti-war Minnesota Senator Eugene McCarthy to run against Johnson. An intellectual who had once considered becoming a monk, McCarthy particularly appealed to college students. Hundreds of them decided to 'be clean for Gene': they shaved off their beards, swapped their jeans for suits and ties, and campaigned for McCarthy in the New Hampshire **primary**. McCarthy won 42 per cent of the votes, Johnson 49 per cent. That was an unprecedentedly low percentage for an incumbent president. It showed how vulnerable Johnson was to a liberal Democrat challenger and tempted Bobby Kennedy to run for the Democrat nomination.

President Johnson was reluctant to leave the White House, but his popularity had so plummeted that, on 31 March, he declared that he would not seek the Democratic Party's nomination but focus on peace in Vietnam. Although Kennedy's friend Arthur Schlesinger Jr told him if he ran he would be criticised as 'a Johnny-come-lately trying to cash in after brave Eugene McCarthy had done the real fighting' and advised him to endorse McCarthy instead, Bobby responded, 'I can't do that. It would be too humiliating … Kennedys don't act that way.' He declared his candidacy on 16 March 1968:

> *I run to seek new policies, policies to end the bloodshed in Vietnam and in our cities, policies to close the gap that now exists between black and white, between rich and poor, between young and old in this country.*

 KEY TERMS

Middle America A term invented by the media to describe ordinary, patriotic, middle-income Americans.

Primary Before a presidential election, the Democrats and Republicans hold an election in each state (mostly called a primary) to decide which candidate they would like to represent their party in the election.

Kennedy's appeal

President Kennedy's assassination changed Robert Kennedy. Many of the less privileged thought he developed a unique empathy with them and their suffering. 'You know', said African-American Kenneth Clark, 'it is possible for human beings to grow. This man had grown.' Kennedy's support of the striking Mexican-American farmworkers in California impressed their leader, Cesar Chavez ('we loved him … He was able to see things through the eyes of the poor … It was like he was ours') and his assistant Dolores Huerta ('Robert didn't come to us and tell us what was good for us. He came to us and asked two questions … 'What do you want? And how can I help?''). Native Americans were similarly smitten when Kennedy investigated the appalling poverty on reservations in Oklahoma and New York State. A Seneca tribesman said, 'Loving a public official for an Indian is almost unheard of, but we trusted him … We had faith in him.' NAACP lawyer Marion Wright was similarly impressed by Kennedy when he visited a Mississippi cottonpicker's hovel in 1967:

> He did things that I wouldn't do. He went into the dirtiest, filthiest, poorest black homes … and he would sit with the baby who had wet open sores and whose belly was bloated from malnutrition, and he would sit and touch and hold those babies … I wouldn't do that! I didn't do that! But he did … That's why I am for him.

Kennedy declared that 'today in America we are two worlds', a prosperous white one and the 'dark and hopeless place' in which lived those forgotten by Johnson because he was preoccupied with Vietnam. On 4 April, Kennedy defied advisers, went into the Indianapolis ghetto, and made a moving speech about Martin Luther King Jr's assassination. He said he too had lost someone that he loved, that his brother had been killed by a white man, and asked them not to blame all whites.

SOURCE A

From Robert Kennedy's speech to the Cleveland City Club, 5 April 1968 (the day after Martin Luther King Jr's assassination) (available from www.jfklibrary.org/Research/Research-Aids/Ready-Reference/RFK-Speeches/Remarks-of-Senator-Robert-F-Kennedy-to-the-Cleveland-City-Club-Cleveland-Ohio-April-5-1968.aspx).

This mindless menace of violence in America which again stains our land and every one of our lives … is not the concern of any one race. The victims of the violence are black and white, rich and poor, young and old, famous and unknown. They are, most important of all, human beings whom other human beings loved and needed. … And yet it goes on and on … we seemingly tolerate a rising level of violence that ignores our common humanity and our claims to civilization alike. We calmly accept newspaper reports of civilian slaughter in far off lands. We glorify killing on movie and television screens and call it entertainment. We make it easy for men of all shades of sanity to acquire weapons and ammunition they desire … violence breeds violence, repression brings retaliation, and only a cleaning of our whole society can remove this sickness from our soul.

Using Source A and your own knowledge, would you conclude that Robert Kennedy was saintly or seeking votes in 1968?

For there is another kind of violence, slower but just as deadly, destructive as the shot or the bomb in the night. This is the violence of institutions; indifference and inaction and slow decay. This is the violence that afflicts the poor, that poisons relations between men because their skin has different colors. This is a slow destruction of a child by hunger, and schools without books and homes without heat in the winter. This is the breaking of a man's spirit by denying him the chance to stand as a father and as a man among other men …

Kennedy versus McCarthy

McCarthy seemed arrogant, cold and distant in comparison to Kennedy. He said nothing about King's assassination and failed to relate to minorities. Kennedy appealed more to the poor, McCarthy more to the middle class. Kennedy won the Democrat primary in Indiana, a state full of factory workers and ghettos. Then he won Nebraska, but said of predominantly white, middle-class Oregon, 'There is nothing for me to get hold of. Let's face it, I appeal best to people who have problems.' McCarthy won Oregon.

By now the once sceptical press was increasingly pro-Kennedy. Tom Wicker, head of the Washington office of the *New York Times*, said that Kennedy was an 'easy man to fall in love with' and warned his writers not to be too adulatory. However, Kennedy had infuriated many in the Democratic Party. Democrat liberals had asked him to challenge Johnson and he had left it to McCarthy. Liberals now feared he would split the liberal vote and open the way for the nomination of former liberal darling Vice President Hubert Humphrey. Humphrey had loyally supported Johnson's Vietnam policies and was expected to continue them if he got the nomination.

SOURCE B

? What does Source B suggest about US society and politics in 1968?

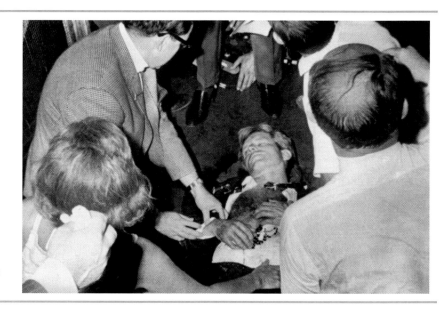

Bobby Kennedy lies dying on the floor of a Los Angeles hotel, 5 June 1968. He had just won the California primary.

Kennedy soon emerged as a stronger candidate than McCarthy. When he attacked both racial prejudice and riots, criticised the rise of welfare and praised hard work, he began to win some middle-class support. Partly because of the glamour of the Kennedy legacy, he stirred intense affection among crowds that often left him with torn clothes and bleeding hands as they grabbed at him to indicate their support. Kennedy narrowly won the crucial California primary, but was assassinated by a disturbed Palestinian, Sirhan Sirhan, who claimed that Bobby was too pro-Israel.

The impact of the Democratic National Convention in Chicago

There was much disillusion with the American Dream in 1968. 'I won't vote. Every good man we get they kill', said one New Yorker after Martin Luther King Jr and Bobby Kennedy were assassinated. The **Youth International Party** (Yippies) sought to show their contempt for the American political process by calling on young people to come to Chicago to disrupt the Democratic National Convention. They spread rumours that they were going to put the hallucinogenic drug LSD in the city's water supply and produced a squealing, rotund young pig ('Pigasus') as their presidential candidate.

KEY TERM

Youth International Party
A radical student group that wanted to show contempt for the political system during the Democratic Party Convention at Chicago in 1968.

The Yippies and the more numerous anti-war protesters who converged on Chicago only numbered around 10,000, but Chicago's Democrat Mayor Daley mobilised around 12,000 police and banned marches. Some protesters threw bags of urine at police officers. They, in turn, removed their badges and nameplates and retaliated, shouting, 'Kill, kill, kill.' A British reporter recorded that some young protesters 'were beaten to the ground by cops who had completely lost their cool'.

Outside the Convention Hall, protesters chanted '*Sieg Heil*'. Inside, Johnson and Humphrey's control of the party machinery and manipulation of the convention ensured that Humphrey won the Democratic presidential nomination, even though he had not won a single primary. That infuriated many other Democrats, including Connecticut Senator Abraham Ribicoff, who took to the platform to nominate South Dakota Senator George McGovern. Ribicoff looked at Chicago's Democrat Mayor Daley and said, 'With George McGovern, we wouldn't have Gestapo tactics on the streets of Chicago.' Daley responded, 'Fuck you, you Jew son of a bitch, you lousy motherfucker.' Lip readers ensured that Daley's response and Democrat divisions hit the national headlines.

The Democrats were tainted by events at Chicago:

- It reminded voters how violence and disorder had become endemic on Johnson's watch. News pictures and reports of students targeting the police (calling them 'pigs', blowing marijuana smoke in their faces and giving them the finger) and having sex in public places, combined to help the Republican, 'law and order' candidate Richard Nixon. Nixon shot ahead of Humphrey in the polls.

- Many Democrats were embittered and weakened by Humphrey's campaign. McCarthy refused to endorse him. Many anti-war Democrats were resentful about the way their anti-war candidates had been treated and rejected at the convention. Hating the war even more than they hated Nixon, they continued to attack Humphrey ('Dump the Hump'). They disrupted his meetings and made it impossible for his speeches to be heard. They told reporters they would probably vote for Humphrey in the end, but wanted to 'push him toward the left'. They pushed him towards defeat and introduced procedural reforms that led to another Nixon victory in 1972.

> ### George Wallace's candidacy
>
> In a further sign of the splintering of the Democratic Party, former Democrat Governor of Alabama George Wallace (see page 121) ran as an independent. He gained a 20 per cent approval rating, with support from Southern segregationists and Northern working-class whites. However, Wallace erred in choosing Air Force Chief Curtis LeMay as his running mate. LeMay wanted to 'bomb Vietnam back into the Stone Age' and told reporters, 'I don't believe the world would end if we exploded a nuclear weapon.'

Why the Republican Richard Nixon won the 1968 election

Nixon won the presidency through his Eisenhower association, moderation, party loyalty, Southern strategy (page 195) and, most importantly, his appeal to a Middle America alienated by Johnson's policies. In 1970, *Time* magazine would describe Nixon as 'the embodiment of Middle America'.

Winning the Republican nomination

After his defeat in 1960 (see page 97), Nixon half-heartedly ran for governor of California and was heavily defeated. In an emotional press conference that made some, including President Kennedy, question his sanity, he said he was retiring from politics and that the media would no longer have Nixon to kick around. *Time* magazine said, 'Barring a miracle, Richard Nixon can never hope to be elected to any political office again.'

In 1968, Nixon made what contemporaries called the most amazing comeback American politics had ever seen. He began by winning the Republican nomination.

Nixon won the Republican nomination because:

- Throughout his 'retirement' (from 1962 to 1968) Nixon won over party loyalists by tireless party fundraising and campaigning.
- In 1964, the right-wing Old Guard (see page 60) took control of the Republican Party, but after their nominee Barry Goldwater was crushingly defeated by Johnson in the 1964 presidential election, they knew the party needed a moderate candidate in 1968.

Richard Milhous Nixon

1913	Born in Yorba Linda, California
1940	Married Pat Ryan
1947–50	Congressman; served on House Un-American Activities Committee (HUAC)
1950–2	Senator
1953–61	Vice president, specialising in foreign visits
1960	Narrowly defeated by Kennedy in presidential election
1968	Defeated Democrat Hubert Humphrey in presidential election
1972	First US president to visit China and the USSR; Soviet–American **SALT** I treaty slowed nuclear arms race. Re-elected in landslide victory over Democrat George McGovern in November
1973	Ended US involvement in Vietnam. Announced resignation in August and was succeeded by Vice President Gerald Ford who, as president, pardoned him in September
1994	Died

Richard Nixon was born to a struggling Californian family in 1913. After university, he practised law, then after naval service in the Second World War, he was elected to the House of Representatives, then to the Senate. He gained national fame through his work in pursuit of Communists on HUAC (see page 34). Although an impressive vice president (see page 64), he was narrowly defeated by the Democrat John Kennedy in the 1960 presidential election (see page 97). He made an amazing political comeback in 1968, defeating the Democrat Hubert Humphrey in the presidential election. He was re-elected in a landslide victory in 1972.

Despite his socially conservative campaign rhetoric, President Nixon was helpful to the less fortunate. However, he had little success with America's economic problems. He (slowly) ended the Vietnam War and improved relations with the USSR and China. However, the scandal generated by his attempted cover-up of the Watergate burglary (in which his men broke into the Democratic Party headquarters) overshadowed his achievements.

In his early political career, Nixon contributed greatly to America's Cold War paranoia. A moderate on social issues, he did not want to dismantle the federal government safety net established by previous Democrat presidents, and from 1968 to 1972, he helped keep the Republican Party out of the hands of right-wingers who favoured minimal government intervention to help the less fortunate. He helped win many ex-Democrats to the Republican Party, especially in the South. However, he is best remembered for the Watergate scandal. Watergate became synonymous with Nixon, dishonesty and disgrace.

- 'Old Guard' Republicans liked Nixon's extreme anti-Communism, and moderate and liberal Republicans found his position on domestic issues acceptable.
- As a former vice president, Nixon had governmental experience and was associated with the prosperity and calm of the Eisenhower years.
- Nixon articulated the concerns of Middle America with highly effective attacks on Johnson's leadership throughout 1967 and 1968. His campaign slogan was, 'FOR THESE CRITICAL YEARS, AMERICA NEEDS NEW LEADERSHIP'.

 **KEY TERM**

SALT The Strategic Arms Limitation Treaty signed by Nixon and the Soviet leader Brezhnev in 1972.

Were the problems listed in Source C due to Johnson's leadership?

SOURCE C

From Richard Nixon's August 1968 acceptance speech at the Republican national convention (available from www.presidency.ucsb.edu/ws/?pid=25968).

When the strongest nation in the world can be tied down for four years in the war in Vietnam with no end in sight, when the nation with the greatest tradition of respect for the law is plagued by random lawlessness, when the nation that has been a symbol of human liberty is torn apart by racial strife, when the President of the United States cannot travel either at home or abroad without fear of a hostile demonstration, then it is time America had new leadership.

Winning Middle America

The people of Middle America earned between $5000 and $15,000 a year and constituted around 55 per cent of the population. Most were blue-collar workers, low-level bureaucrats, schoolteachers and white-collar workers. Although not poor, they existed precariously near to the poverty line. From 1956 to 1966, the amount they borrowed rose by 113 per cent, while their income increased by only 86 per cent. Inflation (4.7 per cent) made it hard for them to maintain their standard of living. Night after night, Middle America watched the riots on television (see page 169), and lost patience with rioters and with a federal government they perceived as taxing them heavily to give the money away to the undeserving poor. While Middle America's children were drafted and sent to Vietnam, student protesters lived comfortably and avoided the draft. 'We just seem to be headed towards a collapse of everything', said one small-town Californian newspaper.

Much of Middle America traditionally voted Democrat, but Nixon appealed to many of them. In a 1984 interview, he said, 'My source of strength was more **Main Street** than **Wall Street**'. In 1970, he was described as having appealed to the 'unyoung, unpoor, and unblack … middle-aged, middle-class, and middle-minded' – in other words, all who opposed 1960s' radicalism, change and disorder.

When Nixon accepted the Republican nomination in August 1968, he clearly distinguished between liberal elites, hippy protesters and ghetto rioters on the one hand, and Middle America, whom he would soon christen the 'silent majority' on the other:

SOURCE D

From Richard Nixon's acceptance speech at the Republican National Convention in Miami in August 1968 (available from www.presidency.ucsb.edu/ws/?pid=25968).

As we look at America, we see cities enveloped in smoke and flame. We hear sirens in the night. We see Americans dying on distant battlefields abroad. We see Americans hating each other; fighting each other; killing each other at home

What might Middle America find appealing in Source D?

… Listen to … another voice. It is the quiet voice in the tumult and the shouting. It is the voice of the great majority of Americans, the forgotten Americans – the non-shouters; the non-demonstrators. They are not racists or sick; they are not guilty of the crime that plagues the land. They are black and they are white – they are native born and foreign born – they are young and they are old. They work in America's factories. They run America's businesses. They serve in government. They provide most of the soldiers who died to keep us free. They give drive to the spirit of America. They give lift to the American Dream. They give steel to the backbone of America. They are good people, they are decent people; they work, and they save, and they pay their taxes, and they care … America is in trouble today not because her people have failed but because her leaders have failed … it's time for new leadership for the United States of America.

Nixon's promises and policies

Nixon won votes through three promises in particular. He promised:

- to bring peace with honour in Vietnam
- to restore law and order in the cities (he repeatedly and effectively cited statistics such as, 'In the [past] 45 minutes … this is what has happened in America. There has been one murder, two rapes, 45 major crimes of violence, countless robberies and auto thefts')
- less and cheaper government (he attacked the massive bureaucracy that implemented welfare and poverty programmes, leading some voters to hope that he would dismantle the Democrats' welfare state).

Nixon's Southern strategy and the Sun Belt

As one might expect of a Californian, Nixon was in tune with opinion in the increasingly important **Sun Belt**. The intellectual, economic and political powerhouse of the nation had traditionally been the predominantly coastal area of the Northeast that stretched southwards from Boston through New York City, Philadelphia and Baltimore to the nation's capital, Washington DC. However, the population of the South and Southwest had doubled between 1945 and 1968 and high-tech industries were booming because:

- increased use of air-conditioning made these hotter regions more habitable
- the federal government made these areas far more accessible through the massive expansion of the interstate highway system
- the federal government (frequently prompted by Lyndon Johnson) had awarded many defence and space contracts to the region in the 1950s and 1960s.

Nixon appealed to Sun Belt voters for three reasons:

- After Johnson's role in ending segregation in the South, many Southern white voters no longer felt at home in his Democratic Party. Nixon wooed them by

 **KEY TERM**

Sun Belt States in the South, Southeast and Southwest, with warm climates, ranging from North Carolina in the East to California in the West.

rejecting Johnson's policy of cutting off federal funds to school districts that refused to desegregate, and by promising to slow down the pace of school desegregation in the South. This so-called **Southern Strategy** was very effective; it transformed Southern voting patterns.

- Nixon proposed **New Federalism**, a recalibration of the balance of power between the states and the federal government. He wanted to share federal revenue directly with the states and thereby decrease the red tape and bureaucracy traditionally involved in the distribution of federal funds. Voters across the nation liked this, but it particularly appealed to Southern whites with their traditional emphasis upon states' rights. However, the Democrat-controlled Congress was unenthusiastic.
- Many inhabitants of the sunshine states were **evangelical** Protestants and social conservatives who disliked liberal intellectuals from the Northeast. They believed that the liberal elite wanted to give away hard-earned taxpayers' money to the idle poor. They resented the fact that while many ordinary American boys had been drafted or volunteered to serve in Vietnam, the children of the elite went to Harvard and Yale and indulged in anti-war protests, safely cushioned by daddy's wealth and influence. Like many Sun Belt voters, Nixon was socially conservative and disliked what he called the 'establishment' or 'elite' of the Northeast.

Nixon's campaign: an improvement

Nixon had learned much about campaigning since 1960. First, he did not exhaust himself with too many public appearances (see page 99). Everyone knew him, so there was no need to appear in shopping centres and school gyms. Instead, he appeared statesmanlike, dignified and experienced, speaking in large auditoriums, with audiences over 1000, or reaching wider audiences through television. Second, he mastered the medium of television. Now he knew to keep his tan topped up in Florida (see page 99) and to keep away from hostile, probing journalists. His campaign concentrated on the production of edited, televised footage of question sessions with ordinary voters, whom Nixon handled with ease.

Eisenhower's support

Many Republicans had long dreamed of a match between Nixon's younger daughter Julie and Eisenhower's grandson David. Julie and David initially resisted such matchmaking efforts, but met for the first time in years on election night in 1966 and found they liked each other. Their 1967 announcement of marriage plans was front-page news and gave Nixon's campaign a big boost. In early 1968, one reporter noted that Julie and David provided the glamour that Nixon lacked. When David arrived at St Louis airport, a crowd of teenage girls met him. 'I touched him', squealed a 14-year-old girl, 'I actually touched him.' Furthermore, David persuaded his dying grandfather to endorse Nixon. Julie's older sister Tricia and their mother Pat were pleasing personalities and valuable campaigners, but Julie was the greatest asset to Nixon's campaign. Her response when hecklers asked her about her father's vagueness on Vietnam was masterly:

> *Daddy wants the peace talks to succeed so much he thinks he shouldn't talk about the war. When he becomes President, he'll put pressure on the Soviet Union. Remember, Daddy was in the Eisenhower Administration and they got us out of one war [Korea].*

Nixon's running mate

Nixon's surprising choice as running mate in 1968 was Spiro Agnew. 'Spiro who?' asked the press.

Maryland's Governor Agnew had gained some national attention and white plaudits when, after the spring 1968 riots in Baltimore, he had summoned leaders of the black community and castigated them as 'circuit-riding, Hanoi-visiting, caterwauling, riot-inciting, burn-America-down type of leaders' who had been 'breaking and running' instead of stopping the riots.

Agnew enlivened the campaign with some gaffes. Asked why he was not campaigning in ghetto areas, he replied, 'When you've seen one slum, you've seen them all.' When Nixon won the election, he triumphantly told his staff that they had picked the right man in Agnew, a man with capacity, brains, energy and quality. 'Well, we sure concealed that from the American people during the campaign', muttered one aide.

Agnew was to Nixon as Nixon had been to Eisenhower: the 'hatchetman' who did the president's political dirty work in his speeches (cynics christened Agnew 'Nixon's Nixon'). In 1972, Nixon kept Agnew on the ticket, impressed by his hard-hitting attacks on radicals and liberals. Agnew appealed to Middle America and right-wing Republicans with his attacks on the East Coast liberal establishment.

The 1968 election results

The race between Nixon and Humphrey was close and nasty. A Republican television commercial showed Hanoi battle scenes, black ghetto rioters, a starving child, then Hubert Humphrey talking about the 'politics of joy'. A Democrat radio commercial sounded a thump, thump, thump, and then a voice-over said in an incredulous tone, 'Spiro Agnew? A heartbeat from the presidency?'

Nixon had been considerably ahead of Humphrey for much of the autumn, but Humphrey rallied dramatically in the final days of the campaign. When he broke from Johnson on Vietnam and advocated a bombing pause, anti-war Democrats came back to him.

Although he won comfortably in the **electoral college**, Nixon took only 43.4 per cent of the popular vote, to Humphrey's 42.7 per cent: the lowest winning margin since 1912. Nixon had to share the white Southern and Northern blue-

 **KEY TERM**

Electoral college Under the Constitution, each state's voters vote for delegates who then vote on behalf of that state in the electoral college. The number of delegates depends on the state's population. The leading candidate in a state takes all that state's delegates. Whoever wins a majority of delegates becomes president.

collar workers with George Wallace, who had campaigned like Nixon on anti-big government, anti-inflation, anti-welfare, anti-riots and anti-liberal **planks**. Wallace won 13.5 per cent of the vote. With quite a low turnout (under 60 per cent), Nixon had won the support of fewer than 27 per cent of American voters – but his election signalled that traditional American values had been reasserted. As malcontents on the left had become increasingly extreme, conservative reaction had set in on the right.

The personalities of the Nixon administration

President-elect Nixon quickly chose his first cabinet. His appointments were moderate, sensible and generally well received. However, his most influential advisers were Henry Kissinger (see page 213), Bob Haldeman and John Ehrlichman, who were not in the cabinet. Many people believe they reflected and intensified the worst aspects of Nixon's personality: vindictiveness, cynicism and amorality.

Kissinger versus Rogers

Kissinger was a Harvard University professor who specialised in international relations. Desperate to serve in the government, he tried but failed to attach himself to the Kennedys, then offered himself to Nixon, who made him his national security adviser. Kissinger told a journalist, 'What interests me is what you can do with power.' He enjoyed the company of glamorous Hollywood actresses, declaring that 'power is the ultimate aphrodisiac'.

Nixon considered foreign policy the most important and interesting presidential task and worked closely with Kissinger on it. Both had exceptional knowledge of foreign affairs and favoured bypassing the traditional diplomatic machinery. Nixon chose his old friend and supporter William Rogers as Secretary of State. Rogers knew little about foreign policy, but Nixon told Kissinger this was an advantage as it would ensure White House control. When Rogers got his first pile of foreign policy papers to read, he was amazed: 'You don't expect me to read all this stuff, do you?' The Kissinger–Rogers relationship was tempestuous. Nixon said:

> I'm sorry about how Henry and Bill get at each other. It's really deep-seated. Henry thinks Bill isn't very deep, and Bill thinks Henry is power-crazy. And in a sense, they are both right.

Years later, Nixon wrote:

> Rogers felt that Kissinger was Machiavellian, deceitful, egotistical, arrogant, and insulting. Kissinger felt that Rogers was vain, uninformed, unable to keep a secret, and hopelessly dominated by the State Department bureaucracy.

It was commonly said in Washington that Kissinger treated his staff as mushrooms: kept in the dark, stepped on and frequently covered with manure.

Haldeman and Ehrlichman

Haldeman managed Nixon's 1968 presidential campaign, then ran the White House as Nixon's chief of staff. Ehrlichman joined Nixon's campaign staff in 1960, and in 1969 became Nixon's domestic affairs adviser. Haldeman and Ehrlichman physically controlled access to Nixon.

After Watergate (see page 218), Nixon put a great deal of blame on Haldeman and Ehrlichman. He said they were responsible for the cover-up, and that he had not sacked them early enough because of his personal loyalty to them. Another influential figure in the Watergate scandal was Nixon's Attorney General John Mitchell.

John Mitchell

Lawyer John Mitchell helped manage Nixon's 1968 presidential campaign, was Nixon's attorney general from January 1969 to March 1972, then headed Nixon's Committee to Re-Elect the President (**CREEP**). Attorney General Mitchell approved **wiretaps** without court authorisation, prosecuted anti-war protesters and tried to block publication of the **Pentagon Papers**. Like Nixon, he was antagonistic towards the press. When the *Washington Post*, owned by Katharine Graham, was about to publish something on Watergate, Mitchell threatened 'Katie Graham's gonna get her tit caught in a big fat wringer if that is published.' Mitchell's outspoken, heavy-drinking wife loved gossip. Nicknamed 'Martha the mouth' by the press, she was always in the news.

> ## Presidency and media
>
> Nixon said, 'In the modern presidency, concern for image must rank with concern for substance,' and that the media were 'far more powerful than the President in creating public awareness and shaping public opinion'. He was convinced that the press hated him and declared himself 'prepared to do combat with the media'. Given all this, choosing the inexperienced 29-year-old Ron Ziegler as press secretary was unwise. Ziegler had worked with Haldeman at an advertising agency.

🔑 KEY TERMS

CREEP Committee to Re-Elect the President, established by the Nixon administration prior to the 1972 presidential election.

Wiretaps Bugging a telegraph wire or a telephone line in order to overhear conversations.

Pentagon Papers A collection of government documents that reflected badly on the Democratic presidents who had got America into Vietnam. The papers were leaked to the press by civil servant Daniel Ellsberg.

Summary diagram: The 1968 presidential election and reasons for Nixon's victory

Democrat divisions
- McCarthy vs LBJ
- McCarthy vs Kennedy
- McCarthy vs Humphrey
- Daley vs liberals

+

Nixon
- Effective attacks on LBJ
- Eisenhower factor
- Won Middle America – law and order
- Southern strategy and Sun Belt appeal
- Promised to end war
- Less and cheaper government
- Improved campaigner

The domestic policies of the Nixon administration

▶ *How successful were Nixon's domestic policies?*

When Nixon became president, the most pressing domestic issues were:

- social problems (poverty, race and law and order)
- protest movements
- the economy.

The restoration of conservative social policies?

Nixon's rhetorical campaign attacks on the expense of the Great Society (see page 143) assisted his electoral appeal and his victories in 1968 and 1972, but Democrat control of Congress and his own moderate, pragmatic Republicanism ensured that he left Johnson's programmes basically intact.

Welfare and anti-poverty programmes

During the 1968 presidential election campaign, Nixon made it clear that he wanted to eliminate the more wasteful, inefficient Great Society programmes, especially what he called the 'welfare mess'. He told his advisers that the American people were 'outraged' by the welfare system, 'and, in my view they should be'. In 1968, polls revealed that 84 per cent of Americans believed 'there are too many people receiving welfare money who should be working'. After the Great Society raised awareness of entitlements, the number of Americans receiving AFDC (see page 144) rose from 3 million in 1960 to 8.4 million by 1970. One in nine children, and one in three black children, were on welfare. While Johnson thought such statistics constituted proof of progress, Middle America resented the expense.

As president, Nixon attacked Great Society programmes and principles from several angles:

- He successfully shrank OEO (see page 143), closed 59 Job Corps centres, and cut federal funding for housing and youth programmes.
- He tried to reform the welfare system. Polls showed that 80 per cent of Americans believed over half of those on welfare could get a job if they wanted it, and Nixon hoped he could make welfare recipients work through his Family Assistance Plan (FAP). Conservatives liked three aspects of FAP: first, welfare recipients would only have received $1600 a year; second, there were work requirements; third, the number of bureaucrats who administered the system was decreased. Liberals disliked those provisions, but were pleased that the plan would have made 13 million more Americans eligible for federal aid. That, in turn, alienated conservatives. There were so many criticisms of Nixon's FAP that Congress rejected it.

- Nixon vetoed the 1971 Child Development Act, which would have provided free childcare to enable poor mothers to work. He said it was too expensive and smacked of Communism.

Having been brought up in poverty, Nixon was basically sympathetic to the poor. Despite all his anti-Great Society campaign rhetoric, he increased federal expenditure on education, private health care, Social Security, Medicare and Medicaid (see page 144), and actually spent more on social programmes than Johnson.

Racial equality

Middle America felt that the Johnson administration had gone too far in appeasing African-Americans and hoped that Nixon would prove far more conservative on race relations.

School desegregation and busing

Johnson sought a Great Society characterised by racial equality. In pursuit of this, Supreme Court rulings in 1971 and 1973 supported the **busing** of students from one neighbourhood to a school in another neighbourhood in order to end *de facto* segregation of schools in the North in particular. However, Americans opposed busing by eight to one, and Nixon attacked it as 'wrenching' children from their families. When the Justice Department began to respond to the Supreme Court's ruling, Nixon told them to 'Knock off this crap. Do only what the law requires and not one thing more.' He was initially unsuccessful in his attempts to slow down school desegregation, as when Congress rejected his request for a constitutional amendment against busing. However, his appointment of conservative Supreme Court justices led to the *Milliken* v. *Bradley* (1974) ruling that halted busing in the Detroit area after 1974 and justified the continuance of *de facto* segregation of schools.

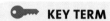 **KEY TERM**

Busing Supreme Court rulings on integrated education meant some white children were sent (by bus) to black schools, and vice versa.

Nixon's Southern strategy and Supreme Court nominees

In 1968, Nixon promised Southern Republicans he would select judges who would slow down the pace of integration. In 1969, he successfully nominated conservative Warren Burger as chief justice. However, although, no Supreme Court nominee had been rejected since 1930, two of Nixon's racially conservative Southern nominees were rejected by the Senate, including G. Harrold Carswell, whose lack of ability was attested by a White House aide: 'They think he is a boob, a dummy ... He is.' One Republican senator tried to support Carswell by saying that even if he were mediocre, 'there are a lot of mediocre judges and people and lawyers. They are entitled to a little representation, aren't they, and a little chance?' However, thirteen other Republicans joined in the successful Senate rejection of Carswell.

Affirmative action

Nixon claimed to dislike affirmative action (see page 164), which he described as reverse discrimination, but in practice his administration gave minorities considerable help. For example, he put pressure on federal contractors to employ more minority workers. As so often with Nixon, there was a gap between what he said and what he did. In many ways, his record on race was quite impressive. His promotion of affirmative action helped ensure its entrenchment in federal government agencies and contractors for many years to come.

Law and order

Nixon and Middle America believed violence and crime had escalated because liberals had been 'soft', for example, in liberal Supreme Court rulings such as the 1966 **Miranda** ruling that seemed to give the accused more rights than the victim.

On the second day of Nixon's presidency, a *New York Times* headline called the nation's capital a 'city of fear and crime', and the Washington *Daily News* asked him to root out the 'fear that stalks the streets of Washington'. A White House secretary was mugged just outside the East Gate and Nixon's secretary Rose Mary Woods had $7000 worth of jewellery stolen from her apartment in Washington DC's new Watergate complex when she accompanied Nixon to Europe. Nixon put forward a bill to decrease crime in Washington, and Congress responded with the District of Columbia Crime Control Act of 1970, which facilitated search procedures and made bail harder to obtain.

KEY TERMS

Miranda Supreme Court ruling that improperly obtained confessions be excluded from trials.

Chicago Eight In 1969, the Nixon administration charged eight New Left leaders with conspiracy. They included Tom Hayden of SDS and Bobby Seale of the Black Panthers. Five were convicted, by an exceptionally hostile judge. Eventually their convictions were overturned on appeal.

Law and order in the USA: statistics

- 1969: 602 bombings or attempted bombings.
- Spring 1969: 300 colleges had demonstrations, 20 per cent of which included bombings or trashing of buildings.
- 1970: 1577 bombings or attempted bombings.
- 1969–70: 56 per cent of bombings resulted from campus disorders, 19 per cent from black extremists, 14 per cent from white extremists, 8 per cent from criminal attacks. There were 41 deaths and 37,000 bomb threats.
- Autumn 1970: Boston University evacuated buildings on 80 occasions because of bomb threats.

The Nixon administration dealt harshly with radicals such as the Black Panthers (see page 172) and the **Chicago Eight**. Middle America was delighted when 28 Black Panthers were killed by the police, and hundreds more of them were imprisoned during 1969. The Chicago Eight were prosecuted in 1970 for travelling across state lines to foment anti-war riots during the 1968 Democrat National Convention (see page 191).

Middle America was most antagonistic towards student protesters, whom they perceived as the privileged children of the middle and upper classes.

The reaction to protest movements and forces of social change

Nixon said he aimed 'to bring the American people together', but his presidential inauguration demonstrated how difficult that would be. His inauguration was the first in American history to be marred by protest. Hundreds of young anti-war protesters shouted, 'Ho, Ho, Ho Chi Minh, the **NLF** is going to win', burned American flags, spat at the police, and threw sticks, stones, beer cans and bottles at the presidential limousine. Middle America was disgusted. A 1969 *Newsweek* poll showed that 84 per cent of Americans believed that student demonstrators were treated too leniently.

The protests seemed never ending. In October and November 1969, America's greatest ever anti-war protests took place. In this **Moratorium**, tens of thousands of Americans of all ages marched on the White House and in every major city. Nixon was also faced with pro-civil rights, pro-Black Panthers and anti-capitalism protests:

- Radical students blew up buildings at the University of Colorado because scholarship funds for black students were frozen.
- Students at San Diego, California, set fire to banks.
- Ohio State students demanded the admission of more black students and the abolition of Reserve Officer Training Corps (ROTC) (see page 177): in a six-hour battle with the police, seven students were shot, thirteen injured and 600 arrested, after which the State Governor called in the National Guard.
- A pro-Black Panthers demonstration set Yale Law School library books on fire.

When Nixon appeared to be extending the Vietnam War to Cambodia in spring 1970 (see page 210), anti-war protests erupted again in more than 80 per cent of American universities. Police and National Guardsmen frequently clashed with students, most famously at Kent State, Ohio.

Kent State and Jackson State

After Kent State students rioted downtown and firebombed the ROTC building, some Kent State students held a peaceful protest rally on 4 May, 1970. The National Guard panicked, shot four students dead and wounded eleven others. Two of the girls were simply walking to class. In the next week, two more students were killed and twelve wounded at predominantly black Jackson State, Mississippi (opinions differ as to whether the students had been violent a few hours before).

Reactions varied. On the one hand, some Americans felt that the government was deliberately murdering dissenters. Nixon antagonised students (and some middle-class parents) when he talked of 'these bums … blowing up the campuses'. The father of one of the students shot dead at Kent State hit the

KEY TERMS

NLF Vietnamese Communist National Liberation Front.

Moratorium In this context, suspension of normal activities to facilitate national anti-Vietnam War protests in 1969.

national headlines when he said four days later, 'My child was not a bum.' Nixon did not handle the Kent State and Jackson State tragedies well, blaming the 'politics of violence and confrontation' and failing to express sorrow at the deaths. On the other hand, over half of Americans blamed the students for what had happened at Kent State.

How Nixon dealt with the protests

With varying degrees of success, Nixon used several strategies for dealing with students. His attempts to communicate with them were unsuccessful. He made an impromptu visit in the middle of the night to the Lincoln Memorial, where he tried to convince a group of amazed students, who had driven all night to come to Washington to protest against the Vietnam War, that he understood them and wanted the same things they did. One girl told a reporter:

> I hope it was because he was tired, but most of what he was saying was absurd. Here we had come from a university [Syracuse] that's completely uptight – on strike – and when we told him where we were from, he talked about the football team and surfing.

In April 1970, Tricia Nixon hosted a White House tea for her fellow Finch College alumni. Invited guests included Grace Slick of the acid-rock group Jefferson Airplane. Slick planned to bring along Yippie (see page 191) leader Abbie Hoffman as her date and to lace the punch with LSD, which would be hidden under her fingernails. The journalist whom Slick told of the idea tipped off the White House. The invitation was withdrawn. Most Americans sympathised with the Nixons.

Nixon also won sympathy when he defied protesters while campaigning during the 1970 congressional mid-term elections. Demonstrators beat on the walls outside the building where he spoke in San Jose, in support of California's Republican Governor Ronald Reagan. When Nixon walked out to the car he climbed atop the presidential limousine and gave them his traditional V-for-victory sign (as used by Churchill during the Second World War). Amid jeers and boos, eggs and rocks the size of baseballs were thrown at the presidential car – an unprecedented occurrence.

Nixon and Agnew tried to discredit protesters by deliberately failing to differentiate between the mainstream anti-war movement and increasingly violent splinter groups. However, it was threats, surveillance, litigation and the withdrawal of American troops from Vietnam that proved most effective in decreasing the protests. Exhaustion and division among the radicals were also important factors.

Nixon's success against protesters

Nixon successfully decreased the number of protests when he

- timed US troop withdrawals from Vietnam to forestall proposed anti-war protests

- adjusted the draft (August 1972) so that students aged over 20 were no longer called up, and then removed it completely in 1973
- threatened to end federal scholarships and loans for convicted student criminals or those who had 'seriously' violated campus regulations
- ordered surveillance of disruptive groups
- took protesters to court. In spring 1970, 10,000 people were arrested in Washington DC. Although most of the arrests were thrown out of the courts because they violated the demonstrators' civil rights, the litigation kept the protesters too busy (and broke, due to the legal fees) to cause more trouble.

Exhaustion and divisions among the radicals

Along with the prosecutions, surveillance and the end of the draft, the exhaustion of many radicals dramatically decreased the number of campus protests. The New Left (see page 131) student movement imploded because the authorities were clearly not going to grant any of their demands and the students were divided. Groups such as the Weathermen favoured revolutionary terrorism, while other groups felt that politics was a farce and activism was a waste of time.

SOURCE E

What do you suppose were the aims of Presley and Nixon when they posed for Source E?

President Nixon greets singer and actor Elvis Presley in the Oval Office in 1970. Presley (whose secret addiction to prescription drugs was to hasten his early death) had offered to help in the war on drugs. Several great rock stars, Janis Joplin, Jim Morrison and Jimi Hendrix, all died from drug overdoses within a ten-month period from 1970 to 1971.

Economic change and the end of the post-war boom

Nixon inherited a faltering economy with a massive federal deficit, inflation at 4.7 per cent, declining productivity in American industry, and a flood of imports from Japan and Germany that endangered America's balance of trade.

Although Nixon tried to halt inflation by cutting federal spending, he had record annual budget deficits. By August 1971, the economy was in big trouble. High rates of inflation and unemployment and the rising trade deficit left the dollar under attack from speculators in the international money market. Nixon's **New Economic Policy (NEP)** of August 1971 introduced the first peacetime wage-price freeze and devalued the dollar. The devaluation made US exports cheaper and more competitive and was designed to help the balance of trade. The NEP received a 75 per cent approval rating, but did not help solve the underlying problems of the American economy. A fuller devaluation of the dollar in July 1973 was equally ineffective, and when Nixon abandoned the wage and price controls, prices rocketed in what became known as the great inflation of 1973. By that time, however, he was too preoccupied with Watergate (see page 218) to focus on the nation's economic problems, which were exacerbated by a developing energy crisis.

The energy crisis

In the three decades after the Second World War, the United States went from energy self-sufficiency to an energy deficit situation. America contained 6 per cent of the world's population yet consumed one-third of the world's oil production. Roughly 30 per cent of the oil Americans used was imported, mostly from the Middle East. The resulting American economic vulnerability was exposed when Nixon's support of Israel in the 1973 **Arab–Israeli War** led to an Organisation of Petroleum Exporting Countries (OPEC) oil embargo on the United States. The end of the embargo was followed by a 387 per cent hike in the price of oil that greatly damaged the American economy (although US oil companies benefited). Cheap oil had been vital to the post-Second World War economic growth and prosperity. When the cost of energy rocketed, it had a massive impact on the lives of many Americans, who now paid around 30 per cent more for heating oil and petrol. That contributed to a rise in the cost of living. Although their standard of living remained the highest in the world, Americans were increasingly gloomy about the nation's economy.

Re-election in 1972

Nixon got re-elected in 1972 because of

- the continued support of Middle America
- his foreign policy triumphs
- Democrat problems.

Foreign policy triumphs

Nixon had three foreign policy triumphs that appealed to voters:

- He improved relations with the USSR, and the SALT agreement (see page 217) was the first meaningful attempt to put a brake on the Soviet–American nuclear arms race.
- His restoration of relations with Communist China, after 20 years of tense hostility, was statesmanlike. He exploited it effectively, obtaining the Chinese government's promise that 'no Democrat is to go to China before the President' and ensuring saturation media coverage of his 1972 visit (when he returned from China, he waited for nine hours in Alaska so his plane could land in Washington DC at the 9p.m. primetime television news hour).
- Nixon's troop withdrawals from Vietnam pleased voters, as did Henry Kissinger's announcement that 'peace is at hand' in Vietnam, on the eve of the election.

> ### A hostile press
>
> Nixon had a point when he claimed the press was unfair to him. When he visited China, the press reported that he had looked at the famous Great Wall and said, 'This is a great wall'. They omitted the rest of the sentence ('and it had to be built by a great people'), without which the statement was inane.

Democrat problems

Nixon was faced with less formidable opposition in 1972 than in 1968. The 1972 Democratic National Convention greatly damaged the Democrats. Middle America watched in horror as some delegates booed Humphrey and Johnson and shouted their support for Vietnamese Communism. Due to new party rules governing the selection of the presidential candidate, the Democrats chose their most left-wing candidate, George McGovern.

McGovern seemed to be the 'counterculture candidate': he wanted to legalise marijuana and abortion, pardon Vietnam War deserters and **draft dodgers**, cut defence spending, and give $1000 to every American to redistribute income and decrease poverty. Republicans played on conservative fears of McGovern, christening him the '3As' candidate: **'acid, abortion and amnesty'**.

The 1972 election results

In an unpleasant campaign, McGovern likened Nixon to Hitler, while the Nixon administration organised a break-in at the Democratic campaign headquarters (see page 220). The administration did not need to spy on the Democrats: Nixon won by a landslide, with 60.7 per cent of the popular vote. He carried every state except Massachusetts and was the first Republican presidential candidate ever to gain the majority of Catholic votes. The traditionally Democrat unions rejected McGovern because he opposed the Vietnam War and defence spending,

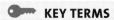 **KEY TERMS**

Draft dodger One who avoided being called up to fight in the Vietnam War.

'Acid, abortion and amnesty' In 1972, Republicans accused Democratic presidential candidate George McGovern of favouring drugs ('acid'), irresponsible sex ('abortion') and unpatriotic draft dodgers (to whom he would give 'amnesty' – freedom from prosecution).

so Nixon carried 52 per cent of the blue-collar vote (compared to 38 per cent in 1968). Several Southern governors, including Jimmy Carter of Georgia, refused to support McGovern because Southerners so disliked his liberalism. Nixon's Southern white support rose from 38 per cent in 1968 to 72 per cent in 1972.

The elections left the Democrats in control of Congress. Nixon was the only president ever to win two terms without his party ever having a majority in either the House of Representatives or the Senate. When combined with the Watergate scandal, this caused Nixon tremendous problems in his second term.

Summary diagram: The domestic policies of the Nixon administration

Problem	Nixon's response	Success?
Great Society expense and inefficiency	Some cuts but spent even more than Johnson	No
Racial inequality	Opposed busing but supported affirmative action	Some
Law and order, protests	Tough on radicals and protesters	Considerable
Economy	Tried to cut federal government expenditure, devalued dollar, wage/price freeze	No

3 The limits of US world power

▶ *How successful was Nixon's foreign policy?*

Richard Nixon recognised that there were limits to American power. He therefore aimed to end the Vietnam War and to decrease tensions with the USSR and China, which would help slow the costly arms race.

Peace negotiations and the continuation of the war in Vietnam and Cambodia

Nixon had long been a hardline Cold Warrior on Vietnam. Throughout the 1960s he urged Johnson to escalate, insisting, 'Vietnam is essential to the survival of freedom.' And yet, as president, he withdrew the US from Vietnam because:

- The Tet Offensive (see page 155) convinced him that America needed to withdraw and hand the conduct of the war over to the South Vietnamese (the '**Nixon Doctrine**' or '**Vietnamisation**'). He said:

KEY TERMS

Nixon Doctrine
Also known as 'Vietnamisation'; belief that America's Asian allies should fight their own battles. Announced by President Nixon at Guam in 1969.

Vietnamisation President Nixon's policy; South Vietnam was to take over all the fighting against the Communists.

> *The nation's objective should be to help the South Vietnamese fight the war and not fight it for them. If they do not assume the majority of the burden in their own defence, they cannot be saved.*

- The world had changed since Eisenhower had established South Vietnam. Sino-Soviet divisions had destroyed the supposedly monolithic Communist bloc and thereby decreased the Communist threat.
- In his inaugural address, Nixon said, 'The greatest honor history can bestow is the title of peacemaker.'
- He knew that Vietnam had ruined Johnson's presidency: 'He has been under such pressure because of that damn war, he'd do anything … I'm not going to end up like LBJ … I'm going to stop that war. Fast!'

Determined not to be the first American president to lose a war, Nixon sought a 'peace with honour' that would allow the continued existence of an anti-Communist South Vietnam, under the leadership of **Nguyen Van Thieu**. Nixon's intended methods were:

- Vietnamisation
- diplomatic pressure on the USSR and China
- military pressure on North Vietnam until it agreed to his peace terms.

Nixon was also forced into unplanned concessions to make North Vietnam agree to peace and to quieten American anti-war protests.

KEY FIGURE

Nguyen Van Thieu (1923–2001)

President of South Vietnam 1965–75.

1969

From February, Nixon bombed the Ho Chi Minh Trail (see page 113) to sever enemy supply lines and pressure North Vietnam into a peace agreement. He excluded Thieu from the peace talks in Paris because he was offering North Vietnam concessions to which Thieu would not have agreed. He dropped Johnson's insistence that American troops would only withdraw from South Vietnam six months after the North Vietnamese troops withdrew, but North Vietnam simply said it had no troops in South Vietnam and demanded that Thieu give way to a coalition with Communist representation.

Nothing worked. Peace was no nearer and despite Nixon's troop withdrawals, millions participated in the anti-war protests of autumn 1969 – the 'Moratorium'. On 3 November, Nixon appealed for national unity and for time to end the war (Source F). While most Americans responded positively to that appeal, the protests continued. In November, 250,000 peaceful marchers converged on Washington: 40,000 walked past the White House, each carrying a candle and proclaiming the name of a dead person. Nixon wondered whether helicopters could be flown low over them to blow out their candles and drown out their voices. The exposure of the massacre of civilians by American soldiers at the South Vietnamese village of My Lai back in 1968 divided Americans further. Some were disgusted; others felt that these things were inevitable during wartime.

? Why do you suppose
Americans responded
positively to the speech in
Source F?

SOURCE F

From President Nixon's televised address to the American people, 3 November 1969 (available from www.pbs.org/wgbh/americanexperience/features/primary-resources/nixon-vietnam/?flavour=full).

For the United States … [a] first defeat in our Nation's history would result in a collapse of confidence in American leadership, not only in Asia but throughout the world … I can order an immediate, precipitate withdrawal of all Americans from Vietnam without regard to the effects of that action. Or we can persist in our search for a just peace through a negotiated settlement if possible, or through continued implementation of our plan for Vietnamization if necessary … I have chosen this second course. It is not the easy way … And so tonight, to you, the great silent majority of my fellow Americans – I ask for your support … Let us be united for peace. Let us be united against defeat. Because let us understand: North Vietnam cannot defeat or humiliate the United States. Only Americans can do that.

1970

In January 1970, Nixon appeared to be escalating the war: even as he withdrew troops, he carpet-bombed North Vietnamese anti-aircraft bases and the Ho Chi Minh Trail in Laos and Cambodia, and sent 30,000 American and South Vietnamese soldiers into Cambodia (the Communist forces simply melted away). Peace seemed no closer and the Cambodian offensive caused many protests and much controversy: 50 per cent of Americans polled approved of the offensive, 39 per cent disapproved. Exasperated by the increase of presidential power in the Cold War (the '**imperial presidency**'), Congress threatened to cut off Nixon's money for the war in Southeast Asia.

1971

Nixon tested Vietnamisation in 1971: 5000 elite South Vietnamese troops began the Lam Son Offensive in Laos, but the Communists routed them with the help of new Soviet equipment. American television viewers saw South Vietnamese soldiers hanging on to American helicopter skids to escape the battle, and American pilots greasing their skids to stop them lest they bring down the helicopters. This helped generate more protests: in spring, 300,000 marched in Washington. Negotiations with North Vietnam went badly, even though Nixon conceded that North Vietnam would not have to withdraw its troops from South Vietnam. The only progress Nixon made was in **detente**. Desirous of detente with the USA, the USSR and China urged North Vietnam to compromise, but North Vietnam refused.

1972

In March, the Communists staged a great offensive in the face of which the South Vietnamese forces crumbled. Nixon therefore decided that these 'bastards have never been bombed like they are going to be bombed this time'.

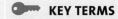

KEY TERMS

Imperial presidency
During the Cold War, presidential power increased so much that some commentators thought the president was becoming like an emperor – hence 'imperial'.

Detente Policy of relaxation of tensions with enemies, associated with President Nixon's improvement of relations with China and the USSR.

He bombed Hanoi, and bombed and mined the North Vietnamese port of Haiphong. While Congress once again threatened to cut off his money, he tried to rally the American people:

> If the United States betrays the millions of people who have relied on us in Vietnam … it would amount to renunciation of our morality, an abdication of our leadership among nations, and an invitation for the mighty to prey upon the meek all around the world.

Despite the protests, Nixon was right in believing the silent majority was behind him. Polls showed that 55 per cent supported continued heavy bombing of North Vietnam, 64 per cent supported the mining of Haiphong, and 74 per cent thought it important that South Vietnam not fall to the Communists.

North Vietnam was finally being driven towards a settlement by

- the destructive bombing
- the failure of the offensive
- American concessions
- Sino-Soviet pressure
- Nixon's likely re-election.

At the peace negotiations in Paris, North Vietnam now conceded that Thieu could stay in power, but insisted on a say in the South Vietnamese government. Kissinger therefore offered a Committee of National Reconciliation (one-third South Vietnamese, one-third Communist, one-third neutral) to oversee discussions of a constitution and elections. This constituted recognition that the Communists were a legitimate political force in South Vietnam, something Thieu had always denied.

In October, Kissinger announced that peace was at hand, but Nixon backed out – Thieu opposed the agreement, and Nixon was unsure that the agreement was truly 'peace with honour'. He feared that he might be seen as giving in to protesters.

Once re-elected in November 1972, Nixon caused worldwide uproar when he bombed and mined Haiphong again over Christmas. Nixon probably aimed to reassure Thieu of US support, weaken North Vietnam so it could not attack South Vietnam soon after peace was signed, and disguise America's retreat from Vietnam and concessions in the peace negotiations. Several US congressmen and newspapers questioned his sanity.

The Paris Peace Accords

The peace settlement negotiated by Kissinger in Paris and signed in January 1973 was basically the same as that agreed in October 1972. The settlement stipulated:

- a ceasefire
- a prisoner of war exchange

- that North Vietnamese forces could stay in South Vietnam but could neither fight nor be increased
- that South Vietnam would continue to exist, and Thieu would remain in power
- that the Committee of National Reconciliation would contain Communists.

As a final concession to ensure a settlement, Nixon secretly promised billions of reconstruction aid to North Vietnam.

This settlement was 'peace with honour' in the sense that South Vietnam and Thieu survived, well supplied with US war materiel (Thieu had the world's fourth largest air force). On the other hand, it could be argued that it was not 'peace with honour' in that the settlement said that Communist forces could remain in South Vietnam. However, it is doubtful that Nixon could have done any better, because of the pressure from Congress. At least he had withdrawn American troops, which benefited the United States, if not Thieu and South Vietnam. The problem was the lack of viability of the South Vietnamese 'state' that had cost Americans and Vietnamese so dearly.

Death and destruction

- Of the 3 million Americans who served in Vietnam, about 46,000 were killed in action ('Now it's all gone down the drain and it hurts. What did he die for?' asked the parent of one dead American soldier), 10,000 died through accidents and around 300,000 were wounded.
- 137,000 South Vietnamese soldiers were killed, 300,000 were wounded.
- Around 400,000 South Vietnamese civilians died and three-quarters of a million were wounded.
- Perhaps as many as 2 million Communist soldiers died.
- Around 2.5 million Vietnamese died and 1.5 million were wounded, out of the total population of about 32 million.
- Many Vietnam veterans who returned home suffered acute psychological problems.

The influence of Kissinger on US policies towards the USSR, Latin America and China

Henry Kissinger and Richard Nixon had exceptional knowledge of international relations, but proved an unfortunate combination: both thought in terms of US national interest, with little apparent regard for moral considerations. Their practice of *realpolitik* can still arouse shock. When Nixon ordered the bombing of North Vietnam, neither seemed to worry (as Johnson had) about the deaths of either Vietnamese civilians or American soldiers. Kissinger declared contemptuously of conscientious objectors, 'Conscientious objection must be reserved only for the greatest moral issues, and Vietnam is not of this magnitude.'

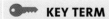
KEY TERM

Realpolitik Emphasising national interest rather than legalism and moralism in foreign policy.

Henry Kissinger

1923   Born in Germany
1954–69   Harvard academic
1969–74   Headed President Nixon's National Security
           Council (NSC)
1973–4   President Nixon's Secretary of State
1974–7   President Ford's Secretary of State
1977   Became an international consultant, writer
           and lecturer

Henry Kissinger was born in Germany. In 1938, his
family fled to the USA to escape the Nazi persecution
of Jews. Kissinger served in the US Army in the Second
World War then, after gaining a Harvard University
doctorate degree, lectured in international relations and
government and became a professor at Harvard. He
served as defence consultant to several administrations.

As President Nixon's National
Security Advisor (1969–74)
and then as his Secretary
of State (1973–4), Kissinger
played a major role in
Vietnamisation, in the peace negotiations that finally
ended the Vietnam War (for which he received the
Nobel Peace Prize), and in the establishment of detente
with the USSR and China. As President Ford's Secretary
of State (1974–7), Kissinger indicated that detente with
the USSR was generally recognised as a failure, although
improved relations with China constituted a necessary
and long-lasting achievement.

Kissinger worked closely with President Nixon and
many commentators believe they brought out the
worst in each other. Both have been criticised for an
overemphasis on US national interests at the expense of
morality, as in Vietnam and Latin America.

Kissinger and Nixon did not believe in explaining their personalised, secret
diplomacy: Kissinger said foreign policy was for the most part 'too complex'
for 'the ordinary guy' to understand, and Nixon agreed. As a result, Nixon did
not always ensure popular and congressional support for his policies, and this
contributed to the collapse of South Vietnam in 1975 (see page 248).

Kissinger and Nixon worked closely together in engineering 'peace with honour'
in Vietnam. Nixon was furious that Kissinger always got more respect than he,
whether from the press or from those who awarded Kissinger the Nobel Peace
Prize for his conduct of the peace negotiations in Paris. Kissinger was certainly
a skilled negotiator, but he shared with Nixon that commitment to what seemed
rational and in America's national interest, yet was considered by many to be
of dubious morality. Both saw the bombing in Southeast Asia as the way to
demonstrate that the retreating USA still had awesome power, and to force
North Vietnam to agree to let Thieu remain in power. Both also saw equally
distasteful policies towards Latin America as essential for US national security.

Latin America

Kissinger dismissed Latin America as 'a dagger pointed at the heart of –
Antarctica … What happens in the South is of no importance'. Nevertheless, he
feared that the USA was losing control in the **Western Hemisphere**. He and
Nixon decided that support for authoritarian national governments in Latin
America was in the US national interest.

 **KEY TERM**

Western Hemisphere
The North and South
American continents.

Chile

In 1970, Kissinger and Nixon feared that the socialist Salvador Allende might win the presidential election in Chile. American-owned copper mining companies and US communications giant International Telephone & Telegraph feared that they might suffer if Allende nationalised industries. Nixon quoted an Italian businessman as saying, 'If Allende should win the election, and then you have Castro in Cuba, what you will in effect have in Latin America is a red sandwich, and eventually it will all be red.' Nixon therefore decided an Allende regime was 'not acceptable' and granted the CIA $10 million to prevent his coming to power or to unseat him if he did.

However, Allende was elected, and the Nixon administration then responded by trying to destabilise his government. Kissinger said Allende's election constituted 'a challenge to our national interest'. Nixon said he wanted to make the Chilean economy 'scream', and stopped all aid and **World Bank** and **Inter-American Development Bank** loans to Chile. Within Chile, the CIA funded media criticism of Allende, opposition parties, and strikes by truckers and taxi drivers, and encouraged demonstrations by middle-class housewives.

In September 1973, General **Augusto Pinochet** led a bloody coup. Allende apparently killed himself. A democratically elected government had been overthrown. It is possible that the coup might have succeeded without US aid because Allende had many problems. However, the US Senate investigation chaired by Democrat Senator Frank Church in 1975 concluded that US economic policy under Nixon was a 'significant factor' in Chile's economic problems, and that the United States had made 'massive' efforts to destabilise Allende's government by funding opponents. It found no 'hard evidence' of direct US involvement in the coup, but felt the US attitude had stimulated the opposition.

SOURCE G

From the Church Report of 1975 (available from http://fas.org/irp/ops/policy/church-chile.htm).

Covert US involvement in Chile in the decade between 1963 and 1973 was extensive and continuous … The CIA attempted, directly, to foment a military coup in Chile [in 1970] … The pattern of US covert action in Chile is striking but not unique. It arose in the context not only of American foreign policy, but also of covert United States involvement in other countries within and outside Latin America. The scale of CIA involvement in Chile was unusual but by no means unprecedented … We had moved finally to advocating and encouraging the overthrow of a democratically elected government … Did the threat posed by an Allende presidency justify covert American involvement in Chile? Did it justify the specific and unusual attempt to foment a military coup to deny Allende the presidency [in 1970]? … On these questions Committee members may differ … Given the costs of covert action, it should be resorted to only to counter severe threats to the national security of the United States. It is far from clear that that was the case in Chile.

Operation Condor

Operation Condor was a Chilean initiative launched in 1975 by the right-wing dictatorships in the **Southern Cone** of Latin America. It was an integrated intelligence system, designed to counter 'transnational subversive elements', to get rid of socialist and Communist influence, and to control opposition to the participating governments. Pinochet used Condor to kill or terrorise political opponents who might challenge his rule. The countries involved in Operation Condor co-operated closely in political assassinations and the kidnapping and 'transfer' of political refugees to their countries of origin. The military governments exchanged information about leftists residing in each other's countries so that, for example, a foreign leftist might 'disappear' in Chile. When Operation Condor ended in 1983 with the fall of the Argentine dictatorship, it had been responsible for around 50,000 deaths, large-scale torture and the disappearance of thousands.

The United States has been slow to declassify information on the Cold War, but information released in the last decade reveals the importance of the US provision of important organisational, financial and technical aid to Operation Condor. Kissinger not only knew about Condor but also covertly encouraged and perhaps abetted Pinochet's behaviour. In the twenty-first century, several Latin American courts and a French judge have tried but failed to obtain information from Kissinger on Operation Condor.

Seeking detente

While historians have been critical of the Nixon administration's policies in Latin America and Southeast Asia, they have been more inclined to praise the pursuit of detente. Knowing that Nixon's impeccable Cold Warrior credentials would pre-empt conservative opposition, Nixon and Kissinger sought detente because:

- Detente would demonstrate that Nixon was a peace-loving world statesman and help him win re-election in 1972.
- Nixon and Kissinger considered it a great and unrealistic error to allow ideology to dominate foreign policy. Kissinger felt that the traditionally legalistic and idealistic US foreign policy style had often been against America's national interest. It made sense to improve relations with the Communist powers and to use traditional balance of power diplomacy and play them off against each other. This was particularly important now that US power was in relative decline, due to financial problems, economic problems and Soviet parity.
- The Cold War world had changed. In the old **bipolar** world it seemed that only Soviet–American relations mattered. In the new **multipolar** world, China and the USSR were enemies, the Western alliance had been deeply divided over the Vietnam War, and the United States seemed to be losing old friends and in need of new ones. Nixon and Kissinger hoped to exploit the Sino-Soviet split to maintain the balance of power in the America's favour.

KEY TERMS

Southern Cone
Southernmost states of South America, for example Chile, Argentina.

Bipolar Prior to the 1960s the Cold War world was focused on two superpowers: the USA and the USSR.

Multipolar Prior to the 1960s, the Cold War world was bipolar (focused on the USA and the USSR); after the Cuban missile crisis and the rise of China, the Cold War world was increasingly multipolar (multiple centres of power and influence).

- Nixon hoped that Moscow and Beijing's desire for detente would encourage them to press North Vietnam to make peace.

China

When Nixon became president, Sino-American relations were hostile (see page 24). For the reasons given above, and in the hope that China could help counterbalance Soviet power and the belief that it was foolish and dangerous to leave a potential superpower outside the international community, Nixon and Kissinger pursued detente with China. For his part, Mao Zedong (see page 21) now considered the Soviets China's greatest enemy and sought to counter them through improved relations with the United States.

Nixon relaxed restrictions on Sino-American trade during 1969–70, then in April 1971 the Chinese invited the American table tennis team to China. This 'ping-pong diplomacy' helped prepare the way for Nixon's 1972 visit (see page 207).

The Nixon administration had opened a dialogue with a potentially dangerous enemy and Beijing duly pressed North Vietnam to agree to peace. However, tensions remained. China resented Nixon's insistence upon maintaining a close relationship with Taiwan, and worried about Soviet–American detente.

The Soviet Union

Nixon and Kissinger had three particular concerns in relation to the Soviets:

- growing Soviet power
- the stability of Europe, especially Germany
- the arms race.

Nixon and Kissinger feared growing Soviet military strength and Kissinger stressed that because the Soviets were now truly a global superpower, they needed 'managing'. Detente would be a new form of containment (see page 14) and it would help slow down the arms race, which would enable cuts in defence expenditure that would ameliorate US economic problems. That, in turn, would please American taxpayers, who were increasingly insistent that West Europeans should finance their own defence. For his part, the Soviet leader **Leonid Brezhnev** feared the growing power of the Chinese and sought to stabilise Europe and to acquire American technological and agricultural expertise.

Nixon's January 1969 inauguration speech had emphasised an 'era of negotiations' with the Soviets. The first area in which progress was made was Europe, where the West Germans had become keen on detente under the leadership of Willy Brandt (1969–74). In September 1971, the USA, USSR, Britain and France signed the Four-Power Agreement in which the Soviets recognised Western access rights to West Berlin (see page 19), and the West conceded that West Berlin was not part of West Germany. This was followed by a Basic Treaty between West Germany and East Germany in 1972, in which both recognised

 **KEY FIGURE**

Leonid Brezhnev (1906–82)

Leader of the USSR 1964–82.

the permanence and validity of the other's frontiers. These German agreements signalled that the USA and the USSR recognised the European *status quo*: the West acquiesced in Soviet domination of Eastern Europe, and the Soviets tacitly agreed not to destabilise Western Europe.

The relaxation of tensions over Germany and Europe was followed by the Strategic Arms Limitation Treaty (SALT) agreement of May 1972, which:

● ended the race over defensive anti-ballistic missile systems
● froze the number of Soviet and American nuclear missiles (the Soviet numerical advantage in missiles was far outweighed by the American ability to put multiple warheads on each missile) and strategic bombers (the United States had three times as many).

SALT was an important step in nuclear arms control but was soon criticised by Cold Warriors. Nixon and Kissinger were surprised when the Soviets tested multiple warheads on a missile just a year later, as this suggested that the Soviets might eventually take the lead in the number of warheads.

The significance of Soviet–American detente

Soviet pressure on North Vietnam assisted the American exit from Vietnam, Europe was increasingly stable, and detente helped Nixon gain re-election. Nevertheless, a series of crises, beginning with the Arab–Israeli War of 1973, demonstrated the limitations of detente.

When Egypt and Syria attacked Israel in 1973 and an Israeli counterattack forced Egypt to seek Soviet aid, the Soviets mobilised their conventional forces. Nixon warned Brezhnev not to use them, and put US nuclear strike forces on alert (some believed he was trying to distract Americans from Watergate). However, Nixon and Kissinger simultaneously restrained Israel, while Kissinger improved relations with Egypt. This American involvement stabilised the region, while excluding the Soviets.

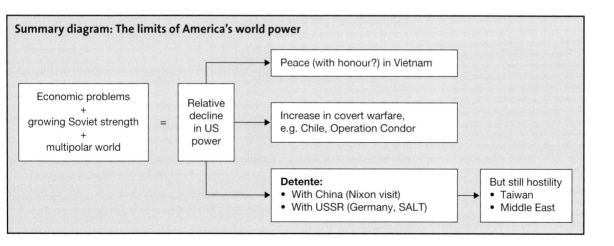

Summary diagram: The limits of America's world power

Economic problems + growing Soviet strength + multipolar world = Relative decline in US power

→ Peace (with honour?) in Vietnam

→ Increase in covert warfare, e.g. Chile, Operation Condor

→ **Detente:**
● With China (Nixon visit)
● With USSR (Germany, SALT)

→ But still hostility
● Taiwan
● Middle East

4 The Watergate affair and its aftermath

▶ *Why was Watergate so important?*

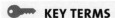
DNC Democratic National Committee, which had its headquarters in the Watergate building in Washington DC.

IRS Internal Revenue Service, the US tax collection agency, which monitors taxpayers, checking whether they pay the correct sum.

Brookings Institution A liberal Washington think-tank.

Watergate is an office complex in Washington DC that housed the Democrat National Committee (**DNC**) headquarters. It has also become a kind of shorthand that sums up Nixon's illegal actions while president. The story of how the name of an office building came to symbolise corruption, illegality and abuse of power is long and complicated.

The Watergate conspirators

Some consider Nixon's employment of vindictive cynics such as Mitchell, Haldeman and Ehrlichman (see page 199) disastrous. They helped bring out the worst in him. Nixon was already and perhaps understandably deeply cynical about the political system (he told one aide, 'You are never going to make it in politics. You just don't know how to lie'). He felt he had been robbed of the presidency in 1960 (see page 98) by dubious electoral practices in Mayor Daley's Chicago and Lyndon Johnson's Texas (Eisenhower wanted him to contest the issue but he said he did not want to destabilise the nation). He himself suffered vindictive cynicism under the Kennedy administration, which had harassed him with an **IRS** audit and an investigation into a loan to his brother, and probably bugged his phone. Given Nixon's experiences and advisers, it is not surprising that the Watergate scandal occurred.

Along with Haldeman, Ehrlichman and Mitchell, other important individuals in Watergate included:

- John Dean: White House Counsel from 1970, he gave Nixon legal advice over Watergate.
- Jeb Magruder: appointed special assistant to Nixon in 1969, he encouraged positive phone calls and telegrams to the White House whenever the president felt in need of support, and worked closely with Haldeman and with Mitchell in CREEP (see page 199).
- James McCord: an ex-FBI and CIA employee, appointed security director of CREEP in 1972.
- Charles Colson: appointed as counsel to Nixon in 1969, then worked on CREEP. Haldeman recalled rumours of wild schemes hatched by Colson, for example, feeding LSD to an anti-Nixon commentator just before he went on television. 'If Nixon said, "Go blow up the Capitol", Colson would salute and buy loads of dynamite', said Ehrlichman. 'That fucking Colson is going to kill us all', opined Attorney General Mitchell, when Colson wanted to burgle, firebomb or set fire to the **Brookings Institution** to access foreign policy documents.

- Gordon Liddy: campaigned for Nixon in 1968, joined the White House staff in 1971 and ran CREEP's surveillance (see below). He suggested electronic eavesdropping, kidnapping of political opponents, disruption of Democratic political meetings and employing prostitutes to compromise Democratic delegates to the National Convention. One of the **'plumbers'**, he organised the break-in of **Daniel Ellsberg**'s psychiatrist's office (see page 199) with Hunt. When the Watergate scandal broke in 1973, Liddy held a lighted candle to his arm to show a lawyer that nothing could induce him to 'spill the beans'.
- E. Howard Hunt: writer of spy novels, appointed to the White House staff by Colson and Ehrlichman after his retirement from the CIA in 1971. Working under Gordon Liddy, he was a member of the 'plumbers' whose job was to stop White House leaks. With a red wig, thick glasses and a speech-alteration device provided by the CIA, he took charge of surveillance of potential Democrat presidential candidate Senator **Edward Kennedy** in 1971–2, in the hope of exposing some sexual escapade.

CREEP

The administration's main preoccupation in 1972 was the presidential election. Nixon was not confident of victory because many disliked his prolongation of the Vietnam War. He therefore established the Committee for the Re-Election of the President (popularly known as CREEP), which engaged in the following:

- Illegal fundraising – it collected over $60 million in campaign contributions. For example, the chairman of fast-food chain McDonald's donated $255,000 and so was allowed to continue an unauthorised price increase on a quarter-pounder cheeseburger.
- Political subversion – CREEP worked to discredit moderate Democratic candidates such as Senator Edmund Muskie (it misled the press into believing he had insulted **Canucks**).
- Criminal surveillance – notably in the office of Daniel Ellsberg's psychiatrist, and in the DNC headquarters in the Watergate building.

According to historian Iwan Morgan, the 'dirty tricks' of the Nixon campaign 'went far beyond the customary rough-and-tumble of American elections'.

CREEP, Ellsberg and the Pentagon Papers

Nixon was concerned that information he wanted kept secret about his Vietnam policies was being leaked to the press. The administration therefore ordered the FBI to wiretap eleven officials (including the Secretaries of State and Defence), four journalists and Don Nixon (Don, whom the president called his 'poor damn, dumb brother', obtained financial favours by using his brother's name). Nixon said that nothing the president ordered done on grounds of internal order and national security could be considered illegal.

The White House Special Investigation Unit (better known as the 'plumbers') was set up in summer 1971 after Daniel Ellsberg leaked the Pentagon Papers.

KEY TERMS

'Plumbers' Those on the White House staff whose job was to halt leaks of information.

Canucks French-Canadians, of whom New Hampshire had a sizeable population.

KEY FIGURES

Daniel Ellsberg (1931–)
Washington bureaucrat who leaked the classified documents on the Johnson administration's Vietnam policies. The documents became known as the Pentagon Papers after their publication by the *New York Times* in 1971.

Edward ('Ted') Kennedy (1932–2009)
Younger brother of John and Robert Kennedy, Ted was senator for Massachusetts from 1962 to 2009. A liberal, he was an (unsuccessful) candidate for the Democratic nomination in 1980.

Although they made Democrat presidents look disreputable over Vietnam, Kissinger convinced Nixon that national security required that classified documents always be kept secret. Fearing more leaks, Nixon sought to discredit Ellsberg. The FBI refused to tap Ellsberg's phone and to undertake surveillance, so the 'plumbers', along with Liddy, Hunt and Colson, were set up to do this.

The 'plumbers' broke into the Los Angeles office of Ellsberg's psychiatrist on 3 September 1971, but found nothing to discredit Ellsberg. Liddy and Hunt had borrowed cameras and burglary equipment from the CIA. Hunt photographed Liddy standing proudly outside the psychiatrist's office (complete with name sign on the door), and then gave the camera back to the CIA with the film left in. 'Idiots', said Dean to the president. As subsequent testimony from Ehrlichman, Dean and Colson varied, it is hard to tell how much Nixon knew about all this.

CREEP and the Watergate break-ins

CREEP organised an illegal break-in at the DNC headquarters in the Watergate building on 17 June 1972. The break-in was discovered by Frank Willis, a security guard. The five burglars (James McCord and four Cuban-Americans) were arrested, along with Liddy and Hunt, who were caught in the building opposite with walkie-talkies, co-ordinating the burglary. Initially, Nixon was unworried: 'I think the country does not give much of a shit when somebody bugs somebody else.'

Why break into the Watergate building?

As Nixon later said, in 1990, the DNC headquarters was 'a pathetic target'. It did not contain any documents about Democratic electoral strategy. Suggested explanations for the break-in include:

- Colson and Hunt wanted to expose Democrat links to radical groups.
- Dean ordered the break-in to get hold of a DNC list of expensive prostitutes that mistakenly included his fiancée.
- It was hoped that the 'plumbers' would find out about a prostitution ring supposedly operating out of DNC and about the prominent Democrats who used it.
- Magruder said, 'We were really after everything', especially, some believe, information on Nixon's involvement in Castro assassination plots in 1959–60 (see page 115) and his financial dealings with reclusive billionaire Howard Hughes.
- When the break-in was authorised, in early 1972, Nixon was behind the Democratic front-runner, Edmund Muskie, in the polls – therefore any information on the Democratic campaign would be useful.

Did Nixon know about the break-ins?

We will probably never know for sure if and how much the president knew about the break-in, but there is no doubt that he was involved from the start in the cover-up. He complained to aides that the Democrats had been doing this sort of thing for years – 'they never got caught … every time the Democrats accuse us of bugging, we should charge that we were being bugged and maybe even plant a bug and find it ourselves'. On the White House taping system, which Nixon knew was in operation, the President asks Haldeman:

'Did Mitchell know [about the break-in]?'

'No.'

'Well who was the asshole that did? Is it Liddy? He must be a little nuts.'

'He is.'

Getting caught

Within days of the break-in, the FBI traced **laundered money** found on the plumbers to CREEP. On 23 June 1972, Nixon and Haldeman discussed using the CIA to stop the FBI: a clear obstruction of justice. The CIA would not co-operate, so Nixon tried to pay the burglars $430,000 to keep quiet: obstruction of justice again. The burglars were indicted in September 1972, then convicted in January 1973. Their sentences ranged from 20 years (Liddy) to 40 (the Cubans).

> ### The role of the media
>
> The press worked hard to uncover the plot. *Washington Post* reporters Bob Woodward and Carl Bernstein wrote a bestseller, *All the President's Men*, which rather suggested that they had done all the work themselves. What made their myth particularly appealing was the mysterious character '**Deep Throat**', the unidentified (until 2005) administration leaker, who gave them stories.
>
> The media followed the unfolding scandal exhaustively. Television networks covered over 300 hours of testimony in the subsequent Senate hearings.

The role of Congress

Following the burglars' conviction, the Senate established the bipartisan Select Committee on Presidential Campaign Activities in February 1973. Also known as the Watergate Committee, it was chaired by Sam Ervin (a Democrat senator from North Carolina, whom Nixon called an 'old fart'). By this time, some of the Watergate conspirators were willing to talk: on 23 March 1973, McCord had agreed to talk about Magruder, Mitchell, Dean, Haldeman and Colson, then Magruder and Dean agreed to talk. From 17 May to 7 August, Ervin's committee held 37 days of hearings. Former Attorney General John Mitchell admitted meeting the conspirators three times before the break-in. The nation watched the television coverage, transfixed: Ervin ('I'm just a country lawyer') and Republican committee member Howard Baker ('What did the President know and when did he know it?') became national heroes.

 **KEY TERMS**

Laundered money
When money is to be used illegally, it is frequently laundered or 'made clean' by being put into a bank not connected with the payer. In this case, the campaign money was laundered through a Mexican bank with the aim of disguising that it came from CREEP.

Deep Throat
The unidentified (at the time) FBI source who gave Woodward and Bernstein vital information during Watergate. In 2005, former FBI employee Mark Felt confessed to being Deep Throat.

On 30 April, John Dean (who had managed the Watergate cover-up) was fired and Haldeman and Ehrlichman resigned. On 22 May, Nixon announced that they had been involved in the cover-up without his knowledge. Dean testified that Nixon was involved in the cover-up, but Haldeman, Ehrlichman and Mitchell denied this.

The judge in the Ellsberg case now revealed the break-in at Ellsberg's psychiatrist's office. Then, on 16 July, White House aide Alexander Butterfield revealed the existence of Nixon's White House taping system, which had been kept highly secret (even Nixon's own family were not aware that their private conversations were being taped).

Congress and the special prosecutors

In May 1973, Congress forced Nixon to appoint the first ever special prosecutor, Harvard law professor Archibald Cox, a Democrat and a Kennedy family friend. Cox and his team (nicknamed the 'Coxsuckers' by the White House) concentrated on getting hold of the Nixon tapes.

Nixon sacked Cox and abolished his office on 20 October 1973, which was constitutionally 'right', but unwise. When Attorney General Elliot Richardson resigned rather than carry out the sacking, there was public outrage at this **'Saturday Night Massacre'**. Nixon's approval ratings sank to 17 per cent. He received a record near-half a million telegrams, mostly hostile. Under this pressure, Nixon named Leon Jaworski as special prosecutor (31 October). The House Judiciary Committee gave $1 million to hire 106 staff, including Yale lawyer Hillary Rodham Clinton, for an **impeachment** investigation. Faced with the public outcry, Nixon decided to surrender seven White House tapes.

Disgrace and disarray

In October 1973, Spiro Agnew, the champion of law and order (see page 197), became the first vice president to resign (for tax evasion and accepting bribes while governor of Maryland). The Nixon administration was in increasing disgrace and disarray. Nixon's own finances came under investigation. Investigators said he had received $1.1 million in income in his first term, but had paid less than $80,000 in taxes. Furthermore, his houses at Key Biscayne and San Clemente had greatly increased in value due to improvements financed by the public purse.

Nixon was under tremendous strain. Outside the White House, pickets carried signs saying 'Honk for Impeachment', so car horns sounded throughout every day. There was talk that Nixon was drinking heavily and emotionally unstable. Invited to an informal dinner at the White House, Barry Goldwater, sickened by Nixon talking 'gibberish', embarrassed the president's family when he cried out, 'Act like a President'. When briefing congressional leaders on the Arab–Israeli War in 1973, Nixon started to roll his head and make jokes about Kissinger's sex life. Kissinger frequently discussed the president's 'stability' with colleagues.

KEY TERMS

'Saturday Night Massacre' When Nixon sacked the Watergate special prosecutor and the Attorney General resigned.

Impeachment Under the US Constitution, Congress has the power to bring an errant president to trial, to impeach him.

The surrender of the White House tapes

The seven White House tapes that Nixon surrendered on 26 November 1973 contained an eighteen-and-a-half-minute gap in a Nixon–Haldeman conversation. Nixon's loyal secretary, Rose Mary Woods, said she had accidentally deleted this. Subsequent expert testimony said the tapes had been tampered with. Nixon claimed that two other subpoenaed tapes did not even exist. Nixon's assurance to reporters that 'I am not a crook' was mercilessly mocked by the media.

Indictments and more tapes

On 1 March 1974, seven of Nixon's aides were indicted for the cover-up. It was subsequently discovered that the president was named as a co-conspirator but not indicted. Rather than face impeachment, Nixon surrendered edited transcripts of other requested tapes in April 1974. The transcripts included many 'expletives deleted', but nothing incriminating. Jaworski wanted the actual tapes and asked the Supreme Court to rule on this. On 24 July, the Supreme Court ruled unanimously, in *United States* v. *Richard M. Nixon, President of the United States*, that the subpoenaed tapes must be released and that the president could not claim executive powers. The 23 June tape (one aide called it the 'smoking gun') proved that Nixon had ordered the cover-up and engaged in a conspiracy to obstruct justice.

After the proof that the president had ordered the cover-up, the House Judiciary Committee approved three articles of impeachment on the grounds of:

- obstruction of justice (by participating in the cover-up)
- abuse of power (by invading the civil rights of individuals such as Ellsberg, by misuse of government agencies such as the FBI, CIA and IRS, and by authorising wiretapping)
- abuse of Congress (by ignoring subpoenas issued by the Judiciary Committee).

Polls suggested that 75 per cent of Americans believed Nixon guilty of the first charge, and 66 per cent favoured impeachment.

The charges against Nixon examined by the House Judiciary Committee

Possible involvement in: obstruction of justice; conspiracy to obstruct justice; conspiracy; conspiracy to misuse government agencies; cover-ups; illegal wiretaps; destruction of evidence; election fraud; forgery; perjuries; money-laundering; bribery; financial misdealings; break-ins; offers of clemency; providing political favours for contributions; failure to fulfil the oath of office; failure to answer subpoenas; interference with federal prosecutors; obstruction of Congressional investigations; secretly bombing Cambodia; illegal impounding of funds.

Abuse of power

In August 1971, John Dean sent a memo to staff that clearly demonstrated willingness to abuse presidential power:

> *How can we maximize the fact of our incumbency in dealing with persons known to be active in their opposition to our Administration? Stated a bit more bluntly – how can we use the available federal machinery to screw our political enemies?*

The authorisation of the break-ins of Ellsberg's psychiatrist's office and the Watergate building are probably the best known examples of the abuse of power. An example of the president's (attempted) involvement occurred in summer 1971 when a Long Island newspaper published a series on the finances of Nixon's best (some say only) friend, Bebe Rebozo. Nixon ordered Haldeman to 'figure out a plan … to harass [the newspaper] … Use the power we have', particularly that of the IRS. Ironically, although the Kennedys used the IRS to embarrass political enemies such as Nixon, the IRS usually refused to be used by Nixon, so in this case he was guilty only of attempting to misuse power. On the other hand, owners of newspapers hostile to Nixon were hounded by the IRS (as Nixon himself had been).

Abuse of Congress

Nixon was certainly uncooperative in responding to Ervin's Senate committee investigating his misdemeanours. He also tried to circumvent congressional power, for example over the appointment of directors of government agencies, for which Congress took him to court. He delayed, evaded and on 27 occasions flat-out ignored congressional requests for information on executive actions. His predecessors had occasionally claimed executive privilege in keeping certain actions quiet, but Nixon went much further.

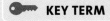 **KEY TERM**

Impounding When the president refuses to spend money allocated by Congress.

Nixon also challenged Congress by **impounding** money that Congress had allocated to spend on programmes such as the Clean Water Act of 1972. He only wanted to spend 25 per cent of what Congress had appropriated, because he was concerned about balancing the budget and/or because he wanted to increase presidential power, depending on one's viewpoint. In 1974, the House Judiciary Committee wanted to include impoundment in the impeachment charges, but lawyers said that Nixon's position was supported by the Constitution and statutory powers. Those sympathetic to Nixon say that the water pollution legislation was used by the Democratic Congress to embarrass the president on a popular issue in an election year, and that the amount they wanted to spend was unrealistically high and probably could not have been spent.

Abusive towards Congress

While possibly guilty of 'abuse of Congress', Nixon was definitely abusive. He was unusual in that he was a Republican president who never had a Republican Senate or House of Representatives with which to work, but he could not even get on with the Republicans in Congress. An aide of Gerald Ford said, 'Nixon couldn't hide his disdain for the Congress and he treated some individuals in Congress very badly.' In 1970, Nixon repeatedly accused Congress of bringing the federal government into disrepute by opposing his programmes. He described Congress as 'cumbersome, undisciplined, isolationist, fiscally irresponsible, overly vulnerable to pressures from organized minorities, and too dominated by the media'.

Ehrlichman described congressmen as 'a herd of mediocrities' and Congress as a place where:

> members consume time in enormous quantities in their quaint Congressional processes. They recess; they **junket**; they arrive late and they leave early; they attend conferences out of town, fly off to give speeches, sip and chat and endlessly party. And only sometimes do they focus on legislation.

Explanations for Nixon's behaviour

The following are possible explanations that can be offered for President Nixon's behaviour.

A pressured president

Nixon faced exceptional strain during his presidency, with unprecedented protests, riots and disorder. His daughter Julie Nixon received dozens of kidnap and murder threats. Unable to attend her graduation because of threatened protests, Nixon resorted to holding a make-believe graduation in spring 1970. Even without him at her official graduation, students had chanted, 'Fuck Julie'. In a 1977 interview, British journalist David Frost told Nixon that he was 'perhaps … the last American casualty of the Vietnam War' (in that Vietnam bore responsibility for much of the unrest).

Guilty of getting caught

Nixon's predecessors had behaved similarly in many ways – but they had not been caught. Both Kennedy and Johnson had ordered a great deal of wiretapping. Kennedy even had his brother Bobby's office bugged. As Nixon said, 'most people around the country think it's [bugging] probably routine, everybody's trying to bug everybody else, it's politics.' Nixon saw nothing wrong in any of this.

'It was us versus them'

Nixon had a point when he described the Democrats as holding 'all four aces in Washington – the Congress, the bureaucracy, the majority of the media, and the formidable group of lawyers and power-brokers who operated behind the scenes in the city'. This led to what Colson subsequently called a 'siege mentality' in the Nixon White House: 'It was us versus them.' CREEP was out to get 'them': Congress, the bureaucracy and the media. Nixon felt that the president, not Congress, represented the American people. Before Watergate, he continually

KEY TERM

Junket The taking advantage of political office by accepting perks such as lavish entertainments.

received high approval ratings while Congress did not, so he felt he had the popular mandate to do what he saw fit.

Disloyalty as normal practice

In December 1971, Ehrlichman discovered that the JCS (see page 78) had been spying on the NSC (see page 23), using naval officer Charles Radford to steal classified documents from the NSC files. The Radford case confirmed Nixon's belief that the federal government bureaucracy was 'crawling with … at best unloyal people and at worst treasonable people'. Radford, when caught, claimed that this military intelligence operation aimed at 'bringing Nixon down' – or at least, getting rid of his national security adviser Henry Kissinger. Clearly, Nixon's methods were commonplace.

The hostility of the press

The media was often unfair to Nixon (see page 207). He had a point when he said, '75 per cent of these guys hate my guts'. For example, in spring 1970, the magazine *Parade* reported that he had made the nation pay for a $60,000 'wind wall' around his swimming pool at his San Clemente home, to protect him from the strong prevailing offshore wind. The wall was in fact a bullet-proof glass shield on which the Secret Service insisted, and which Nixon had not wanted. *Parade* refused to print a retraction. Press hostility continued after Nixon's disgrace. Readers of Woodward and Bernstein's 1976 book on *The Final Days* of Nixon's presidency were agog at the depiction of a dangerously unstable drinker, who talked to portraits on the White House wall, and had not had sexual relations with his (drunken) wife for fourteen years. Despite her husband's protests, Pat Nixon read it, then suffered a stroke. Nixon is frequently quoted as having said in the 1977 interview with Frost, 'When the president does it, that means it's not illegal', but it is rarely mentioned that he was talking about actions in a national security context.

The resignation of the president

On 8 August 1974, Nixon resigned because the Watergate scandal gave him financial and legal concerns and lost him Republican support.

Financial and legal concerns

If Nixon resigned he would get his $60,000 presidential pension and $100,000 for staff expenses, but if impeached, 'I'll be wiped out financially' by legal fees and a $500,000 bill for unpaid taxes. He had paid virtually no tax while president, obtaining a large tax write-off in exchange for donating his vice presidential papers to the National Archives, and making dubious capital gains in selling property without paying any tax. Nixon also feared criminal prosecution if impeached. Anxious about the national trauma, the House Judiciary Committee promised Nixon on 6 August 1973 that he would face no further charges if he resigned.

Loss of Republican support

Nixon was not sure whether Republican senators would continue to support him and deny the necessary two-thirds majority required in the Senate to secure his impeachment. Initially, Republican Senator Barry Goldwater said, 'Well, for Christ's sake, everybody bugs everybody else.' However, when the 23 June 1972 tape of the conversation between Nixon and Haldeman was released and showed Nixon's complicity in the cover-up (see page 223), Goldwater said, 'Dick Nixon has lied to me for the very last time. And to a helluva lot of others in the Senate and House. We're sick to death of it all … Nixon should get his ass out of the White House.'

Polls showed that 66 per cent of Americans favoured impeachment, while only 27 per cent opposed it.

Nixon's political legacy

Nixon was the first president to resign while in office. He left the presidency with an unprecedentedly villainous reputation. When scholars rank presidents, Nixon always comes out at or near the bottom. Historian Melvin Small considered the Nixon administration:

> the most scandal-ridden administration in American history … Whereas some presidents participated in some of those illegal activities much of the time, and others did almost all of them on occasion, none of them committed all the illegitimate acts that constituted Watergate all the time.

While the break-in and the cover-up are remembered, the second article of impeachment, the abuse of (presidential) power, is not. Some historians believe that Nixon was responsible for the worst abuse of presidential power in American history, and that Watergate was not simply a scandal but a constitutional crisis of enormous magnitude.

Nixon's legacy included damage to the government, to the Republican Party, and to his successor Gerald Ford and the presidency.

Damaged government

Nixon contributed greatly to increased popular cynicism towards and distrust of government. In March 1977, Nixon confessed to David Frost:

> I let down my friends, I let down the country. I let down our system of government and the dreams of all those young people that ought to get into government but think it's all too corrupt and the rest.

Although government agencies were perhaps more important in exposing the affair, the press believed that their role in the Watergate scandal made them the great guardians of democracy. Woodward and Bernstein (see page 221) inspired a generation of reporters to seek similar fame by digging away at potential political scandals that invariably had the word 'gate' (from Watergate) stuck on the end of their names. This exacerbated the popular cynicism about the government that began with Johnson and the credibility gap (see page 155) then increased with Watergate. It was reflected in the decreased electoral turnout in the 1970s (see page 243).

Nixon's biographer Joan Hoff contended that Watergate was 'a disaster waiting to happen', the inevitable product of what she calls the **'aprincipled** American political system'. She lamented that the popular belief that it was all Nixon's fault stopped much-needed reform of the American political and constitutional system, in which the executive could easily abuse its power.

KEY TERM

Aprincipled Unable to see what was acceptable and what was unacceptable behaviour.

Damaged Republican Party

The Republican Party suffered greatly in the 1974 congressional elections: the four Republicans on the House Judiciary Committee who had voted against impeachment lost their seats. Nixon also bore responsibility for the Republican Party's move to the right. First, conservatives took the opportunity to associate the disgraced president with his moderate policies. Second, when Nixon's successor President Gerald Ford pardoned Nixon (see below), it probably cost him the 1976 election. Republican conservatives chose to interpret Ford's defeat as the electorate's rejection of moderate Republican policies, and proceeded to take control of the Republican Party. That dramatically affected American politics, government, economic affairs and foreign policy for many years afterwards (see page 264).

Damaged presidency

Congress enacted several laws to try to limit presidential power and avoid another Watergate, for example, the Budget and Impoundment Control Act (1974) and the Ethics in Government Act (1978). While historians disagree over the effectiveness of such legislation, the presidency of Nixon's successor, Gerald Ford, certainly demonstrated the damage Nixon had done to the prestige of the office.

When in October 1973 Spiro Agnew became the first vice president to resign (see page 222), Nixon chose Republican House Minority Leader Gerald Ford as vice president. (Haldeman claimed that Nixon chose Ford believing that the House knew Ford's ability so well that they would never impeach the president lest Ford replace him.) When Nixon resigned in August 1974, Ford became president, declaring, 'Our long national nightmare is over.'

While Nixon's resignation averted an impeachment trial, a presidential pardon enabled him to avoid any criminal prosecution. On 8 September 1974, President Ford pardoned Nixon. The pardon caused national outrage and Ford's approval rating to plummet from 71 to 49 per cent. He was then subjected to exceptionally disrespectful media treatment (see page 234).

Why did Ford pardon Nixon?

Ford pardoned Nixon because:

- Ford said this was the best way to end the 'American tragedy', because the national trauma would be prolonged if Nixon went on trial. Ford thought it better to let the slow process of healing begin.
- The trial of a former president in a criminal court would degrade the presidency.
- The antagonism towards Nixon was so great that it would be difficult, even impossible, to meet Supreme Court standards for an unbiased jury.
- The indictment and trial would take a long time and the nation would continue its unhealthy and divisive obsession with Watergate.
- If Nixon was found guilty of criminal activities, whoever was president would have to pardon him (in order to avoid setting the precedent of prosecuting a president for his policies and actions), so why not sooner rather than later?
- A Ford envoy to Nixon suggested that Nixon was, 'an absolute candidate for suicide; the most depressed human being I have ever met'. Nixon's family confirmed that. The pardon made Nixon more depressed and for a dangerously long time he refused hospitalisation, despite the possibility of a life-threatening embolism. In his speech announcing the pardon, Ford said, 'I feel that Richard Nixon and his loved ones have suffered enough.'
- It was Christian to show mercy.
- Ford believed resignation from office was an admission of guilt (he always carried a Supreme Court decision in his wallet that a pardon 'carries imputation of guilt, acceptance, a confession of it').
- Ford was possibly concerned for Republican electoral prospects in 1976 if Nixon's misdemeanours were still being pored over by the press.
- Many contemporaries were convinced that Nixon and Ford had made a deal, a pardon in exchange for the presidency. There is no evidence of any deal.

When Gerald Ford died in 2007, Senator Edward Kennedy, who had opposed the pardon at the time, said he now felt it to be the right decision. Pardoning Nixon certainly helped finish Ford's political career (see page 243).

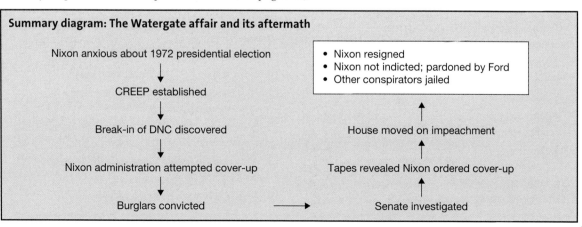

Summary diagram: The Watergate affair and its aftermath

Nixon anxious about 1972 presidential election
↓
CREEP established
↓
Break-in of DNC discovered
↓
Nixon administration attempted cover-up
↓
Burglars convicted →

Senate investigated
↑
Tapes revealed Nixon ordered cover-up
↑
House moved on impeachment
↑

- Nixon resigned
- Nixon not indicted; pardoned by Ford
- Other conspirators jailed

Chapter summary

Democratic Party divisions and association with disorder and costly Great Society programmes helped Nixon win the 1968 presidential election. Middle America voted for Nixon in 1968 and 1972 because they felt he shared their antagonism to the changes, violence and protests that characterised the 1960s.

Nixon had promised to demolish the Great Society but never did, partly because of a Democrat Congress, partly because he sympathised with the poor. Although he wooed racist Southerners over school desegregation, he promoted affirmative action.

The protest movements declined during his presidency because the protesters were increasingly exhausted and divided, Nixon was tough on them, and he removed a major cause of dissatisfaction when he wound down the Vietnam War.

Nixon ended the war through unprecedented bombing (which seemed to some to be expanding the war), detente and concessions. It was a slow process, partly to disguise the US retreat and partly because North Vietnam was reluctant to compromise. As Secretary of State, Kissinger played an important role in foreign policy. He and Nixon rarely disagreed on international relations. The Nixon administration supported the overthrow of a democratically elected leader of Chile and the murderous Operation Condor in Latin America. Detente with the Soviets and Chinese was helpful in stabilising Europe, in the US exit from Vietnam and in slowing the nuclear arms race, but relations remained tense.

The dark side of Nixon's personality was accentuated by advisers with similar faults, especially Kissinger, Haldeman and Ehrlichman. CREEP's break-in at the Democrat offices in the Watergate building and the Nixon administration's attempted cover-up was symptomatic of the administration's frequent abuse of power. Congress and the press pursued the issue and Nixon was forced to resign, having damaged the government, the presidency, the Republican Party and his successor.

 Refresher questions

Use these questions to remind yourself of the key material covered in this chapter.

1 How did the Democrats contribute to Nixon's election as president in 1968?

2 Why did Nixon appeal to Middle America?

3 In what ways were Haldeman and Ehrlichman important?

4 What did Henry Kissinger contribute to the Nixon administration?

5 Did President Nixon dismember the Great Society poverty programmes?

6 Were President Nixon's policies on race conservative?

7 How did President Nixon deal with protesters?

8 What economic problems were faced by President Nixon?

9 Why did President Nixon prolong and apparently extend the Vietnam War?

10 Why did the USA lose the Vietnam War?

11 Why and with what results did the Nixon administration pursue detente?

12 In what ways could Nixon and Kissinger be accused of demonstrating amorality in foreign policy?

13 What was the role of Congress in the Watergate affair?

14 What was Nixon's political legacy?

Question practice

ESSAY QUESTIONS

1 'Richard Nixon won the 1968 presidential election because of Johnson's policies.' How far do you agree with this view?

2 'President Nixon restored conservative social policies.' Assess the validity of this view.

3 'Henry Kissinger thoroughly deserved the Nobel Peace Prize.' To what extent do you agree with this view?

4 'Richard Nixon has received too much blame for Watergate.' Assess the validity of this view.

SOURCE ANALYSIS QUESTION

1 With reference to Sources E in Chapter 4 (page 151) and Sources A (page 189) and D (page 194) in this chapter, and your understanding of the historical context, assess the value of these three sources to a historian studying Nixon's presidential election victories in 1968 and 1972.

CHAPTER 6

The USA after Nixon 1974–80

The Vietnam War, Watergate and the deteriorating economy convinced many Americans that the nation was in decline. Hopes that Republican President Gerald Ford (1974–7) and then Democrat President Jimmy Carter (1977–81) might arrest the decline proved unfounded. This decade of disappointment in and disillusion over the American Dream is covered in sections on:

★ Ford and Carter as presidents

★ The position of the USA as a world power

★ African-Americans in the North and the South

★ The USA by 1980

Key dates

1974	Ford became president	**1978**	63 per cent of Americans considered inflation their greatest concern
	Ford pardoned Nixon		
	Acute racial tensions over busing in Boston	**1978–9**	$40 billion trade deficit
		1979	Concerned Women for America established to oppose women's rights
	Supreme Court ruling and congressional legislation against busing		Petrol availability crisis
1975	South Vietnam fell to Communists		Carter's 'crisis of confidence' speech
1976	Carter defeated Ford in presidential election		Iran took 60 Americans hostage
			USSR invaded Afghanistan
1977	Supreme Court supported anti-abortion legislation	**1980**	'Billygate'
			Race riots
1978	Supreme Court supported affirmative action but not quotas in *Bakke*		Reagan defeated Carter in presidential election

1 Ford and Carter as presidents

▶ *Did Americans lose faith in the American Dream in the 1970s?*

The revulsion generated by Nixon and Watergate prompted Presidents Gerald Ford (1974–7) and Jimmy Carter (1977–81) to try to differentiate and distance themselves from Richard Nixon and the 'imperial presidency' (see page 210 and Source A) with a new style of leadership.

SOURCE A

From the *Gettysburg Times*, 29 January 1970. Printed in a small Pennsylvania town, the *Gettysburg Times* had a small circulation.

President Nixon's August idea of European-style formal dress garb for White House police has bloomed in late January – to a cold reception from some critics.

The new $95 outfits ordered for about 100 policemen are described by the Secret Service as 'a white cream tunic, made out of elastique, with a double-breasted cut, three buttons, a stand-up collar, gold nylon trim and a vinyl cap.'

Nixon apparently was pleased by the uniforms since he had four of the police in their new outfits at the front door of the White House when British Prime Minister Harold Wilson arrived for a state dinner Tuesday night …

Some critical comments from bystanders … ranged from … 'They look like extras from a Lithuanian movie' … [to] 'Nazi uniforms'.

Nixon's suggestion for new uniforms came last summer after he noticed the palace guards and policemen during his European tour.

> **To what extent does Source A suggest the 'imperial presidency'?** ?

Regular guys

After Nixon, the American public hoped for a 'regular guy' in the White House. Nixon had emphasised the ceremonial aspects of the presidency, most famously with the White House guards (see Source A), but his two successors played down the ceremonial aspects in an attempt to suggest a new leadership style.

Gerald Ford was a respected and popular congressman from 1948 to 1973. He accepted the vice presidency after Spiro Agnew's resignation (see page 222) with the self-deprecatory joke that he was **'a Ford not a Lincoln'**. When Nixon resigned and Ford became president in August 1974, Americans felt strangely reassured when the pyjama-clad president-elect picked up his own newspaper off his front porch and waved to the press. *Newsweek* magazine said he was, 'nothing any different from your next-door neighbor'. Some Americans related to his family (his lively and outspoken wife would be photographed pushing him fully clothed into the Camp David pool). The American people wanted to believe in their president, but the honeymoon period ended when Ford pardoned Nixon (see page 229). His popularity never recovered. The 'regular guy' was just another politician after all.

Jimmy Carter too rejected excessive formality. A successful and homely Governor of Georgia, he and his family walked down **Pennsylvania Avenue** after his presidential inauguration: an unprecedented and highly informal gesture. Carter sold the presidential yacht and wore casual clothes for a televised broadcast.

Despite their attempts to offer a new kind of leadership, both Ford and Carter are considered to have been exceptionally poor leaders. However, they were unlucky in that they faced:

🔑 KEY TERMS

'A Ford, not a Lincoln'
Ford was saying that he was not going to be a great president like Abraham Lincoln, playing on the public's familiarity with cars. Fords were the cars of ordinary Americans; Lincolns were expensive, prestige cars.

Pennsylvania Avenue
A street in Washington DC that joins the White House and the Capitol building.

Gerald Rudolph Ford

1913	Born in Omaha, Nebraska
1948	Married Betty Warren
1948–73	Republican congressman in the House of Representatives
1973	Became vice president after Agnew resigned
1974	Became president after Nixon's resignation and then pardoned Nixon
1976	Won Republican nomination, but greatly damaged by Reagan's conservative challenge
	Defeated by Jimmy Carter in presidential election
1976–7	Retired from politics
2007	Died

Born in Omaha, Nebraska, Gerald Ford attended the University of Michigan on an athletics scholarship. He worked at a hospital and sold his blood every eight or ten weeks to finance his liberal arts degree. From 1935 to 1938, he coached Yale University's football team (one of the best college football players in the country, Ford rejected offers from professional teams because 'professional football probably wouldn't lead me anywhere'). During his presidency, the media often mocked his intellect, but he studied law at Yale (1938–41) and graduated in the top third of his class.

He served in the navy in the Second World War, then had a distinguished career in Congress, so much so that Richard Nixon considered him the consummate legislator and asked him to be his running mate in 1968. Ford declined, because he hoped to be Speaker of the House. After Vice President Spiro Agnew resigned and Ford became vice president, he was very loyal to President Nixon until the 'smoking gun' tape (see page 223).

President Ford had few concrete achievements. There was no landmark legislation during his presidency and he seemed unable to cope with US economic problems and Congress. Contemporaries felt that he had no great foreign policy achievements, but their criticisms of the Helsinki Agreements (see page 250) were perhaps short-sighted.

Ford was the first American president who had not been elected as either president or vice president. It was a tribute to the strength of the American system that he took over office so smoothly. Ford lost popular support after he pardoned Nixon. He then suffered much media mockery. However, Ford was highly significant in that he helped to restore stability after Watergate. He was probably right when he claimed during the 4 July 1976 **Bicentennial** celebrations, 'I guess we've healed America.' That was his greatest achievement.

(see page 223)... (see page 250)

🔑 KEY TERM

Bicentennial The USA's 200th birthday was on 4 July 1976. Americans had made their declaration of independence from Britain on 4 July 1776.

- great and growing economic problems
- several international crises
- congressional determination to rein in the 'imperial presidency' that Congress felt had reached its peak with Richard Nixon
- decreased respect for the presidency
- increased social divisions.

Decreased respect for the presidency

Ford was an easy target for disrespectful media coverage because of his informality and because he had not been elected president. Lyndon Johnson's joke that Ford had played football once too often was frequently cited. Ford was shown on television falling over on ski slopes and stumbling down a plane ramp – one network showed the latter 11 times in one newscast.

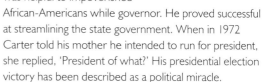

James Earl 'Jimmy' Carter

1924	Born in Plains, Georgia
1963–6	Served in Georgia State Senate
1970–4	Governor of Georgia
1974	Began presidential campaign
1976	Won Democratic nomination
	Defeated Gerald Ford in the presidential election
1978	Brokered peace between Egypt and Israel
1979	Iranian students took hostages from US embassy in Tehran
1980	Unsuccessful Iranian hostages mission
	Defeated by Reagan in presidential election
1981–	Mediated several international conflicts; wrote books

James 'Jimmy' Carter was born in Georgia. His father was a successful peanut farmer and Georgia legislator, his mother was a registered nurse and exceptionally liberal on race and poverty. In 1946, Jimmy Carter graduated from the US Naval Academy at Annapolis and married Rosalynn. After naval service, he returned to Georgia on his father's death to manage the peanut business. He served in the Georgia State Senate (1963–6), then as Governor of Georgia (1970–4). Although he had campaigned on a segregationist platform, he was helpful to impoverished African-Americans while governor. He proved successful at streamlining the state government. When in 1972 Carter told his mother he intended to run for president, she replied, 'President of what?' His presidential election victory has been described as a political miracle.

Carter is generally considered to have been an ineffective president. He made little effort to get along with Congress and had a poor legislative record. He helped bring greater stability to the Middle East but had few other foreign policy successes. He seemed unable to deal with the most pressing contemporary issues (the economy, the energy crisis and Iran). 'Can Carter cope?' became a common refrain.

Carter was important in that his election represented disillusionment with the tainted nature of Washington politics, and because he reflected the increasing political and social conservatism of many Americans. Often far removed from the liberal wing of his Democratic Party, he anticipated President Reagan in his criticism of big government.

Responses to social divisions

During the 1960s, America seemed to have become a nation deeply scarred by social divisions. Protests had led to some improvements in the position of African-Americans and women, but this had generated a socially conservative reaction that had helped put Richard Nixon in the White House (see page 194).

When Ford became president, *Time* magazine wrote that a 'time for healing' was needed, but bitter divisions were hard to overcome. This was demonstrated over clemency for Vietnam draft dodgers. Ford believed that clemency would help heal the nation, but conservatives were infuriated by the whole idea and liberals called it 'shamnesty' because Ford did not offer unconditional amnesty. Other socially divisive issues included poverty, race and the rights of women.

Women's rights

By the 1970s, over two-thirds of female college students agreed that 'the idea that the woman's place is in the home is nonsense'. Most women now expected to work for most of their lives. More women entered traditionally masculine occupations such as medicine and law, but they only received 73 per cent of the salaries paid to professional men. Women remained overwhelmingly dominant in low-paid jobs and constituted 66 per cent of adults classified as poor. The greatest preoccupation of women activists in the 1970s was the passage of the Equal Rights Amendment (ERA), which they hoped would bring greater economic equality by guaranteeing equal rights under the law.

> ## The ERA
>
> - Section 1. Equality of rights under the law shall not be denied or abridged by the United States or by any state on account of sex.
> - Section 2. The Congress shall have the power to enforce, by appropriate legislation, the provisions of this article.
> - Section 3. This amendment shall take effect two years after the date of ratification.

The ERA

KEY TERM

Nuclear family Husband, wife and children.

The Democrat-controlled Congress voted overwhelmingly for the ERA in 1972. Liberals were delighted, but opponents said it would lead to gay marriages, women in combat, unisex toilets and the end of the **nuclear family**. Perhaps the single most influential opponent of women's rights, including abortion, was Catholic lawyer and mother of six Phyllis Schlafly, who

- was nicknamed 'Sweetheart of the Silent Majority'
- campaigned for women's skirts to be two inches below the knee
- established a 'Stop ERA' organisation in 1972, which attracted 50,000 members (when 20,000 feminists met in Houston, Texas, for a National Women's Conference in 1978, Schlafly's counter-rally drew 8000 supporters)
- said, 'The American people do not want the Equal Rights Amendment, and they do not want government-funded abortion, lesbian privileges, or … universal … childcare.'

Many conservative states agreed with Schlafly and the ERA never obtained the assent of the 75 per cent of states required for an amendment to the Constitution, even though the issue remained high on the political agenda throughout the 1970s.

Although Betty Ford championed the ERA, her husband did nothing to help women. Carter was more sensitive to women's rights (he insisted that at least one female candidate be considered for each cabinet post and appointed two female cabinet members and more women to high-level posts than any previous president). Carter supported the ERA, but many women voters felt that he should have spoken out more (he let his wife Rosalynn speak for him). Some were also annoyed by his opposition to federal funding of abortion except in cases of rape, incest or the endangerment of the mother's life.

Reproductive rights

Before 1973, abortion was:

- a crime in 30 states
- legal in cases such as rape, incest or a threat to the woman's health in twenty states.

In the 30 states where abortion was a crime, many women risked backstreet abortions in which unqualified practitioners used primitive instruments and harsh chemicals. By the 1960s, college students could usually obtain safe abortions performed by sympathetic doctors, but poor women lacked such access. Many feminists considered the right to abortion the most important of women's rights: one said, 'We can get all the rights in the world … and none of them means a doggone thing if we don't own the flesh we stand in.' From 1971, the National Abortion Rights Action League lobbied state legislatures for the legalisation of abortion.

The case of a Texas woman who did not want to bear a child that would grow up in poverty led to the Supreme Court's ***Roe v. Wade*** (1973) ruling, which legalised abortion in the first thirteen weeks, when a foetus could not sustain life on its own. The ruling was politically and socially divisive: feminists, women who feared unplanned pregnancies, liberals and organisations such as NOW (see page 179) and **Planned Parenthood** were thrilled, but conservatives were outraged and actively opposed the ruling. Betty Ford called *Roe* v. *Wade* a 'great, great decision', but Presidents Ford and Carter kept quiet about it.

Conservative opposition to abortion

Conservative organisations such as the National Right to Life Committee (set up in 1967 by the Catholic Church to oppose abortion) campaigned against *Roe* v. *Wade* in the courts, in elections and in the streets. Anti-abortion activists proved highly effective fundraisers and recruiters. They used mass mailings containing highly emotive language. One 1978 anti-abortion mailing contained graphic pictures and pleaded:

> STOP THE BABY KILLERS … *Abortion means killing a living baby, a tiny human being with a beating heart and little fingers … killing a baby boy or girl with burning deadly chemicals or a powerful machine that sucks and tears the little infant from its mother's womb.*

In 1979, San Diego housewife and bestselling author Beverly LaHaye established Concerned Women for America (CWA) to fight against the ERA and abortion. CWA had 500,000 members by the mid-1980s. LaHaye and her supporters wanted women to stay at home, look after the family and not deprive men of possible employment. She was representative of a resurgent social conservatism that was beginning to greatly affect American politics.

This social conservatism was closely associated with the Republican Party. In 1976, Republican Representative Henry Hyde led Congress in the passage of a

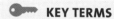

KEY TERMS

Roe v. Wade The Supreme Court decision legalising abortion.

Planned Parenthood Organisation established in 1916 to promote reproductive health and care.

law that banned the use of federal funds for abortion. In 1977, the increasingly conservative Supreme Court ruled Hyde's measure constitutional, and extended the ban on federally funded abortions to military and Peace Corps personnel. Around 70 per cent of those contacted by the National Right to Life Committee turned out to vote in the congressional elections in 1978 (twice the national average) and 50 per cent of them donated at least $25 to the committee. The conservative campaign against abortion affected the 1980 congressional elections: several liberals were defeated, including George McGovern (see page 207). *Roe* v. *Wade* had played a big part in mobilising the social conservatism that revitalised the Republican Party and would contribute greatly to so-called 'culture wars' between liberals and conservatives in the 1980s.

Poverty

In 1978, Senator Edward Kennedy said the development of a 'permanent underclass in our society' constituted 'the great unmentioned problem of America today'. The less sympathetic criticised the 'welfare mentality' – the way in which welfare became an accepted way of life for successive generations. While the Republican President Ford was a firm believer in self-help and had no real ideas or impact on poverty and welfare, the Democrat Carter was expected to care and do more about poverty. However, Carter faced several problematic demographic trends:

- The fastest growing section of the American population was the elderly, which necessitated increased federal government expenditure on Social Security and health care. Keen to balance the federal budget, Carter wanted to rationalise and reform those government programmes without increasing federal expenditure.
- The continuing 'white flight' of middle-class taxpayers (many from the Northern or 'Snow Belt' cities to the Sun Belt) exacerbated urban blight in poverty-stricken Northern city centres.
- Owing in particular to the economic recession of 1973–5, the number living below the poverty line was growing. It rose from 11.2 per cent in 1974 to 12.5 per cent in 1976. It included 50 per cent of all black female heads of household. The numbers eligible for food stamps grew from 18.5 million in 1976 to 20 million in 1980, when the United States suffered another recession.

Carter made little progress on these problems, despite the allocation of $4 billion for public works in 1977 and increased federal aid to the poor (for example, food stamps). The problem was that taxpayer voters did not want to subsidise the poor, of whatever age, colour or sex, while Carter, a fiscal conservative, wanted to balance the budget.

The growth of homelessness

The number of homeless Americans grew during the 1970s. Estimates of the total number in 1980 vary from 200,000 to 1 million. There were several reasons behind the increase:

- The number of institutions for mentally ill people decreased. This was because liberals campaigned successfully for inmate discharges on the grounds of their right to greater personal freedom and independence. Additionally, the unpaid labour that had helped finance the institutions was ended by a 1973 federal district court ruling that patients in mental health institutions had to be paid for their labour. Conservatives wanted to decrease expenditure on such institutions and were reluctant to make up for the shortfall. With fewer institutions, many former residents ended up homeless and on the streets.
- As a result of continuing urban renewal policies (see page 128), many inner-city '**skid row**' hotels that had housed the exceptionally poor were demolished. Former residents struggled to find alternative accommodation.
- Rising unemployment (see Figure 6.1) led some people into depression, despair and life on the streets. Budget cuts and lower welfare benefits restricted the 'welfare safety net', which contributed to the sense of hopelessness.
- The number of homeless women increased because of declining marriage rates and the increased number of single mothers. Without support from a partner and with unsympathetic authorities, many simply gave up and lived on the streets.
- The increased use of crack cocaine in the inner cities resulted in addicts who spent all their money on drugs and could not afford or access regular living accommodation.

KEY TERM

Skid row An impoverished urban area inhabited by marginalised people.

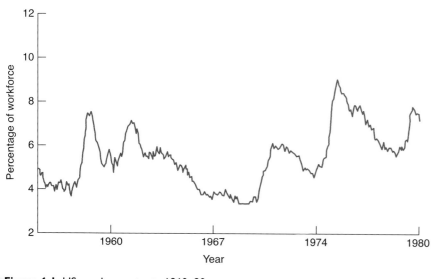

Figure 6.1 US employment rate 1960–80.

As always, African-Americans constituted a disproportionate number of the poor.

African-Americans

By the 1970s, 35–45 per cent of black families were classified as middle class and many statistics suggested that African-Americans were making great gains:

- African-Americans in Congress: 1959 – 4; 1969 – 10; 1980 – 18.
- Cities with African-American mayors: 1960 – none; 1970s – many, including Los Angeles, Detroit, Cleveland, Birmingham, Oakland and Atlanta.
- Proportion of black families earning over $10,000 (in **constant dollars**): 1947 – 3 per cent; 1960 – 13 per cent; 1971 – 31 per cent.

However, other statistics suggested continuing problems in the 1970s:

- Black male teenage unemployment averaged 50 per cent.
- Continuing 'white flight' (see page 54) made ghetto communities even more rundown.
- Half of all black teenagers in New York City dropped out of high school before graduation.
- Compared to a white child, a black child was twice as likely to die before reaching the age of one, twice as likely to drop out of school, and four times as likely to be murdered.

Liberals remained convinced that integrated education was essential for progress.

In 1969, the Supreme Court ruled that separate but equal schools were 'no longer constitutionally permissible'. By 1974, the percentage of segregated schools in the South was down from 68 to 8 per cent. However, *de facto* segregation continued in the North, where it was a divisive issue. This was demonstrated by events in Boston.

Desegregation: the case of Boston

Boston's public schools were clearly separate and unequal. While in 1965, 25 per cent of Boston students were African-American, only 0.5 per cent of teachers were – and none were principals. NAACP initiated a federal district court case, complaining about inferior educational materials and a textbook in which the song 'Ten Little Niggers Sitting on a Fence' was used to teach arithmetic. In June 1974, the federal district court found Boston guilty of unconstitutional segregation of schools. It ordered busing (see page 201) of black students from Boston's Roxbury area to the predominantly white South High School in neighbouring Irish-American South Boston, but the city authorities refused to comply. White anti-busing groups such as Restore Our Alienated Rights (ROAR) sprang up. They were encouraged by President Ford when he said that 'I respectfully disagree with the judge's order' and that there would be no federal government intervention to keep order. When Massachusetts Senator Edward Kennedy advocated busing (his children attended private schools), ROAR marchers chased him into the federal building where he had his office and pounded on the barricaded glass doors until they shattered.

(see page 54)

KEY TERM

Constant dollars To make comparisons between dates more meaningful, economists factor in changes in the cost of living or the value of the currency, and so on.

On Boston's first desegregated day, many black and white students were frightened to go to school. Black parents greeted white students, but South Boston High parents surrounded the school, jeered and threw objects at black students. Nine children were injured, eighteen buses damaged. Whites then boycotted city schools. White adults 'welcomed' black students to school throughout the year by holding bananas, calling them apes and chanting obscenities. Schools installed metal detectors because knife fights became common. President Ford opposed busing, but had troops ready in December 1974 when riots erupted: a white South Boston High student was stabbed, white parents surrounded the school, and black students had to escape through the back. Although there was sporadic violence in the next few years, it decreased when increasing numbers of white students enrolled in schools outside the Boston public school system.

While educational opportunity remained limited for many African-Americans, there was considerable progress with affirmative action.

Carter and affirmative action

From the mid-1960s, affirmative action laws based upon the Civil Rights Act (1964) were passed to help minorities and women in education and employment. More sensitive to minority rights than Ford, Carter:

- insisted that at least one minority candidate be considered for each cabinet post
- chose African-American Patricia Harris as Secretary of Housing and Urban Development
- appointed more black federal judges than any previous president (38)
- made Martin Luther King Jr's associate Andrew Young US ambassador to the United Nations
- channelled government contracts to minority firms
- strengthened Justice Department enforcement of voting rights laws
- made the work of the EEOC (see page 122) against discrimination in the labour force more effective
- supported the 1977 Public Works Act, which said that minority contractors should get 10 per cent of federal grants for public works.

Affirmative action proved socially divisive, as demonstrated in the *Bakke* case. Allan Bakke was a 33-year-old white male who sought to be a medical student. He claimed that the University of California's Davis medical school had discriminated against him by accepting minority students with lower grades. His litigation led to a Supreme Court ruling (*Bakke* v. *Regents of the University of California*, 1978) that upheld affirmative action but not quotas (sixteen Davis places were reserved for disadvantaged students). After *Bakke*, affirmative action programmes continued basically unchanged.

African-American dissatisfaction

African-Americans disliked *Bakke* and complained that Carter was insufficiently committed to:

- busing
- a 1977 bill that encouraged lenders to assist minorities (this became the Community Reinvestment Act)
- the **Humphrey–Hawkins** bill, which attempted to increase employment opportunities (the bill became an ineffective Act)
- the expansion of social welfare programmes.

African-Americans suffered disproportionately during the great recession of the Carter years. When hundreds of black teenagers reported for snow-shovelling work in Washington DC in 1979 and found the jobs already filled, they broke into and looted shops. The same thing happened in Baltimore. Black officials told Carter they blamed him for not helping the poor and unemployed. In 1980, economic problems prompted the worst summer of racial violence since the 1960s. In Liberty City, Miami, Florida, an all-white jury acquitted four white policemen charged with beating to death a black insurance salesman. Three days of looting, shooting, overturning of cars and burning of property followed. Sixteen people died, over 400 were injured and an estimated $100 million of property was damaged. 'Black folks ain't worth a damn in this country', said NAACP leader Benjamin Hooks. There was sporadic violence in Miami throughout the year and similar scenes in Chattanooga, Boston and Wichita.

Democrat divisions

Social divisions elicited conflicting responses from Democrats during the 1970s. On the more liberal wing were those such as Senator Edward Kennedy, who wanted to offer more to the poor, while on the right were those such as Carter, who felt that the country could not afford it.

Political corruption and the loss of national self-confidence

Watergate generated great public disillusionment and disrespect for politicians. A series of scandals, beginning with Ford's pardon of Nixon, convinced many that American politics was irredeemably corrupt.

Ford's pardon of Nixon

Ford's pardon of Nixon irreparably damaged relations with Congress, the public and the media. Republican congressmen blamed the pardon for the loss of 43 House seats in 1974 and right-wing Republicans openly criticised Ford. A conservative New Hampshire newspaper called him 'Jerry the Jerk'. By late 1974, Republican Governor Ronald Reagan of California was privately asserting that Ford was a 'caretaker' who had been 'in Congress too long'. Backed by other Republican right-wingers, Reagan challenged Ford for the Republican presidential nomination in 1976. Reagan ran as an outsider untainted by the corruption of Washington DC. Ford eventually won the nomination, but Reagan humiliated him and weakened him for the fight against the Democrat presidential candidate, Jimmy Carter.

Corruption, disillusion and the 1976 presidential election

In the lowest presidential election turnout since 1948 (only 54 per cent of eligible Americans voted), Carter won 49.9 per cent of the vote, to Ford's 47.9 per cent. Neither candidate excited the electorate: when polled on whether the candidates had presidential quality, just over three-quarters of Americans thought both Ford and Carter lacked it. Ford staffers told the president that 'vast numbers' of voters saw 'no practical difference' between him and Carter. The low turnout and public opinion polls demonstrated the electorate's disillusionment.

'Why don't people vote? Because it's doesn't make a difference', said one welfare worker. In the Carter years, around half of the electorate never bothered to vote, clearly feeling alienated from the political process. Polls illustrated Americans' loss of confidence in politicians and the government.

Table 6.1 Americans' views of their government in 1969 and 1979

US public views	1969	1979
Percentage who felt that government will 'do what is right most of the time'	56%	29%
Percentage believing government officials were 'smart people who know what they are doing'	69%	29%
Percentage who felt that US affairs were run for the benefit of a few big interests rather than all the people	28%	65%
Percentage who agreed that the 'people running the country do not really care about what happens to you'	26%	60%

Why Carter won

Carter's victory owed much to:

- Reagan's divisive and exhausting challenge to Ford
- the perception that Ford was a weak and indecisive leader who had lost ground to the Soviets (see page 250)
- economic problems (inflation was in double figures and Americans were worried about oil shortages and gasoline prices).

It also owed much to the perception that Ford's administration was corrupt. Many felt that there had been some secret deal with Nixon over the pardon. When the head of the FBI was accused of using an agency man to install a window sash for free in his home, Carter criticised Ford for not sacking him. Ford also suffered from talk that corporate friends with whom he played golf received special favours, and had excessive access to him. John Dean (see page 218) damaged Ford when he claimed that Ford had moved to stop investigations into Watergate. Finally, Ford's running mate Robert Dole was dogged by press stories of an illegal corporate contribution to his 1973 election.

Carter made much of the corruption issue, emphasising that he had not been part of the corrupt Washington scene. His campaign exploited the nation's anti-Washington mood. Many considered the federal government meddlesome, inflexible, bureaucratic, out of touch, untrustworthy and immoral. Carter appealed to the American public to help him improve it.

President Carter and corruption

Carter had run on an anti-Washington platform and pledged to end the **pork-barrel politics** that characterised Capitol Hill. However, he too was involved in scandals, the worst of which was 'Billygate'.

The president's older brother Billy Carter was commonly lampooned as a beer-bellied **redneck**. His self-deprecatory humour made him a popular talk-show guest and lecturer.

In 1978, Billy and other Georgia businessmen and legislators visited Libya. In January 1979, Billy hosted a reception for a Libyan 'friendship delegation'. His pro-Libya and pro-Arab sentiments were interpreted as anti-Semitism, to which Billy responded, 'The only thing I can say is there is a helluva lot more Arabians than there is Jews.' President Carter said he hoped that the American public would 'realise that I don't have any control over what my brother says' and that 'he has no control over me'. 'If Billy is not working for the Republican Party, he should be', joked one Atlanta newspaper.

After several weeks in an alcohol treatment centre, Billy was sober (which made the celebrity circuit lose interest in him) and short of money. In July 1980, he admitted receiving a $220,000 'loan' from the Libyan government. This was investigated by the Senate and Justice Department. 'Billygate' raised a political storm. The media speculated on the president's involvement.

The Senate acquitted President Carter of all involvement other than unwisely trying to use Billy's Libyan contacts to try to help free the Iranian hostages (see page 252). The American public decided that President Carter was not corrupt – just incompetent.

KEY TERMS

Pork-barrel politics
When a legislator will not pass legislation unless he is given particular benefit for his own constituents.

Redneck Poorly educated, working-class white Southerner, frequently characterised by racism and beer drinking.

> ### Corrupt Congress?
> In February 1980, it was revealed that FBI agents posing as wealthy Arabs in a sting operation had successfully persuaded twelve government officials and seven members of Congress to take bribes from a fictitious oil sheik in return for political favours.

The loss of national self-confidence

Many Americans thought well of Presidents Eisenhower (1953–61) and Kennedy (1961–3). Many initially considered President Johnson's leadership reassuring after his predecessor's assassination. However, the protest movements of the 1960s reflected and generated a more critical view of American society and politics. Then the credibility gap over Vietnam, the Watergate scandal, Ford's pardon of Nixon and Carter's apparent inability to cope, all combined to create growing voter disillusion and a sense of a nation in crisis. This was exacerbated by international problems (see page 251) and an economic crisis.

Economic crisis

After the Second World War, the United States was the world's wealthiest nation. However, there were worrying economic trends by the 1960s. While America still led the world in manufacturing industries that employed many Americans, those industries were in decline. The expense of the Vietnam War and to a lesser extent of the Great Society raised the federal government deficit from $1.6 billion in 1965 to $25.3 billion in 1968, leading to inflation and a weakened dollar.

By 1973, countries such as Japan and West Germany seemed poised to overtake the United States as the world's leading economic power. The American economy suffered from inflation (mostly due to rising oil prices and federal government overspending), a **balance of trade deficit** and a weakened currency. All this impacted on the lives of many Americans, many of whom had an insatiable appetite for the consumer goods and oil (for cars and heating) that they now struggled to afford.

Inflation and unemployment

Gerald Rafshoon, assistant to the president for communications, told Carter in 1977:

> *It is impossible to overestimate the importance of the inflation issue … It affects every American in a very palpable way. It causes insecurity and anxiety. It affects the 'American Dream'.*

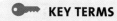

KEY TERMS

Balance of trade deficit
When the value of the goods imported by a nation exceeds the value of the goods exported.

Rust Belt The traditional manufacturing areas of the Eastern seaboard and the Midwest, where the old industries had declined and mostly disappeared.

Table 6.2 Highest and lowest figures for US inflation rate 1955–81

Year	Highest rate	Lowest rate
1955	0.7%	0.4%
1961	1.7%	0.7%
1963	1.6%	1.0%
1969	6.2%	4.4%
1974	12.3%	9.4%
1977	7.0%	5.2%
1981	11.8%	8.9%

During the years 1973–80, Americans experienced unprecedented inflation, in or near double figures for much of the decade. It made everything more expensive – mortgages, loans, food and energy. During July 1974 alone, prices rose by 3.7 per cent. A 1978 poll showed that 63 per cent of Americans considered inflation their greatest concern.

As the cost of living rose at a yearly average of 8.2 per cent between 1973 and 1983, inflation greatly affected family incomes. The hardest hit were those in the areas of declining manufacturing output known as the **Rust Belt**. Increasing numbers previously accustomed to well-paid manufacturing work found themselves unemployed.

Unemployment rose across the nation throughout the decade. For example, it rose from 6.5 per cent in December 1974 to 8.9 per cent by May 1975. The increase was due to two main factors. First, increased mechanisation in American industry meant machines were replacing men. Second, countries such as Germany and Japan were producing manufactured goods at lower prices and often superior quality. Some car workers attacked Japanese-manufactured Toyotas with sledgehammers, United Auto Workers asked President Carter to restrict Japanese car imports, and some sported BUY AMERICAN: THE JOB YOU SAVE MAY BE YOUR OWN bumper stickers – all to no avail.

It was difficult for those who lost manufacturing jobs to find alternative employment, apart from within the service industries. Service jobs constituted 60 per cent of employment opportunities in 1970 but 70 per cent by 1980. Many were low paid. Although the federal minimum wage rose from $2.10 an hour in 1975 to $3.35 an hour in 1981, it failed to keep pace with rising prices. Many mothers had to work in order to maintain the usual family income: 38 per cent of women worked in 1960, 43 per cent in 1970, 52 per cent in 1980.

The oil crisis and the end of cheap energy

Cheap oil had been vital to America's post-Second World War prosperity and economic growth. However, in the three decades after the Second World War, the United States went from energy self-sufficiency to an energy deficit situation. Although constituting only 6 per cent of the world's population, Americans consumed one-third of the world's oil production. Roughly 30 per cent of the oil Americans used had to be imported, mostly from the Middle East. The resulting American economic vulnerability was exposed when Nixon's support of Israel in the 1973 Arab–Israeli War (see page 217) led to an Organisation of Petroleum Exporting Countries (OPEC) oil embargo on the USA. The end of the embargo was followed by a 387 per cent hike in the price of oil that greatly damaged American industry (apart from US oil companies). The end of the era of cheap energy hit Americans' standard of living. Probably one-third of the alarming rise in prices was due to the increased cost of oil.

Several dramatic events illustrated the seriousness of the energy crisis during the decade:

- In 1974, a strike by 100,000 independent truckers demanding lower fuel prices brought the nation's roads to a standstill for eleven days and left stores with empty shelves.
- In the exceptionally harsh 1976–7 winter, a natural gas shortage forced closure of schools and factories, especially in the eastern USA. Fuel stations closed on Sundays or cut their hours in order to conserve supplies, and long queues developed at the petrol pumps. The first American energy riot

occurred in Levittown, Pennsylvania, when truckers barricaded expressways: 100 were injured and 170 arrested in two nights of violence.

- In 1977, 165,000 United Mine Workers began a three-month strike. The consequent coal shortage led to school closures and shortened working weeks in the eastern USA.
- In 1979, half of the nation's petrol stations were without fuel. Those that had it were charging 50 per cent more than the year before. Drivers were queuing for petrol on specified days, often for several hours.

Politicians and the energy crisis

The energy crisis provided politicians with an apparently insoluble problem. Voters wanted them to 'do something about it' but rejected the obvious option of the increased taxes on fuel that would have cut consumption and ended fuel shortages. The inability of Ford, Carter and Congress to solve either this conundrum or the nation's other economic problems contributed to the growing political disillusion and the feeling that the United States was in an unprecedented decline.

SOURCE B

From President Carter's televised speech to the nation on 15 July 1979.

It's clear that the true problems of our Nation are much … deeper than gasoline lines or energy shortages … inflation or recession … All the legislation in the world can't fix what's wrong with America. So, I want … to talk…about … a crisis of confidence … that strikes at … our national will. We can see this crisis in the growing doubt about the meaning of our own lives and in the loss of a unity of purpose for our nation.

The erosion of our confidence in the future is threatening to destroy the social and the political fabric of America … We've always had a faith that the days of our children would be better than our own. Our people are losing that faith … In a nation that was proud of hard work, strong families, close-knit communities, and our faith in God, too many of us now tend to worship self-indulgence and consumption … The symptoms of this crisis of the American spirit are all around us … Two-thirds of our people do not even vote. The productivity of American workers is actually dropping … there is a growing disrespect for government … churches … schools, the news media, and other institutions …

These changes did not happen overnight. They've come upon us gradually over … shocks and tragedy [such as assassinations and Vietnam] … We respected the presidency as a place of honor until … Watergate … Ten years of inflation began to shrink our dollar and our savings. We believed that our nation's resources were limitless until 1973, when we had to face a growing dependence on foreign oil … [The] gap between our citizens and our government has never been so wide.

Study Source B. Why do you suppose the public reaction to Carter's speech was initially positive but then turned negative?

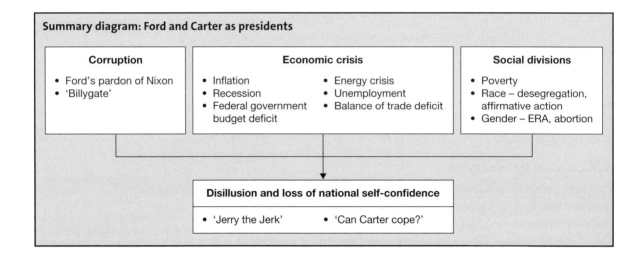

Summary diagram: Ford and Carter as presidents

Corruption	Economic crisis		Social divisions
• Ford's pardon of Nixon • 'Billygate'	• Inflation • Recession • Federal government budget deficit	• Energy crisis • Unemployment • Balance of trade deficit	• Poverty • Race – desegregation, affirmative action • Gender – ERA, abortion

Disillusion and loss of national self-confidence

• 'Jerry the Jerk'　　• 'Can Carter cope?'

(2) The position of the USA as a world power

▶ *Was the USA a superpower in decline during the 1970s?*

After Nixon's disgrace, Ford retained Henry Kissinger as Secretary of State and relied heavily on him. However, many of the policies with which Kissinger and Nixon had been associated became discredited, including support for Thieu and South Vietnam.

The final withdrawal from Vietnam

Nixon and Kissinger had supposedly brought 'peace with honour' at Paris in 1973 (see page 211). However, the Paris Peace Accords contained no provisions for Communist resumption of the war in South Vietnam. Under the settlement, America could protect South Vietnam through financial aid, but Congress cut the aid by 50 per cent in 1973 and then again in 1974. American taxpayers felt that the $150 billion spent on Vietnam had been wasted money and opposed further expenditure.

In winter 1974–5, the Communists began a major offensive against South Vietnam. Nixon had secretly promised Thieu American support if the peace collapsed, but neither Congress nor the public were interested when Ford appealed for help for South Vietnam. Thieu fled the country on 21 April, after a speech in which he accused the United States of selling out. Ford responded with a carefully calibrated speech that combined admission that the war was over with more positive sentiments (Source C).

SOURCE C

From President Ford's 23 April 1975 speech at Tulane University (available from www.presidency.ucsb.edu/ws/?pid=4859).

Today, America can regain a sense of pride that existed before Vietnam. But it cannot be achieved by re-fighting a war that is finished as far as America is concerned … Instead of my addressing the image of America, I prefer to consider the reality of America. It is true that we have launched our Bicentennial celebration without having achieved human perfection but we have attained a very remarkable self-governing society that possesses the flexibility and the dynamism to grow and undertake an entirely new agenda, an agenda for America's third century … We are, of course, saddened indeed by the events in Indochina. Events, tragic as they are, [that] portend neither the end of the world nor of America's leadership in the world … I am determined as a president can be to seek national rediscovery of the belief in ourselves. I ask that we stop fighting the battles and the recriminations of the past. I ask that we look now at what is right with America.

Study Source C. What do you suppose were the differences between 'the image of America' and the reality?

All that remained was to evacuate the 6000 American personnel left in South Vietnam, along with their Vietnamese wives, children and in-laws. They numbered 40,000 and Ford arranged for their exodus. The US Navy also rescued over 32,000 Vietnamese 'boat people' who fled by sea. Ford welcomed some refugees personally in San Francisco, but few Americans shared his enthusiasm for the influx.

An interesting footnote to the exodus occurred when, in 1994, a businessman friend of Ford found the ladder that the 40,000 had ascended to reach the embassy roof and the helicopter flights out of Saigon. Amid a heated debate among the trustees of the Gerald Ford Foundation as to whether the ladder should be displayed in the Ford Museum, two contrasting visions of America's identity emerged. Kissinger was furious about the ladder, asking, 'Why would you want to remind visitors about this horrible chapter in American history?' Ford saw it differently: 'To some, this staircase will always be seen as an emblem of military defeat. For me, however, it symbolises man's undying desire to be free.'

Relations with the USSR and China

Initially, Ford and Kissinger sought to continue detente with the Soviets. In November 1974, Ford met with the Soviet leader Brezhnev at the Vladivostok summit meeting on arms control. They agreed on the basic principles of another Strategic Arms Limitation Treaty (SALT) agreement, designed to put limits on missiles and bombers. However, Americans were becoming so opposed to detente that in 1976 Kissinger called it 'a word I would like to forget'.

Why Americans turned against detente

Americans turned against detente with the Soviets for several reasons:

- Detente suffered from its association with disgraced President Nixon.
- Conservatives particularly opposed the **Helsinki Agreement** (1975), saying that it constituted 'appeasement' of the Soviet Union. The Helsinki Agreement was arguably the nearest the Second World War victors ever came to making a European peace settlement, in that both sides recognised the post-war European *status quo*. In exchange for that implicit Western recognition of Soviet domination of Eastern Europe, the Soviets agreed on a human rights provision. Although some in the West felt the agreement was a sell-out, the human rights provision encouraged agitation for human rights in Eastern Europe and caused the Soviet Union considerable international embarrassment.
- Americans perceived the Communists as having taken advantage of detente to build up their nuclear arsenal and to increase their influence in Africa and Vietnam.
- Americans had grown dissatisfied with SALT I because the Soviets had attained parity on multiple warheads.

KEY TERM

Helsinki Agreement
1975 accord where the West recognised Soviet control of Eastern Europe in exchange for Soviet concessions on human rights.

The Helsinki Agreement (1975)

- The West recognised the current national boundaries in Eastern Europe.
- West Germany recognised the legitimacy of East Germany.
- NATO and the Warsaw Pact (see page 20) countries agreed that each should have observers at the other's military exercises.
- There would be more trade, more co-operation in economic, scientific and technological endeavours, and a free exchange of people and ideas between the Soviet bloc and the West.
- Both sides opened their human rights records to public scrutiny.

Why the Soviets turned against detente

The Soviets turned against detente for a number of reasons:

- They resented President Carter's repeated criticisms of the Soviet Union's human rights record. For example, when in 1979 Brezhnev allowed an exceptional number of Jews to emigrate from the Soviet Union (something the Americans had long demanded), Carter responded by conducting a high-profile correspondence with a Soviet dissident. The Soviets retaliated by criticising the US human rights record, citing widespread racial prejudice, unemployment and organised crime in the West as indicative of Western hypocrisy.
- The Soviets resented their exclusion from Carter's Middle East peace process in 1978 (see below).

- The USSR considered Carter too friendly with China. When the Americans and Chinese finally established full diplomatic relations in January 1979, the Soviets blamed Sino-American plotting for the subsequent Chinese invasion of Vietnam (a Soviet ally). The Soviets had hoped to isolate China through detente, but the Chinese were buying military hardware from the West and improving relations with Japan (America's ally).
- The Soviets had hoped that detente would do more to help their economy.
- Worst of all, the Helsinki Agreement had led to unrest in Eastern Europe and worldwide criticism of the USSR on the human rights issue.

The demise of detente was illustrated when Congress refused to ratify the **SALT II** treaty that Carter and Brezhnev agreed on at the Vienna summit (1979). Congress felt the Soviets had taken advantage of detente to become more aggressive, as demonstrated in Afghanistan.

The response to crises in the Middle East

The 1973 Arab–Israeli War (see page 217) had clearly demonstrated the limitations of detente, particularly when Nixon put America on full nuclear alert. It affected Ford and Carter in that it demonstrated the West's increasing vulnerability to Arab oil power: when the United States had supplied weapons to the great Arab enemy, Israel, and used NATO bases in Western Europe as transportation points, the Arab nations had retaliated by imposing an oil embargo which damaged the American, West European and Japanese economies (oil prices rocketed). Under the pressure of this oil crisis, Japan and Western Europe seemed increasingly pro-Arab, which worried Ford and confirmed the dangers of the multipolar world that had made Nixon seek detente.

Whereas the importance of oil had led President Eisenhower to woo the Arab nations (see page 80), the United States was far more closely associated with support of Israel by the 1970s. Carter proved a brilliant negotiator in bringing about an Israeli–Egyptian detente at Camp David in 1978, but US problems with the Middle East were demonstrated in the Iranian crisis.

Iran and Afghanistan

Iran and Afghanistan were the international crises most responsible for the media and public refrain of 'Can Carter cope?' Iran was the greatest crisis of Carter's presidency.

Iran

In 1978, Islamic fundamentalists led a revolution against the repressive, pro-American Shah Mohammad Reza Pahlavi. In January 1979, the Shah fled Iran. Iranians resentful of American military and political support for the Shah stormed the US embassy in Tehran and held it for several hours. Many Americans felt powerless, and 50 per cent of them felt that Carter was 'too soft' on Iran.

KEY TERM

SALT II Treaty signed by Carter and Brezhnev (1979) but not ratified by the USA after the Soviet invasion of Afghanistan; the treaty aimed to slow down the arms race.

On 4 November 1979, Iranian militants seized the US embassy in Tehran and took 60 Americans hostage in protest against Carter allowing the Shah into America to receive cancer treatment. Carter tried to negotiate the hostages' release, stopped Americans buying Iranian oil, and froze Iranian assets. His approval rating rocketed to 61 per cent. Then, in April 1980, he attempted a military rescue. It was a disaster.

One of the American rescue mission helicopters broke down as it entered Iranian airspace. A second got lost in a sandstorm. A third developed hydraulic problems and so the mission was aborted. Then one of the helicopters crashed, setting the others on fire. Eight Americans died, four were badly burned. Among the criticisms were:

- The plan was too complex.
- The plan was dependent on too many variables.
- The mission needed more than six helicopters and two spares.

Carter's painstaking diplomacy effected the release of the hostages, but only after he had left the White House.

For many Americans, the crises in Iran and Afghanistan seemed to confirm that America was a power in decline.

Afghanistan

Afghanistan was a Muslim state on the southern border of the Soviet Union. In 1979, its pro-Soviet government was divided into two factions and plagued by tribal risings. On 27 December 1979, the Soviets invaded Afghanistan in support of the more moderate faction. Soon 100,000 Soviet troops were fighting Muslim guerrillas who opposed the pro-Soviet government.

The Soviet Union intervened in Afghanistan because it:

- had a Muslim population in the southern USSR and wanted to stop unrest spreading there
- sought to avoid an anti-Soviet state on its southern border.

As this was the first time Soviet troops had been used outside Eastern Europe since 1945, the United States thought it signalled a new phase of Soviet expansionism and reacted with hostility. Congress refused to ratify SALT II and Carter

- stopped exports to the USSR and American participation in the 1980 Moscow Olympics
- dramatically increased US defence expenditure
- pledged US intervention if the Soviets threatened Western oil interests in the Persian Gulf.

In 1979, 41 per cent of Americans believed their country was 'in deep and serious trouble'. By 1980, it was 64 per cent. That change owed much to the crises over Iran and Afghanistan.

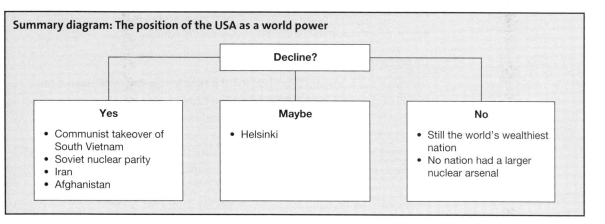

Summary diagram: The position of the USA as a world power

Decline?

Yes	Maybe	No
• Communist takeover of South Vietnam • Soviet nuclear parity • Iran • Afghanistan	• Helsinki	• Still the world's wealthiest nation • No nation had a larger nuclear arsenal

③ African-Americans in the North and the South

▶ *Had African-Americans attained equality by 1980?*

The position of many African-Americans improved greatly between 1945 and 1980, but the dream of equality was not yet achieved.

The impact of civil rights legislation

The civil rights legislation of 1964–5 in particular (see page 160) and supportive Supreme Court rulings led to improvements in the social, economic and political status of black Americans by 1980.

Social status in the South

The social status of African-Americans in the South had greatly improved through the 1964 Civil Rights Act, which ended the social inferiority enshrined in the Jim Crow laws. That act had mandated the acceleration of school desegregation and, coupled with Supreme Court rulings, had helped to increase the number of African-Americans who graduated from high school and obtained degrees. African-Americans were slowly closing the educational gap on whites, although they were still far behind:

- In 1970, 31 per cent of African-Americans (and 55 per cent of whites) aged over 25 years completed four or more years of high school. By 1980, 51 per cent of African-Americans (and 69 per cent of whites) had done so.
- In 1970, 4 per cent of African-Americans (and 11 per cent of whites) completed four or more years of college. By 1980, 8 per cent of African-Americans (and 17 per cent of whites) had done so.

The percentage of African-American children in segregated schools in the South fell from 68 per cent to 8 per cent during Nixon's presidency (see page 201) and the desegregation of schools in the South peaked later in the 1970s. However, *de facto* segregation in the North proved harder to combat.

De facto segregation in the North

Although the Supreme Court had ruled it time for the full implementation of school desegregation in 1971 (*Swann* v. *Charlotte-Mecklenburg*), and had specified the busing of black and white children to each other's schools as a way to achieve racially mixed schools, the courts and Congress grew more conservative on busing. In *Milliken* v. *Bradley* (1974), the Supreme Court ruled by five to four that white suburbs had no constitutional obligation to merge with predominantly black cities such as Detroit in order to facilitate school integration. In 1974 and 1975, the Democrat-controlled Congress approved anti-busing legislation.

As demonstrated in the Boston anti-integration riots (see page 240), busing was a bitterly divisive issue. The white backlash generated by busing made an important contribution to the revival of social conservatism and to the culture wars of the 1980s. Conservatives criticised 'limousine liberals' such as Senator Edward Kennedy (see page 219) for imposing principles of racial harmony on others while cushioned against such issues themselves. In 1971, the Ku Klux Klan bombed and destroyed ten school buses in Pontiac, Michigan. Opposition to integrated schools caused private school numbers to rise across America (Boston's public schools contained 45,000 whites in 1974 but only 16,000 by 1987) and 'white flight' to accelerate (6 per cent of the population moved to the suburbs in the 1970s).

SOURCE D

What does Source D suggest about the impact of the civil rights legislation upon the North?

From Supreme Court Justice Thurgood Marshall's dissent to the Supreme Court ruling in *Milliken* v. *Bradley* (available from http://en.wikisource.org/wiki/Milliken_v._Bradley/Dissent_Marshall).

This Court recognized [in Brown] … that remedying decades of segregation in public education would not be an easy task. Subsequent events, unfortunately, have seen that prediction bear bitter fruit … the Court today takes a giant step backwards … [The state of Michigan has] engaged in widespread purposeful acts of racial segregation in the Detroit School District … Negro children have been intentionally confined to an expanding core of virtually all-Negro schools immediately surrounded by a … band of all-white schools … [The Milliken ruling will increase segregation in Detroit when] white parents withdraw their children from the Detroit city schools and move to the suburbs to continue them in all-white schools … [and guarantee] that Negro children in Detroit will receive the same separate and inherently unequal education in the future as they have been unconstitutionally afforded in the past … Today's holding, I fear, is more a reflection of a perceived public mood that we have gone far enough in enforcing the Constitution's guarantee of equal justice than it is the product of neutral principles of law.

Clearly, as Eisenhower had said, racial tolerance and social equality could not be legislated into existence.

Economic status

Following the civil rights legislation of 1964–5 in particular, the federal government had focused on the promotion of affirmative action and anti-discrimination measures in higher education and employment, in an attempt to improve the economic status of African-Americans. In this, the government was supported by the judiciary and many city officials and university authorities.

The combination of affirmative action (especially 'set-asides' that guaranteed a certain percentage of contracts to minority-owned businesses) and EEOC pressure to decrease discrimination in hiring, accelerated the growth of the black middle class across the nation. Similarly, affirmative action in universities increased the educational opportunities available to upwardly mobile African-Americans. By 1980, around one-third of African-Americans were middle class. However, a white backlash developed against affirmative action in university entrance (see page 241) and in employment. For example, a federal judge's 1975 ruling against the Detroit police department's 'last hired, first fired' principle, which protected recently employed black officers, caused a 'police riot' in which several white police officers attacked one African-American officer.

Furthermore, the civil rights legislation and the affirmative action that followed it did not solve all black economic problems. Although the median household income of whites increased slightly during the decade, that of black Americans did not: by 1980, median black household income was only 60 per cent that of whites, a similar figure to 1965. The proportion of African-Americans in poverty remained at around 33 per cent, three times that of whites. One-third of black Americans had low-status, low-skilled jobs in low-wage occupations, and average black earnings were half those of whites. As a consequence of poverty, the black infant mortality rate remained twice that of whites, even though Medicaid lowered the black infant mortality rate and raised life expectancy. While black life expectancy in 1980 was 68.1, white life expectancy was 74.4 and there had been little closing of the gap since 1970. A further consequence of inferior socio-economic status lay in the crime statistics: African-Americans constituted 12 per cent of the US population but 43 per cent of arrested rapists, 55 per cent of those accused of murder and 69 per cent of those arraigned for robbery. Ghetto crime, poverty and unemployment remained insoluble problems that even black mayors could not solve.

Table 6.3 Life expectancy in the USA 1960–90

Year	Average age at death for black Americans	Average age at death for white Americans
1960	63.6	70.6
1970	64.1	71.7
1980	68.1	74.4
1990	69.1	76.1

By 1980, many African-Americans were disheartened by the opposition to desegregation and affirmative action, and disillusioned with the American Dream.

Political status

The Voting Rights Act helped ensure that African-Americans in the South could vote. This had a great impact: Maynard Jackson was elected mayor of Atlanta and even Birmingham elected a black mayor (1979). Indeed, African-Americans became mayors in several major cities across the nation, including Detroit (1973), Los Angeles (1973) and Washington DC (1974). Over twenty African-Americans sat in the US House of Representatives from 1973 to 1980, but they represented congressional districts with predominantly black populations. Because it was difficult for a black candidate to obtain state-wide votes, the sole African-American in the Senate in this period was Edward William Brooke III, who represented liberal Massachusetts from 1967 to 1979. Nationally, only 1 per cent of elected officials were black in 1980.

The Supreme Court worked to promote equal political status across the nation by ruling that no redrawing of political boundaries should leave ethnic minorities worse off in terms of political representation (*Beer* v. *United States*, 1976). Some states went further and created districts in which black American voters were grouped together to help ensure the election of black officials. However, the Supreme Court weakened the Voting Rights Act (see page 160) when it ruled that discriminatory effect had to be accompanied by discriminatory intent (*City of Mobile* v. *Bolden*, 1980). This made it harder to challenge discriminatory voting laws and, overall, African-American political inequality continued.

Change and continuity in the New South

KEY TERMS

New South Originally used to describe the transformed South during Reconstruction, and occasionally used to describe the changes in the South after the civil rights legislation of 1964–5.

Born-again Christian A Christian who has experienced a spiritual rebirth; particularly fashionable in the USA from the late 1960s.

Contemporary claims of a **New South** during Reconstruction were silenced by the arrival of Jim Crow, and by the mid-twentieth century the South was commonly perceived as regressive (see page 162). That perception was confirmed by media coverage of the reaction of Southern white bigots to the civil rights movement of the early 1960s. However, the Civil Rights Act (1964) and the Voting Rights Act (1965) changed the South. Public places were no longer legally segregated. Indeed, by the 1970s, the South led the nation in school integration. Southern governors such as Jimmy Carter of Georgia (see page 235) no longer used the racist rhetoric of previous decades. In 1974, George Wallace (see page 121) declared himself a **born-again Christian**, and apologised to the Selma marchers for his segregationist past. In the 1970s, the South was also characterised by economic growth. The lower wages and less powerful unions of the South had attracted industries since the Second World War, and the attraction increased after the reforms of 1964 and 1965.

Many claimed that the combination of greater racial tolerance and economic growth constituted a New South that Martin Luther King Jr's old friend Bayard

Rustin considered transformed by 1980 (see page 162). Such change and transformation in the South was well illustrated in Atlanta, Georgia.

Change in Atlanta

In 1973, Maynard Jackson became Atlanta's (and Georgia's) first black mayor, and he remained in office until 1981. Black political control had a great impact on African-Americans in the city:

- It reinforced black middle-class involvement in the city's business and social affairs. For example, Jesse Hill became the first black officer at the Atlanta Chamber of Commerce and became its president in 1977.
- Black employment in public departments rapidly increased. Jackson hired Atlanta's first affirmative action officer, and the proportion of black public employees in professional positions rose from 19.2 to 42.2 per cent between 1973 and 1978. The proportion of black managers more than doubled from 13.5 to 32.6 per cent. Here, Jackson was assisted by the 1972 Equal Employment Opportunities Act, which expanded the prohibition against discrimination in the 1964 Civil Rights Act to include state and local government jobs.
- Jackson increased the percentage of city contracts awarded to black firms by around 25 per cent. During his first term, the proportion of city funds paid to black firms soared from 2 to 33 per cent. For the first time, some city funds were deposited in black-owned banks. Jackson withdrew city money from one bank that refused to accept affirmative action. A city ordinance was passed with minority hiring goals for all companies that sought to conduct business in Atlanta.

Perhaps Jackson's grandfather was right when he argued during the 1960s that 'eventually, and ultimately, most of our problems will be solved and settled at the ballot box'.

Continuity

Despite the advances evidenced in Atlanta, it is unrealistic to see the South as totally transformed. By 1980, the increase in black voter registration had still not led to a great increase in the number of black elected officials in Deep South states such as Georgia. Although African-Americans constituted 27 per cent of registered voters in Georgia in 1980, Georgia had only 249 black elected officials – 3.7 per cent of the state total. This was less than the average of 5 per cent across the South as a whole. In 1980, nine of Georgia's 23 majority black counties still lacked black elected officials.

Social and economic deprivation continued. One-third of black Atlantans remained below the poverty line in 1980. African-American Judge Edith Ingram, elected by Hancock County's black community in 1968, said:

I have to write checks [cheques] for them, pay bills, buy groceries, take them to the doctors, balance check-books, certify them for welfare, make doctors' appointments, read letters, answer letters, and fix loan papers for houses. A good 85–90 percent of the work that we do is non-office related work, but the people have no one else to depend on.

In 1980, black unemployment in Georgia was 12.5 per cent: three times the percentage proportion for whites. Within Atlanta, black unemployment was double the white unemployment rate, and of those employed, 70 per cent had blue-collar jobs. Around 33 per cent of Atlanta's black families were below the poverty line, compared to 7 per cent of white families. Despite all the efforts and progress since 1945, black economic, social and political inequality continued.

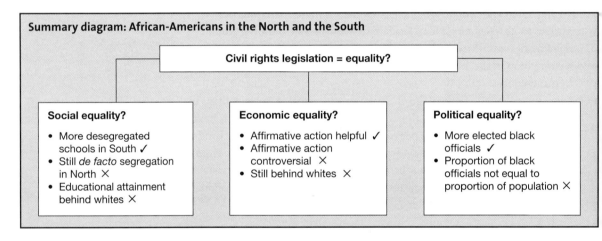

Summary diagram: African-Americans in the North and the South

Civil rights legislation = equality?

Social equality?
- More desegregated schools in South ✓
- Still *de facto* segregation in North ✗
- Educational attainment behind whites ✗

Economic equality?
- Affirmative action helpful ✓
- Affirmative action controversial ✗
- Still behind whites ✗

Political equality?
- More elected black officials ✓
- Proportion of black officials not equal to proportion of population ✗

4 The USA by 1980

▶ *How far had the USA changed between 1945 and 1980?*

In 1945, the United States emerged victorious from a war universally acknowledged to be a 'good' war against evil regimes. Americans felt pride in their image and identity abroad, and confidence in the strength of their nation and the American Dream. By 1980, the pride, confidence and strength seemed somewhat tarnished.

The US position as a superpower

In 1945, America was by far the most powerful nation in the world due to its wealth and monopoly on atomic weaponry. However, by 1980 many thought that supremacy was at or near an end. Americans felt humiliated over South Vietnam ('lost' to Communism in 1975 after several decades of US aid) and over the Iranian hostage taking in 1979 (a new form of warfare against which conventional forces and nuclear arsenals seemed useless). The hostage taking was a result of increasingly unfavourable perceptions of American identity abroad. The United States had long perceived itself as a peace-loving beacon of democracy and freedom to an admiring world that frequently required its benevolent patronage and assistance. However, by 1980 many in the non-Communist world considered America a frequently aggressive power that sought to impose its will on others. While that perception owed much to US action in Vietnam between 1955 and 1973, many in Latin America in particular had long been uneasily resentful of US interventionism.

By 1980 it seemed that while America was in decline, the Soviet challenge was greater than ever: the Soviets had gained nuclear and naval parity and appeared frighteningly confident and aggressive. Although subsequent events would demonstrate the unstable foundations of the Soviet Union, many Americans were convinced that the United States was unprecedentedly vulnerable: by 1980, 54 per cent of Americans believed the US world position was only 'fair' or 'poor'; 62 per cent felt their country was 'becoming weaker'; 81 per cent believed the nation was in serious trouble. Such perceptions were excessively pessimistic: America remained by far the wealthiest and most powerful nation in the world, but it no longer had the massive lead over other nations that it had enjoyed in 1945.

The extent of social and economic change

For two decades after the Second World War, the American economy boomed, but by 1980 it seemed to be in decline.

Economic change

The economic boom of the post-war decades was over because:

- Increased federal government expenditure on the Vietnam War and on social programmes had led to a federal budget deficit and inflation.
- The energy crisis and the greatly increased price of oil had damaged American industry and households.
- American manufacturing industries had declined in the face of foreign competition, which had led to increased unemployment (it had risen to 8.2 million in summer 1980) and a trade deficit (around $40 billion during 1978–9). The mounting trade deficits had a negative impact on the dollar, causing it to slump on the world currency markets.

Nevertheless, although Americans felt economically squeezed, the United States remained easily the world's most affluent society, with a far higher GNP than its nearest rivals.

Case study: the car industry

The impact of foreign competition was demonstrated in the car industry. Inexpensive and well-made Japanese car imports were extremely attractive to American consumers. By 1981, Japanese companies had 23 per cent of the American car market (in 1978–9, over a quarter of the US trade deficit was due to Japan's trade surplus). American car companies were slow to adapt. Even as the sales of American cars fell, manufacturers continued to produce 'gas guzzlers' that used a great deal of petrol, while Japanese cars were smaller and more economic. Chrysler lost billions and needed a controversial $1.5 billion government bailout in 1980. By 1980, foreign competition contributed to the 24 per cent unemployment in the car manufacturing city of Detroit, where the number of permanent jobs in the car industry fell from 940,000 in 1978 to 500,000 in 1982.

Many American companies moved production abroad or bought finished products from foreign manufacturers for whom labour was cheaper and less assertive.

American economic problems led the **AFL-CIO** to describe the United States as 'a nation of hamburger stands, a country stripped of industrial capacity and meaningful work … A service-economy … a nation of citizens busily buying and selling cheese-burgers.' While this is clearly an exaggeration, the union leaders had correctly identified a long-term economic trend: the decline of skilled manufacturing jobs and the increasing dependence of American workers on low-paid, insecure jobs in the service industry.

Social change

Prior to the 1960s, America seemed to be a stable society in which:

- over two-thirds of the population lived in unprecedented affluence
- the race problem was under control, with African-Americans safely segregated by law in the South and by residence in the North
- protests were rare
- gender inequality was the generally accepted norm.

By 1980 there had been considerable social change. President Johnson's Great Society failed to eradicate poverty but had made it more visible by drawing the nation's attention to it. Thanks to Johnson, Americans in 1980 had a greater welfare safety net than in 1945. Social Security and free medical care programmes had been expanded. However, the Great Society had failed to improve the inner-city ghettos that had mushroomed since the middle of the century due to the impact of the Great Migration, discrimination in post-war federal mortgage loans (they were not usually given to black families), white opposition to black neighbours and white flight.

The legal segregation and disfranchisement with which African-Americans had been afflicted in the South had been ended by 1980. Most schools were desegregated in the South by that date, but efforts to eradicate the impact of *de facto* housing segregation on education in the North by introducing busing had lost momentum by 1980. The busing controversy demonstrated continuing racism: cities retained 'chocolate' centres ringed by 'vanilla' suburbs. However, although one-third of African-Americans remained below the poverty line,

KEY TERM

AFL-CIO The American Federation of Labour and the Congress of Industrial Organizations are combined in an umbrella organisation for all US labour unions.

the civil rights legislation had accelerated the introduction of affirmative action policies that contributed to a growing black middle class. Furthermore, the number of elected black officials was increasing across the nation.

Women's lives had also changed dramatically since the early 1960s. The skyrocketing divorce rate (40 per cent) and new attitudes to work, sex, family and personal freedom, constituted a cultural revolution that upset conservatives.

Table 6.4 Percentage of women in the US workforce 1960–90

Year	Percentage of women in the workforce
1960	38%
1970	43%
1980	52%
1990	58%

The economic status of women was improving but remained inferior to that of men. Although women's wages were rising (they were 62 per cent of men's wages in 1980), they remained markedly unequal. Furthermore, although more women were working and in a wider variety of jobs than in 1945, they still held fewer executive, managerial and professional positions. Like African-Americans, women were greatly underrepresented in politics, even though the number being elected was increasing. There were still only sixteen women in the US House of Representatives and no women in the US Senate in 1979–80.

Despite continuing economic and political inequality, feminists thought they had achieved reproductive rights when the Supreme Court ruled in favour of contraception for married couples in 1965 (see page 182) and legalised abortion in 1973 (see page 237). However, the changing status of women, and *Roe* v. *Wade* in particular, stimulated a formidable reaction among social conservatives who resented the recent and dramatic changes. Many of these conservatives belonged to the **Religious Right**, and they played an important part in the presidential election victory of Ronald Reagan in 1980.

Reasons for Reagan's victory in the presidential election

Ronald Reagan's victory in the 1980 presidential election owed much to the perceived inadequacies of President Carter, but also a great deal to his own personality and to the support of social conservatives.

'Can Carter cope?'

Carter was weakened by a challenge from the liberal Democrat Edward Kennedy during the 1980 presidential election campaign. Liberal Democrats were displeased by Carter's words in his second State of the Union address:

> *Government cannot solve our problems. It cannot eliminate poverty, or provide a bountiful economy, or reduce inflation, or save our cities, or cure illiteracy or provide energy.*

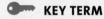

KEY TERM

Religious Right Influential, late 1970s movement in reaction to the liberalism and counterculture of the 1960s.

Ronald Reagan

1911	Born in Tampico, Illinois
1932	Graduated from Eureka College; sports commentator in Iowa
1937	Started a Hollywood acting career
1947–52	Became a conservative Republican
1954–62	Hosted the *General Electric Theater* television programme
1967–74	Served two terms as governor of California
1968	Unsuccessful bid for the Republican nomination
1976	Second unsuccessful bid for the Republican nomination
1980	Won the Republican nomination; defeated the Democrat incumbent Jimmy Carter (51 to 41 per cent of the popular vote)
1981–9	President for two terms
2004	Died

Born in Illinois in 1911, Ronald Reagan supported Franklin Roosevelt's New Deal (see page 2) in the 1930s, but paying around 90 per cent tax on his film-star salary turned him into a conservative Republican. A practised performer after his media career, he appealed to voters with his easy charm and his repeated attacks on big government, liberals and protesters.

Reagan helped restore national self-confidence and the prestige of the presidency after Vietnam, Watergate and the unimpressive presidencies of Ford and Carter. Since Roosevelt's New Deal in the 1930s, America had been moving in the direction of the welfare state and some historians think Reagan successfully halted and reversed that process. He contributed greatly to the ending of the Cold War. Most Americans rate him highly: right-wingers generally approve of his policies and often consider them successful; left-wingers generally consider him likeable and appreciate his restoration of the prestige of the presidency.

Carter was a fiscal conservative, while liberal Democrats unrealistically sought greater government expenditure on social problems. However, the main reason for Carter's defeat was that he frequently seemed incapable of handling the economic and international problems that faced him. By 1980, only 18 per cent rated Carter 'a very strong leader'. The economy seemed to be spinning out of control and Reagan made great political capital out of Carter's apparent inability to solve economic problems. In 1980, 47 per cent of registered voters simply stayed at home: many were poor and/or unemployed and would normally have voted Democrat but were disillusioned with politics and with the leadership of Jimmy Carter.

The great communicator

Ronald Reagan's previous career as broadcaster and film star had helped make him a genial and inspirational speaker, who over the years had perfected his attacks on big government and high taxes. Despite Reagan's reputation as the 'great communicator', Carter felt that he had to debate with him (October 1980). Unusually, Reagan made no gaffes, and came across as warmer than Carter with his frequent 'aw shucks' and 'there you go again' interjections. Reagan asked Americans whether they felt anything was better after four years of Carter. That was highly effective and polls suggested that Reagan had won the debate. The 'great communicator' had come across as a warm personality, optimistic about American international and domestic capacities, in contrast to the earnest, moralistic Carter who told Americans that they were suffering crises of confidence and spirit.

SOURCE E

From presidential candidate Ronald Reagan's comments during the October 1980 debate with President Carter.

Are you better off now than you were four years ago? Is it easier for you to go and buy things in the stores than it was four years ago? Is there more or less unemployment in the country than there was four years ago? Is America as respected throughout the world as it was? Do you feel that our security is as safe, that we're as strong as we were four years ago? And if you answer all of those questions 'yes', why then, I think your choice is very obvious as to whom you will vote for. If you don't agree, if you don't think that this course that we've been on for the last four years is what you would like to see us follow for the next four, then I could suggest another choice that you have.

> What are your answers to the questions posed in Source E?

The socially conservative vote

Reagan's electoral victory owed much to the support of social conservatives, who rejected the more liberal social attitudes of the 1960s and envisioned a return to 'traditional family values'. Reagan had clearly aligned himself with them by 1980. He emphasised his disgust at 1960s' excesses and permissiveness and his opposition to feminism and the ERA. Despite his divorce in 1952 and his difficult relationships with two of his four children, Reagan was the apostle of the nuclear family. Although he rarely attended church, he supported school prayer (the Supreme Court had ruled against it in 1962) and criticised the federal courts for not allowing **creationism** to be taught (some extreme religious conservatives believed in creationism and opposed the teaching of **Darwinism** in schools). He told an audience of evangelical ministers that he was a born-again Christian.

Such social issues mobilised conservative voters. The well-organised **New Right** or 'Religious Right' was already one of America's most visible and powerful political forces, and it backed Reagan. An estimated 5 million evangelical Christians who had never voted before now voted for Reagan.

The Religious Right opposed:

- feminism, which they blamed for damaging paternal authority and weakening the family
- divorce (divorce rates doubled between 1965 and 1985 from 25 to 50 per cent of all marriages)
- mothers going out to work (the Religious Right lamented that fewer than 50 per cent of women were full-time **homemakers**, believing this adversely affected family life)
- the ERA (see page 236)
- drug taking

🔑 KEY TERMS

Creationism A biblical account of the origins of the earth and the life on it.

Darwinism Creationists believe that Darwin's theories of evolution go against the Bible.

New Right This group of right-wing voters became influential in the late 1970s; their beliefs were a reaction to the counterculture of the 1960s, and included opposition to abortion, busing and Darwinism.

Homemakers Mothers who stay at home to look after their families, rather than going out to work.

- abortion and *Roe* v. *Wade* (see page 237) (there were four abortions for every ten live births between 1974 and 1977)
- sexual liberalisation (roughly 500,000 unmarried couples lived together in 1970, around 1 million by 1980)
- premarital sex and sexual promiscuity
- unmarried mothers, many of whom relied on welfare payments (the percentage of children born to unmarried mothers rose from 11 per cent in 1970 to 18 per cent in 1980 and 28 per cent in 1990)
- homosexuality
- popular culture's preoccupation with sex
- pornography
- the teaching of sex education in schools.

Table 6.5 Percentage of US marriages ending in divorce 1955–90

Year	Percentage of divorces
1955	23%
1960	22%
1970	33%
1980	52%
1990	49%

KEY TERM

Coattails Americans talking of a president whose popularity helps other members of his party get elected, say those other members got in on the president's coattails.

The Religious Right had great political and social importance. First, it increased the polarisation of American politics and society when it campaigned to promote traditional values in what some called 'culture wars'. Second, it affected the outcome of elections, as in 1980.

The results and significance of the 1980 election

Greatly assisted by Reagan's **coattails** and the Religious Right, the Republicans took control of Congress as well as the White House in 1980. However, Reagan's was not a decisive victory. Only 28 per cent of the potential electorate voted for him (25 per cent voted for Carter). The 47 per cent of voters who stayed at home constituted the biggest group in American politics. Most were poor and/or unemployed and were the traditional Democratic constituency. These statistics suggest disillusionment with politics in general, Democrat disillusionment with Carter in particular, and resurgent social conservatism. Among the many divisions that the 1980 elections illustrated were the divisions over the American Dream. By 1980, fewer Americans believed in it or thought it had been achieved.

The American Dream: reality and illusion 1945–80

From 1945 to 1980, America faced many challenges at home and abroad. During this period, Americans experienced varying degrees of uneasiness about issues such as inequality at home and Communism abroad.

Some Americans offered individual versions of the American Dream, notably President Johnson with his 'Great Society'. However, most Americans defined the American Dream as the opportunity for each individual to fulfil his or her potential and obtain material gain. The prosperity that followed the Second World War made many Americans think that they had achieved the American

Dream. However, around a quarter of the population remained poor, and many of the more prosperous suffered a deteriorating standard of living in the 1970s, by which time the post-war boom was over. Some Americans felt that economic and social inequality made the American Dream an illusion, and despite progress towards greater equality between 1945 and 1980, there were Americans who remained dissatisfied and disillusioned in 1980.

The version of the American Dream articulated in the Truman Doctrine (see page 17) and by President Johnson over Vietnam (see page 157) envisaged the United States as exporting what it considered to be its superior political, social and economic system to other nations. However, by 1980, events in nations such as Vietnam and Iran (see page 251) were helping to dispel American illusions about favourable foreign perceptions of America's identity.

Summary diagram: The USA by 1980

1945	1980
Most powerful nation in world	Still most powerful, but felt less so, e.g. Vietnam, Iran, Soviet nuclear parity
Reasonable image abroad	International image damaged, e.g. bully over Vietnam
Economy on verge of amazing boom	Inflation, recession, unfavourable balance of trade, federal government budget deficit, energy crisis
Led world in manufacturing	'Nation of hamburger flippers'
African-Americans quiet but unequal; legal segregation in South; *de facto* segregation in North	Some progress towards equality; no legal segregation, but still *de facto* segregation
Women: homemaker ideal	Some progress towards economic and social equality
Very liberal president	Very conservative president elected

Chapter summary

Americans remained divided over poverty, the rights of women and race. During the 1970s, homelessness increased, the Equal Rights Amendment was rejected, and abortion, desegregation and affirmative action were highly controversial. Although the social, economic and political status of African-Americans had improved between 1945 and 1980, they had still not attained equality in those areas. The 'New South' was economically and racially transformed, but there was continuity in that many African-Americans still suffered discrimination and poverty.

Americans were increasingly disillusioned with politics, as shown by the low voter turnout and anti-Washington victories in the presidential elections of 1976 and 1980. Many Americans believed that US politics was characterised by increasing corruption. Both President Ford and President Carter seemed unable to cope with inflation, recession, unemployment, and crises over energy and foreign policy. All this combined to contribute to a loss of national self-confidence.

Americans rejected Ford's pleas to assist South Vietnam, which fell to the Communists in 1975, and turned against detente, mostly because it seemed to have benefited the Soviets more.

The combination of Carter's inability to secure the release of the US citizens taken hostage by Iranians and the Soviet invasion of Afghanistan made Americans feel powerless.

By 1980, America's position as a military and economic superpower seemed to have deteriorated, but the United States remained the most powerful nation in the world. Between 1945 and 1980, the extent of the American economic lead over other countries had decreased, but America remained the world's wealthiest nation in spite of the decline in manufacturing industries, the federal budget deficit and the unfavourable balance of trade.

Between 1945 and 1980, American society had greatly changed, but the increased liberalism led to a resurgence of social conservatism that was crucial to Reagan's defeat of Carter in the 1980 presidential election. That social conservatism was particularly focused on the role of women.

Overall, confidence in the American Dream had greatly decreased by 1980.

Refresher questions

Use these questions to remind yourself of the key material covered in this chapter.

1 Suggest reasons for media disrespect towards President Ford.

2 Why was Phyllis Schlafly important?

3 How did Americans react to *Roe* v. *Wade*?

4 Why had homelessness increased during the 1970s?

5 What statistics suggest a) African-American equality and b) African-American inequality?

6 What was the significance of the rioting in Liberty City, Florida, in 1980?

7 List reasons for the crisis in national self-confidence.

8 Give five examples of corruption in American politics in the 1970s.

9 How significant for Americans was the fall of South Vietnam to Communism in 1975?

10 Why did Americans turn against detente?

11 In what ways did President Carter seem unable to cope?

12 What was the impact of civil rights legislation during the 1970s?

13 Was there ever a 'New South'?

14 Was the USA a superpower in decline by 1980?

15 How far had the US economy changed between 1945 and 1980?

16 How far had American society changed between 1945 and 1980?

17 Why did Reagan win the 1980 presidential election?

 Question practice

ESSAY QUESTIONS

1 'President Carter was justified in saying that America was experiencing a crisis of confidence in 1979.' Assess the validity of this view.

2 'The presidential election victories of Carter in 1976 and Reagan in 1980 were primarily due to popular disillusion with Washington politicians.' Assess the validity of this view.

3 'Between 1945 and 1980, African–Americans had gained much in theory but little in practice.' Assess the validity of this view.

4 'The international standing of the United States had changed little between 1945 and 1980.' Assess the validity of this view.

SOURCE ANALYSIS QUESTION

1 With reference to Sources B (page 247), C (page 249) and E (page 263), and your understanding of the historical context, assess the value of these three sources to a historian studying the crisis in national self-confidence in the USA in the 1970s.

AQA A level History

Essay guidance

At both AS and A level for AQA Component 2: Depth Study: The American Dream: Reality and Illusion, 1945–1980, you will need to answer an essay question in the exam. Each essay question is marked out of 25:

- for the AS exam, Section B: answer **one** essay from a choice of two
- for the A level exam, Section B: answer **two** essays from a choice of three.

There are several question stems which all have the same basic requirement: to analyse and reach a conclusion, based on the evidence you provide.

The AS questions often give a quotation and then ask whether you agree or disagree with this view. Almost inevitably, your answer will be a mixture of both. It is the same task as for A level – just phrased differently in the question. Detailed essays are more likely to do well than vague or generalised essays, especially in the Depth Studies of Paper 2.

The AQA mark scheme is essentially the same for AS and the full A level (see the AQA website, www.aqa.org.uk). Both emphasise the need to analyse and evaluate the key features related to the periods studied. The key feature of the highest level is sustained analysis: analysis that unites the whole of the essay.

Writing an essay: general skills

- *Focus and structure*. Be sure what the question is asking and plan what the paragraphs should be about.
- *Focused introduction to the essay*. Be sure that the introductory sentence relates directly to the focus of the question and that each paragraph highlights the structure of the answer.
- *Use detail*. Make sure that you show detailed knowledge, but only as part of an explanation

being made in relation to the question. No knowledge should be standalone; it should be used in context.

- *Explanatory analysis and evaluation*. Consider what words and phrases to use in an answer to strengthen the explanation.
- *Argument and counter-argument*. Think of how arguments can be balanced so as to give contrasting views.
- *Resolution*. Think how best to 'resolve' contradictory arguments.
- *Relative significance and evaluation*. Think how best to reach a judgement when trying to assess the relative importance of various factors, and their possible interrelationship.

Planning an essay

Practice question 1

'Vietnam was Johnson's war.' Assess the validity of this view.

This question requires you to analyse whether Johnson's predecessors in particular (but also Robert McNamara, Congress or the JCS) bore as much if not more responsibility than Johnson for the American involvement in Vietnam. You must discuss the following:

- The extent of Johnson's responsibility (your primary focus).
- The extent of the responsibility of Truman, Eisenhower and Kennedy, and, to a lesser extent, of McNamara, Congress and the JCS (your secondary focus).

A clear structure makes for a much more effective essay and is crucial for achieving the highest marks. You need several paragraphs to structure this question effectively. In each paragraph you could deal with persons responsible for the war. At least one of these *must* be the person in the question.

A very basic plan for this question might look like this:

- Paragraph 1: Ways in which Johnson can be blamed for the war.
- Paragraph 2 : Ways in which Truman and Eisenhower could be blamed.
- Paragraph 3: Ways in which Kennedy could be blamed.
- Paragraph 4: Ways in which others might be blamed.

It is a good idea to cover the factor named in the question first, so that you don't run out of time and forget to do it. Then cover the others in what you think is their order of importance, or in the order that appears logical in terms of the sequence of paragraphs.

The introduction

Maintaining focus is vital. One way to do this from the beginning of your essay is to use the words in the question to help write your argument. The first sentence of question 1, for example, could look like this:

The fact that it was President Johnson who sent the first American ground troops to Vietnam suggests that it was indeed 'Johnson's war'.

This opening sentence provides a clear focus on the demands of the question, although it could, of course, be written in a more exciting style.

Focus throughout the essay

Structuring your essay well will help with keeping the focus of your essay on the question. To maintain a focus on the wording in question 1, you could begin your first main paragraph with 'it was Johnson's war'.

It was 'Johnson's war' in that while there were simply American 'advisers' in South Vietnam when he became president, there were 535,000 American ground troops there by the end of his presidency.

- This sentence begins with a clear point that refers to the primary focus of the question (Johnson's war) while linking it to the commitment inherited from Johnson's predecessors.
- You could then have a paragraph for each of the other presidents who started or increased the US commitment.
- It will be important to make sure that each paragraph focuses on analysis and includes relevant details that are used as part of the argument.
- You may wish to number your presidencies, for example, by beginning a paragraph with, 'President Truman was the first president to get the United States involved in Vietnam.' This helps to make your structure clear and helps you to maintain focus.

Deploying detail

As well as focus and structure, your essay will be judged on the extent to which it includes accurate detail. There are several different kinds of evidence you could use that might be described as detailed. These include correct dates, names of relevant people, statistics and events. For example, for question 1 you could use statistics such as 'fewer than 700 advisers under Eisenhower' and 'over 16,000 advisers under Kennedy'. You can also make your essays more detailed by using the correct technical vocabulary, for example, by referring to Senate hearings.

Analysis and explanation

'Analysis' covers a variety of high-level skills including explanation and evaluation; in essence, it means breaking down something complex into smaller parts. A clear structure which breaks down a complex question into a series of paragraphs is the first step towards writing an analytical essay. The purpose of explanation is to provide evidence for why something happened, or why something is true or false. An explanatory statement requires two parts: a *claim* and a *justification*.

For example, for question 1, you might want to argue that one important reason for the war and a major turning point was Eisenhower's rejection of the Geneva Accords and his creation and support of the new state of South Vietnam. Once you have made your point, and supported it with relevant detail, you can then explain how this answers the question. For example, you could conclude your paragraph like this:

Eisenhower's creation and support of the South Vietnamese state suggests that this could well be called 'Eisenhower's war'[1], because[2] his successors felt obliged to continue the commitment to that state lest it seem that America was weak and ineffective in its opposition to Communism and an unreliable ally of anti-Communist states[3].

1 The first part of this sentence is the claim while the second part justifies the claim.
2 'Because' is a very important word to use when writing an explanation, as it shows the relationship between the claim and the justification.
3 The justification.

Evaluation

Evaluation means considering the importance of two or more different factors, weighing them against each other, and reaching a judgement. This is a good skill to use at the end of an essay because the conclusion should reach a judgement which answers the question. For example, your conclusion to question 1 might read as follows:

Clearly, Johnson massively escalated the war through his dispatch of ground troops and through Rolling Thunder. However, he was a victim of the commitment trap bequeathed by his predecessors: Truman had made the containment of Communism in Vietnam important to the United States; Eisenhower had created the anti-Communist state of South Vietnam and guaranteed to support it through SEATO; Kennedy had sent thousands of advisers to assist South Vietnam and his administration's collusion in the assassination of the South Vietnamese leader left America morally bound to support his successor. Therefore, Johnson had little choice but to continue and escalate the American commitment.

Words like 'however' and 'therefore' are helpful to contrast the importance of the different factors.

Complex essay writing: argument and counter-argument

Essays that develop a good argument are more likely to reach the highest levels. This is because argumentative essays are much more likely to develop sustained analysis. As you know, your essays are judged on the extent to which they analyse.

After setting up an argument in your introduction, you should develop it throughout the essay. One way of doing this is to adopt an argument–counter-argument structure. A counter-argument is one that disagrees with the main argument of the essay. This is a good way of evaluating the importance of the different factors that you discuss. Essays of this type will develop an argument in one paragraph and then set out an opposing argument in another paragraph. Sometimes this will include juxtaposing the differing views of historians on a topic.

Good essays will analyse the key issues. They will probably have a clear piece of analysis at the end of each paragraph. While this analysis might be good, it will generally relate only to the issue discussed in that paragraph.

Excellent essays will be analytical throughout. As well as the analysis of each factor discussed above, there will be an overall analysis. This will run throughout the essay and can be achieved through developing a clear, relevant and coherent argument.

A good way of achieving sustained analysis is to consider which factor is most important.

Here is an example of an introduction that sets out an argument for question 1:

The fact that it was President Johnson who sent the American ground troops to Vietnam suggests that it was indeed 'Johnson's war'[1]. Similarly, he began Rolling Thunder, a bombing campaign of unprecedented intensity that further demonstrated and escalated the American commitment to the defeat of Communism in South Vietnam[2]. However, a study of the extent and nature of his predecessors' involvement in South Vietnam demonstrates that this was not 'Johnson's war'. Johnson was simply the unfortunate victim of the commitment trap'[3].

1 The introduction begins with a claim.
2 The introduction continues with another reason.
3 Concludes with an outline of the argument of the most important reason.

● This introduction focuses on the question and sets out the key factors that the essay will develop.
● It introduces an argument about which factor was most significant.
● However, it also sets out an argument that can then be developed throughout each paragraph and is rounded off with an overall judgement in the conclusion.

Complex essay writing: resolution and relative significance

Having written an essay that explains argument and counter-argument, you should then resolve the tension between the argument and the counter-argument in your conclusion. It is important that the writing is precise and summarises the arguments made in the main body of the essay. You need to reach a supported overall judgement. One very appropriate way to do this is by evaluating the relative significance of different factors, in the light of valid criteria. Relative significance means how important one factor is compared to another.

The best essays will always make a judgement about which was most important based on valid criteria. These can be very simple, and will depend on the topic and the exact question.

The following criteria are often useful:

● Duration: which individual or factor was important for the longest amount of time?
● Effectiveness: which individual or factor achieved most?
● Impact: which individual or factor led to the most fundamental change?

● Removal: which individual or factor, if removed, would have made the outcome unlikely?

As an example, you could compare the presidents in terms of the extent and duration of their commitment to Vietnam, asking at which stage any of them fundamentally changed the US position. You could remove each president in turn and see whether you think that his removal would have been crucial. A conclusion that follows this advice should be capable of reaching a high level (if written, in full, with appropriate details) because it reaches an overall judgement that is supported through evaluating the relative significance of different factors in the light of valid criteria.

Having written an introduction and the main body of an essay for question 1, a concluding paragraph that aims to meet the exacting criteria for reaching a complex judgement could look like this:

Clearly, Johnson massively escalated the war through his dispatch of ground troops and through Rolling Thunder. However, he was a victim of the commitment trap bequeathed by predecessors who made Vietnam seem vital in the Cold War for thirteen years before Johnson came to the White House. Eisenhower and Kennedy each had the opportunity to withdraw without any great loss of American face. Eisenhower could have ended the US involvement after Dien Bien Phu, when it would have seemed that the French were to blame for the Communist victory. Kennedy could have pointed out that Eisenhower had warned Diem from the first that continued US support depended on his willingness to introduce social and economic reform, and that the Buddhist demonstrations in spring 1963 were clear proof that Diem had not reformed and therefore no longer deserved American aid. Instead, Eisenhower and Kennedy both so escalated the US involvement that, in the Cold War context, Johnson understandably felt that he had little choice but to continue the state created and sustained by two revered predecessors. Indeed, given that it was Eisenhower who created the state that Kennedy and Johnson felt bound to support, it is surely most persuasive to argue that this was Eisenhower's war.

Sources guidance

Whether you are taking the AS exam or the full A level exam for AQA Component 2: Depth Study: The American Dream: Reality and Illusion, 1945–1980, Section A presents you with sources and a question which involves evaluation of their utility or value.

AS exam	A level exam
Section A: answer question 1, based on two contemporary sources. (25 marks)	Section A: answer question 1, based on three contemporary sources. (30 marks)
Question focus: with reference to these sources and your understanding of the historical context, which of these two sources is more valuable in explaining … ?	Question focus: with reference to these sources and your understanding of the historical context, assess the value of these three sources to a historian studying …

Sources and sample questions

Study Sources 1–3. They are all concerned with American anti-Communism.

SOURCE I

From Truman's March 1948 speech to Congress (available from http://trumanlibrary.org/publicpapers/index. php?pid=1417).

Since the close of hostilities,* the Soviet Union and its agents have destroyed the independence and democratic character of a whole series of nations in Eastern and Central Europe.

It is this ruthless course of action, and the clear design to extend it to the remaining free nations in Europe, that have brought about the critical situation in Europe today … I believe that we have

reached the point at which the position of the United States should be made unmistakably clear … There are times in world history when it is far wiser to act than to hesitate … We must be prepared to pay the price for peace, or assuredly we shall pay the price of war.

* The Second World War.

SOURCE 2

From an article by former Socialist turned militant anti-Communist Max Eastman, published in *The Freeman*, 1 June 1953.

Red Baiting – in the sense of reasoned, documented exposure of Communist and pro-Communist infiltration of government departments and private agencies of information and communication – is absolutely necessary. We are not dealing with honest fanatics of a new idea, willing to give testimony for their faith straightforwardly, regardless of the cost. We are dealing with conspirators who try to sneak in the Moscow-

inspired propaganda by stealth and double talk, who run for shelter to the Fifth Amendment* when they are not only permitted but invited and urged by Congressional committee to state what they believe. I myself, after struggling for years to get this fact recognized, give McCarthy the major credit for implanting it in the mind of the whole nation.

* The right not to incriminate oneself.

SOURCE 3

From an article by former president Harry Truman, published in the *New York Times*, 17 November 1953.

It is now evident that the present Administration has fully embraced, for political advantage, McCarthyism. I am not referring to the Senator from Wisconsin. He is only important in that his name has taken on the dictionary meaning of the word. It is the corruption of truth, the abandonment of the due process law. It is the use of the big lie and the unfounded accusation against any citizen in the name of Americanism or security. It is the rise to power of the demagogue who lives on untruth; it is the spreading of fear and the destruction of faith in every level of society.

AS style question

With reference to Sources 1 and 2, and your understanding of the historical context, which of these sources is more valuable in explaining the extent of the Communist threat in the years 1945–54?

A level style question

With reference to Sources 1, 2 and 3, and your understanding of the historical context, assess the value of these sources to a historian studying the Red Scare in the United States after the Second World War.

The mark schemes

AS mark scheme

See the AQA website (www.aqa.org.uk) for the full mark schemes. The summary of the AS mark scheme below shows how it rewards analysis and evaluation of the source material within the historical context.

Level 1	Describing the source content or offering generic phrases.
Level 2	Some relevant but limited comments on the value of one source or some limited comment on both sources.
Level 3	Some relevant comments on the value of the sources and some explicit reference to the issue identified in the question.
Level 4	Relevant well-supported comments on the value and a supported conclusion, but with limited judgement.
Level 5	Very good understanding of the value in relation to the issue identified. Sources evaluated thoroughly and with a well-substantiated conclusion related to which is more valuable.

A level mark scheme

This summary of the A level mark scheme shows how it is similar to the AS, but covers three sources. The wording of the question means that there is no explicit requirement to decide which of the three sources is the most valuable. Concentrate instead on a very thorough analysis of the content and evaluation of the provenance of each source, using contextual knowledge.

Level 1	Some limited comment on the value of at least one source.
Level 2	Some limited comments on the value of the sources or on content or provenance, or comments on all three sources but no reference to the value of the sources.
Level 3	Some understanding of all three sources in relation to both content and provenance, with some historical context; but analysis limited.
Level 4	Good understanding of all three sources in relation to content, provenance and historical context to give a balanced argument on their value for the purpose specified in the question.
Level 5	As Level 4, but with a substantiated judgement on each of the three sources.

Working towards an answer

It is important that knowledge is used to show an understanding of the relationship between the sources and the issue raised in the question. Answers should be concerned with

- provenance
- arguments used (and you can agree/disagree)
- tone and emphasis of the sources.

The sources

The two or three sources used each time will be contemporary – probably of varying types (for example, diaries, newspaper accounts, government reports). The sources will all be on the same broad topic area. Each source will have value. Your task is to evaluate how much – in terms of its content and its provenance.

You will need to assess the *value of the content* by using your own knowledge. Is the information accurate? Is it giving only part of the evidence and ignoring other aspects? Is the tone of the writing significant?

You will need to evaluate the *provenance* of the source by considering who wrote it, and when, where and why. What was its purpose? Was it produced to express an opinion; to record facts; to influence the opinion of others? Even if it was intended to be accurate, the writer may have been biased – either deliberately or unconsciously. The writer, for example, might have only known part of the situation and reached a judgement solely based on that.

Here is a guide to analysing the provenance, content and tone for Sources 1, 2 and 3 (pages 272–3).

Analysing the sources

To answer the question effectively, you need to read the sources carefully and pull out the relevant points as well as add your own knowledge. You must remember to keep the focus on the question at all times.

Source 1 (page 272)

Provenance:

- The source is an extract from a speech given by President Truman a few weeks after the Communist takeover of Czechoslovakia, while Congress was considering voting to fund Marshall Aid.
- The extract is taken from his speech to Congress. Truman is therefore trying to persuade Congress to fund the Marshall Aid that his administration considered necessary for the revitalisation of Western Europe.

Content and argument:

- The source argues that the Soviet Union is an expansionist power that has designs on the West European nations.
- The peace-loving United States must give economic aid to Western Europe and pay the financial price to avoid an even more expensive future war.

Tone and emphasis:

- The tone is hostile. The issue is presented in black and white – the expansionist Soviets must be opposed with money or it will eventually require full-scale war to stop them.

Own knowledge:

- Use your knowledge to agree/disagree with the source, for example: details about the Red Army's imposition of and support for Communist regimes in Hungary, Bulgaria, Romania, Poland, Czechoslovakia and the Soviet zone of Germany, in the period 1944–8.

Source 2 (page 272)

Provenance:

- The source is from an article by the prolific writer Max Eastman, formerly left wing, now right wing.
- It provides the viewpoint of someone familiar with the tactics and threat from the far left, who supports McCarthy and the methods many

(including Truman and Eisenhower) considered abhorrent.

Content and argument:

- The source warns that Red baiting is essential to deal with the Communist traitors who do Moscow's dirty work in America.
- The source argues that McCarthy deserves credit for raising American awareness of this threat.

Tone and emphasis:

- The tone shows the author's loathing of Communism and impatience with Americans who pay insufficient attention to warnings from people such as McCarthy and himself.

Own knowledge:

- Use your knowledge to agree/disagree with the source, for example: McCarthy did not give 'reasoned, documented' proof that the Truman State Department was crawling with traitorous Communists.

Source 3 (page 273)

Provenance:

- The source is an extract from the writings of former Democrat President Harry Truman.
- Truman has used a prominent, leading and respected newspaper, widely read across the nation, to criticise the administration of the Republican President Eisenhower.

Content and argument:

- The source argues that the Republican administration has wholeheartedly committed itself to McCarthy-style accusations.
- It says that Republican scaremongering is characterised by lies, illegality and unsubstantiated accusations.

Tone and emphasis:

- Truman's article is highly partisan in tone, as it claims that Eisenhower's Republican

administration exploits anti-Communism for political advantage over Democrats.

Own knowledge:

- Use your knowledge to agree/disagree with the source, for example: Eisenhower disapproved of McCarthy but did little or nothing to discredit him, and many Republicans (including Vice President Nixon) gained great 'political advantage' from McCarthy. However, the Truman administration had also condoned unpleasant and often unjustified investigations of innocent Americans during the Red Scare.

Answering AS questions

You have an hour to answer the question. It is important that you spend at least one quarter of the time reading and planning your answer. Generally, when writing an answer, you need to check that you are remaining focused on the issue identified in the question and are relating this to the sources and your knowledge.

- You might decide to write a paragraph on each 'strand' (that is, provenance, content and tone), comparing the two sources, and then write a short concluding paragraph with an explained judgement on which source is more valuable.
- For writing about content, you may find it helpful to adopt a comparative approach, for example when the evidence in one source is contradicted or questioned by the evidence in another source.

At AS level you are asked to provide a judgement on which is more valuable. Make sure that this is based on clear arguments with strong evidence, and not on general assertions.

Planning and writing your answer

- Think how you can best plan an answer.
- Plan in terms of the headings above, and compare the two sources.

As an example, here is a comparison of Sources 1 and 2 in terms of content and tone, with the focus on the similarity:

The two sources have similar viewpoints, despite their differing provenance. Both are vehemently anti-Communist in tone and see Communism as a great threat to the USA. In Source 1, the president sees Soviet expansionism as threatening America's friends and security in Western Europe, while in Source 2, a journalist sees Communists as a great domestic threat, because they infiltrate federal government departments and the media.

You could then go on to compare the content of Sources 1 and 2, using your own knowledge to emphasise the difference in the value of what they assert. For example:

However, in reality, Truman points up a far greater threat than Eastman. As the Red Army marched towards Berlin in the winter of 1944–5, it colluded with local left-wing organisations in the establishment of Communist regimes. Then, by March 1946, as Winston Churchill pointed out, the Soviets had brought down an 'Iron Curtain' between East and West Europe. The Iron Curtain was finally and fully completed with the destruction of the non-Communist parties in Czechoslovakia in February 1948, just before Truman spoke. The Truman administration feared US security would be endangered if Western Europe, economically prostrate after the war, were to succumb to the Red Army. If that happened, American security would be threatened through the loss of democratic friends and potential trading partners and the Soviets would probably be encouraged to promote Communism in other countries. While Truman perhaps exaggerated the Soviet threat (the Soviets were exhausted after the war and initially keen to have Marshall Aid), Eastman's argument is far weaker. As is often the case with political converts, Eastman demonstrates extremism in agreeing with McCarthy that America is flooded with fanatical Communist

conspirators. Yes, there were some – Alger Hiss in the State Department and those such as the Rosenbergs (and British diplomats based in Washington) who had leaked atomic secrets to the Soviets, but they were few in number and did not merit the large-scale persecution for which McCarthy bore so much responsibility.

Which is more *valuable*? This can be judged in terms of which is likely to be more valuable in terms of where the source came from; or in terms of the accuracy of its content. However, remember the focus of the question: in this case, the Communist threat.

While both sources explain the Communist threat, the president's assessment of the perceived Soviet threat to American national security through past and likely Soviet actions in Europe is the more valuable source, because it helps us to understand the underlying reason for the hysterical anti-Communism demonstrated in the writing of the poacher turned gamekeeper, Max Eastman.

Then check the following:

- Have you covered the 'provenance' and 'content' strands?
- Have you included sufficient knowledge to show understanding of the historical context?

Answering A level questions

The same general points for answering AS questions (see 'Answering AS questions') apply to A level questions, although of course here there are three sources and you need to assess the value of each of the three, rather than choose which is most valuable. Make sure that you remain focused on the question and that when you use your knowledge it is used to substantiate (add to) an argument relating to the content or provenance of the source.

If you are answering the A level question on page 27 with Sources 1, 2 and 3 (pages 272–3):

- Keep the different 'strands' explained above in your mind when working out how best to plan an answer.

- Follow the guidance about 'provenance' and 'content' (see the AS guidance).
- Here you are *not* asked to explain which is the most valuable of the three sources. You can deal with each of the three sources in turn if you wish.
- However, you can build in comparisons if it is helpful, but it is not essential. It will depend to some extent on the three sources.
- You need to include sufficient knowledge to show understanding of the historical context. This might encourage cross-referencing of the content of the three sources, mixed with your own knowledge.
- Each paragraph needs to show clarity of argument in terms of the issue identified by the question.

Glossary of terms

38th parallel The line of latitude that formed the border between North and South Korea prior to the Korean War.

'A Ford, not a Lincoln' Ford was saying that he was not going to be a great president like Abraham Lincoln, playing on the public's familiarity with cars. Fords were the cars of ordinary Americans; Lincolns were expensive, prestige cars.

Acceptance speech A candidate's speech accepting that he is his party's nominee for the presidency.

Access routes Land routes that crossed East Germany *en route* to West Berlin.

'Acid, abortion and amnesty' In 1972, Republicans accused Democratic presidential candidate George McGovern of favouring drugs ('acid'), irresponsible sex ('abortion') and unpatriotic draft dodgers (to whom he would give 'amnesty' – freedom from prosecution).

Administration When Americans talk of 'the Truman administration', they mean the government as led by that particular president.

Affirmative action Giving disadvantaged minorities extra opportunities (even if others were better qualified) in education and employment in order to compensate for previous unfair treatment.

AFL-CIO The American Federation of Labour and the Congress of Industrial Organizations are combined in an umbrella organisation for all US labour unions.

Age of majority Age at which an American legally became an adult (ranging from 18 to 21 years, depending on the US state).

American Dream Belief that the nature of US society enables an individual to fulfil his or her potential, especially through wealth.

American Friends of Vietnam US organisation that lobbied in favour of South Vietnam 1955–75.

Amendment The Founding Fathers wrote out rules by which the United States was to be governed in the Constitution. New rules or amendments can be added.

Anti-Catholicism The influx of Catholic immigrants from Ireland and southern Europe in the nineteenth century generated great anti-Catholic prejudice in the USA.

Ap Bac Battle between Vietnamese Communist guerrillas and the army of South Vietnam, which was assisted by US 'advisers' (1963).

Appeasement Placating Nazi Germany.

Aprincipled Unable to see what was acceptable and what was unacceptable behaviour.

Arab–Israeli War War in the Middle East, started in 1973 when Egypt and Syria attacked Israel; also known as the Yom Kippur War.

Armistice Agreement to stop fighting, usually a prelude to a peace treaty.

Attorney General Head of the Justice Department in the federal government.

Baby boom Post-Second World War population boom following the soldiers' return home.

Balance of trade deficit When the value of the goods imported by a nation exceeds the value of the goods exported.

Baloney Nonsense.

Beat generation Participated in, or supported, a countercultural movement of the late 1950s, characterised by spontaneity, free love and general defiance of authority and convention; famous published figures included the poet Allen Ginsberg and the novelist Jack Kerouac.

Bell hops Hotel porters.

Berlin Wall The wall divided Communist East Berlin from pro-Western West Berlin.

Bicentennial The USA's 200th birthday was on 4 July 1976. Americans had made their declaration of independence from Britain on 4 July 1776.

Big Three The leaders of the USA, USSR and Britain in the Second World War.

Bill   Suggested legislation is passed to Congress in the form of a bill. When passed by both the Senate and the president, the bill becomes an Act or law. The president can veto a bill, but if there are sufficient votes, Congress can override his veto.

Bipartisan   When Republicans and Democrats forgo political partisanship and co-operate on an issue.

Bipolar   Prior to the 1960s the Cold War world was focused on two superpowers: the USA and the USSR.

Black Panthers   A group of militant black activists who used revolutionary rhetoric, ostentatiously carried guns, monitored police brutality and distributed free meals to the ghetto poor.

Black Power   A vaguely defined black movement with aims including separatism, and greater economic, political, social and legal equality for African–Americans.

Border state   States such as Kansas and Missouri, situated on the edge of the American South and sharing similar characteristics.

Born-again Christian   A Christian who has experienced a spiritual rebirth; particularly fashionable in the USA from the late 1960s.

Brinkmanship   John Foster Dulles defined 'massive retaliation' as 'getting to the verge without getting into the war' in order to defeat Communist ambitions. Critics decried this as dangerous 'brinkmanship'.

Brookings Institution   A liberal Washington think-tank.

Brown nosing   Flattering and kowtowing to someone in order to gain favour.

Budget deficit   When a government's spending exceeds its income.

Busing   Supreme Court rulings on integrated education meant some white children were sent (by bus) to black schools, and vice versa.

Camp David   Presidential retreat in the rural hills of Maryland.

Canucks   French-Canadians, of whom New Hampshire had a sizeable population.

Cape Cod   A seaside resort in northeast USA.

CENTO   Anti-Soviet organisation, formerly known as the Baghdad Pact, but reconstituted as the Central Treaty Organisation in 1959. Its members included Turkey, Pakistan, Iran, Britain and the USA.

Chapters   Local branches of an association.

Che Guevara   Argentine revolutionary, closely associated with Fidel Castro and Cuba.

Chicago Eight   In 1969, the Nixon administration charged eight New Left leaders with conspiracy. They included Tom Hayden of SDS and Bobby Seale of the Black Panthers. Five were convicted, by an exceptionally hostile judge. Eventually their convictions were overturned on appeal.

CIA   The Central Intelligence Agency was set up in 1947 to monitor Communist threats early in the Cold War.

Citizens' Councils   Southern organisations set up in protest after the *Brown* ruling.

Civil rights movement   The predominantly black movement for equal rights for African-Americans.

Coattails   Americans talking of a president whose popularity helps other members of his party get elected, say those other members got in on the president's coattails.

Cold War   The struggle between the capitalist USA and the Communist Soviet Union.

Cold Warrior   One who wanted the US to wage the Cold War with even more vigour.

Commander-in-chief   Under the US Constitution, the president is commander-in-chief of the nation's armed forces.

Communist   Believer in economic equality brought about by revolutionary redistribution of wealth.

Congress   The US equivalent of Britain's Parliament. It consists of the House of Representatives and the Senate. Each US state selects two senators, and a number of congressmen proportionate to its population.

Congressional mid-term elections   Congressional elections are held every two years, so some are held along with the president's election, some are held in the middle of the president's term.

Consciousness-raising   Procedure adopted by feminists to raise awareness of women's issues.

Constant dollars   To make comparisons between dates more meaningful, economists factor in changes in the cost of living or the value of the currency, and so on.

Consumerism   Great interest in acquiring consumer goods such as cars and kitchen gadgets.

Containment   US Cold War doctrine advocating military and diplomatic action to limit the expansion of Communism.

Counterculture   An alternative lifestyle to the dominant culture; in the case of 1960s' America, the 'drop-out' mentality, as compared to the dominant, materialistic, hard-working culture of the students' parents.

Covert warfare   Undermining an enemy through subversion, for example with coups and spies.

Creationism   A biblical account of the origins of the earth and the life on it.

CREEP   Committee to Re-Elect the President, established by the Nixon administration prior to the 1972 presidential election.

Darwinism   Creationists believe that Darwin's theories of evolution go against the Bible.

***De facto* segregated**   Black and white people segregated in residential areas and some other public places in practice if not in law.

***De jure* segregation**   Racial segregation by law.

Deep South   States such as Mississippi, Alabama and Georgia, where segregation and racism were most deeply entrenched.

Deep Throat   The unidentified (at the time) FBI source who gave Woodward and Bernstein vital information during Watergate. In 2005, former FBI employee Mark Felt confessed to being Deep Throat.

Democrat   Member of one of the two main political parties. In comparison to Republicans, more supportive of government interventionism and more on the left of the political spectrum.

Detente   Policy of relaxation of tensions with enemies, associated with President Nixon's improvement of relations with China and the USSR.

Dixiecrats   Southerners who broke away from the Democratic Party in 1948 because the Democrats were increasingly liberal on civil rights.

DNC   Democratic National Committee, which had its headquarters in the Watergate building in Washington DC.

Domino theory   President Eisenhower's belief that if one country fell to Communism, neighbouring countries would fall soon after.

Draft   The US equivalent of British conscription; compulsory service in the nation's armed forces.

Draft dodger   One who avoided being called up to fight in the Vietnam War.

Electoral college   Under the Constitution, each state's voters vote for delegates who then vote on behalf of that state in the electoral college. The number of delegates depends on the state's population. The leading candidate in a state takes all that state's delegates. Whoever wins a majority of delegates becomes president.

Equal Employment Opportunities Commission (EEOC)   A federal agency established to deal with unequal employment opportunities for ethnic minorities.

Equal Rights Amendment (ERA)   Congress passed the ERA in 1972. Designed to help women and minorities in employment and education, it was never ratified by sufficient states.

Evangelical   Some would say a more fanatical and/or enthusiastic kind of Protestant, with tendencies towards social conservatism, often taking the Bible very literally.

Executive powers   The US Constitution gives the president various powers. Cold War presidents contended that in such a time of national emergency, they, as the executive branch of government, needed certain executive privileges, such as keeping some things secret because of the demands of national security.

FBI   The Federal Bureau of Investigation was set up in 1924 to help deal with crime.

Federal government   The national or federal government, based in Washington DC, consists of the President, Congress (which makes laws) and the Supreme Court (which interprets laws).

Federal government deficit   When the federal government is spending more than it is receiving in taxes.

Federal Reserve   The US central bank.

Feminist   Advocate of equal political, social, economic and legal rights for women.

Filibuster   Tactic prolonging congressional debates to stop bills being voted on.

Fissionable   Material with which to construct nuclear weapons.

Food stamp programme   First used during the Great Depression, revived by President Kennedy, made permanent by the Food Stamp Act (1964); impoverished individuals present stamps provided by the government for food.

French Indochina   Cambodia, Laos and Vietnam were French colonies from the late nineteenth century to 1954, when they gained their independence and 'French Indochina' ceased to exist.

Gestapo   Infamous Nazi secret police force.

Ghetto   Area inhabited mostly or solely by (usually poor) members of a particular ethnicity or nationality.

GNP   A country's gross national product is the aggregate value of goods and services produced in that country.

Great Depression   Beginning with the 1929 Wall Street crash, the US economy was characterised by unprecedented unemployment in the 1930s.

Great Migration   The Northward movement of Southern African-Americans during the twentieth century.

'Great Society'   President Johnson said he wanted to create an American society free from the racism and poverty which were particularly prevalent in the urban ghettos.

Ground troops   In March 1965, President Johnson sent the first few thousand regular soldiers (rather than just 'advisers') to Vietnam.

Gubernatorial   Pertaining to being a state governor in the USA.

Gulf of Tonkin resolution   1964 congressional authorisation for the president to do as he saw fit in South Vietnam.

Happenings   1960s' events such as rock concerts and festivals attended by hippies, among others.

Harlem   New York City's African-American ghetto.

Hash   Also known as marijuana, cannabis or pot.

Head of state   Chief public representative of a country such as a monarch or president.

Head Start   A federal government programme to help economically disadvantaged pre-schoolers, providing educational, health, social and other services.

Helsinki Agreement   1975 accord where the West recognised Soviet control of Eastern Europe in exchange for Soviet concessions on human rights.

Hippies   Young people (often students) who, in the 1960s, rejected the beliefs and fashions of the older generation, and favoured free love and drugs.

Homemakers   Mothers who stay at home to look after their families, rather than going out to work.

Hooey   Nonsense.

House Minority Leader   Leader of the political party in the minority in the House of Representatives.

House of Representatives   One of the two congressional chambers. Each state sends a number of congressmen proportional to its population to the House.

HUAC   The House (of Representatives) Un-American Committee investigated suspected Communists within the USA.

Humphrey–Hawkins   This bill said the federal government should be the employer of last resort during a recession. The final Act (October 1978) was a much watered-down version of the original bill.

Impeachment   Under the US Constitution, Congress has the power to bring an errant president to trial, to impeach him.

Imperial presidency   During the Cold War, presidential power increased so much that some commentators thought the president was becoming like an emperor – hence 'imperial'.

Impounding   When the president refuses to spend money allocated by Congress.

In loco parentis   In place of parents.

Inaugural address   Speech made by the president or state governor after he has been inaugurated.

Inauguration Day   The president usually undergoes an elaborate inauguration ceremony on Capitol Hill, at which he is sworn into office.

Infant mortality   The proportion of infants who die before a certain age is taken as an indication of a nation or group's health and well-being.

Inter-American Development Bank   Established in 1959 by the USA, which subsequently dominated it. Lends to Latin American governments.

Interposition resolutions   Assertions of states' right to oppose federal government actions deemed unconstitutional.

IRBMs   Intermediate-range ballistic missiles.

Iron Curtain   Cold War accusation, notably by Churchill (1946), that the USSR had made the Soviet bloc countries (East Germany, Czechoslovakia, Poland, Romania, Bulgaria, Hungary) inaccessible and repressed.

IRS   Internal Revenue Service, the US tax collection agency, which monitors taxpayers, checking whether they pay the correct sum.

Isolationist   Long-standing US foreign policy tradition (for example, Jefferson opposed entangling alliances); the avoidance of foreign entanglements.

'It's not the Pope I'm afraid of, it's the pop'   Truman was more frightened of John Kennedy's powerful father, noted for his advocacy of appeasement of Hitler, than of the possibility that the Roman Catholic Kennedy would put loyalty to the Pope before loyalty to America.

JCS   The Joint Chiefs of Staff were the heads of the army, navy and air force.

Jim Crow   An early 1830s' comic, black-faced, minstrel character developed by a white performing artist that proved popular with white audiences. Southern state laws that legalised segregation in the late nineteenth century were known as 'Jim Crow laws'.

Junket   The taking advantage of political office by accepting perks such as lavish entertainments.

Karl Marx   First great theorist of Communism.

Kinsey Reports   US academic Alfred Kinsey published widely read reports (1948, 1953) on the sexual mores of Americans.

Labour   Blue-collar (manual), unionised workers.

Laos, Congo and Indonesia   During Kennedy's presidency, Laos was bitterly divided between Communists and non-Communists; the Congo had a civil war after one province seceded; President Sukarno of Indonesia pursued aggressive policies towards neighbouring countries.

Laundered money   When money is to be used illegally, it is frequently laundered or 'made clean' by being put into a bank not connected with the payer. In this case, the campaign money was laundered through a Mexican bank with the aim of disguising that it came from CREEP.

'Long Telegram'   US diplomat George Kennan's 1946 telegram to Washington analysing Soviet expansionism and urging US resistance.

Lynching   Unlawful killing (usually by hanging) of African-Americans.

Main Street   A synonym for the usually conservative, average, ordinary, small-town US resident.

Mandate   The authority to do something.

Mass direct action   Large-scale protest movements, for example the Montgomery bus boycott.

Materialism   Excessive preoccupation with material goods and consumerism.

McCarthyism   Anti-Communist hysteria triggered by Senator McCarthy.

Medicaid   Introduced under President Johnson in 1968; the federal government gave financial assistance to states to help them provide medical treatment to impoverished residents who could not afford essential medical services.

Medicare   Introduced under President Johnson in 1965; provided federally funded health insurance for over-65s and those with disabilities, regardless of their income or existing medical conditions.

Middle America   A term invented by the media to describe ordinary, patriotic, middle-income Americans.

Military–industrial complex   Influential figures in the armed forces and defence industry, who profited from war.

Minority Leader   Leader of the minority party in the House of Representatives or the Senate.

Miranda   Supreme Court ruling that improperly obtained confessions be excluded from trials.

Missile gap   Used in the USA for the perceived superiority of the number and power of the USSR's missiles in comparison with its own.

Moratorium   In this context, suspension of normal activities to facilitate national anti-Vietnam War protests in 1969.

More bang for a buck   Eisenhower administration policy emphasising reliance upon nuclear weapons rather than excessive expenditure on conventional forces.

MRBMs   Medium-range ballistic missiles.

Multipolar   Prior to the 1960s, the Cold War world was bipolar (focused on the USA and the USSR); after the Cuban missile crisis and the rise of China, the Cold War world was increasingly multipolar (multiple centres of power and influence).

NAACP   The National Association for the Advancement of Colored People was the oldest and most respected black civil rights organisation.

Nation of Islam (NOI)   Black separatist religion that considered all whites evil. Also known as Black Muslims.

National Convention   A few weeks before the presidential election the Republicans and Democrats both hold National Conventions in which each party selects or confirms its candidate for the presidency.

National Guard   State reserves that can be federalised by the president during an emergency.

NATO   The treaty establishing the North Atlantic Treaty Organisation was signed in April 1949 by the USA, Canada, Britain, France, Belgium, Luxembourg, Holland, Norway, Italy, Portugal, Iceland and Denmark. Other nations became NATO members later, for example, Germany (1955).

Neo-colonialism   The use of political and economic (rather than military) pressure to force a weaker country to do what the more powerful country desires.

New Deal   Roosevelt's plan to get the USA out of the 1930s' Depression; an unprecedented programme of federal aid to those most in need.

New Economic Policy (NEP)   Nixon's new policy of August 1971 froze wages and prices for 90 days. When he discovered that Lenin had had an NEP, he dumped the phrase but not the policy.

New Federalism   Nixon's plans to redirect power away from Congress and the federal bureaucracy, and back to the states and local communities, who could spend revenue on education and other local issues as needed.

New Left   Student group of the early 1960s, who wanted greater racial and economic equality and an end to social conformity.

New Right   This group of right-wing voters became influential in the late 1970s; their beliefs were a reaction to the counterculture of the 1960s, and included opposition to abortion, busing and Darwinism.

New South   Originally used to describe the transformed South during Reconstruction, and occasionally used to describe the changes in the South after the civil rights legislation of 1964–5.

Nixon Doctrine   Also known as 'Vietnamisation'; belief that America's Asian allies should fight their own battles. Announced by President Nixon at Guam in 1969.

NLF   Vietnamese Communist National Liberation Front.

NSC The National Security Council advised the President on foreign policy.

Nuclear family Husband, wife and children.

Old Guard Conservative Republicans such as Senator Robert Taft.

'Pactomania' Eisenhower's Secretary of State John Dulles made so many treaties with other anti-Communist foreign nations that contemporaries joked about his obsession with pacts.

Pennsylvania Avenue A street in Washington DC that joins the White House and the Capitol building.

Pentagon Papers A collection of government documents that reflected badly on the Democratic presidents who had got America into Vietnam. The papers were leaked to the press by civil servant Daniel Ellsberg.

Pink Having Communist sympathies.

Planks Stated policies of a candidate in an election. Each plank is a component of the platform.

Planned Parenthood Organisation established in 1916 to promote reproductive health and care.

Platform Consists of the different policies or planks of a candidate or political party.

'Plumbers' Those on the White House staff whose job was to halt leaks of information.

Politicking Focusing on elections.

Poll tax A tax levied on would-be voters, which made it harder for African-Americans (who were usually poorer) to vote.

Pork-barrel politics When a legislator will not pass legislation unless he is given particular benefit for his own constituents.

Poverty line An amount set by the US government; those whose annual family income is below this are legally defined as 'poor', which is important for federal aid entitlements.

Primary Before a presidential election, the Democrats and Republicans hold an election in each state (mostly called a primary) to decide which candidate they would like to represent their party in the election.

Realpolitik Emphasising national interest rather than legalism and moralism in foreign policy.

Reconstruction The process of rebuilding and reforming the eleven Southern states after their defeat in the Civil War.

Red Army The Soviet Union's army (the Soviet/ Communist flag was red).

Red Scare Periods of hysterical anti-Communism in the USA; the first was after the Russian Revolution, the second in the late 1940s to early 1950s.

Redneck Poorly educated, working-class white Southerner, frequently characterised by racism and beer drinking.

Religious Right Influential, late 1970s movement in reaction to the liberalism and counterculture of the 1960s.

Reproductive rights A woman's right to know about and have access to contraception and abortion.

Republican Member of one of the two main political parties. More conservative than Democrats, and generally opposed to federal government interventionism.

Reservations Lands to which white Americans confined Native Americans from the nineteenth century onwards.

Roe v. Wade The Supreme Court decision legalising abortion.

Rollback Republican policy, much talked about in the 1952 presidential election; it suggested the Democrat Truman's 'containment' was insufficiently dynamic, and that Communist expansion should not be simply stopped, but reversed.

Running mate The individual chosen to be a political party's presidential candidate has to choose a running mate, who will be vice president if the presidential candidate wins the election.

Rust Belt The traditional manufacturing areas of the Eastern seaboard and the Midwest, where the old industries had declined and mostly disappeared.

Saigon regime The South Vietnamese government was based in Saigon, South Vietnam's main city.

SALT   The Strategic Arms Limitation Treaty signed by Nixon and the Soviet leader Brezhnev in 1972.

SALT II   Treaty signed by Carter and Brezhnev (1979) but not ratified by the USA after the Soviet invasion of Afghanistan; the treaty aimed to slow down the arms race.

'Saturday Night Massacre'   When Nixon sacked the Watergate special prosecutor and the Attorney General resigned.

Sears   A US department store chain.

SEATO   Southeast Asia Treaty Organisation established in 1954 and consisting of Australia, France, New Zealand, Pakistan, Philippines, Thailand, the UK and the USA.

Senate   One of the two chambers of Congress; two senators are elected from each state.

Senate Majority Leader   Leader of the majority party in the Senate.

Service industries   Businesses that serve customers but are not involved in manufacturing, for example restaurants, motels and petrol stations.

Sharecroppers   Tenant farmers who give a share of the crops produced to the landowner as rent.

Sino-Soviet alliance   Alliance between Communist China and the USSR, dating from 1950 treaty.

Sit-ins   When protestors sat in the 'wrong' seats in restaurants and refused to move, causing the establishment to lose custom and then, hopefully, desegregate.

Skid row   An impoverished urban area inhabited by marginalised people.

Socialised medicine   Conservative Americans opposed giving medical assistance to the poor, claiming that it smacked of socialism and Communism.

Socialist   Believer in a political philosophy that favours a more equal distribution of wealth than is attained under pure capitalism.

Solid South   Before the Democratic Party became more liberal on race, the Southern states were dominated by the Democratic Party.

Southern Cone   Southernmost states of South America, for example Chile, Argentina.

Southern Strategy   Nixon's plans to win Southern voters from the Democrats.

Soviet bloc   The USSR's East European Empire (East Germany, Poland, Czechoslovakia, Romania, Bulgaria, Hungary) from about 1945 to 1989.

Sovietised   Made to resemble the social and political structure of the USSR.

State of the Union   Annual speech by the president, usually boasting of his achievements and setting out his future plans.

States' rights   Belief that the states have certain rights that the federal government in Washington should never diminish.

Status quo   The current state of affairs.

Student Peace Union   National student organisation, active from 1959 to 1964.

Subpoena   Order to appear before a court as a witness.

Sun Belt   States in the South, Southeast and Southwest, with warm climates, ranging from North Carolina in the East to California in the West.

Supreme Court   Issues rulings on whether or not laws and actions are in line with the Constitution.

Surgical air strike   Air strike on specified targets.

Tennessee Valley Authority   New Deal programme that modernised the Tennessee Valley through electrification.

Term   A US president is elected for a four-year term. Since FDR, he or she can only be re-elected for a second term.

Tet festival   Vietnamese New Year, celebrating the arrival of spring.

Tet Offensive   Great Communist offensive in South Vietnam in early 1968.

Third World   The term used for less-developed nations during the Cold War, when America and its allies constituted the first world, the Communists the second world, and the non-aligned and less developed nations were the third group of countries.

Title VII   The anti-sex discrimination section of the 1964 Civil Rights Act.

Uncle Tom   A black person who behaves in an overly subservient way to whites. Based on a character in Harriet Beecher Stowe's *Uncle Tom's Cabin*.

Upward Bound   Federal government-financed programme linking higher education institutions to poor students with college potential; established by President Johnson.

USSR   Several years after the Russian Revolution of 1917, Communist Russia became known as the Union of Soviet Socialist Republics (USSR) or the Soviet Union.

Viet Cong   Vietnamese Communist guerrillas.

Vietnamisation   President Nixon's policy; South Vietnam was to take over all the fighting against the Communists.

Voice of America   US government's broadcasting vehicle targeted at foreign nations since 1942.

Wagner Act   1935 legislation that assisted the establishment and work of labour unions.

Wall Street   The financial centre of the United States, whose big-earners traditionally vote Republican.

War by proxy   During the Cold War, the USA and the USSR often supported opposing sides in a war that was not initially a Cold War conflict but then became one as in the Korean War (see page 21) and the Vietnam War (see page 112).

War materiel   Military equipment such as guns, ammunition and so on.

Western Hemisphere   The North and South American continents.

White ethnics   Groups of Americans such as Irish-Americans, Italian-Americans and Polish-Americans.

White flight   The post-Second World War exodus of white Americans from inner-city areas, which were then left to minorities such as African-Americans.

Wiretaps   Bugging a telegraph wire or a telephone line in order to overhear conversations.

World Bank   UN organisation, established in 1944 to aid developing nations; dominated by the USA.

Youth International Party   A radical student group that wanted to show contempt for the political system during the Democratic Party Convention at Chicago in 1968.

Further reading

Books of overall relevance

Jean-Christophe Agnew and Roy Rosenzweig, editors, *A Companion to Post-1945 America* (Blackwell, 2006)
Useful collection of essays that summarise research on all aspects of post-war American history

Harold Evans, *The American Century* (Jonathan Cape, 1998)
Lively, lavishly illustrated (but only in black and white) series of vignettes of American politics and society

Adam Fairclough, *Better Day Coming: Blacks and Equality, 1890–2000* (Penguin, 2001)
Excellent overview, full of sympathetic biographies that enliven the narrative

Walter LaFeber, *America, Russia and the Cold War, 1945–2006* (McGraw-Hill, 2008)
Lively, cynical, revisionist account of US foreign policy

James Patterson, *Grand Expectations: The United States, 1945–1974* (Oxford University Press, 1996)
An excellent synthesis of social, economic, political and international developments

James Patterson, *Restless Giant: The United States from Watergate to Bush v Gore* (Oxford University Press, 2005)
Another excellent synthesis

Robert Schulzinger, *US Diplomacy Since 1900* (Oxford University Press, 2007)
Solid, readable

Natasha Zaretsky *et al.*, editors, *Major Problems in American History Since 1945* (Cengage, 2013)
Interesting, useful collection of documents on much debated issues

Chapter 1

David Halberstam, *The Fifties* (Random House, 1993)
Halberstam is a journalist with a good ear for good stories, often biographies, that bring the decade to life

Steven Hugh Lee, *The Korean War* (Longman, 2001)
Good, brief study that combines international and national perspectives well

David McCullough, *Truman* (Simon & Schuster, 1990)
Sympathetic biography that really brings Harry Truman alive

Arnold Offner, *Another Such Victory: President Truman and the Cold War, 1945–1953* (Stanford University Press, 2002)
Highly critical of Truman's worldview. Most historians are more sympathetic than this to what Truman perceived as his foreign policy dilemma

Chapter 2

Stephen Ambrose, *Eisenhower: Soldier and President* (Simon & Schuster, 2003)
Ambrose is a good biographer. Detailed, balanced and quite an easy read

David Anderson, *Trapped by Success: The Eisenhower Administration in Vietnam* (Columbia University Press, 1993)
Highly critical of Eisenhower's Vietnam policy

Jean Edward Smith, *Eisenhower in War and Peace* (Random House, 2013)
Interesting depiction of Eisenhower as the consummate politician even while he was a soldier

Chapter 3

Robert Dallek, *John F. Kennedy: An Unfinished Life, 1917–1963* (Penguin, 2003)
Exhaustive, sympathetic biography

Lawrence Freedman, *Kennedy's Wars* (Oxford University Press, 2000)
Detailed study of Kennedy's foreign policy leads the author to conclude that he would have got the USA out of Vietnam

David Garrow, *Bearing the Cross* (William Morrow, 1986)
Excellent biography of Martin Luther King Jr, full of contemporary quotations that give the reader a real 'feel' for the civil rights movement in the years of King's ascendancy

Chapter 4

Robert Dallek, *Flawed Giant: Lyndon Johnson and his Times, 1961–1973* (Oxford University Press, 1998)
Balanced, detailed biography

Michael Heale, *The Sixties in America* (Edinburgh University Press, 2001)
Easy, entertaining read

Nancy MacLean, *The American Women's Movement, 1945–2000* (Bedford/St Martin's, 2008)
Excellent coverage and useful documentary sources

Manning Marable, *Malcolm X* (Penguin, 2011)
Currently considered the definitive biography

Chapter 5

Stephen Ambrose, *Nixon: The Triumph of a Politician, 1962–1972* (Simon & Schuster, 1989) and *Nixon: Ruin and Recovery, 1973–1990* (Simon & Schuster, 1991)
Detailed, readable, balanced and often sympathetic biography in two volumes

Peniel Joseph, *Waiting Til the Midnight Hour: A Narrative History of Black Power* (Henry Holt, 2006)
Interestingly, white historians generally seem content to leave writing about the Black Power movement to black historians such as Joseph. Joseph does a reasonable job

Melvin Small, *The Presidency of Richard Nixon* (Kansas University Press, 1999)
Small is one of those historians whose disgust over Nixon's deeds occasionally bursts through what is otherwise a reasonably balanced narrative

Chapter 6

John Robert Greene, *The Presidency of Gerald R. Ford* (Kansas University Press, 1995)
Another good biography in Kansas University Press's reliable series

Burton Kaufman and Scott Kaufman, *The Presidency of James Earl Carter* (Kansas University Press, 2006)
Another good volume in the Kansas series

Michael Schaller and George Rising, *The Republican Ascendancy: American Politics, 1968–2001* (Harlan Davidson, 2002)
While geared to explaining (with exceptional clarity) the history of the Republican Party in those years, this also gives an excellent account of US politics in general

Some useful websites

www.casahistoria.net
Good links to topics for students studying the Cold War

http://avalon.law.yale.edu/subject_menus/coldwar.asp
Good sources on the Cold War

http://memory.loc.gov/ammem/index.html
A portal with thousands of sources on ethnic minorities and women

www.teachersdomain.org/special/civil/
Includes transcripts, film and interviews

www.malcolm-x.org/docs/
An interesting source collection

www2.iath.virginia.edu/sixties/HTML_docs/Sixties.html
Useful on the protest movements of the 1960s

Index

Acknowledgements: American Presidency Project. *Evening Citizen*, 21 November 1949. Federation of American Scientists. *Gettysburg Times*, 29 January 1970. Harcourt, Brace & World, *The City in History* by Lewis Mumford, 1961. Harry S. Truman Library and Museum. Harvard University Press, *LBJ: Architect of American Ambition* by Randall Bennett Woods, 2007. Hodder, *Stalin and Khrushchev: The USSR 1924–64* by Michael Lynch, 1990. Humanities & Social Sciences Online. John F. Kennedy Presidential Library and Museum. Lillian Goldman Law Library. Longman, *Russia, America and the Cold War, 1949–91 by* Martin McCauley, 2004. *Lyndon Baines Johnson Library and Museum*. Marxists Internet Archive. New American Library, *Lyndon B. Johnson: The Exercise of Power* by Rowland Evans and Robert Novak, 1966. *New York Times*, 17 November 1953. Organisation for Economic Co-operation and Development. Oxford University Press, *Flawed Giant: Lyndon Johnson and His Times, 1961–1973* by Robert Dallek, 1998; *From Colony to Superpower: US Foreign Relations since 1776* by George Herring, 2008; *Grand Expectations: The United States, 1945–1974* by James Patterson, 1996; *Lone Star Rising* by Robert Dallek, 1991. Pearson, National Organisation of Women's Statement of Purpose, 1966. Penguin, *John F. Kennedy: An Unfinished Life 1917–1963* by Robert Dallek, 2003; *The Feminine Mystique* by Betty Friedan, 2010. Public Broadcasting Service (PBS). Random House, *The Passage of Power* by Robert Caro, 2012. Routledge, *British Political History 1867–2001* by Malcolm Pearce and Geoffrey Stewart, 2002. Simon & Schuster, *Eisenhower: Soldier and President* by Stephen Ambrose, 2003; *Truman* by David McCullough, 1992. *The Freeman*, 1 June 1953. University of Minnesota Law Library. Wikisource.